Anthony J. Lauck, CSC
Notre Dame, IN

D0915835

# THE WORD MADE FLESH

OTHER BOOKS BY CHARLES E. MILLER, C.M.

*Opening the Treasures*, A Book of Daily Homily Meditations, Alba House.

*Living in Christ*, Sacramental and Occasional Homilies, Alba House.

*Making Holy the Day*, a Commentary on the Liturgy of the Hours, Catholic Book Publishing Co.

*Love in the Language of Penance*, A Simple Guide to the New Rite of Penance, Alba House. (Also published in Spanish.)

# THE WORD MADE FLESH

## Homilies for the Sundays of the Three Cycles

Compiled from:
*Announcing the Good News, Breaking the Bread,*
and *Communicating Christ*

### by

### Charles E. Miller, C.M.
### Oscar J. Miller, C.M.
### Michael M. Roebert

"In the beginning was the Word. And the Word became flesh and made his dwelling among us, and we have seen his glory: the glory of an only Son coming from the Father, filled with enduring love" (John 1:1, 14).

Library of Congress Cataloging in Publication Data

Miller, Charles Edward, 1929-
   The Word made flesh.

   A compilation of three previous books, "Announcing
the good news, Breaking the bread, and Communicating
Christ"—Pref.
   Includes bibliographical references.
   1. Catholic Church—Sermons. 2. Sermons, American.
I. Miller, Oscar J., 1913-      . II. Roebert,
Michael M. III. Title.
BX1756.A2M57      1983      252'.02      83-8819
ISBN 0-8189-0436-4


Imprimi potest:
John A. Grindel, C.M.
Provincial, Province of the West

Nihil Obstat:
Newman C. Eberhardt, C.M.
Censor Librorum

Imprimatur:
Cardinal Timothy Manning
Archbishop of Los Angeles
August 31, 1982


The Nihil Obstat and Imprimatur are
a declaration that a book or pamphlet is considered
to be free from doctrinal or moral error. It is not implied
that those who have granted the Nihil Obstat and
Imprimatur agree with the contents,
opinions or statements expressed.

Designed, printed and bound in the United States of
America by the Fathers and Brothers of the
Society of St. Paul, 2187 Victory Boulevard,
Staten Island, New York 10314, as part of their
communications apostolate.


   2 3 4 5 6 7 8 9 (Current Printing: first digit)

# Introduction

It speaks well for a volume when it is said to be "out of print." It speaks better for it when its publishers decide to reprint. This has been the fortune of the three volumes of homilies on the Sunday readings which are now combined in this present volume, *The Word Made Flesh*.

There are three authors. The major number of reflections come from the pen of Father Charles Miller, C.M. He is a man of deep spiritual resources and a responsible Seminary Rector. Father Oscar Miller, C.M., is his brother and served our Seminary faculty for fifteen years. Father Michael Roebert is a priest of the Archdiocese of Los Angeles and currently a faculty member of the Seminary. It is a privilege to be associated with them in the prefacing of this book. May it follow, in its reprint, the furrows of grace ploughed through its predecessors.

TIMOTHY CARDINAL MANNING
Archbishop of Los Angeles

# Preface

This is not a new book. It is a compilation of three previous books, *Announcing the Good News, Breaking the Bread,* and *Communicating Christ*, all of which are now out of print. Some of the homilies have been revised and a number of new ones have been added.

Preaching is not merely one among many forms of communication; rather, preaching is unique as being prophetic. The core of authentic preaching is not words about God, but the Word of God itself. It is a faith experience for both preacher and hearer. Preachers in the past have been admonished that they must never preach themselves. In a humanistic sense this warning is needed but in a theological sense it is off the mark. The effective preacher is an embodiment of the Word of God, Christ himself. He must allow the Word, who is part of his being by ordination and should also be such by the holiness of his life, to be spoken from the depths of his Christian identity as minister of the Word.

Preaching as prophetic is also incarnational, for the Word of God comes clothed in the words of men. It is in the incarnational aspect that this collection is meant to help a priest in preaching, but it is only a help and not a short cut to a fully prepared homily. It cannot substitute for one's own creative work after study and prayer over the scriptural readings in the light of people's current needs. These homilies are one approach to the day's liturgy and are intended only to provide a spark or stimulus to a priest's own thinking as he prepares his homily. At best the words in this book are nothing more than cold, black print on a page. Only the preacher can make what is contained in them come alive as real spiritual communication in a new enfleshment of the Word.

The office of preaching is a gift from God by which we are "to utter his praises in the vast assembly" (Ps 22:26). May this book by God's grace be a help in fulfilling that office.

Charles E. Miller, C.M.

# TABLE OF CONTENTS

# THE WORD MADE FLESH

# THE ADVENT SEASON

**First Sunday of Advent (A)**

## *BEGINNING WITH THE END*

Almost everybody likes to read a mystery story. If you are like me, you are sometimes tempted to flip to the last chapter to see how the story turns out, and the longer the book, the greater the temptation. If you do give in and peek at the last chapter, of course you will spoil the story because all the suspense is gone.

Our lives, and the life of our whole world, is a mystery. We are not quite sure how they will turn out, but we would certainly like to know. Well, we do know how they are supposed to turn out and we even know how our world will turn out. Knowing this in no way spoils the story of life; it is just too important to be in suspense about it. The truth is that knowing what life's end is helps to guide and direct us through this life on earth.

Today we begin the season of Advent. We start our preparation to commemorate once again the coming of Christ into the world. The Church sees the coming of Christ in three phases. The first phase is his birth into this world, the beginning of the mystery of our salvation. The second phase is the one we experience right now, in which Christ comes to each one of us in many ways: through Holy Communion, through the Scriptures, through each other. The final phase, and this is the one emphasized in today's liturgy, is his coming at the end of time when he will come in glory and triumph to raise us from the dead so that we may be joined, body and soul, with him in happiness forever.

It may seem strange to begin Advent by talking about the end of the world. After all, Advent leads up to Christmas, the feast of the beginning of our salvation. The truth is that the Church is giving us a little look at the final chapter of the great mystery of salvation. Today we are getting at least some idea of how the story will turn out. And knowing how the story will turn out is very important to us.

We have to live on this earth with the realization that we are meant for a greater life, body and soul, with Christ in heaven. The Vatican Council reminds us that "The Church [and that means us] . . . will attain her full perfection only in the glory of heaven" (*Dogmatic Constitution on the Church*, 48). Someone has compared our lives to being in a sunken submarine (cf. Louis Evely in *That Man Is You*). Somehow in the submarine everything is working except the apparatus that raises the submarine to the surface. While in the sunken submarine, there are two things you must do. The first is that you must survive. You must eat and drink, sleep, recreate and so on. The second thing you must do is to work to get the submarine back to the surface, and you will no doubt make every effort to get some kind of contact with the surface. If you fail to do either thing, you are doomed. If during the long time that it will take to make repairs you fail to take care of yourself, you will die before the work can be accomplished. On the other hand, if you become so satisfied with life in the sunken ship that you give up working to get it back to the surface, you are indeed very foolish and will be destroyed on the bottom of the sea.

In this world we must carry on our everyday activities, but we must do so with the idea that we are working to reach heaven, to get to the surface, so to speak. God wants us to live as true human beings: to eat, drink, work and enjoy ourselves. But it would certainly be a very sad thing to become so satisfied with our present existence as to forget all about heaven.

The Vatican Council speaks of the Church as a Pilgrim Church. This is to say that we are people on a pilgrimage, a journey to heaven. In the Mass we have a symbol of our journey. As you come to receive Communion this morning you will walk in procession to the altar. This procession is a sign of our journey through life to heaven. And on this journey we have a special food to sustain us, the Body of Christ in Holy Communion. The Mass is also our chief "contact with the surface," for in the Mass we speak to God in our prayers and he speaks to us in the words of Scripture and the homily.

As we look forward to the feast of Christmas, the beginning of our salvation, we should do so with the realization of how God wants the story to end. He wills that through our resurrection we be joined with his Son in glory and happiness forever.

C.E.M.

**First Sunday of Advent (B)**

# A SECOND CHRISTMAS

As we begin Advent today, the Church tells us that Christmas is coming. It looks like the Church is pretty late, however, with her announcement. All the stores have long ago put up their decorations and displays, and every now and then you can catch a Christmas carol on the radio. Some children are by now on the fourth or fifth revision of their list of presents they want from Santa Claus, and little boys and girls are already eagerly asking, "How many more days to go?" Anybody who doesn't know that Christmas is coming must have been living on another planet, and it seems about time that the Church has finally gotten around to telling us to get ready.

And yet, we can look pretty hard at today's scriptural readings without finding any idea about the birth of Jesus. The reason is that there are two Christmases we have to think about. The first is the one we know so well, the coming of Jesus Christ into the world through his birth at Bethlehem. Jesus was born a man like us in all things but sin in order to teach us how to live both by his words and by his example. He won for us our freedom from sin and gave us the means to fulfill the purpose of human existence. Now he has left his human home, this earth, to go to his Father's home in heaven. But he will return. There will be a second Christmas. This second Christmas is the coming of Christ into the world at the end of time. Maybe we don't give that coming enough thought, and so the Church wisely on this first Sunday of Advent calls our attention to this second coming.

When Jesus does return, he will want to know how we have followed the teachings and what use we have made of the means he has given us to make something of our lives. However, our expectation of the second Christmas should be a joyful and happy one, in much the same spirit as we await our celebration of Christmas day. Though Jesus is certainly no Santa Claus, he will come as a gift-giver, and we should have our list of desired presents ready for him, a list that may need a little revising. Of course we all want the gift of happiness, but perhaps in the past our list has been a trifle childish in what we have been asking for in prayer—things like financial success, health, the overcoming of loneliness and frustrations. All these things are worth asking for, but we must remember that they are like so many presents we get at Christmas which don't last very long. In comparison with what Jesus has to offer, they are actually scarcely better than some inexpensive toy with which a child plays for a while but soon breaks or tires of. The gift that Jesus wants to give is eternal life—something impossible for us to imagine, for no ear has ever heard, no eye has ever seen the wonderful gift that God has for those who wait for him.

And wait we must, with perseverance and patience. "Stay awake," Jesus says in the gospel. "Do not let him come suddenly and catch you asleep." You have seen little children who on Christmas eve want desperately to stay awake for the coming of Santa Claus but who just can't keep their eyes open, despite all their eagerness and impatience. We cannot afford to fall asleep because of weariness in our struggle to be faithful to the teaching of Christ. Nor must we grow impatient, thinking that Jesus will never come to right the wrongs of this world and to give us the present he has promised.

Maybe if we knew just when Jesus will come again, we could be more enthusiastic and zealous. "How many more days, or years, to go?" To that question, Jesus refuses to give an answer. He simply says, "You do not know when the appointed time will come. Be constantly on watch!" Part of our faith and trust is to believe that Jesus will come at what is the best time in his divine plan. Our concern must be to keep watching, well prepared for his return. We have a pledge that, if we but cooperate, God will strengthen us to the end, so that we will be blameless on the day of Christ's coming.

We have the power to make the Second Christmas either joyful and happy, or fearful and terrifying. If we are loyal and persevering, we can be eager about the coming of Christ—eager, not anxious, for anxiety means a painful uneasiness of mind over an impending evil. Jesus does not will evil for us. He wants to give us a marvelous Christmas present, eternal life. The spirit that we should have—the spirit of the Second Christmas—is summed up in our prayer following the "Our Father": "In your mercy keep us free from sin and protect us from all anxiety as we wait in joyful hope for the coming of our Savior, Jesus Christ."

C.E.M.

**First Sunday of Advent (C)**

# *WHEN HE COMES AGAIN*

Advent is a time of preparation for the coming of Christ. The very word "Advent" means coming. But there are two comings of Christ: his first coming, when he was born of Mary in Bethlehem, and his second, when he will come again in glory at the end of time. And so the Church divides Advent into two parts.

The first part, which begins today and goes until December 16th, emphasizes preparation for the second coming of Christ. The second part, from December 17 through Christmas eve, emphasizes preparation for the celebration of his birth (cf. *Calendarium Romanum*, p. 61).

Advent should be a joyful time, since expectation of a happy event is always a happy thing. Though the "Gloria" is not said in the Mass, it is omitted not because we are sad or sorrowful, but only so that on Christmas our singing of this great song of the angels may in a certain sense be a new experience for us (cf. *Calendarium Romanum*, p. 61). Today we begin the joyful expectation of the final coming of Christ at the end of time.

But there is something of a problem here. The picture that many of us have of the final coming is, at best, short of joy. We have the idea that it will be a terrifying experience: a great, awesome cataclysm with the world engulfed in fire and the fearsome judge of all men calling us to account for the least wrong we have done. How can we be expected to want the end of the world, and to look forward to it? And yet the early Christians had an intense yearning for it. That is strange to our present outlook. If the early Christians looked forward to the end of the world, and we dread it, it seems obvious that our notion is different from theirs.

It is not surprising that we are troubled by the thought of the end of the world. In the gospel we have just heard, St. Luke paints an awesome picture. Frankly, we are not quite sure what this picture means. The images in the gospel are taken largely from the Old Testament, and they refer to a judgment by God. But God's judgment destroys one thing only: sin, not goodness. And the world, the universe is good. That is the view the early Christians had. That there will be a change, even an upheaval, at the end of time seems clear, but not in the sense of the annihilation of the universe, but in the sense of the final fulfillment of all things in

Christ. All sin, all evil will be removed from the universe by the coming of Christ.

Notice what the gospel says: "When these things begin to happen, stand up straight and raise your heads, because your redemption is at hand." And redemption here refers not only to people, but to all of creation. Jesus saves us not by taking us out of the world and out of our own history, as if the world and all that men have done are evil. Rather his redemption purifies and perfects all created things. Complete redemption means that in Christ this universe will reach the purpose for which God created it, and in Christ all of human history will find its meaning and fulfillment. We do not know just how all this will happen any more than we know when it will happen.

There is much fear in our times that the whole world may just blow up through gigantic atomic or hydrogen explosions. There is no guarantee that this will not occur. But we must not be afraid that God is going to lose control of his creation or that men through their foolish genius will upset God's plans for the universe. Whatever may happen from the human angle, God will send his Son in glory again when he has decided that the time has come for the end of our present world. But that time will be a new beginning for all of creation, a time of perfection without sin.

And what of ourselves? Naturally, we live in hope that we will be part of that perfection without sin. And we will be, if we live according to the words of today's gospel: "Be on guard lest your spirits become bloated with indulgence and drunkenness and worldly cares. Pray constantly. . . ." We will have confidence and joy if we try to live in accord with the prayer of St. Paul in today's epistle: "May the Lord make you overflow with love for one another. May he strengthen your hearts, making them blameless and holy before our God and Father at the coming of our Lord Jesus. . . ."

Today we begin a new Church year. During this year, we will celebrate all the saving events of the life of Jesus Christ. But today as we begin, we look to the end. We look to the completion of all the good that Jesus began by his life on this earth, a completion that will come only at the end of time.

Like the early Christians, we should have an intense yearning for the final coming of Christ. As we will pray in the Preface, we should "watch for the day hoping that the salvation promised us will be ours when Christ our Lord will come again in his glory'' (First Advent Preface).

*(For support for this approach, cf. the* Pastoral Constitution on the Church in the Modern World, *paragraph 39).*

C.E.M.

## Second Sunday of Advent (A)

## *BETTER THINGS TO COME*

In the tradition of the Church, St. John the Baptist has always figured prominently within the liturgy of Advent. He has also been afforded a place of honor among all the saints. Many magnificent churches have been named in his honor. And yet John the Baptist is not Jesus. It might even be observed that John is a foil for Jesus, which is to say that he tends by contrast to set off Jesus to advantage.

The gospel gives the impression that John was a very serious man, a person without a sense of humor, a really no-nonsense type. He has been caricatured by the Bible pounding, hell and brimstone preacher who exists more completely in movies and literature than in real life. John had a vital message to proclaim, but I doubt very much if you had heard him preach that you would be eager to meet him personally or to invite him over to your home for dinner.

John openly proclaimed that the one to follow him was more powerful than he was. Indeed, Jesus is not only more powerful than John; he is more of everything that is good. We have no way of knowing for certain how much John understood about Jesus. It does not seem that he was aware of the uniqueness of Jesus, who united divinity and humanity in himself. John prepared the way for Jesus but the reality was much greater than John expected.

And such is God's way, to surprise us with something much better than we could have hoped for. We can be confident about the future, about better things to come, because in looking to the past we can see how God has been at work. The circumstances behind the first reading today were that King Ahaz, a very weak and unfaithful ruler, had brought the country to such a ruinous state that it was like the stump of what had once been a flourishing tree. The prophet Isaiah promised that God would make a shoot sprout from the stump to begin a new, luxurious growth. This shoot was to be an ideal king of the house of David, upon whom would come the spirit of the Lord so that the kingdom could be renewed. Isaiah foresaw a human king, but the Church has a deeper understanding. Reading this passage of Isaiah in the light of fuller revelation, the Church sees the promise fulfilled in the person of Christ the King who proclaimed the kingdom of heaven. And that is God's way: his fulfillment is always greater than his promise.

Perhaps at times we become a little dubious about awaiting a better future, especially an eternal one. The reason is that in our human lives we very often experience the opposite of God's way. People who make promises frequently do not keep them. Advertisements and commercials exaggerate the quality of their products. When something is being given away, there is usually some catch. We must not let our unhappy human experiences dictate our outlook on God and his promises.

During the first part of Advent (through December 16), the Church focuses our attention on the second coming of Christ at the end of time when he will bring his kingdom to perfection. This part of Advent, like life itself, stands somewhere between the two comings of Christ, the first being his humble birth and the second being his glorious return. No one in the Old Testament era suspected that the Messiah would be divine, the very Son of God. As the first coming of Christ far outshone anything the people had hoped for, so his second coming will far outshine anything we can imagine.

In every Mass, we pray that God the Father may deliver us from all anxiety "as we wait in joyful hope for the coming of our Savior, Jesus Christ." Our expectation should be a joyful one, filled with confidence in God's goodness. And our anxiety about the future should be replaced with a trust that God always does more than merely keep his promises. For people of faith better things are yet to come.

C.E.M.

## Second Sunday of Advent (B)

## *BEGINNING AND END*

Today's gospel reading was the beginning of the holy gospel according to Mark. During this liturgical year we will be hearing more of

Mark's gospel than of the other three, as the mystery of Christ is unfolded Sunday after Sunday. Since you would expect the beginning of a gospel to center around the birth of Jesus, the verses we just heard seem to be a strange starting point. Mark takes up his narrative when Jesus was already a grown man, heralded by John the Baptist. Mark is not so much concerned with the fact that Jesus was born as he is with the reason why he was born and came into our world. His main purpose was to present Jesus as the Savior, as the Man-God who came to lead man back to God.

Mark's approach is of great value. It should make us stop and think. Certainly we treasure the beautiful stories of Christ's birth as found in Matthew and especially in Luke, but for some people Christmas seems to mean little more than a charming narrative which serves as a setting for a myriad of carols. No doubt this year we will again hear the plea, "Put Christ back into Christmas." And it is a plea which needs to be made. But that plea is not heeded merely by making sure our Christmas cards depict a nativity scene or even by placing a crib next to the tree. These things we should do, but they have meaning only if we do them with the realization of why God the Father gave us the first Christmas gift, his own Son, and with faith in what Jesus came to accomplish.

In the beginning, God made man in his own likeness, and set him over the whole world to serve him and to rule over all creatures. Our first parents had the ability to know God and to love him—to be his friends. But they lost God's friendship through sin, something that human beings have been doing ever since. As a result our world fell into turmoil, filled with confusion, hatred and greed, leading to death. And yet at no time did God give up on his creation or abandon the human race. Again and again God offered a renewal of friendship, and through the prophets taught men to hope for salvation. Slowly and gradually, people began to realize that one day God would send a personal savior to right the wrongs of the world, and firmly reestablish a relationship of love and friendship between himself and the human race.

Mark began his presentation of Jesus with the story of John the Baptist, the last of the Old Testament prophets. In a sense, John summed up in his preaching the message of all the other prophets. "Get ready," he said, "the savior is here, the one who is greater than I." As Mark developed his gospel, he showed that Jesus Christ is the expected savior; not just another prophet, but God himself who became a man like us in all things but sin. Most importantly, he emphasized that Jesus saved us through his death and resurrection. Jesus destroyed death and restored life, as he bridged the gap separating mankind from God.

The beginning of Mark's gospel makes us think back to the past, to the beginning of our human history. Jesus came as a savior because of a long history of failure on the part of human beings. Jesus has beyond doubt given us the means of salvation, but anyone who has eyes to see can perceive that our world is still filled with confusion, hatred and greed leading to death. As a matter of fact, the coming of Jesus stands between two extremes of human history, its beginning and its end. It took long centuries of waiting for God to send Jesus into the world, and it is taking long centuries of waiting before the saving work of Jesus takes full effect.

In today's second reading St. Peter, like an Old Testament prophet, teaches us to hope for the complete salvation promised by God. He begs us not to be impatient or to think that God is delaying his work unnecessarily. God has a plan which he is carefully working out. St. Peter says, "What we await are new heavens and a new earth where, according to his promise, the justice of God will reside." John the Baptist preached repentance as a preparation for the first coming of Christ, and St. Peter preaches the same message as a preparation for the second coming of Christ. He says, "So, beloved, while waiting for this, make every effort to be found without stain or defilement, and at peace in his sight."

In a short time we will once again commemorate the birth of Jesus, a coming which marked the turning point in human history. We should celebrate Christmas in the traditional way, with all its decorations and carols in a spirit of joy. But we should realize that the happiness of Christmas is only a shadow of what still awaits us in the second coming of Christ. We are a people of hope who yearn for the saving work of Jesus to take its full effect, as we look for a new heaven and a new earth.

C.E.M.


**Second Sunday of Advent (C)**

## *PREPARE!*

At first hearing, today's gospel seems to contain a lot of obscure details about little known people in far-off places. Actually, St. Luke, who wrote the gospel, was trying to pinpoint a moment in history. He was saying, in the language of the day, that Christ came at a precise moment in time, a time predetermined by God the Father.

If St. Luke were writing this gospel today, he would not include the names of Tiberius Caesar, and Annas and Caiaphas, and the rest of them. Rather, he would use the name of the Pope, the President, and perhaps the mayor. That would be his way of giving his message a realistic and historical context. He would then proclaim to us that the word of God is coming to us, that the Lord is near, and that we must prepare the way for him.

As a matter of fact, this description is not mere imagination on my part. There is precise truth in what I have just said. The word of God comes to us in this Mass just as surely as it did to John the Baptist in the wilderness. That word tells us that the Lord is near and that we must prepare for his coming. We must be prepared for the celebration of his coming at Christmas so that we will be prepared for his coming at the end of time.

First, the celebration of his birth at Christmas. This Christmas day, Jesus will just as truly come to us as he did to the people of the gospel story. Jesus was born many centuries ago, but this Christmas through the Liturgy he will be born once again in our hearts, and he will bring to us his love, his truth, and his help. But we have to be ready for him. We simply cannot afford to pass him up, to fail to recognize him, to say that there is no room in our lives for him. Do we need Jesus? I can hardly think of a time when we needed him more. The whole world needs him, and each one of us in particular needs him.

The only catch is that we have to be prepared; that is the warning that the word of God gives us today. It has now become a cliché to observe that we must keep Christ in Christmas. We all know how materialism has taken over. I do not say that we should do away with all the decorations and the gift giving. If we did, our economy would collapse. More importantly, a lot of the spirit of joy and enthusiasm surrounding Christmas would probably be lost. What I suggest is that we "baptize" once again the whole situation of Christmas; we have to have a right attitude.

Why do we decorate? Because we want to celebrate the coming of the Savior. It is a happy occasion. We just have to remember why we decorate in a spirit of joy. Why do we give gifts? It should be in commemoration of the greatest gift God has ever given us: God so loved the world that he sent his only begotten Son. Our gift giving at Christmas should be in imitation of the great generosity of God our Father.

But above all, we must try to make this Christmas primarily a religious experience by letting the Christmas Mass be the center of our celebration. I suggest that you plan your day around the Mass rather than a Christmas dinner. It is the spirit of the way in which you approach the Mass that will make the difference. And finally, I suggest that we all make the effort to go to confession before Christmas. A good, sincere, humble confession is the means we have to make our crooked ways straight, and our rough ways smooth.

The Church teaches us that Advent is more than a preparation for Christmas; it is also a preparation for the final coming of Christ. All that we do now prepares us for the final coming. The good confession we make, the way in which we try to make Christmas primarily a religious experience, the Christian spirit of generosity and joy with which we give gifts and decorate our homes—all these things are meant to direct us to the final coming of Christ.

All of the joy, all of the happiness, all of the good things we associate with Christmas, the first coming, will reach a fullness and completion and satisfaction in the second coming far beyond our poor powers to imagine—provided we are prepared by the good life we live now.

C.E.M.

## Third Sunday of Advent (A)

### *A PATIENT LONGING*

As people of faith, we are called not to be satisfied with this present world, but to look forward with patient longing toward a better future. It has always been so for people of faith. We see an example in the first reading today, which is a poem of hope.

This poem with its vivid and lush images was composed for the people of God who were exiles in Babylon, far from their homeland, and who were subjected to a state of slavery. The situation was not only painful. It seemed devoid of hope. Apparently there was no future for a people living in an alien land. They had few if any rights, and no opportunity to rise above their impoverished condition. Most serious of all, they were far removed from the holy city of Jerusalem and its temple, the symbol of their religious unity as the people of God. Their only light came from the prophetic word, the poem of hope, which we heard in our first reading.

That poem applies to us, especially during this season of Advent. We are a people in exile, far from our home in heaven. Our hands tend to be feeble as they try to ward off evil, our knees weak with carrying the burdens of life. Our hearts may be frightened in the face of an uncertain economic and social future. The prophetic word calls out to us: "Be strong, fear not! Here is your God." But in reply we perhaps are compelled to ask, "Where is God?" We do not see him and we do not feel him. A God there must be, but who is he? With John the Baptist we can turn to Jesus and ask, "Are you 'He who is to come' or do we look for another?"

Indeed, the nature of our society calls out to us to look for another rather than Jesus as our source of happiness and meaning in this life. The poet Wordsworth wrote, "The world is too much with us." The constant tugging of the world at our hearts produces tension and worry. Its unrelenting temptations cause anxiety and confusion. Evil is near us; God seems far away. We need to reflect again on the significance of the event we are preparing to celebrate on the twenty-fifth of this month.

The celebration of Christmas is more than a delightful holiday laden with custom and sentiment. Traditionally, we will gaze into the crib and see the representation of an infant. Only the coldest heart will remain untouched by this tender scene. But we must with the eyes of faith see beyond the veils of this simple, humble picture to the truth of the Christmas event: in human flesh has come the savior of the world. We need look for none other. Jesus is indeed the one who was promised to come.

And yet, we must admit that we do not see the glory of the Lord or the splendor of our God. The signs of the kingdom are that the blind recover their sight, cripples walk, lepers are cured, the deaf hear, and dead men are raised to life. But we do not witness these signs as events which have transformed the world into God's kingdom. The fact is that in his first coming in the flesh, Jesus laid the foundation for his kingdom after the fashion in which a farmer plants seed for a crop. A farmer must be patient while the soil receives the rains in order to bring the seed to fruition. And we must be patient until the Lord comes again to bring his kingdom to fruition.

In one sense, we are the soil in which the seed of the kingdom has been planted. In our gathering for Mass each Sunday, we do have a sign that the kingdom is here and growing among us. As Jesus foretold, ''the poor have the gospel, the good news, preached to them.'' We are those poor: people who are poor in the eyes of the world but who are rich in the sight of God, people who depend on God and not on worldly values. The proclamation of the gospel is part of every Mass. The word which we hear is like a seed and that seed is nourished, not by the rains, but by the body and the blood of the Lord. The means of growth are with us. We must be patient and cooperative.

In the gospel today, Jesus added a short but important declaration: ''Blest is the man who finds no stumbling block in me.'' As people of faith, we are called not to be satisfied with this world the way it is, and we are equally called to be satisfied with the plan being followed by Jesus. A farmer may want his crop to ripen overnight, but he must be patient. We too must be patient as we wait in joyful hope for the coming of our Savior, Jesus Christ.

C.E.M.

## Third Sunday of Advent (B)

### DO YOU RECOGNIZE HIM?

When a man has something important on his mind, something that is really bothering him, he finds it pretty hard to hold it back. If he is talking to you, he probably will bring up the subject before very long. When St. John composed his gospel, it took him only eleven verses to get to something that was bothering him. After proclaiming that the eternal Son of God came into our world, he made this melancholy statement: ''To his own he came, yet his own did not accept him.'' And just a few verses later, he quoted the words of the Baptist which we heard read only moments ago: ''There is one among you whom you do not know.'' The failure of people to recognize and accept Christ was still on John's mind when he came to the conclusion of the gospel. Because he wanted to make sure that his listeners would not make the same mistake as others, he said: "These things have been recorded to help you believe that Jesus is the Messiah, the Son of God. . . ."

John's gospel was not written down until the end of the first century. By that time, its central message had been preached and proclaimed for about sixty years. Moreover, many passages from the Old Testament, such as the one we heard today as our first reading, had been read and understood by the Church in the light of a further and full revelation which brought the figure of Jesus Christ into a gradually sharper focus. For John the Apostle, the truth of Jesus Christ was a clear, living reality. It must have been absolutely incredible to him, as he neared the end of his life, that many people still failed to recognize or to accept Jesus Christ.

If John the Apostle were alive today, I wonder what he would think of people and their faith. Would he observe that all of his apostolic efforts had produced results in the twentieth century? Perhaps we can agree that he would find it incredible that in our modern world so many people still fail to recognize or accept Christ. But maybe we have arrived at the right answer while looking in the wrong direction. If we are thinking of all the irreligious people, the atheists, the pagans of our own times as a cause for John's disappointment, we are not focusing on the real problem. John would want to know whether we who profess to be Christians have really accepted Christ. Could it be that he would find it necessary to quote the words of the Baptist to us: "There is one among you whom you do not recognize"?

We believe that Jesus is the Messiah, the Son of God. We accept the reality of his presence in the Blessed Sacrament. But there should be more. Jesus is not only glorified in heaven and sacramentally present in the Eucharist. He is among us today. Do we recognize him? When Jesus walked this earth, his divinity was hidden beneath the veils of his humanity. Only faith could see through those veils to his true identity. Today, Jesus is hidden beneath the humanity of the persons with whom we live. Only faith can see through that humanity to the person of Jesus Christ.

We will soon renew our faith in Jesus through the celebration of Christmas. We will profess our belief that the little baby born of Mary in Bethlehem is the Messiah, the Son of God. Once again, the "Christmas spirit" will fill us with the feeling of good will toward our fellow men as we write cards, give gifts, and greet others with a joyful "Merry Christmas." One of the nicest things about Christmas is the effort that everyone makes to be pleasant, agreeable, and helpful. No one wants to be another Scrooge at this time of the year. But the birth of Jesus is not just another historical event of the past which is commemorated each December. Jesus is born again and again in our fellow human beings. The Christmas spirit of love should not be confined to the last two weeks of this month. Rather, it should endure all year. Why can't we keep that spirit in January and through all the other months? I don't think the basic reason for our failure is that we are bad or that we don't care about others or that we are selfish. I think the basic problem is that we don't have real faith that Jesus is living in others, that what we do, good or bad, to even the least of his brethren, we do, good or bad, to him.

St. Paul today had a Christmas wish for us: that we may be found irreproachable at the coming of Jesus Christ. When Jesus comes again to judge us, he will have something on his mind and it will not take him long to get to the point. He will want to know, not only whether we have recognized him as the Messiah, but also whether we have recognized him as he truly lives in our fellow human beings.

C.E.M.

### Third Sunday of Advent (C)

## *THE CHRISTIAN CHALLENGE*

A friend of mine once said to me, "If only God did not demand so much from us, life would be much easier." If only God did not demand so much from us. . . . Does it seem that God does demand much? If not, then maybe we have missed something of the meaning of Christianity. As a matter of fact, God wants everything. If all we had to do was to come to Mass and to tell God that we loved him, it would be a snap. Words are cheap; they come easy.

The people of today's gospel seemed to have realized that more than words was required of them. They had heard John preach repentance. They had listened to his call for a change of life. In a spirit of enthusiasm generated by the challenging preaching of the Baptist, they cried out, "What ought we to *do*?" And John quickly replied with equal enthusiasm. He told them to be generous; to share their goods with others. He urged them to be fair, to be just, to be charitable.

But that is nothing new. We have heard it all before—many times. And I am sure that we all want to be generous, fair, just and charitable with others. We tell God in our prayers that we love him, and that we want to do his will. But maybe that is nothing new to God either. Maybe he has heard it all before—many times.

But what must we do? Perhaps you feel that it would be a wonderful thing if a preacher like John the Baptist were standing in the pulpit today, to tell you exactly what you must do to please God. Perhaps you wish that the Church could go back to the old way of pointing out to us precisely what to do and what not to do. The old way was so comfortable and convenient. No meat on Friday, go to confession and Communion at least once a year, come to Mass every Sunday, don't go to places of amusement that show lewd entertainment—there seemed to be a nice, neat answer for every question of what we could or could not do.

Today, almost everything seems so different. One priest may tell you one thing, while another gives a completely opposite story. Yes, the old way certainly was convenient, but it was dangerous and it was deadening. It was dangerous because it made it possible for us to feel complacent, to feel satisfied in doing just the minimum that a precisely formulated law required of us. It was deadening because it took the challenge out of Christianity. It tended to treat us like children who need to be told every little thing, who cannot make decisions that require generosity and maturity.

I am not saying that the Church has abandoned her role as a moral guide. I am not suggesting that two priests are both right when they contradict each other. I am not hinting that each one of you should just go ahead and do whatever you want and then try to square your conscience with your actions, instead of squaring your actions with your conscience.

What I am saying is that God demands much of us. He is not satisfied with a strict legalism, with a mere sticking to the letter of the law. We must not become complacent and self-satisfied because we think we have kept the ten commandments and the precepts of the Church. We must not sit back and wait to be told what to do, as if we were little children. It would be convenient if God were to tell us exactly what we must do and must not do in every moment of our lives, but in such a situation there would be no challenge and no chance for maturity.

Take a couple who say they are truly in love. What kind of a married life will they have if they are content with merely not offending each other? Suppose the wife complains to her husband, and he says, "What's the matter? I haven't done anything." And the wife says, "That's just the problem. You haven't done anything—you haven't done anything to show your affection, your concern, your love for me." If we want to be Christians, we cannot stand before God and say, "What's the matter? I haven't done anything." Christianity is not a question of what we have *not* done, but of what we do in trying to be generous with God.

I am always struck by a phrase in the third eucharistic prayer. Following the consecration, after we have offered Christ as our gift to God, we pray, "May he make us an everlasting gift to you. . . ." An everlasting gift! When you have given a gift to someone, you relinquish all claim to that gift. It belongs entirely to the person to whom you have given it. When we pray, "May he make us an everlasting gift to you," we are giving ourselves completely and irrevocably to God. It is not that only a part of our lives belongs to God; *everything* about our lives belongs to him.

C.E.M.

## Fourth Sunday of Advent (A)

## *SPIRITUAL LIBERATION*

The early 70's may go down in history books as the high point in the emancipation of womanhood. The woman's liberation movement has propelled women into the political limelight. Commercials remind women of their newly discovered freedom in fashions and housekeeping. But what is heralded as a breakthrough in this century is only part of a long line of history.

It started ages ago—in fact some seven hundred years before the birth of Christ. The status of women indeed needed elevating, especially in Palestine. Politically and religiously it was truly a man's world. Even the hope for a Messiah, a great new leader, was founded on David's dream that one of the long line of male descendants would be the Messiah. So the thinking went until the day the prophet Isaiah was moved by God to confront Ahaz, the reigning monarch. Ahaz was a shrewd statesman. He had made alliances with all the great states surrounding Palestine. Each agreed to protect Palestine against the others' countries. Ahaz was proud of his shrewdness, and that is what disturbed Isaiah. Ahaz had given up any notion of needing God.

Isaiah came to ask Ahaz to put his trust in God and promised to give him a sign. Ahaz proudly refused to comply, under the pretense of not wanting to tempt God. But Isaiah gave him a sign anyway, a sign of God's continued protection and guidance by promising that a young woman would bring forth a Savior, and his name would be Emmanuel, ''God-with-us.'' This passage as read by the Church and understood in the light of further and full revelation brings the figure of the woman, Mother of the Savior, into a gradually sharper focus. When looked at in this way, Mary is the virgin who is to conceive and bear a son, whose name will be Emmanuel.* So it was that Christ our Lord was to be born of the House of David, but through Mary's side of the family. And woman's road to dignity began.

Yet even modern feminists will admit that women can't do everything alone. Not even Mary, the chosen mother of the Messiah, could do so. A holy and good man was chosen, a loving husband, Joseph. And Joseph was no dim-witted husband out of a kitchen cleanser commercial. To begin with, he didn't suddenly discover that Mary was pregnant. Mary was obviously in love with Joseph and would have confided the angelic revelation. Nor was Joseph afraid that Mary would be punished for bearing a child out of wedlock, for Jewish law recognized engagement as a solemn binding contract and allowed the couple to live as husband and wife. What Joseph feared was his own unworthiness to act as father of a child who came from God, and he did not think himself holy enough to care for Mary since God had personally chosen her for a great task. The only answer he could see was to back out of the picture with a divorce. Then he was told to have no fear about taking Mary as his wife, and he was instructed to accept the child by giving him his name, Jesus.

And a good balance began: a humble man caring for his young wife, and together in God's providence raising and offering to the world its Messiah. They were a man and a woman sharing a great responsibility.

*Cf. Vatican II's *Dogmatic Constitution on the Church*, 55.

Mary and Joseph became an example to all of us, not dictating to God how they would like their lives to go, but accepting life's events as gifts for growing closer to God.

Yet Mary and Joseph are not unique. God the Father can work miracles in all of us by placing his Son in our minds and hearts. And he will do so, if we offer ourselves to God as Mary and Joseph did. Christ can be born in us only if we lay aside basic human pride, and admit we need help. This is why we are here at Mass: to receive the gift of Christ, to discover that someone really cares about us, not just during the Christmas season, but for the rest of our lives. And we assume our true dignity as Christian brothers and sisters, equal before God our Father. No need for a spiritual liberation movement. The Father frees us from the bondage of sin with his forgiveness at the beginning of Mass, and makes us worthy to stand around the altar with Christ his Son. Christ prepares himself and us to be a gift to the Father. What a fine preparation for Christmas: Christ and we become the gift and the givers, giving ourselves to the Father and each other.

Perhaps the decade of the 70's will go down in history as the awakening, the liberation of men and women to their highest dignity as mature Christians called by the Father to accept one another with equal worth, while anticipating our final glory in the second coming of Christ, the final liberation of all men and women to live as one with the Father.

M.M.R.

**Fourth Sunday of Advent (B)**

## GOD'S CHRISTMAS PREPARATIONS

The time before Christmas is a time of preparation: writing last minute Christmas cards, purchasing a tree, and planning a menu. Most important of all is the selecting of gifts for relatives and friends. We spend the most thought, time, trouble, and expense on the gifts that will go to the persons whom we love the most.

Of course, we give gifts at Christmas only because God started the whole idea. The gifts that we give others should be a reminder of the great Gift God gave to us on the first Christmas. That first Christmas was a long time in coming. God in a sense spent much thought on his Gift. His plan was a mystery hidden for ages (second reading). God had the intention of giving us his Gift all along, even before he created the world, but when sin became a reality his Gift took on a new value and preciousness.

God put a lot of time and trouble into the preparation for his Gift. In fact the entire Old Testament is the story of his preparation. First God selected a man, Abraham, to be the father of his chosen people, the Hebrews. Abraham had a son Isaac, and Isaac had a son Jacob, who in turn had twelve sons, from whom came the twelve tribes of Israel. These people, in time of famine, went into Egypt where they enjoyed the protection of one of the twelve sons, Joseph. Following the death of Joseph, the Israelites became enslaved in Egypt until they were led by Moses to freedom in the Exodus. After wandering in the desert for forty years, the Israelites were established in the promised land where God made a further selection in preparation for his Gift. He decreed that the savior would come from among one of the twelve tribes, that of Judah. From among the members of that tribe, the Jews, he chose one family, that of David. The prophecy of Nathan, which we heard in the first reading, formed the basis for Jewish expectation of a Messiah. The promise that David's kingdom and throne would endure forever was brought to a focus through Mary in the event described in today's gospel. Mary was told that the child to be conceived in her womb by the Holy Spirit would be given the throne of David, his father. Nine months later the Messiah was born in Bethlehem, David's home town. Throughout the lengthy history of salvation in the Old Testament, God was very patient and painstaking in his preparations. The Gift took a long time in coming, but all the waiting was worth it. God gave us a wonderful Gift. He loved us so much that he gave us his own Son.

When some people give you a Christmas gift, they go to great trouble to wrap it as elegantly as possible. Once in a while, the wrappings are so extravagant that you are disappointed when you open the gift. God did just the opposite with his Gift. He wrapped his Gift in a plain, ordinary way, for Jesus did not come robed in the finery of regal elegance amid the splendid trappings of a royal court in a leading city of the world. He was born just as human as we are except for sin, of a humble Jewish girl in an out-of-the-way place within the little known town of Bethlehem. One of the great appeals of Christmas is that the eternal Son of God in the simplest manner possible became flesh and made his dwelling among us.

We are the ones who benefit by all the preparations God made. We are the ones who enjoy his precious Gift. Jesus has really been given to us. He has entered our history, our world, our lives. Though Jesus came at one point in history, and in one definite place, his coming has value and significance for all men of all times and places. Jesus means everything to us. It is no wonder that at Christmas we are joyful and happy. But besides being joyful and happy, we should be grateful to God for his Christmas gift to us. In the preface we will say, "Father, all-powerful and ever-living God, we do well always and everywhere to give you thanks. . . ." When we reflect on the meaning of Christmas, we know that we have a special motive for thanksgiving at this time of the year. In this Mass, we should lift our minds and hearts and voices in gratitude to God who has been so generous with us.

And as we go about our final preparations for Christmas, we should let those preparations be a reminder to us of all the thought, time and trouble that God put forth in preparing to send us our great Gift, his own son.

C.E.M.

## Fourth Sunday of Advent (C)

## *THE SACRED MYSTERY*

There is a certain mystery and even a sacredness about a woman who is carrying a child in her womb. What an amazing thing to reflect on—that a new, tiny human being is living within her body. Life is a sacred gift from God. How mysterious it is that this sacred gift grows and develops within the dark secrecy of the womb. Only a woman who has borne a child can begin to appreciate this marvel. Only she can know the feeling of awe at the first movement within her. Only she can experience the increasing sense of eager longing for the birth of the child. What an incredible thing the beginning of human life is!

Today's gospel centers around two expectant mothers, Mary and Elizabeth. The episode took place several months before the birth of Jesus. When Mary learned that her elderly cousin had conceived, she felt that it was her duty to visit the older woman and offer her help. When Mary arrived, Elizabeth greeted her with these words, "Blessed are you among women, and blessed is the fruit of your womb," words that have come to form part of the "Hail Mary."

Elizabeth's greeting is not surprising. She herself had an exquisite appreciation of motherhood. For many years of her life with her husband, Zechariah, she had been without a child. Then in her old age by the special power of God she conceived John the Baptist. Her many years of patient waiting made her value all the more the mysterious sacredness of begetting a child. She had an even greater sense of sacredness and mystery when she realized how God's special power had been at work.

And so when she saw Mary, all of her own awareness, her own appreciation, overflowed in her exuberant greeting. If every new life is sacred, how much more sacred was the life Mary was carrying in her womb. If God's power had been at work in Elizabeth's conceiving of John, how much greater was God's power at work in Mary's conceiving of Jesus. No wonder, then, that Elizabeth exclaimed, "But who am I that the mother of my Lord should come to me?"

In just a few days, we will celebrate the birth of Christ. We will try to renew all our spirit of awe and wonder at the mysterious sacredness of the birth of Jesus. The birth of Jesus in all of its magnificent reality is beyond our ability to comprehend. It is something we simply cannot grasp. And we can ask, "Who are we that the Lord himself should come to us in human flesh like our own?"

In the preface of this Mass you will hear these words, "In his love he has filled us with joy as we prepare to celebrate his birth, so that when he comes he may find us watching in prayer, our hearts filled with wonder and praise." Indeed, our hearts should be filled with wonder when we think about the meaning of Christmas. "Wonder" means astonishment, even surprise. And it is astonishing that the God who made the universe, who controls the movement of the stars and planets, and shapes the destiny of all men, became a tiny infant. It is surprising that the all-powerful, all-knowing God who holds all life in his hand, went through the whole mysterious process of conception and birth. Astonishing, surprising—and true!

And because of this, our hearts should be filled not only with wonder, but also with praise. On Christmas day we will sing, "Glory to God in the highest." God is worthy of our praise and glory. What a magnificent thing he has done in sending his Son into our world to be our Savior.

Soon it will be Christmas once again. In the little time that remains we should all try to collect our thoughts, despite the many distractions, so that we may realize what the celebrating is all about. We will have another Christmas this year, so that we may grow in our sense of wonder at the sacred mystery of the birth of Jesus, and so that we may praise our God for his magnificent Christmas Gift.

C.E.M.

# THE CHRISTMAS SEASON

## Christmas (A)

(The following two homilies can be used separately for Midnight Mass or Christmas Day. They can also be combined for a slightly longer homily.)

## *THE GREAT CHRISTMAS GIFT*

For the last four weeks, we have been like children expecting a large package in the mail. We've known it was coming. It was just a matter of waiting for the day. And tonight the Gift has arrived. And like children, even before the official presenting of the Gift, we've peeked inside. We know already the Gift is Jesus Christ, sent to us from God our Father.

But even knowing that it is the Son of God arriving, we can't help but be stunned by the special way the Gift is wrapped. For the Father presents his Son wrapped in the clothes of a baby. What hardened person, what calloused Scrooge isn't moved by the sight of a newborn child? Instant welcome, instant love is felt for the child—a far cry from the rejection to be experienced by this child when he reaches his manhood.

And how amazing that during this birth celebration in which we receive the Eucharistic Bread, the Child should be born in a city whose name means House of Bread, Bethlehem. And more, he is laid in the manger, a symbol of nourishment. The Father suggests that he gives us the Son to become a part of us, to be our Food of life.

And tonight we experience history's greatest exchange of gifts. Jesus Christ takes the gift of our humanity with all its vibrance and beauty, and gives to each of us in return a share in his divinity, making us his brothers. Our simple humanness takes on a glow. We are no longer creatures staring up at a giant creator. We become different—going from confused orphans of this world, to richly rewarded, adopted children of a great Lord. Our destiny becomes clear. Our inheritance guarantees eternity for us: an eternity of knowing we are loved, wanted, accepted and treasured by God. After all, we are members of his family.

And like a child showing a new gift, we ought to share our confidence and sense of hope with our brothers in this world who have no hope, no vision of the future. How good it is that many people choose Christmas as the one time of year to visit a Catholic service. During the greeting of peace, we ought to share not only the peace of Christ, but our confidence, our hope, our happiness which comes through Christ, our Gift. Again and again we could invite our neighbors and friends to attend Mass, to become close to the experience of God among men.

And tonight, we have the opportunity to complete the giving cycle by offering anew the body and blood of Christ to the Father, but with an added dimension. The Gift is not Christ alone, for we have become one with Christ. The Gift is not just the perfection of Christ but our added imperfections—our willing to try to be people of hope, proud possessors of a precious gift: Jesus Christ. Our one body in Church this night is made up of new friends, new faces, those not able to attend often, those who may be avoiding Christ. All of us join together in our weakness as children, happy to be here and thankful for the Father's Christmas Gift: Jesus Christ.

M.M.R.

## Christmas (A)
(Alternate homily: Midnight Mass or Christmas Day.)

# *THE AMBASSADOR*

A century ago, it was the custom of great nations to send their young sons to foreign countries to learn the customs and temperament of another people. Then when the youngster grew up, he would be in a unique position to understand both his own country and the land to which he had been sent. He would have the delicate role of negotiating treaties and trade agreements. And as remarkable as it would seem, he would be loved by both countries.

With all the beauty, warmth, and flourish that the Christmas season can provide, a great young Ambassador has come to our land. He has come to be like us in all aspects. In learning our qualities, he will be able to share with us his background. He comes as the Son of a Great Ruler who wishes to establish ties of love, who places full trust and authority in his Son. God our Father has sent his Son Jesus Christ as a boy child to become a man like us in all things except sin. He is the greatest Christmas gift mankind has ever received: a Child who is God himself. How many thousands of generations have longed to look at the face of God. And in one simple gesture of birth, God shows himself to our time: a Father who loves, a Son who loves. That Son will love enough to offer up his precious human life on a hill in Palestine to bring the love of the Father to us. And the joyful, generous Father will seal this gift with the eternal promise of the resurrection, not only for his Son who deserves it, but for all who believe in his Son, for all who call themselves brothers and sisters of Jesus Christ.

Christmas is a passing day, and seldom are Christmas gifts long lasting. But today we receive the Gift of Life. As the coming of a child into a family is a beginning with the promise of growth, so the real Christmas is receiving Christ on a permanent basis, first as the Ambassador from the Father, and secondly as a Brother who cares. Christ comes as a Child to convince us that he will not hide behind his divinity in a kind of diplomatic immunity from human want, worry and pain. He will go before us, experiencing the problems of life. Then he will turn back and suggest a way for us to travel.

Christmas for us is people: family, friends. But more, Christmas is a Person: Jesus Christ. He comes to show us how to live by loving; how to grow by suffering. In greeting others with "Merry Christmas," we become envoys of Christ, spreading not just Christmas cheer, but extending his loving concern. Perhaps some day world powers may come to recognize our Ambassador Christ. Then truces can turn into lasting peace, and we can celebrate an Eternal Christmas.

M.M.R.

## Christmas Day (B)

## *THE BIRTH OF HOPE*

Christmas celebrates light overcoming darkness. The darkness of the night can suggest danger and hostility. It can arouse feelings of fear, uncertainty and loneliness. It often is an especially difficult time for those who are sick, and yet the night can be a turning point for them. Those few who are keeping a quiet vigil at the bedside observe that the patient becomes restful; his temperature goes down; the crisis passes, and there is born in their hearts a new hope for recovery, health and happiness.

Some seven hundred years before Christ, Isaiah wrote in prophecy: "The people who walked in darkness have seen a great light; upon those who dwelt in the land of gloom a light has shone; you have brought them abundant joy and great rejoicing . . . for a child is born. . . ." Christmas is the perfect fulfillment of those words, an event of great hope which took place in the dark stillness of night. It was the turning point for the whole human race, sick almost to death with the illness of sin. The crisis passed with the birth of a child. Only a few observed the event: Mary, Joseph and the shepherds—but they knew with joy beyond description that with the birth of Jesus there was born a new hope for recovery from sin, and a new hope for spiritual health and eternal happiness.

A newly born child is a natural sign of hope. His parents pray that he will grow and develop into someone important and famous, someone of value and worth. Many a father has looked at his new son and said, "This kid can be President some day." We do not exactly know what the thoughts of expectation were in Mary's mind as she looked upon her son for the first time. We are not quite sure whether Mary even then had an image of how her son was to be of value and worth to his fellow human beings. As she looked on the smooth, soft infant's flesh which she had given him, did she know that she would see that flesh torn and lacerated in the crucifixion? Did she realize that the precious blood which was then giving a healthy hue to her baby's face would one day be drained from his body on the cross? These things we are not certain of, but when the day of sacrifice did come Mary understood that her son was giving himself for all of us, for our spiritual health and eternal happiness.

Mary at Christmas looked to the future with hope. We now look to the past, not only upon the birth of Jesus, but also upon his death and resurrection, the means of our salvation. But we wonder where is the spiritual health, where is the happiness he came to bring? The world still seems sick with the illness of sin. There is poverty, hatred and war, rather than peace on earth.

The reason for all this is that salvation does not occur automatically. Each one of us must learn to live like Jesus, to share his love for God and for our fellow human beings. With his birth the turning point was indeed reached, the crisis was over. But much remains to be done before the world fully recovers. Each one of us individually must contribute to that recovery by the way in which we live. Our flesh will be torn and lacerated in the struggle against sin. Even our blood will be drained in the battle against hatred and war.

This Christmas, however, is a sign of joyful hope, because Christmas is meant to be a new birth for Jesus. Jesus gives us his flesh and blood in communion, with the plea that we will give him our flesh and blood so that his goodness and love may continue in the world today. He wishes to be born again in us like a little baby, a baby who is a sign of hope.

C.E.M.

**Christmas Day (C)**

# *LIGHT AND WARMTH*

Today we are celebrating a birthday. Everybody likes a birthday, and is usually willing to join in the party. But this birthday is unique. It is celebrated not only by a few relatives and close friends, but by millions of people. It is celebrated not merely in the person's birthplace, but throughout the entire world from Bethlehem in Judaea to Bethlehem in Pennsylvania, all the way from earth to heaven. For it is the birthday of God himself, the Word made flesh.

The center of a birthday celebration is usually the cake topped by the birthday candles. We do not have a cake, but we have the candles burning on the altar; at home and on the streets lights make up the major portion of the Christmas decorations. Light is an excellent symbol of the meaning of Christmas. In fact, Christmas is very much a feast of light.

Just a few days ago there occurred the shortest day in the year, December 21, when the least amount of sunshine is possible. From now on, however, the days grow longer and the hours of sunshine increase in number. This is taken to be a symbol of the coming of Christ to be the Light of the world. Christ, the Son of God, is the shining sun of our lives.

The sun does two main things for us; it brings light and it brings warmth, both of which are necessary for life. Christ brings the light of God's truth into our lives. Darkness is really a frightening thing that panics a child and can even on occasion terrify an adult. With our artificial lighting it is difficult to realize the meaning of darkness, but just imagine that some night all the electricity fails. You are in total darkness. You can't see where you are going or what you are doing. You stumble around and bump into things. You feel very much alone, confused, almost in despair. Such was the condition of the world without Christ. Men were confused about the meaning and purpose of their existence. They stumbled through life, not knowing clearly where they were going or what they should do.

It was a long, dark night from the first sin until the bright day of Christ. Christ's coming was like the sun rising in the morning with its fresh brilliance. This light of Christ was his teaching about God his Father and his divine plan for us.

The sun is not only a source of light but of warmth as well. Again with our artificial heating it is difficult to appreciate fully the effect of cold, especially extreme cold. In extreme cold all life processes slow down; a kind of lethargy and listlessness comes over nature itself. A man who is freezing can think only of himself. Instinctively he wraps his arms around himself in an attempt to generate a little heat. Without warmth he must die.

Christ as the Light of the world also brings to us the warmth of his love. Without his love we cannot live as we should. Without his love we go through life in a kind of lethargy and listlessness, thinking only of ourselves and loving only ourselves. But what a wonderful thing to know and to feel the love of God for us in the Person of Christ. That love opens us up and lifts us from the despair of selfishness. Everyone wants and needs love, and it is only the love of God that can completely fill and satisfy us.

Christmas should make us appreciate the meaning of the coming of Christ. It is the celebration of a great event that took place not only a long time ago, but which continues to take place every day, especially in the Mass. Christ is still among us as the light and warmth of our lives.

In the Mass, Christ is present in the words of the scripture readings and in the homily to enlighten our minds. His words are truth to live by. Christ comes to us in Holy Communion to warm our hearts with the love of God. We can and should have the effect of Christmas every time we participate in the Mass.

Yes, we are celebrating a birthday unique in many ways. Ordinarily we give a gift to the person whose birthday it is; but today, on his birthday, Christ gives us the gift of himself. He comes to us with the light of his truth and the warmth of his love.

C.E.M.

**Feast of the Holy Family (A)**

## THE FATHER'S FAMILY

Think how easy it was for Jesus to grow up as a perfect young man. He was raised by two saints: Mary and Joseph. Or to turn it around, Mary and Joseph found it easy to be saints as parents simply because Jesus Christ, Son of God, was their child. No problems. Except there were the poor living conditions at Bethlehem. And the time Jesus was "lost" in the temple—certainly a lack of communication there. Or Mary "forcing" her son into action at Cana, simply because he was unwilling to "show off." Or more seriously, the biting shame of having her son arrested as a criminal and the tragic loss when her son was executed. Every family has problems, even the best family.

But the Holy Family is special. And sociologists today would suggest an additional reason why the Joseph of Nazareth Family is special: it's a Jewish family. In fact, of all the ethnic groups in the United States, Jewish families have the smallest number of juvenile delinquents. The style of Jewish family life may present a clue. Jewish children grow up experiencing their father as the representative of God in the family. Many Jewish feastdays are times of family celebration and the father presides over the prayers. He blesses the children as God's representative. Then growing up, the children can accuse their father of getting bald, not being the greatest ball player in the world, but they can never deny that he represents God.

How many Catholic fathers lead their families in prayer, or bless them before they go to bed? Without slighting a mother's role in the family, more fathers could recognize their God-given authority to be a family-teacher, a family-prayer-leader. Most fathers try year after year to provide the best of everything for their family. And they become "unknown" heroes since they are gone from the family for most of the day. But how impressive it would be for any family to have the father's presence be a joyful reminder of God, as Joseph reminded his family of the Father. All fathers aren't perfect, but each one reflects the loving care, the protection of our Father in heaven. Each father has a special patron in heaven, God the Father, and should make demands on the Father. And if more families could rely on the blessings flowing from the head of the family, perhaps less disunity and mistrust would be present.

Mothers and fathers try hard to make family life happy. But all families aren't bursting with joy. And some homes wind up being miserable places to live. Yet, ultimately all of us, whether we have a perfect family situation or not, can be happy in the bigger family we belong to. As St. Paul says: ". . . You are God's chosen ones, holy and beloved.'' All baptized Christians are adopted children of the Father. All the love that adopting parents bestow on their long-awaited children is ours. This love and concern from the Father should prod us, as Paul suggests, to have "beautiful mercy . . . kindness, humility, meekness, and patience'' at home. We ought to "bear with one another, forgive whatever grievances you have against one another. Forgive as the Lord has forgiven you.''

The Christmas season is very much a time for family celebration. It is sad when a person is alone at Christmas time. So this Mass is a family celebration. Someone may meditate well alone on a mountain top, but when he wants to celebrate he comes together with others—as we are gathered here. And the sign of our familyhood is that we gather around our Father's table. As one family, we sing from our hearts in psalms, hymns, and other inspired songs. And the Father nourishes us with life-giving Food: his own Son. Mass by Mass our own sonship grows. Let us pray during this Mass for our own families, but especially for each other—that we may long for the day when all of us will finally be home with the Father.

M.M.R.

**Feast of the Holy Family (B)**

## *MISSION: IMPOSSIBLE*

"Your mission, Ted and Teri, if you decide to accept this marriage agreement, is to form a holy family." Very truthfully, these words could be addressed to each couple during their wedding ceremony. And, if they were spoken by the presiding minister, almost everyone attending the wedding, including the bride and groom, would shout out, "Mission: Impossible." Our society has become more and more pessimistic about the possibility of forming a holy and happy family life. And yet, this feast today in honor of the holy family of Jesus, Mary and Joseph, presents us with just such a possibility.

The liturgy today offers us a good image of family life. The wisdom of the Old Testament of the Bible is condensed in the first reading. It seems to me it would be advantageous to hear this read again slowly and meditatively. (*Read.*) You see, the image presented here is one of a positive and constructive view of the problems that usually confront our families today. Unfortunately, it has become more and more profitable, especially on television, to create laughs at the expense of the family image. If the laughter from the live audience is not loud enough, it is amplified with previously taped laughter. And so, a previously tarnished image is made still more dull and uninspiring.

Obviously, the recommendations in both the first and second readings seem to present an impossible task. And yet, even if in your family you have not seen happiness work out, still you do know some families where it has. If you say that you don't know any, then one would have to reply that your experiences are not broad enough, or you are taking superficially imperfect situations as the norm, and not realizing the deeper happiness that is present, but seldom expressed to you. The fact that a priest is not married and thus does not experience directly the problems of achieving happiness in marriage must be admitted. However, his pastoral experience brings him into contact with a large variety of marriages. The sum total of these contacts is that happiness in family life is possible. Complete and absolute and total happiness? Obviously not. Such happiness is not possible in any human situation. But peace, contentment, enjoyment, good feelings, growing and developing personalities, positive thinking about the challenges of daily living together—all these and more are seen in the broad spectrum of family life that is the joy of any priest who gives his time and energy to the families under his care.

Let's take a few minutes looking at some of these couples who have improved their image of family life. First, they realize the sacredness and permanence of the agreement that they made to be husband and wife, and hopefully, father and mother. For Catholics, this sacredness is further enhanced by the sacrament of marriage received during the Mass.

For some couples this realization was not present at the time of the wedding, but gradually through prayer and study and consultation it came to be one of the main supports of a satisfying living together. The initial sacrament of their family relationship has been added to Sunday by Sunday, by those couples who truly worship together at Mass and develop that feeling of closeness and unity which comes from receiving the bond of unity, Holy Communion. And the main bulwark of many couples against the forces that can tear them apart is that they honestly and openly listen to each other. Consequently there is not the effort on the part of one member to the marriage to make over the other in the image which he or she had that the other should be. When the lines of communication are always open, or if blocked temporarily, then opened again as soon as possible, most of the problems that interfere with the happiness of the family can be resolved. Surely, there are many problems that need outside help, but if the couple are really talking to each other, then they will mutually realize this need and agree to seek such help. God help those who are not willing to be truly honest with one another! Many other good ways to happiness are seen in so many families. But let these few examples suffice for now.

The image of family life as given us by the holy family is a possible image for all those who truly wish it. Let us pray for all our families in this Mass, the beautiful Eucharist of peace, and harmony, and love, and happiness.

O.J.M.

**Feast of the Holy Family (C)**

## *YOUR FEAST DAY*

During the course of the year we celebrate many feast days: Christmas, Easter, Christ the King, different saints. But today is your feast day, the feast of the Holy Family. As parent or child of whatever age, this is your feast.

In the Church we make use of the special term, "Vocation." Usually when we hear this word, "vocation," we think of the priesthood or the religious life. But that is a narrow use of the word. You, parents and children, have a vocation too, the vocation to family life. Vocation means God's plan for you, and his plan for the vast majority of people is family life.

You fathers must have a job. It is your duty to support your family. Your job naturally takes a lot of your time, your talent and your thought. But whatever your job is, no matter how important that job may be to the welfare of others or even of society as a whole, your principal vocation is to be a husband and father.

You mothers these days are often engaged in a lot of activities that take you out of the home. You may even have an outside job or a career. But for you too, your principal vocation is to be a wife and mother.

You children and young adults look forward now or soon will look forward to becoming independent, going out on your own, getting a job, and eventually starting your own family, but right now your principal vocation is within your present family.

Today there is a special need for this feast of family vocation. We all know that the family is under attack because of divorce, anti-child propaganda, and the pansexualism of our age which tends to separate sex from marriage and true love. Some scientists are even predicting that the day will come when husband and wife will not be allowed by law to have children. Instead, sperm and ova banks will be set up. Children will be conceived artificially according to what some scientist thinks is the best possible combination of genes. The baby will then be a "test tube" baby. After birth, he will not be brought up within a family but by professional social workers. Then there will be no need for marriage or the family. So the predictions go, and a sorry, tragic day it will be if they come to pass.

The teaching of the Church is, of course, that marriage and the family are of divine institution. They are God's idea, not man's. As such they are sacred and permanent. The Vatican Council in its *Decree on the Laity* states: "The family has received from God its mission to be the first and vital cell of society" (11). Marriage and the family as instituted by God are necessary for a healthy, normal society, as the lesson of history has so emphatically taught us. Civilizations of the past have crumbled when marriage and the family as the solid foundation of society have been destroyed.

Family life is a full time job, and a difficult one. That is why the Vatican Council stated that the family will fulfill its mission, not only "through the mutual affection of its members," but also through "the common prayer they offer to God.'' Prayer is necessary and absolutely indispensable, both in the home and together here in church at the Mass. Only from prayer and the Mass can a family derive the strength and help needed to fulfill its important vocation in our society. Parents, never hesitate to insist on prayer in your home. And remember that you must do more than "hear" the prayers of your children. I know parents who make sure that their children pray, but their children never see them praying. Pray with your children. Try to come to Mass together. There are problems, especially if you have little ones. But all the trouble involved is worth the benefit of praying together here at Mass every Sunday.

All of us must pray for the success of family life, even if we are living alone. Upon the success of family life depends the welfare of our whole society and of the Church as well. And so all of us here in this Mass today must join together in praying for God's blessings upon family life.

Today, the feast of the Holy Family, could well be called "Family Vocation Sunday," because today God wishes to emphasize the importance of your vocation to family life.

C.E.M.

## Solemnity of Mary, the Mother of God (A)

## *HAPPY NEW LIFE*

Every mother knows the feeling of relief that comes after her child has been born. The several months of worry and concern as to whether the baby will be healthy have made her anxious and tense. Finally the baby comes. Her anxiety turns to love and protection, as she cares for her child. A mother even possesses a special sound system whereby she recognizes her baby's voice during the night or in a crowd. A mother is preoccupied with her child.

Today we celebrate the time when Mary was preoccupied with her child. First were the nine months of waiting, and then the days of watching and listening for her child as she went about her normal duties as Joseph's wife, caring for his home. But always the delightful thought of Jesus was on her mind.

And all this can be a clue for our beginning the new year. Quite simply we need to be aware of Christ, or better, preoccupied with him in a special way. As we go about the normal activities of our lives we should have Jesus on our mind, just as good parents have their children on their mind even as they go about their daily duties. Christ should take a position in our minds and hearts, not like the highway patrolman whom we fear as we drive, or the teacher whom the grammar school student watches out of the corner of his eye. Rather it should be as a child, or perhaps a friend, holds a corner of our mind. Jesus should occupy a part of us.

We welcomed Christ at Christmas. He is here. He has come to be a friend, to join our family, to be a part of our existence. But what do we do with Christ? Is he to be like a picture of a relative who has passed away, a picture hanging on the wall and scarcely ever catching our attention? No, Christ is alive. He comes again in this Mass. He speaks to us in the scriptures. He greets us through the person next to us in the sign of peace. He gives us himself in Communion. At the end of Mass do we smile a good-bye and leave him here in church, or does he go with us through the door?

The beauty of Christ's presence is that he rides lightly on our minds. He is there for a moment's recollection, like remembering a good time we've had or a good friend we've been with. Uniquely Christ is not just a memory, for when we think of him, he is present and as real as he was with his mother and his disciples. The breakthrough was Mary's acceptance. By simply agreeing to be the mother of Christ, she set aside her personal wishes and gained the world. How much more would we gain if we could only learn the art of gracious acceptance, to accept Christ as he is present here in the Mass, in ourselves and in others.

Seeing and accepting Christ, we could then learn to accept others as they are, not as miniature versions of ourselves, without making harsh demands on them. We should begin our year by saying to ourselves, our family, our friends, our world: "The Lord bless you and keep you. The Lord let his face shine upon you and be gracious to you. The Lord look upon you kindly and give you peace" (first reading).

M.M.R.

**Solemnity of Mary, the Mother of God (B)**

## *RENEWAL*

"May God bless us in his mercy." This is one of the nicest responsories we have during the entire year. And it is very appropriate for the beginning of a new year. There are many blessings we all need—in the whole world, in our nation, in our cities and towns, in our families and homes, and in our own individual lives. So, may God bless each of us through this new year.

The blessings in the first reading when spoken by God to Moses were in relation to the renewal of the Hebrew people after their freedom from Egyptian slavery. Actually, the entire history of these chosen people looked toward a freedom which would involve the entire human race. Even though these people thought of freedom only in relation to themselves, nevertheless God had in mind the renewal of all mankind in love and freedom—freedom once again to love God and all men for the sake of God. This universal freedom, this renewal, was realized in the coming of Christ, born of a woman. St. Paul stated, "When the designated time had come, God sent forth his Son born of a woman . . . so that we might receive our status as adopted sons."

The fathers of the Vatican Council reaffirmed the place of Mary, this woman, in God's plan of renewal, "truly the mother of God and mother of the redeemer." They pointed out that "in subordination to Christ and along with him, by the grace of almighty God she served the mystery of redemption" (*Constitution on the Church*, 56).

Mary responded to God's plan of redemption more completely than any other human person. Her example should give encouragement to us in our efforts to cooperate with God in the renewal of ourselves. Following Mary as a model, we should see New Year's resolutions as an expression of our own individual effort with God's grace to make the work of redemption effective here and now. Take anger, for example, anger which does real harm to the person who is angry and through him to others, such as the brutal beating of another, either of a young child by an irate parent, or of an old man by irresponsible youths. Some people say this kind of thing, though deplorable, is inevitable. God's plan of renewal says that gradually the peace of Christ and his meekness will envelop those persons afflicted with the sin of anger. And so with every other sin.

What we may not realize is that we do need the influence and help of a mother to become the better persons we should be through the grace of God. Again the fathers of the Vatican Council remind us of the role of Mary: "In an utterly singular way she cooperated by her obedience, faith, hope, and burning charity in the Savior's work of restoring supernatural life to souls. For this reason she is a mother to us in the order of grace. . . . By her maternal charity Mary cares for the brethren of her Son who still journey on earth surrounded by dangers and difficulties, until they are led to their happy fatherland" (*Ibid.*, 61f.).

Certainly, devotion is in place to anyone so intimately connected with God's renewal. One important form of devotion is imitation. In our devotion, let us imitate Mary's great love for all of God's children. She was willing to become the spiritual mother of every human being, regardless of race, color, nationality, political beliefs, religious creed, looks, health, wealth, poverty, success, failure, appeal, drabness—I need not go on with the litany. Why do we make such distinctions when Mary never did? Mary loved everyone enough to bring Christ into the world for them. Why do we hold back in showing the love of Christ to the world?

On this first day of the new year when we celebrate the Solemnity of Mary, the Mother of God, an excellent resolution would be to imitate Mary in her love. Working toward fulfilling that resolution with God's grace, will be working toward the renewal God has in mind for the entire world.

O.J.M.

**Solemnity of Mary, the Mother of God (C)**

## *BEGINNING AGAIN*

Just one week ago, we celebrated the birth of Christ. On this day, the eighth day after Christmas, the Christ child was circumcised and given the name "Jesus." In Hebrew the name means "God saves," and it indicated that Jesus was to be the Savior of all men. In a sense the day marked a beginning for Mary, as a whole new life with Jesus opened out before her. We are not sure of how much Mary understood at the moment concerning what lay ahead in the future for herself and her child. But she must have started that new life with a great sense of confidence and hope, because she had Jesus with her.

Today is also New Year's Day. Most of us have the practice of making resolutions on this day. I suppose that this practice is based on the idea that all of us like to take the opportunity for a new start, to begin again, with the hope that we will improve ourselves during the new year.

This day should remind us that we need never despair, no matter what our mistakes in the past may have been. We can always begin again. I personally believe that one of the greatest favors of God is the chance to make a new start. God today is giving us a new year. We can take this as a sign that God is always willing to give another chance, not just in the new year but in every new day that he lets us have.

On this first day of the fresh new year, we should forget the past with all of its failures and shortcomings, and look to the future. It is true that we are not certain about what the future will contain for us, but like Mary we should begin today with confidence and hope because we too have Jesus, the Savior, with us. If we had to go it alone, if we had to walk into the darkness of the future all by ourselves, there would indeed be good cause for trepidation. But we are not alone. We have Jesus to help us, especially in the Mass.

We are beginning the new year in the right way by this celebration of the Mass. Here we are praying with Jesus; here we listen to his words; and here we receive him in Communion. God gives us his Son, our Savior, to be with us and to help us in every moment of our lives. That is God's gift to us as we begin this new year.

If you are the kind of person who makes new year's resolutions, you can probably look back over the year and see that you did not keep your resolutions very well. And maybe that is the story for most of us: failures despite good intentions. The message of today's Mass is that we need never despair, that God is a good God, who gives us his Son so that we may have another chance.

C.E.M.

## Solemnity of the Epiphany (A)

# FOLLOW THAT STAR

Isn't it amazing, in this age of science and sophistication, that there is so much interest in horoscopes and astrological signs? It isn't long before most friends discover each other's birthdate and star sign. And all of us are secretly pleased when the newspaper prophet predicts a day to take life easy and be prepared for something grand to happen.

With today's outlook, it isn't too hard to appreciate ancient man's dependence on stars and heavenly occurrences. Any event in the skies caused excited expectation. The heavens were the television screen of the gods predicting in some hidden way man's coming events. It was natural for Matthew to choose the star as the sign of pagan men hoping for answers from heaven.

Whether it was a real or symbolic star isn't important. Matthew's narrative skillfully shows that Christ fulfilled the ancient predictions of the coming Great One. It also shows that nature responds more appropriately to God than man, that foreigners were more adept at recognizing Christ than the Jews, and that the mission of Christ was to extend to a world scene far beyond that of Palestine. And the wise astrologers were blessed. Of all who must have noticed a special star, they were the most eager. They yearned to join the new King.

Longing for something is usually a delightful experience. We all experienced the longing for the warmth and surprises of Christmas. And very often the longing, or expectation of something, is happier than the actual event which comes and goes in a flash. Longing for a home of your own, or planning a vacation in the future, can be a delight.

And on a deeper level, picture the husband and wife who long to get away from the kids just to be alone and appreciate each other. The second honeymoon might never come, but just longing for it is a good sign of the love that exists between husband and wife. It proves that love is there. How sad if that desire ever disappears.

And how many of us would long to get away from job and distraction, just to spend more time with our Lord. "I'd go on a retreat right now, if I could get away." "I'd love to spend more time in prayer at home, but the phone rings, the kids come in. I get so distracted, that Christ seems a million miles away." As disheartening as it seems sometimes, there is a good side. Be happy you have the desire to reach Christ. This desire, this longing only shows how limited things are on this earth. Only in heaven will we possess Christ perfectly. He'll be right there face to face.

Some of the greatest saints in history—St. John of God, both St. Theresas, St. Francis of Assisi—all had to fight the problems of business and distractions. But the struggle of years never dampened their longing for Christ. And in the end, their patience with themselves and their life situation won Christ for them. Epiphany celebrates Christ showing himself to the world. But even Christ our Lord had to be patient to wait for thirty years before the right time came to fulfill what he longed for.

The longing of the wise men brought the reward of the discovery of the Christ child. Our own patience with our longing for Christ will give us Christ. Don't be impatient with your distractions in prayer or even at this Mass. Be happy about this desire you have. Know that Christ will come to us. He comes in this Mass to increase our faith, our hope to be closer, our imperfect love. And don't worry, you're not lost. If you long for Christ, you're following the right star.

M.M.R.

## Solemnity of the Epiphany (B)

## *EQUALITY OF MAN BEFORE HIS CREATOR*

In an unpretentious cemetery in Lancaster, Pennsylvania, you can see the grave of Thaddeus Stevens. Hardly any congressman worked harder for "equality of man before his Creator." He died in 1868, attended by two black nuns. His epitaph, composed by himself, can be read on his tombstone:

I repose in this quiet and secluded spot,
Not for any natural preference for solitude
But, finding other Cemeteries limited as to Race
by Charter Rules,
I have chosen this that I might illustrate
in my death
The Principles which I advocated through a long life:
Equality of Man before His Creator.

(See *Reader's Digest*, July 1971, page 174)

Equality of Man before His Creator. This is one of the truths that the liturgy of the Epiphany is concerned with. It is a truth that concerns us today.

Christians in the early Church were confronted with the problem of exclusiveness. Like us, they had been taught they were a chosen race, a royal priesthood, a special people, a people through whom salvation was to come. The early Christians inherited this idea from the Jewish religion from which most of the first converts came. Were not the Jewish people the chosen ones from whom would come the Savior of the world? Were they not the descendants of Abraham to whom the promise of redemption was given, and passed on through Isaac and Jacob and the twelve tribes that sprang from him? So it was natural for some of them to think of themselves as better than those who did not belong to their ranks. It was easy for them to forget that their faith was a gift from God and something they had not merited. Equality of all men before the Creator was admissible as a theory, but in practice there was a tendency among some Christians toward smugness and an attitude that their salvation was automatically assured, no matter how they led their lives. In theory we, too, readily admit, especially since the Second Vatican Council, the equality of all men before God, but in practice we can have a tendency toward exclusiveness and a complacent attitude of automatic salvation. Let us see how today's liturgy attempts to set straight our thinking in this matter.

According to the first reading, Isaiah sees Jerusalem as the center of God's mercy. At last the time is coming when the glory of the Lord will shine upon this chosen city. Yes, Jerusalem is the chosen city of redemption, but the resulting salvation is not the exclusive right of the citizens of the city. For, "your sons come from afar . . . all from Sheba shall come." And so our response to this word of God was: "Lord, every nation on earth will adore you."

In the second reading, St. Paul speaks very bluntly. "In Christ Jesus the Gentiles [everyone who is a non-Jew] are now coheirs with the Jews, members of the same body and sharers of the promise through the preaching of the gospel." That there is no exclusiveness in God's kingdom is so frequently mentioned by St. Paul as to become a commonplace. He had no difficulty in admitting the equality of man before his Creator. It is because God loves us that we, too, have equality before him. For our part we should recognize this equality in all other persons and strive therefore to give them what is rightfully their due. Even though St. Paul is speaking mainly in a religious sense of equality, nevertheless, the implications of this equality are found in every aspect of life. Within the ambit of our own personal lives, such as the family and the neighborhood, we must exercise personal responsibility to see that we do not infringe on the equal rights of others. In fact, we should positively support these rights in every way we possibly can. This is the lesson of equality of all men before their Creator that the liturgy teaches us today.

The story of the Wise Men in today's gospel is part of St. Matthew's way of teaching the early Christians the universality of God's salvation plan. God does not despise poor Jewish shepherds, or the rich men from the east. How many and what other people came to see the infant, we do not know. But we can be sure that they were all graciously received. It is an interesting tradition that we retain the shepherds in the Christmas crib, even after the time of their visit is passed, while we introduce the Magi into the scene. There is something in this that admits our equality before God.

Like the Magi, we, too, come offering our gifts. Representatives of this congregation will carry to the altar the water, wine and bread, as we prepare to offer ourselves with Christ to the Father. Let this offering of ourselves not be marred by feelings of prejudice, bigotry or discrimination. Rather let us be joyful that before God, our Creator, we stand as equals, redeemed in the precious Blood of Jesus Christ.

O.J.M.

## Solemnity of the Epiphany (C)

### *JESUS, OUR GIFT*

The word "Epiphany" is a Greek word which means "manifestation." On this day Jesus manifested that he was to be the Savior not only of the Jews but of all men. This idea is presented in today's second reading: "God's secret plan . . . has been revealed by the Spirit. . . . In Christ Jesus the Gentiles are now coheirs with the Jews, members of the same body and sharers of the promise through the preaching of the gospel."

This feast also manifests *how* Jesus was to be the Savior of all men, that is, what he was going to do in order to win salvation. The Church, according to a very ancient tradition, sees the gifts of the Magi as symbolic of his mission and his character. Gold of course was the most precious metal of the day. It was intended to manifest the value and preciousness of the person of Christ; that value is infinite since Jesus is God himself. Frankincense, or simply incense, was used in worship, and it was a sign that Jesus would be a priest who would give perfect worship to his Father in heaven. Myrrh was used to embalm bodies in preparation for burial. It symbolized how Jesus would give worship to his Father, that is, by sacrifice, by the offering of his life as a victim.

And so the Epiphany brings out not so much that Jesus was a receiver of gifts from the Magi, but that he himself was to be a most precious gift to his Father in the worship of sacrifice. He was to save all men by the offering of himself as a victim.

In the Mass, at the time of the consecration of the wine into the blood of Jesus, we hear these words: "This is the cup of my blood, the blood of the new and everlasting covenant. It will be shed for you and for all so that sins may be forgiven." Every Mass, then, manifests Jesus as the savior of all men. As we know, the Mass continues the sacrificial worship of Jesus. In each Mass the sacrifice of Christ is made present. Jesus is our gift, the victim we offer to God. And we can have no greater gift. We must remember how precious Jesus is: more precious than gold or anything else we can imagine. We are indeed fortunate in having the perfect gift to offer to God.

But all gift giving is meant to say something. It says something about the giver and the receiver. It says that the giver wants to express his respect, his concern, his love. The preciousness of the gift says something about the receiver. It indicates his position, his dignity, and how high he stands in the esteem of the giver. In the Mass our gift says that we want to express our love, our esteem, our concern for God. And we give him the most valuable thing we can because of who God is.

It follows then, that there must be something behind the gift. For example, if a man gives his wife a gift on their wedding anniversary, no matter how costly the gift, it may mean little or nothing to her. If she rarely sees her husband at home, if he seems to have little time for her, if they are always bickering and quarreling, then the gift is empty, hollow, even hypocritical. The gift should mean that she is first in the affection of her husband. Any woman worthy of her womanhood wants her husband, not just a meaningless present. A gift is meant to be symbolic; to be acceptable, it must represent the giver.

And so with ourselves here at Mass. Even our giving of Jesus as a victim to God may actually be meaningless. If we do not have time for God, if we rarely or never really pray to him and think about him, if we are unfaithful to God in our daily lives, then the Mass does not mean for us what it should. It may be empty, hollow, even hypocritical.

Jesus makes his sacrifice present again in the Mass for our benefit, not his. He offered himself perfectly on the Cross in a total giving of himself in a supreme act of love for his Father. He does not have to do it all over again as if he had not done it perfectly once and for all. The Mass represents that unique offering of Christ. What makes the Mass different from the Cross is what we put into the Mass. A lot is left up to us. Our sincerity, our real effort to please God in all things, the way in which we live—these are the things that will give meaning to what we do here at Mass.

We have a most precious gift to give to God. But that giving must come from the heart. It must be a total giving of ourselves as it was for Jesus in his sacrifice, that sacrifice which is ours in every Mass we celebrate.

C.E.M.

## The Baptism of Our Lord (A)

Sunday following January 6th

## *HERE WE GO AGAIN*

A promising young man is chosen and blessed by God to lead a new people. He walks into the Jordan for a ritual cleansing. He emerges and quickly chooses twelve men to be his assistants. Of course it sounds like Jesus Christ. But a thousand years before Christ, a young man named Joshua emerged from the Jordan to lead the twelve tribes of Israel. He was a prefigurement of Christ. This helps to explain why the sinless Christ should seek the baptism of John. Christ walks into the Jordan to become the new Joshua, or better, the New Israel going through the waters of the Red Sea. As Christ comes out, we have a New Exodus from the old incomplete Judaism to the freedom and potential of the New Israel, the Church.

So today we the Church celebrate a new beginning, probably a more realistic one than the New Year's Eve resolutions. For a week we've been able to rest from the holidays and settle down to routine. Now we can decide if this year is really going to be a different year for us. But it is hard to change, isn't it? The trouble is that so much of what we do is repetitious. We fall into a pattern of getting up, going to work, attending school, making beds, doing the dishes, and all of a sudden it's Christmas again. Another year slips right by us. But rather than look for some spectacular change, we ought to face the core of the problem head on: routine events, monotony, the drab rhythms that carry our days through the year.

Psychologists tell us we need our daily routine, a certain familiar pattern of events. If we had to examine and choose each small detail of our day, we would soon become frayed neurotics with nervous twitches. Our routine, even with its monotony, is the soft familiar support which cushions us against the more disturbing events which need concentration and decisions.

But even granting all this doesn't help much to spare us from the dullness, the lack of color in routine. How many housewives can easily clamor: "We never do anything." How many husbands: "If I didn't have to work this weekend, we could go somewhere." Yet this admittedly mild form of suffering has a value. All of us would like to say next year that during this year we became a better person, closer to Jesus Christ. So why not use the monotony, the dullness of each day to achieve this?

The clue is our own baptism. Baptism is the joining force with Christ. We were baptized into the death and suffering of Christ and shared in his resurrection. We accepted a symbolic drowning, being buried under the water of baptism, in order to rise to a new life. If we could mentally join our daily dull suffering with that of Christ, we could enjoy a new life with him even now.

Today we can easily make a realistic beginning. We can start by facing the routine which fills most of our time, and thereby grow from it rather than try to run from it. We can accept the daily grind with a new intention, with a new purpose, and embrace this mild suffering in order to unite ourselves with Christ, the Suffering Servant. Our monotony is the link which joins us with the Suffering Christ. A slight irritation or dullness can remind us each day of Christ. Christ didn't mind repeating an action already done before by Joshua. We will less and less begrudge repeating our day to day actions if we are in rhythm with the suffering of Christ. By joining the suffering of Christ we will eventually share in the glory of his resurrection.

Even this Sunday celebration of Mass will become routine now until the special beauty of Holy Week and Easter. This very repetition is the journey forward step by step toward the Father. We climb a steep mountain by circling the same sides again and again, but each time on a higher level. Make today a beginning. Renew your baptismal promises within your heart. Ask Christ to accept the ounce of suffering from each day as an investment in your future. Listen especially at the moment of the consecration: "On the night before he suffered, he took bread. . . ." Ask Christ then to take your suffering and offer it with his own. And yearn for the final step: your death and the end of monotony when you will hear the words: "Welcome home; you are my beloved. My favor rests on you."

M.M.R.

### The Baptism of Our Lord (B)
Sunday following January 6th

## *BAPTISM AND HUMILITY*

The human race from the beginning offended God by sin and continues to do so, and therefore is in need of redemption. Regardless of his own personal condition of sinlessness, Jesus knew that the Messiah, the Redeemer, had to take upon himself the sinful condition of mankind. And so the first act of his public life was an act of humility, going down into the Jordan River to be baptized by John. From this first act, every other action was directed toward the completion of redeeming mankind. Christ's death on the cross, made present under the signs of bread and wine in this very Mass, was the culmination of a life of extraordinary humility.

Jesus came for the sake of sinners. Although Jesus knew that his reputation would be stained, he did not hesitate to be friendly with the woman taken in adultery, to allow Mary Magdalene to approach him and to wash and kiss his feet, to go into the house of Zacchaeus and eat with him, to enter the home of the Roman centurion, to sit at the well of Jacob and bring the news of salvation to a foreign woman of ill repute. And sure enough, Jesus' reputation was tarnished, for the accusation was finally made, "He is a friend of sinners and publicans, and eats and drinks with them."

But the seal of approval was put upon Christ by God his Father, and that is all that really counted. When Jesus came up from the waters of the Jordan, his Father declared: "You are my beloved Son. On you my favor rests." When we came from the water of our baptism, God said of us: "You are my beloved. On you my favor rests." And that is what really counts—not what others may think of us or even what we may think of ourselves. But as Jesus did not take the words of his Father as an excuse to refuse to associate with sinful mankind, so we, even though beloved by the Father, must not think that we are too good for any fellow human being. We must not fall into the trap of self-righteousness, thinking that we are better than others. St. Peter's words in the second reading set us on the right track: "I begin to see how true it is that God shows no partiality. Rather, the man of any nation who fears God and acts uprightly is acceptable to him. This is the message he has sent to the sons of Israel, 'the good news of peace' proclaimed through Jesus Christ who is Lord of all."

If we are to follow the humility of Christ, then one thing we must do. In the decisions we make we must be careful lest the opinions of others sway us from the truth or from that which we know we must do. Jesus could have saved himself from death on the cross—yes, but only at the expense of compromising the truth and going back on what he knew was his calling in life, that of redeeming mankind. Many of the decisions we make can be good or bad. A lot depends on what is behind them. The virtue of humility demands that we know the "why" of our decisions, which means that we face up honestly to our motives. Our concern for what others think of us is not necessarily evil, but if it makes us do things we know are wrong, then its influence is bad. We should recognize that we are God's children and that he loves us, but we must never use that truth as an excuse for turning our backs on those who are labeled as sinners or those whom we may find to be displeasing us.

Yes, Christ's death on the cross, made present for us here in the Mass, was the culmination of a life of extraordinary humility. As we now enter upon the eucharistic sacrifice, we should do so with the faith that we are indeed beloved by God, but we must also recognize that our offering will be pleasing only if we share in the humility of Christ.

O.J.M.

## The Baptism of Our Lord (C)
Sunday following January 6th

# *FROM CRIB TO CROSS*

Last Sunday, we celebrated the solemnity of the Epiphany. We saw that the word, "epiphany," means "manifestation." The infant Jesus was manifested as the Savior not only of the Jews but of all mankind. Today, the feast of the baptism of our Lord, is also an epiphany, a feast of a still further manifestation of our Lord.

Today, the Church asks us to leave aside the sweet, touching scene of the crib. We must see Jesus not as a tiny, helpless infant, but as a grown man who takes upon himself a tremendous burden and responsibility. The burden is the weight of the sins of all mankind. The responsibility is to make reparation for those sins.

The fact that Jesus was baptized by John was something of a difficulty for the early Church. John's baptism was a baptism of repentance for the forgiveness of sins. The early Church was keenly aware of the fact that Jesus as divine was absolutely sinless. The question was why should someone who was free of sin submit to a baptism that included an admission of sin. The fact that our Lord was baptized by John showed that he was taking upon himself the sins of the whole world, even though he was perfectly innocent of sin himself.

Jesus took sin upon himself in order to do away with its guilt. As St. John the Baptist proclaimed, "Behold the lamb of God who takes away the sins of the world." His baptism was a self-abasement, a humiliation. But from the waters of the Jordan he emerged as a glorified Savior.

The words of God the Father are also an epiphany, a manifestation: "You are my beloved son. On you my favor rests." They evoke most clearly the Suffering Servant passages of the Old Testament. As we read in the first lesson from Isaiah, "Here is my servant whom I uphold, my chosen one with whom I am well pleased. . . ." In its fullest sense the idea of the servant found its realization in Jesus, and it was Jesus himself who clearly identified himself as the servant of God. As such, Jesus would suffer for the sins of the people, all people.

Today's feast, then, manifests that Jesus came to be our Savior through his obedient and loving acceptance of suffering. But it also manifests what our lives ought to be as Christians, as followers of Christ, as those who live the Christ-life today.

Our Christian life began with our baptism. It too was a self-abasement, a humiliation. But we emerged from the waters of baptism as new people with a new life. Our baptism was an end and a beginning. It was an end of the life of sin and the beginning of the new life of God's favor. It was a sharing in the very death and resurrection of Jesus.

Every time we as baptized people celebrate the Mass we identify ourselves with Jesus, as he renews his sacrificial death on the Cross. We implicitly say that we too wish to be suffering servants of God, that we wish to accept any suffering that is necessary to disassociate ourselves from sin. Each one of us has had the experience of knowing that self-denial and suffering are frequently involved in avoiding sin. Even more importantly the attempt positively to lead a good, Christ-like life means self-sacrifice and generosity. In the Mass we not only identify ourselves with the suffering and generosity of Christ, but we also see the supreme model and example of what our lives should be: a total gift of ourselves to God in obedience and love.

But all of our sacrifice and generosity are worth it, for they will lead us to the fullness of life for which we all yearn. Recalling the words of St. Paul, we should realize that "If we have died with Christ, we believe that we are also to live with him" (Rm 6:8).

Today, then, the Church calls us from the crib of the infant to the Cross of the Savior. But in doing so, the Church does not destroy the joy and happiness that was ours at Christmas. Rather, the Church shows us the goal and purpose of the birth of Christ: the fullness of life that comes from the suffering and death of Jesus. And today that fullness of life is our hope and expectation.

C.E.M.

# THE LENTEN SEASON

**First Sunday of Lent (A)**

## *STAYING ON THE ROAD*

A pessimist can have a field day with the news, whether on TV or in the papers: war, riots, murder, hatred, catastrophes. What is wrong with the world? How did it ever get into such a mess? Can a loving God be charged with all this evil? That is a question which has troubled people of every age.

God revealed to his chosen people that he made all things good in the beginning. Human beings were his special creatures to whom he entrusted all the rest of creation. That is what is meant by the opening verses of today's first reading. Also in the beginning, the relationship between God and man was a wonderful thing. The Bible pictures God and man conversing, as they walked together in the cool of the garden. God communicated his interest in man, his care, his concern, his love. God loved man so much that he gave him a gift which none of the other living beings on this earth enjoyed, the gift of freedom. God desired a voluntary love from man because he wanted him to be his familiar, his friend, his child. But freedom is a two-way street: man could use freedom to get to God or to get away from God. Unfortunately the first man went in the wrong direction, and the human race by and large has continued to make the same mistake. Sin is the root of evil in the world and the consequences of sin are evident today in our homes, on our streets, across the nation, around the globe. How necessary is the prayer of the responsorial psalm: "Be merciful, O Lord, for we have sinned."

In the second reading, St. Paul proclaims that God has been merciful to us. The first man's sin disrupted the relationship with God, but the second man's (Christ's) obedience gives the opportunity of reconciliation. "Just as through one man's disobedience all became sinners, so through one man's obedience all shall become just."

The gospel goes on to give evidence of Christ's obedience. The devil was up to his old tricks again. He tried to get Jesus to abuse his freedom by turning away from God to travel the road of selfishness and greed. But Jesus responded to the devil's temptations with loving obedience to his Father's will. The gospel episode represented a turning point in the history of mankind. In the desert, Jesus reached a decision which set him on the road to the cross, the sacrifice of reconciliation which we celebrate in the Mass.

Lent reminds us that we must follow the road to the cross. The cross, however, is not the end of the road. Rather, it opens up for us a whole new road, a freeway, that leads to resurrection with Christ. It is the only road that can lead us to peace and happiness. To stay on the right road we must keep in contact with God. We must pray. Jesus has opened the lines of communication for us. Because of him our prayers get through to God, as we beg for light and guidance on our journey. And God responds to us if we only listen. And listen we must, for Jesus warns, "Not on bread alone is man to live, but on every utterance that comes from the mouth of God."

The Mass is beyond doubt our best means of communicating with God. Together as his children we talk to him in the Mass of our needs, our love for him, our sorrow for our failures. And God tells us his wishes and gives us his guidance through the words of scripture. But is Sunday Mass enough? During Lent we are to be "more fervent in prayer." One way to be more fervent is to make the effort to get to Mass during the weekdays of Lent. Maybe every day is not possible, but can't you be here two or three times a week? Even once during the week would be good. You will find the word of God in the weekday readings a real source of strength and guidance, and you will be offered the extra opportunity of praying to God.

To be more fervent in prayer also means carrying the spirit of the Mass into all the aspects of our lives. Morning and evening prayers, grace at meals, and especially just trying to be mindful of God at different times—all these things should be an important part of our day. And as we try to make decisions, or when we know we will be faced with temptatio.. or problems that try our patience or our charity, we should turn to God and ask, "What do you want me to do? Show me the way. Help me."

What a wonderful gift God has given us in freedom. But with freedom comes the possibility of sin, and sin alone can get us going in the wrong direction on the road of life. Prayer is what we need, communication between God and ourselves, in order to stay in the right direction on the road that will lead, not only to the cross, but to the glory and happiness of resurrection with Jesus.

O.J.M.
C.E.M.


**First Sunday of Lent (B)**

## *THE CHRISTIAN RAINBOW*

Parents like to tell their children, even their adult children, about things that happened to them when they were infants. Many a child has heard more than once about his being lost for several hours and making everyone frantic, including the neighbors, or about how he would always want to climb into bed with parents during a thunderstorm. Most of us tend to discount the experiences of our earliest days, not only because the stories are usually embarrassing, but also because we have to take events of our infancy on the word of others since, of course, we have no personal memory of them. But I think another reason is that for the most part we feel that only little things happened to us when we were little people. Psychologists, however, generally insist that all the things we have experienced, no matter at how early an age, have had their impact. Their mark is on us.

On this first Sunday of Lent the Church, like an interested and concerned parent, wants to remind us of something that happened to most of us when we were infants, something wonderful and momentous, and that something is our baptism. No matter how little we were, it was a very big thing. But whether we were baptized as infants or later in life, we have to take the significance of that event on the word of the Church as she teaches us God's revelation concerning the importance of this sacrament, an importance we must not discount.

The great value of baptism is that it communicates to us the saving grace of Jesus Christ. To help us appreciate this meaning of baptism, St. Peter (second reading) teaches us that the rescue of Noah from the flood was a prefigurement of baptism. In baptism, God extends his hand to rescue us from the flood of human misery, to save us from drowning in the engulfing waters of sin. Moreover, after God had saved Noah from the flood, he made the rainbow a symbol of his mercy and love. A rainbow is a sign that the storm is over, that the danger has passed. Baptism is the Christian rainbow. Even after our baptism, we will continue to see clouds of evil gathering all around us. We will still hear the distant rumbling of a hatred that wishes to destroy us. But our baptism should make us realize that we need not fear the threatening thunderstorms of life. Baptism is the symbol of God's mercy and love, the sign that he will not allow a flood of hatred and evil to destroy us.

According to a very ancient custom, the Church has always emphasized the sacrament of baptism during Lent. Originally the catechumens, those who were seeking baptism, were required to spend the entire season of Lent preparing to receive this sacrament on Holy Saturday. That is why at the conclusion of Lent we will all be invited to renew our baptismal promises, either within the Holy Saturday liturgy or during the Mass of Easter Sunday.

Notice that the Church will invite us to *renew* our baptismal promises. What are we expected to renew? What did we promise through our godparents or even personally if we were adults? According to St. Peter (second reading) the basic promise or pledge is a good conscience. Baptism is a covenant, an agreement between God and us. God promised his mercy and love, and we promised a life of fidelity. He became our God and we became his people. If our renewal of baptism is not to be merely an empty gesture, we must spend the time of Lent seriously considering our relationship with God. Jesus in the gospel says: "Reform your lives." That is a message the Church continues to preach to all of us without exception. It means that we must have the courage to work at changing whatever needs to be changed about our way of living. Lent should be devoted to an honest appraisal of what we are doing with our time and with our talents. That appraisal is something each one of us must make for himself.

During Lent the official forms of penance have been greatly reduced (in the United States). Only Ash Wednesday and Good Friday are days of fasting and abstinence. Catholics who are fourteen years of age and older are asked to abstain from meat on the Fridays of Lent. This simple penance should remind us that we must turn away from selfishness and turn our minds and hearts to God by striving to be more earnest in prayer. It should also remind us that we must overcome any smallness which prevents us from being considerate of others and generous in works of charity.

In the covenant of baptism, God has promised that evil and hatred will not destroy us; he has given us a pledge of his mercy and love. One of these days after a Spring rain, we may have the good fortune of seeing a rainbow in the sky. It is the sign of God's covenant with us.

C.E.M.

## First Sunday of Lent (C)

## *TEMPTATIONS: FAILURE, SUCCESS, AND . . . ?*

Today as we begin the season of Lent, the Church wants us to think again about the great fundamental facts of our religion. The Church wants us to reflect on the relationship between God and the people of the Old Testament, between God and his Son, Jesus Christ, and between God and ourselves. The three readings we have just read remind us of these relationships.

The first lesson shows the relationship between God and the Old Testament people. It recalls that after Israel had gone down into Egypt where the people were mistreated and enslaved, God brought the people out of slavery in the exodus in order to lead them into the promised land. The exodus was the great saving event of the Old Testament. God revealed himself thereby as Savior of his people. Before the people entered the promised land, however, they wandered in the desert for forty years. There they faced grave temptations, and for the most part they failed God. They were selfish, thinking only of themselves and their own welfare. They wanted God to feed them, and even after he did so miraculously they were not satisfied. They murmured against God and wanted to put him to the test, to have him prove his might and his power. They lacked trust. And despite all that God had done for them, many fell into idolatry and worshipped false gods.

Jesus came as the new Israel, the chosen one of God. In his person he summed up the whole purpose and meaning of the chosen people, and fulfilled and completed all that they should have been and more. Like the chosen people Jesus was led into the desert, and there he spent, not forty years, but forty days. There he underwent temptations similar to those of the Israelites. The devil tempted Jesus to be selfish: "Command this stone to turn into bread." The devil was trying to get him to think only of himself, to use his power for his own convenience and comfort. The devil tempted Jesus to put God to the test, to have God prove his might and his power by saving Jesus from destruction in a leap from the parapet of the temple. The devil even tempted Jesus to idolatry by saying: "Prostrate yourself in homage before me and the world shall be yours."

Yes, Jesus did undergo temptations similar to those of the Israelites in the desert, but where the Israelites had failed, Jesus was triumphant. Jesus showed that his relationship with his Father was based on loving obedience. That loving obedience indeed led Jesus to die on the Cross, but it was through that death that God exalted him and led him into the true promised land, the life of perfect happiness in heaven.

What of our own relationship with God? We are the new chosen people of God. He wants to lead us into the promised land with Jesus, but for a while we must wander in the desert of this world. Here we too undergo temptations. We are enticed by the devil to be selfish, to think only of ourselves, our welfare, our convenience. When our wants and wishes are not satisfied, we are tempted to put God to the test, to demand that he show his power and his might by healing the ills of our society and by solving our own personal problems. We are even tempted to turn from the true God to worship false gods, such as materialism, pleasure, expediency and laziness.

We will fall victim to these temptations if we forget all that God has already done for us and what he promises in the future. God has saved us in Jesus Christ, and as he raised Jesus from the dead and exalted him because of his loving obedience, so God will raise us and lift us up to heaven if we have the same loving obedience as Jesus. That is our faith, and it should be a motive to keep us from failing God.

Lest we become selfish and concerned only with ourselves, we should be more generous in works of charity. Lest we give in to the temptation to put God to the test, to demand that he show his power, we should prepare with joy for the paschal feast, the mystery of our salvation in Jesus Christ. Finally, lest we become worshippers of modern false gods, we must be more fervent in prayer. With these antidotes we will avoid the failure of the Israelites, and will share in the triumph of Jesus.

**C.E.M.**

**Second Sunday of Lent (A)**

## *GOD REACHING OUT TO US*

Last Sunday, we observed that during Lent we should be "more fervent in prayer." Prayer is a dialogue between God and ourselves. The highest form of this dialogue is our Mass, especially when we all gather together, as right now.

The first step in prayer is made by God. We've always begun our prayers, "In the name of the Father, and of the Son, and of the Holy Spirit." God reaches out to us where we are and in some fashion communicates with us.

The first reading in today's Mass is a good example. Man had sinned, a horrible response to God's love. God's reaction was one, not only of justice, but also of mercy. He promised a redeemer, one who could restore the lines of communication between God and man. At one point in man's history, God reached down into the desert country of Haran and touched the life of a man named Abram. And in touching Abram's life, he touched the lives of all of us. In the spirit of Christ we are all children of Abram, later called Abraham, for we are the heirs of God's merciful forgiveness. In the words of the first reading: "All the communities of the earth shall find blessing in you."

In the second reading Paul, in his letter to Timothy, repeats the same idea. "God has robbed death of its power and has brought life and immortality into clear light through the gospel." This thought is God reaching into our lives. Through St. Paul he is communicating to us his mercy and love. Did we realize this sufficiently when we responded a few minutes ago: "Lord, let your mercy be upon us, as we place our trust in you"?

The fact that we have prayed, have even wanted to pray, is a sure sign that God has already touched us. A prayerful man named John R. Coburn has written well of God touching us in our lives (*Prayer and Personal Religion*. The Westminster Press. Philadelphia, 1957):

"Many have been struck by their inability to direct their lives according to their own best intentions. They find themselves caught in patterns of behavior they had firmly resolved to avoid. Yet they have a vague, uneasy sense that something else or someone else is around, and trying to communicate with them. This is God breaking into their lives."

God is reaching out to us today, here in this Mass. We have been listening to his Son coming to us in the readings and homily. At our Sunday Mass we are like Peter, James and John going up the mountain with Christ. According to the gospel account of today's Mass, God communicated something to these three men that they would later communicate in God's name to the Church. This message is well summarized in the second reading of today. "God has saved us and has called us to a holy life, not because of any merit of ours but according to his own design—the grace held out to us in Christ Jesus before the world began but now made manifest through the appearance of our Savior." God the Father is communicating to us in sight and sound just as he did to the three apostles on the mount of transfiguration. "This is my beloved Son on whom my favor rests. Listen to him." Maybe we ought to manifest a little more of the enthusiasm of Peter, "Lord, how good it is for us to be here!"

God is reaching into our lives within this hour. He has been waiting for us on this Sunday, as he does on every Sunday, to communicate to us his love. This is what the Mass is: God reaching out to us in love and we responding in the sacrificial act of Christ. This is prayer at its highest level. Yes, Lord, it is good for us to be here.

O.J.M.

## Second Sunday of Lent (B)

## *A HINT OF GLORY*

Pagan people before the time of Christ thought of their gods as divine beings who had to be paid or even bribed for their help in human affairs. In time of great national distress, some people even sacrificed a firstborn son with the idea that nothing was too good for the gods. They hoped that their gods could not fail to respond to such a sacrifice. Barbaric though the act was, there was a certain heroism about it. Since Abraham, the father of the chosen people, felt compelled to show no less a heroism than his pagan neighbors, he prepared to sacrifice his son Isaac to the one true God. Abraham's intention manifested a special heroism. God had promised Abraham that he would establish his covenant with him and his descendants and that he would make him the father of a multitude of nations (Gn 17:4, 7). Abraham understood that all of God's promises would be fulfilled through Isaac. It was terrible enough to be asked to sacrifice his son. What disturbed him the more was that the death of his young child would seem to render God's promises impossible of fulfillment. The whole idea seemed absurd, something that did not appear to make sense. Abraham was heroic not only in his generosity but in his trust in God as well.

God was pleased with Abraham's good will, but today's first reading indicates that while his people had to be prepared to give up everything, even their most precious possessions, God did not require human sacrifice. He himself provided a ram in place of the firstborn son. And yet what God did not require of his people he did require of himself. We have become so used to the idea of the crucifixion of the Son of God that we are not sufficiently impressed by this sacrifice. St. Paul, however, never stopped reflecting on this great mystery. Fully aware of the Abraham-Isaac incident, he wrote to the Romans: "God did not spare his own Son but handed him over for the sake of us all" (second reading).

St. Paul, of course, reflected on the meaning of the cross in the light of the resurrection. He was impressed with the magnanimity of God's act, but since he clearly understood that the obedient death of Jesus led directly to his glorification, he did not see the cross as either barbaric or absurd (1 Cor 1:23f). Such was not the case for the apostles, who before the resurrection heard Jesus himself predict that he would have to suffer and die on a cross. They were understandably shocked to think that their master would have to undergo so horrible a fate. They were also dismayed because they hoped that Jesus would set Israel free, something they believed a dead leader could not accomplish. The apostles lacked both the generosity and the complete trust of Abraham.

Jesus saw the shock and dismay of his apostles. He knew what a trial his passion and death would be for them. And so it was that six days after he had made the prediction of his crucifixion he took Peter, James and John up a high mountain where he was transfigured before them. The magnificent change that came over his physical appearance was a preview of the glory of his resurrection. Though the transfiguration was really little more than a hint of the glory that would come to Jesus through his death, it was intended to bolster the faith and trust of the apostles, to prepare them for the ordeal of the passion.

During Lent, we ought to think more about the sacrifice of the cross. We should try to appreciate God's love for us by considering that he did not spare his own Son, but handed him over for the sake of us all. But we must also realize that for Jesus, suffering and death led to glory and happiness. Most important of all, we should see that Jesus made the passage through death to eternal life for our sake, so that he might raise us from death to a life of glory and happiness. The transfiguration, together with its fulfillment in the resurrection, is a sign of our own future glory as God's beloved children.

What would life be without God's love for us? Some have thought that human existence is nothing more than a struggle for survival so that we may live some seventy or eighty years with pain and suffering most of the time. For them life is little better than the barbarism of the jungle. Others have judged that life is only a vain search for a drop of temporal happiness amid a torrent of frustration and sorrow, with death at the end as a welcome oblivion. For them life is absurd. How different should be our outlook as Christians! In the words of today's responsorial psalm we must believe even amid the greatest afflictions that we are precious in the eyes of God, and that one day we will walk in his presence forever.

C.E.M.

## Second Sunday of Lent (C)

### *PUTTING THE PIECES TOGETHER*

When many of us here today were children, one of our favorite pastimes was the working of jigsaw puzzles. We would dump all the pieces on the table and start to put the puzzle together. At first it was all confusion, and if some important pieces were missing we could not make sense out of it all. But we always had the picture on the box to show us how the puzzle was supposed to turn out.

The amazing episode of the transfiguration of Christ in today's gospel is somewhat like an important piece of a jigsaw puzzle. It is really just one part of a big picture, and we need all the pieces to make sense out of it. One week before the event Jesus had made the third prediction of his passion to his apostles. He told them that he would go up to Jerusalem and that there he would be mocked, scourged and put to death, but that he would rise on the third day. The prediction of his death was such a shock and a disappointment to the apostles that they scarcely even heard the words about resurrection. They were downcast and dejected.

Jesus realized that his passion would be a difficult experience for his apostles, especially for Peter, James and John, the three who would witness his agony in the garden. And so in the transfiguration Jesus wished to give at least these three apostles a hint of what his future glory through his death would be like. The transfiguration was meant to serve as a bolstering of their faith and hope. This event pointed out the big piece in the puzzle of the life of Christ that would make the whole picture make sense. That one big piece was the resurrection of Christ from the dead. Moreover, the apostles heard the words of God the Father, "This is my Son, my Chosen One." These words should have made them realize that God would not abandon his Son in the grave nor allow his Chosen One to undergo the corruption of the dead (cf. Psalm 16). Death for Jesus, accepted in loving obedience to his Father, would mean life and glory.

The full picture of the life of Christ is as important to us as it was to the apostles. The reason is that our lives are meant to follow the pattern of Christ's life. When Jesus made the prediction of his passion a week before the transfiguration, he added these important words for all of us: "Whoever wishes to be my follower must deny his very self, take up his cross each day, and follow in my steps." To be a Christian means to be like Christ. If he had to suffer, we can expect the same. But if we suffer with Christ in loving obedience, we can also expect to live with him in happiness forever.

Without Christ, life is the craziest of jigsaw puzzles. All of its frustrations and sorrows simply do not make sense. Without Christ it is absurd to be born into this world, to struggle for survival, to work long and hard, and to find but a drop of happiness in the ocean of human misery and suffering. Though it is true that many lives are not that dismal, every human being must face the dark, deep mystery of death. Is life meant to be nothing more than a vain struggle for a modicum of joy and satisfaction, a struggle that is terminated after a relatively short span of time by the awesome conclusiveness of death?

Jesus shows us that life is not absurd, only paradoxical. He teaches us that it is in unselfishness that we will find satisfaction, in suffering that we will come to happiness, and in dying that we will come to eternal life. That is what he meant when he said, "Whoever would save his life will lose it, and whoever loses his life for my sake will save it." In today's gospel, God the Father himself warns us that we must listen to Jesus. And indeed, not only must we listen to him, but also follow his example of taking up the cross in loving, willing obedience to God.

No wonder St. Paul in the second lesson today sounds a warning: "Unfortunately, many go about in a way which shows them to be enemies of the cross of Christ. Such as these will end in disaster." But then St. Paul adds the note of hope for those who follow Christ: "He will give a new form to this lowly body of ours and remake it according to the pattern of his glorified body."

Life is indeed a puzzle, like the jigsaw puzzle we used to play with as kids. The life of Christ is the picture on the box of life that tells us how the puzzle is supposed to turn out. But we cannot complete the puzzle of our own lives until we have fitted in the most important piece of all, our sharing in the resurrection of Christ.

C.E.M.

**Third Sunday of Lent (A)**

## *GOD POURS OUT HIS SPIRIT*

Lake Erie is dead, and Lake Michigan nearly so. This is the estimate of conservationists and ecologists. One has reached the point where it no longer supports life, while the other just barely so. Sometimes the clutter and wastes of human existence deaden, or nearly so, the Spirit, that is the life of God in us. It is then that we need to pray, especially to say our best prayer, the Mass. That is why last Sunday we repeated a couple of times with Peter: "Lord, how good it is for us to be here."

For a people living in a desert land where good water was scarce, living water, such as that found in Jacob's well, was a blessing. The living water, what we would call "fresh water," that bubbled from the rock after Moses struck it, revived a people dying of thirst in the desert. Traditionally both the rock of water in the desert and Jacob's well have been symbols of God showing his mercy to us in the Mass. It is here Christ gives us his life that we may have life.

Our Sunday Mass should be a time of refreshment and rejuvenation for us. Like the woman in the gospel coming to Jacob's well for good, refreshing, life-sustaining water, we should come to Sunday Mass with the same eagerness. Then, perhaps, we could leave Mass renewed in faith that here God has once more reached into our lives. From this living water of the Body and Blood of Christ we should have the energy and enthusiasm to tell all whom we meet: "This is the One you are looking for. He is the Savior of the world." We should leave Mass like people into whom "the love of God has been poured out through the Holy Spirit who has been given to us."

Jesus did not argue with the woman. He simply tried to make her realize the facts of the situation. He is God's gift to men, not in the silly way in which we use those words sometimes, but in the reality of the Incarnation. Perhaps God is saying to us right now: "If only you recognized God's gift. . . ." Certainly the woman was interested in life-giving water. But where was anyone to find a beautiful flowing clear stream in that desert? Jesus disregarded that objection, for he was talking about himself as the giver of eternal life. ". . . the water I will give shall become a fountain within him, leaping up to provide eternal life." Then the woman uttered her first prayer, and even though it was a selfish one ("Give me this water, sir, so that I won't grow thirsty and have to keep coming back here to draw water"), a "gimme" prayer, nevertheless God accepted it. It was a response to his communication, and consequently an acceptable prayer. From that first response, Christ was able to lead the woman to an acceptance of him as Messiah. From that first response, the woman became the instrument of many others believing in Christ.

In the words of this Mass, we repeat the promise of Christ. "I have come that you may have life, and have it more abundantly" (Jn 10:10). In this Mass Christ asks us to believe: ". . . the man who feeds on this bread shall live forever" (Jn 6:58).

We here at Mass, and those at Masses all over the world, are those of whom Christ prophesied: "Yet, an hour is coming, and is already here, when authentic worshippers will worship the Father in Spirit and truth." The Spirit of God does break into our lives with his truth. Let us not be like a rock which does not yield to God's gentle urgings, or even to the heavy striking of his word. "If today you hear his voice, harden not your hearts." "Come, let us sing joyfully to the Lord; let us greet him with thanksgiving. . . . For he is our God, and we are the people he shepherds."

But our Mass, like our other prayers, seems to lack enthusiasm and vigor. If we come here simply out of a sense of duty and obligation, time will hang heavy on us. Everything will seem too long, too different, too mixed-up. We need to realize, by telling ourselves over and over again, who it is that is communicating with us through the Mass. It is necessary that we take to heart the admonition contained in the response we prayed after the first reading: "If today you hear his voice, harden not your hearts." How much better off we would be, if we made our response to God communicating with us, with attention and deep meaning. "Come, let us bow down in worship; let us kneel before the Lord who made us. For he is our God, and we are the people he shepherds, the flock he guides."

O.J.M.

## Third Sunday of Lent (B)

# *TRUE WORSHIP*

Gift giving has become a rather prominent aspect of our society. In addition to the Christian custom, we give gifts for birthdays, anniversaries, graduations, weddings, mother's day and father's day. Every now and then we voice a complaint about how commercialized it has all become, but more importantly we should be concerned about the meaning of gift giving. There must be something behind the gift, because giving a gift is a way of saying something. A husband's gift to his wife on their anniversary, no matter how costly, may have no real significance. The gift should mean that she is first in his affection, but if he is unfaithful to her, the gift is hollow and hypocritical. Any wife worthy of her womanhood wants her husband, not just some meaningless present. A gift is symbolic; to be acceptable, it must represent the giver.

Sacrifice is a form of worship which involves gift giving. When Jesus cleared the temple in Jerusalem of the merchants and their animals, he showed how upset he was that sacrifice there had become commercialized. He complained, "Stop turning my Father's house into a marketplace." Actually the buying and selling of animals to be used in the temple sacrifice was legitimate in the temple precincts, the outer courtyards surrounding the holy places, and was originally intended as a convenience, especially for non-residents of Jerusalem who could hardly have been expected to bring oxen, sheep or doves with them when they had to travel a long distance to get to the city. What Jesus really objected to was the fact that for both buyers and sellers the whole transaction had become devoid of the spirit of worship. For the merchants it was simply a sure way to make money. For the customers the purchase of an animal was the prelude to what had degenerated for many into an empty ritual.

In the time of Jesus, many Jews had forgotten the nature of their calling as the chosen people. The Lord had declared that he would be their God and they would be his people. The Israelites were to be worshippers of the one true God, who said to them: "I, the Lord am your God. You shall not have other gods besides me." According to God's directions, part of worship was the offering of animal sacrifices. There was nothing practical about the offering, in the sense that God certainly did not need oxen or sheep or doves. The offerings were to be symbolic of the affection and loyalty of the people. Sacrifice had to be backed up by a life of loving obedience to God.

Jesus condemned a worship which had become commercialized and largely hypocritical. But he did not stop there. He fully intended to replace it with a perfect form of worship, the sacrifice of himself on the cross. When the temple officials demanded a sign for his authority, Jesus responded, "Destroy this temple and in three days I will raise it up." The statement was admittedly obscure to the officials, but St. John explains for us that Jesus was referring to the temple of his body. It was an apt figure of speech. The inadequate worship of the temple would find perfection in the sacrifice of Jesus, the true temple of God. The animal offerings of Judaism would be replaced by the self-oblation of the Son of God in his death and resurrection.

As Catholics, we are the new chosen people of God. God has called us to be his true worshippers, and in the Mass he himself has provided us with a perfect sacrificial gift, not oxen or sheep or doves, but the body and blood of his own Son. The Mass is more excellent than the Old Testament sacrifices, in the degree that Jesus Christ is more excellent than irrational animals. That is a truth we must always keep in mind when we enter this church, this temple of God. But above all, we must remember that the Mass is a form of gift giving. It must be expressive of our affection, our loyalty, our faithfulness to God. We certainly should try to make our participation in Mass enthusiastic and devout, but the measure of our sincerity will be found in how we live.

Jesus first lived a life of loving obedience to his heavenly Father, and then made the offering of himself on the cross. He needed only one offering because he did it perfectly once and for all. We come to Mass to make a promise that we will live lives of loving obedience, and then we have to try to fulfill that promise. Of course we never make a perfect offering nor do we keep our promise completely. That is why God continually gives us the opportunity to renew our offering in every Mass, and to make a new start at keeping our promise as we leave this temple of worship. The important thing is that we never stop trying, despite our failures. God indeed is well aware of what is in our heart, and he wants to see a reflection of the worship we offer him in the Mass.

C.E.M.

## Third Sunday of Lent (C)

# *REPENTANCE*

In the news, we are constantly learning of terrible tragedies throughout the world with big losses of life: the crash of a jet liner, a hurricane in Mississippi, an earthquake in Peru. These tragedies remind us of the ones mentioned in today's gospel: Galileans slaughtered by Pilate and eighteen people killed by a falling tower. And like the people of our Lord's day, maybe we are tempted to feel that victims of such sudden, unexpected tragedies are receiving just punishment for their sins.

But Jesus today warns us, as he does frequently in the gospels, that it is not ours to judge other people and their guilt in the sight of God. No one but God really knows what is in the human heart. Rather than judge the victims of tragedies, we should turn their experience to our own profit by allowing the tragedy to remind us that we must face the eternal death of damnation unless we are truly repentant. As Jesus warns, "You will all come to the same end unless you begin to reform."

Today fire and brimstone sermons are not popular, if ever they were really popular. No one likes to sit in church and hear dire predictions of eternal damnation hurled at his head by a pulpit-pounding preacher. After all, the people in church are there because they are trying to be good and want to please God. The people in church are not pagans or atheists or profligates. In comparison with many people, those present in church are living saints. Why should they hear about repentance?

The point is that we cannot afford to be complacent. Complacency leads to pride, and, as someone has said, "Pride comes before the fall." That is why St. Paul reminds us in the second lesson, "Let anyone who thinks he is standing upright watch out lest he fall." St. Paul also points out that God showed great favor toward his people in the exodus, and in the desert he fed them miraculously. They knew they had been chosen by God. Nevertheless in the desert they failed God. And that failure did not happen all of a sudden. They lulled themselves into a spirit of complacency in which they felt that all was in good order in their lives, that God would take care of them no matter what they did or did not do. They believed themselves, therefore, to be superior to other people, and from that dizzy height of pride they fell into deep disfavor with God, who punished them severely.

We are the new chosen people. We have passed through a new exodus in our baptism. In the desert of this world we are fed with the body and blood of Christ. We are believers, and yet in the *Constitution on the Sacred Liturgy* we read, "To believers also the Church must ever preach faith and repentance" (9). We too cannot afford to be complacent. It is true that God is patient with us and will give us many opportunities to improve ourselves. That is the meaning of the parable of the fig tree in today's gospel. But notice also that Jesus warns that if the tree does not bear fruit in good time, then it will be cut down. We do not know how much longer God will give to each one of us, but God does give us this season of Lent as a grace to be repentant.

Repentance is not primarily concerned with making up for sins committed in the past. It is intended rather to effect a change of our lives for the better in the present so that we may stand firm in the future. It begins with an act of humility, an honest and forthright admission that without God we cannot succeed. This humble honesty must then extend into an examination of our lives in every detail, but two important areas are appropriate during Lent: prayer and charity.

How can we become more fervent in prayer? We should try to participate actively and intelligently in the prayers of the Mass. We read the prayers from cold, black print. It is up to us to give those words warmth and meaning. Prayer must not be limited to the time we are present in church. Prayer must become a real part of our lives all through the week.

How can we become more generous in charity? We must constantly strive to think less of ourselves and be more concerned with the needs of those with whom we live and work. The love we have for God must overflow into the love that we have for others. But in all we do we must join an invincible confidence in God with a healthy fear of our own weakness. That is why we humbly profess at Communion time, "Lord, I am not worthy to receive you but only say the word and I shall be healed."

Later today or perhaps tomorrow, we will probably learn of some human tragedy. It is not for us to judge the victims. But their misfortune should remind us of the words of Jesus, "You will all come to the same end unless you begin to reform." The time for such reform, for repentance, is now.

C.E.M.

## Fourth Sunday of Lent (A)

# *WASH AND SEE*

Traditionally, Lent has been a time of concentrating on the sacrament of baptism. Today's scripture readings are filled with allusions to this sacrament, because the Church wants us to give close attention to the meaning of our baptism.

As far as we know, the blind man in the gospel was not complaining about his plight. Nor is the man depicted by St. John as crying out after Christ for a cure. Born blind, he really had no way of knowing what he was deprived of. It was Jesus who took the initiative. Notice the little ceremony Jesus went through to cure the man. He made clay of spittle and dust and anointed the man's eyes. It is significant that St. John used the word "anointed" here. John probably chose it as an allusion to the rites of baptism. The earliest Christians recognized that the evangelist intended his readers to see the realization of Jesus' sign in the sacrament of baptism. Jesus also made the point that the man received his sight only after he had fulfilled the command to wash in the pool of Siloam, a washing which also makes us think of baptism.

In our own sacrament of baptism, Jesus took the initiative by giving us the call to become Catholics. For most this call came as infants, for others as adults. In either case it was "as Jesus walked along, he saw a man who had been blind from birth." He knew that we had been born blind spiritually, and he broke into our lives with the sacrament of baptism.

The other readings today also have something to do with baptism. The first speaks of an anointing and its result. God sent Samuel, the Judge, to Jesse of Bethlehem. From among the sons of this man, Samuel was to pick Saul's successor as king. Seven sons were brought before Samuel, but he rejected them all. When he found out that there was still one son, the youngest who was tending sheep, he asked that he be sent for. As soon as Samuel saw this young man, whose name was David, he knew he was the one. Samuel went through a ceremony of anointing not unlike that in baptism. The priest anointed us with the sacred oil, and truly the spirit of God rushed upon us.

In the second reading, St. Paul spoke of the Christian as one coming out of darkness into light, as one born blind gaining the power to see. His words should make us think of the candle the parents and godparents hold for the infant in the ceremony of baptism, as the priest says, "Receive the light of Christ."

In the gospel story there are two reactions to what Jesus did, that of the Pharisees and that of the man born blind. The Pharisees were people who refused to see. At first they would not accept the fact that the man before them had been born blind. His parents had to be dragged into court to prove that he was their son, that he had been born blind, and that he had been cured. Despite all the evidence, the Pharisees did not want to admit the cure because they did not want to have to believe in Jesus. Jesus tried to enter their lives, but they would have none of him. They preferred to remain spiritually blind. When the man told his judges and accusers that Jesus was from God, their response was typical of those who do not have the humility to accept Christ: "You are steeped in sin from your birth, and you are giving us lectures?" They threw the man out and in the process threw out Christ as well.

Faith was God's gift to us in baptism. We were led from darkness into spiritual light. At the conclusion of Lent we will be asked to renew our baptismal vows, but we really do not have to wait until then. We can make that renewal right now. As we stand for the profession of faith, the words should come not only from our lips but also from our hearts. Our "Amen" as a response to the words, "The Body of Christ," at Communion should mean "I do believe, Lord." And when we leave church we should do so with faith that Jesus is our Good Shepherd, as we professed in the responsorial psalm. He will satisfy our needs. We need fear no evil because he is within us. Through all the dark valleys of life he will lead us along the right paths to the house of his Father where we will live forever. How fortunate we were that as Jesus walked along he saw us and stopped to cure us of spiritual blindness. What a blessing it is that we can see Jesus with the light of faith and say, "I do believe, Lord."

O.J.M.

**Fourth Sunday of Lent (B)**

## *GOD SO LOVED THE WORLD*

A play called *Inherit the Wind* was made into a movie starring Spencer Tracy and Frederick March. Every now and then the movie is shown on television, and perhaps you have seen it. The plot revolves around the true story of a high school instructor by the name of John Scopes who in 1925 violated an old law of Tennessee by teaching evolution in his high school biology class. Among other things, John Scopes was accused of having said: "God made man in his own image and likeness and man returned the compliment." The implication was that man had dragged God down to his own level by attributing to him human characteristics.

Whether John Scopes ever really made that statement is uncertain, but its implication is true regarding many religions. It is only natural for people groping to understand God to think of him in anthropomorphic terms. Ancient pagans especially thought of their gods as being ambitious, jealous, even lustful. In opposition to their neighbors the Israelites of the Old Testament maintained a faith in one true God, a transcendent being prior to and exalted above the universe, spiritual and perfect in every way. They arrived at this notion, not through natural groping, but through supernatural revelation from God himself. Of course that revelation was necessarily expressed in human words and in reference to human traits, but far from presenting a god in the likeness of man, that revelation formed an image of God by means of contrast with human imperfections. Where man was small and petty, God was big and generous. Where man was vindictive and hateful, God was forgiving and loving.

Here is an example of the contrast between God and human beings. For human beings there is always a limit to endurance, the last straw. A husband or wife may forgive a single infidelity on the part of a spouse, but repeated affairs are more than anyone can put up with. Not so with God. God looked upon his chosen people as his spouse, but in spite of their repeated infidelities he never gave up on them. Today's first reading is a good example. It was written about three hundred years before Christ, when the author could look back on a long history in which the people "added infidelity to infidelity." And yet he saw that "early and often did the Lord, the God of their fathers, send his messengers to them, for he had compassion on his people. . . ." God's patience and love were much more than anything that could be expected of a human being.

But it took the New Testament revelation in Jesus Christ to bring out how much God really loves the world. Today's gospel illustrates the advance made by New Testament revelation by reference to an incident recorded in the Old Testament book of Numbers. Trying to enter directly into Palestine from the south after the exodus from Egypt, the Israelites found the way blocked and had to skirt Edom so as to come in from the East. The people were not happy about the detour and grumbled against God and Moses. God punished the people by sending poisonous snakes among them. Then in his mercy he commanded Moses to make a bronze serpent and erect it as a standard. The people were saved by turning in faith toward the bronze serpent lifted up by Moses. Jesus himself saw in the lifting up of the serpent a type or sign of his own lifting up on the cross. That is why today's gospel quotes Jesus as saying, "Just as Moses lifted up the serpent in the desert, so must the Son of Man be lifted up, that all who believe may have eternal life in him." Then St. John comments, "Yes, God so loved the world that he gave his only Son." All through the Old Testament, God had shown his love through men like Moses and by means of merciful incidents like that of the bronze serpent. But in the fullness of time God manifested even greater love in the degree that Jesus is greater than Moses and to the extent that his being lifted up on the cross is greater than the lifting up of the bronze serpent in the desert.

St. Paul was almost overwhelmed with the magnitude of God's love as shown in Jesus Christ. It is no wonder that in today's second reading, almost in ecstasy, he cried out: "God is rich in mercy; because of his great love for us he brought us to life with Christ when we were dead in sin. By this favor you were saved." Despite a long history of human perversity, "God did not send his Son into the world to condemn the world, but that the world might be saved through him."

Some of us at times may think that this picture of God makes him out to be too soft or weak. Perhaps the problem is that deep down we know that we ourselves cannot even begin to be as patient and forgiving as God is. Though we would like to be unselfish and generous, we realize that our love for others does not come anywhere near the kind of love God has for us. Subconsciously we fall into the mistake of trying to make God in our own image and likeness. We can begin to have an idea of God's love, not by looking at ourselves, but by turning in faith toward the image of Jesus Christ lifted up on the cross.

C.E.M.

**Fourth Sunday of Lent (C)**

## *THE LOVING FATHER*

The magnificent story we have just heard in the gospel has long been known as the parable of the prodigal son. Actually the story was intended to focus on the father, rather than on either of the two sons in the story, and could perhaps more accurately be termed the parable of the loving father.

The background of the story is that the scribes and the Pharisees were upset to see Jesus associating with known sinners. Jesus told the story in order to bring out the idea that God willed the salvation of sinners and was eager to forgive their sins. He wished to impress on his hearers the truth that God is a loving and understanding Father.

Jesus, however, painted such a true-to-life picture of the younger son that down through the centuries it is this picture that has caught the attention of most people. It is typical for a young person to want to be independent, to be free of parental control, to go out on his own, to see and do and experience all those things that were never a part of home life. The results of this leave-taking are also typical: discovering the value of a dollar, the need for true friends, the importance of a sense of belonging. That is a jolting, disturbing experience.

And we know how the young man felt. We know what it means to be alone, to feel guilty, to be overcome with fear. After he had spent his money, all his shallow, good-time friends deserted him. He was left alone with his misery, his guilt and his fear. He began to realize what a mistake he had made in leaving his father.

The older brother in the story is also a person we can understand. When he returned from work in his father's fields, he was infuriated to discover a party going on for his "worthless" brother. At first sight it looks as though he had been cheated, but there is really little excuse for his jealousy. He should have been happy that his little brother had come to his senses. There is something revealing in his protest to his father: "For years now I have slaved for you. I never disobeyed one of your orders, yet you never gave me so much as a kid goat to celebrate with my friends." He considered working for his father a form of slavery and his obedience was mercenary, not filial. Apparently he did everything with the expectation eventually of some great reward from his father. His work was motivated by selfishness, not love. The older son represents the scribes and Pharisees who complained about our Lord's merciful treatment of sinners.

"But I was going to say when Truth broke in with all her matter-of-fact" about the two sons, that the story was really intended to focus on the father in order to reveal something about God. When the younger boy brought up the idea of leaving home, the father was in turmoil. He knew the dangers that lay ahead for his son. And yet he equally understood the young man's need and right to be free. The father rightly refused to dominate or control his son at this time in his life because he realized that love to be true must be freely given, that it cannot be forced. And so when the boy insisted on his freedom, the father in loving-kindness sadly agreed.

All the while the boy was gone the father was hoping that the experience would teach him a sense of real values, as apparently his fatherly words had not. Every day he went to the top of the hill and scanned the road as far as he could see with the hope that he would catch sight of the boy returning. One day his hope was fulfilled. He rushed to meet his son, threw his arms around him, and with an impetuosity that revealed his deep emotion he would not even let him complete the little speech begging for pardon, which he had so carefully memorized. The boy knew that he deserved to hear his father say, "You were determined to make a fool of yourself, and you succeeded brilliantly. I will have nothing more to do with you." Instead he was overcome with the loving reception he received.

What a great love the father had for this young son. But his love is really no less for the older son. He refused to be forced into taking sides with the one brother against the other. Though each had failed in his own way, the father never stopped loving them both. With all their shortcomings, he regarded them both as his sons.

I suppose that in some ways we are like the younger son, and in other ways we are like the older son. But wherever we stand, Jesus wants us to know that God gives us human freedom because he wants a love that is freely given, not forced. Jesus also wants us to know that after even the most stupid of mistakes and tragic of sins, God will be looking for us with open arms to take us back as his children. Our God is indeed a loving and understanding Father.

C.E.M.

**Fifth Sunday of Lent (A)**

## *HOPE — FOR NOW*

We are not sure what kind of person Lazarus was. We may feel that since he was a friend of Jesus he must have been a good man, but we must remember that Jesus associated with all kinds of people, including some notorious sinners. Actually the point of importance to us is not that Lazarus was good or bad, but that he was dead and was brought back to life. Lazarus received the effect of God's great love, which we hope to receive too.

God does not wait until we are worthy of his love. Jesus himself said, "I was sent not to call the just, but sinners, to repentance." And just two weeks ago at Mass we heard St. Paul telling us: "At the appointed time, when we were still powerless, Christ died for us godless men. It is rare that anyone should lay down his life for a just man, though it is barely possible that for a good man someone may have the courage to die. It is precisely in this that God proves his love for us: that while we were still sinners, Christ died for us.''

Lazarus' condition in the tomb resembles ours before baptism, and his resurrection is like our reception of baptism. A dead person can do nothing for himself. We were like dead persons, but God took the initiative and gave us spiritual life through baptism. The second reading of this Mass told us: "If anyone does not have the Spirit of Christ, he does not belong to Christ. But . . . you are in the spirit [that is, not dead, but alive], since the Spirit of God dwells in you.

Actually it might be a valuable question to ask, "What kind of person was Lazarus after his resurrection?" He was a living witness to the prophecy of the first reading in today's Mass: "Then you shall know that I am the Lord, when I open your graves and have you rise from them"—and that is why the enemies of Jesus tried to kill Lazarus. What kind of life would you lead, if you had been dead and brought back to life? Certainly you would go around telling everyone you met all about it. You would express, in your own words, the sentiment of today's responsorial psalm: "With the Lord there is mercy and fullness of redemption." How great would be your trust in God! It would be so great that you would not fear even enemies who wanted to kill you.

We were in a real sense dead before baptism, spiritually dead. God took the initiative and broke into our tomb to bring us to life, spiritual life. How great should be our trust in God, with fear of no one. Baptism gives us hope. Let me tell you about a woman who knew what real hope is, Carson McCullers, the American novelist. At the time of her death Mrs. McCullers' career was described by a literary critic as a "vocation of pain." Before she was twenty-nine she had suffered three strokes which paralyzed her left side. She was so discouraged that she thought she could never work again. But gradually, a page a day, she resumed her writing, despite her pain. Then her husband committed suicide. In a rare mention of her troubles she said, "Sometimes I think God got me mixed up with Job. But Job never cursed God and neither do I. I carry on.''*

"I carry on." That is a response of real hope and trust. Maybe we

---

* Christopher Notes, no. 170.

are using alcohol, drugs, sexual freedom, excessive pleasure, disregard for the rights of others—maybe we are using all these things or more, simply because we are not responding to God in hope. All evils in the world today are not necessarily God's punishment. Rather, they can be looked upon as a challenge to us to put our trust in God and then go forward with positive and constructive measures of reform and improvement. Hope does not mean only a response to God concerning the next world. It just as surely also means a response to God for now.

Think about the conversation between Jesus and Martha in today's gospel. When Jesus said that Lazarus would rise again, she responded: "I know he will rise again in the resurrection on the last day." Martha found no difficulty in hoping for God's mercy at the end of the world. What she had trouble with was the now. Maybe we are the same.

God has broken into our lives a sufficient number of times to prove that he loves us. Why are there not better proofs of our response in hope and trust? Why do we not have more confidence in our prayers, especially when we pray together as we are doing right now? We pray for mercy many times in the Mass. Why can we not trust God to grant us his forgiveness now? We pray for peace. Do we trust God to answer our prayer this year? Our gathering together in the name of Jesus should itself be a confident prayer that will give us the power to put our hope into action *now*. Let's remember the word of God in the first reading: "I have promised, and I will do it." And that means not only in the future, but even right now.

O.J.M.

## Fifth Sunday of Lent (B)

Suggested use: eucharistic acclamation B

# A LAW OF LIFE

Within Sequoia National Park in California towers the famous General Sherman redwood tree, three hundred and sixty-five feet tall. The tree is so tall that if you were to stand as much as thirty feet away and try to see the top, you would fall over backwards. At its base rests a plaque containing a seed taken from the tree, a seed no larger than the nail on your little finger. A similar seed, buried in the earth, needed sun,

water, soil and about twenty-five centuries to grow to the present height
of three hundred and sixty-five feet.

This tree in America was approximately five centuries old when
Jesus walked the earth in far-off Palestine. At that time it was slowly but
persistently growing heavenward, a living example of the mysterious
words of Jesus in today's gospel: "Unless the grain of wheat falls to the
earth and dies, it remains just a grain of wheat. But if it dies, it produces
much fruit." With these words Jesus proclaimed the paradox of the
Father's plan that death is the source of life. It is a law of sacrifice, that
one can come to a greater life only by dying to a lesser one. It is a law
exemplified in nature—in a grain of wheat and in the seed of a tree. A
seed which does not "die" by being buried in the earth can never grow
into something greater. Jesus was like a seed. He had to die and be buried
in the earth for three days. Then on Easter Sunday he pushed through the
soil, like a growing tree, and reached heaven to enjoy the fullness of new
life.

Today's second reading from the letter to the Hebrews presents the
same law of sacrifice, though less graphically. However, it emphasizes
that accepting the law was not easy for Jesus, who, though divine, was
also as human as we are in all things but sin. The author reminds us that
Jesus prayed with tears to be saved from death. We have only to think of
Jesus in the garden of Gethsemane to feel the full force of these words.
Difficult though it was to embrace death, Jesus did so in loving obedience to his Father. Ironically through his obedience Jesus was indeed
saved from death, not in the sense that he did not have to die at all, but in
the sense that through his resurrection he overcame the effects of death as
he rose to a new, glorified life.

Jesus accepted death in obedience to his Father for our sake. He
made the passage through death before us to take away the effects of
eternal death. Through his exaltation in the resurrection he became the
source of eternal salvation for all who accept him. Jesus said in the
gospel, "And I—once I am lifted up from the earth—will draw all men
to myself." The phrase, "to be lifted up," has a double meaning. It
refers to his being lifted up on the cross in death and to his being lifted up
to life in the resurrection. Jesus wishes to draw us to himself to share in
his death so that we may also share in his resurrection.

Jesus lived and died at a definite point in time, and yet he spans the
centuries before and after his sojourn on this earth. He was planted like a

seed in Old Testament times, a seed of hope. Today's first reading is almost a summary of the entire Old Testament. Again and again God offered a covenant to his people, a pledge of his salvation in return for their obedience. Even as his people broke the covenant by disobedience, God through the prophets taught them to hope for salvation, for a new covenant in which God would forgive sin. That hope of the new covenant was realized in Jesus Christ, and sealed in his blood, ''the blood of the new and everlasting covenant.''

And Jesus still lives today. He stands like a giant redwood, reaching heavenward toward our eternal destiny. Face death we must; it is inevitable. We cannot escape death, but we can overcome it in union with Jesus. He is the only way to salvation. Wherever we go, whatever we do, we will find no answer to the problem of death and sin other than Jesus himself.

In the eucharistic acclamation today we will proclaim our faith in Jesus: ''Dying you destroyed our death; rising you restored our life; Lord Jesus, come in glory.'' That proclamation is an expression of our belief that, no matter how small or insignificant we may seem, we can grow with Jesus to the fullness of everlasting life.

C.E.M.

### Fifth Sunday of Lent (C)

# *REPENTANCE AND FORGIVENESS*

The scribes and the Pharisees in the gospel narratives are not only the enemies of Jesus; they are a foil to him—that is, they set Jesus off to advantage by their contrast with him. They are petty where Jesus is generous; they are snobbish where Jesus is gracious; they are self-righteous where Jesus is understanding and forgiving.

In the story of today's gospel, some of the scribes and the Pharisees hoped to make Jesus look bad in the eyes of the people. They presented him with the case of a woman they said they had caught in the act of adultery. Just how they managed this apprehension induces the imagination to consider their perversity, and perhaps Jesus himself did not fail to attend to that aspect of the situation. It is possible that it was one of the thoughts in his mind when he said to them, ''Let the man among you who has no sin be the first to cast a stone at her.''

Of course their perversity was obvious in the question they proposed to Jesus. It was meant to be a dilemma so that whatever Jesus answered, they hoped to use his statement against him. If Jesus were to indicate that the woman should be released, he would be made to appear in defiance of the law of Moses. If Jesus were to consent to the stoning, he would be made to look like a dissembler who preached forgiveness but did not practice it.

What Jesus wrote with his finger on the ground, we do not know. Probably he merely traced some idle lines to indicate his lack of interest in their pretended concern about his opinion. When they persisted in their question, Jesus set them back on their heels with the words, "Let the man among you who has no sin be the first to cast a stone at her." The challenge was such a shock that even the scribes and the Pharisees did not have sufficient hypocrisy to pretend innocence.

The words of Jesus must not be interpreted as indifference to sin. His point was simply that they had no right to judge and condemn a fellow human being, both because of their own sinfulness and because they could not possibly see into the heart of the woman. And his refusal to condemn the woman himself does not mean that he condoned her sin. He did know what was in her heart and he saw there the spark of repentance. He put into words for the woman what her repentance should be: "From now on, avoid this sin." Jesus was understanding and forgiving, while the scribes and Pharisees were self-righteous in their condemnation of the woman.

One thing we should learn from this gospel is that we must not judge others. In the news media we hear many horrible things about the evils people are guilty of. Though we realize that while condemning the sin we are not the ones to condemn the sinners, we usually find it pretty hard not to sit in harsh judgment on others. Maybe that is one reason we have some fear about the judgment we will receive from God. Perhaps subconsciously we project upon God our own manner of judging. In one sense we ourselves are a foil to God.

More importantly, we should learn from this gospel to be overjoyed that it is God who will judge us and not one of our fellow human beings. Jesus reveals to us today that God is infinitely more understanding and forgiving than human beings could ever possibly be. He sees the temptations to which we are subject. He understands the weakness of our human condition. And he knows the secret workings of the human heart.

We should cry out with great confidence, "Lord, have mercy."

This confidence should not induce us to be indifferent or careless about sin in our lives. Rather, it should make us realize that the repentance to which we are called during Lent is really worthwhile. "From now on, avoid this sin," Jesus tells us. And the sincere, honest effort to avoid sin with God's grace is the spark of repentance that will win from God the response, "Nor do I condemn you."

C.E.M.

## Passion Sunday (A)
(Palm Sunday)

# *LORD OF THE HEREAFTER*

Imagine the small parade of a not too promising, and not too sophisticated group of ordinary people. Some cut branches from the trees along the road and lay them in the path of a man riding on a colt. Others take off their cloaks and lay them along the path. Soon whispers from pages of the Old Testament pass from one to the other. "Fear not, O daughter of Zion! Your king approaches you on a donkey's colt." Not really understanding what is happening to them, the people begin to respond to God working in them. "Hosanna! Blessed is he who comes in the name of the Lord! Blessed is the king of Israel." Soon it becomes a "get-on-the-bandwagon" kind of atmosphere. People begin to dance about, and to shout out that the kingdom of God is about to start. The reign of the Messiah is finally going to begin and the Romans will be driven out of the sacred land of God's people.

The events which followed this short-lived triumphal procession into the city of Jerusalem show how poorly these people understood what God was saying to them through his Son, Jesus from Nazareth in Galilee. Their reactions could serve as guidelines for us in our response to God communicating with us. A study of them might help us improve our prayer of hope, hope in the hereafter, for this is where these people went wrong. Last Sunday we looked at our response of hope in this life, in the right now. We asked that we all try to deal with present problems with a prayer of hope for the now. Today we must look at the other side of the coin. How does hope for the hereafter influence our lives? What is our response to God communicating eternal life to us?

The problem is a sort of "all-this-and-heaven-too" situation. The people in the first Palm Sunday procession wanted a strong, kingly ruler and a government that would make the Jewish nation the conquerors of the whole world. They were unable, or unwilling, to look beyond their own time. When the procession lost its momentum, and nothing more happened, they drifted away. They concluded that nothing much was going to come of this Jesus of Nazareth and his idealistic teachings. So, it was not difficult for them, on the following Friday, to turn against Jesus. The climax of this rejection is found in the Passion account read today, especially in the words, "Crucify him!" What a way to respond to God entering their lives and offering them the promise of eternal life! Even in his trial before Caiaphas when Jesus spoke the truth, he was condemned as a blasphemer. We need God's truth. We need to know with certainty: "Soon you will see the Son of Man seated at the right hand of the Power and coming on the clouds of heaven." It is true we do not easily understand the Jewish figure of speech which Christ used, but nevertheless the truth is that, through Christ, we are to live forever.

The Christian lives his life fully and completely in this world, but with an eye on eternity. The person who "cops out" on either one is not living his life fully, no matter how successfully he may deceive himself. Judas is a good example in today's account of the Passion. Judas took the "short term" view of the situation. Jesus had failed to set up a kingdom. So Judas rejected him, and made what he could out of the shambles—thirty pieces of silver, the price of a slave. For Judas the "short term" did not pay off.

We must not fall prey to the "short term" view of life. In this Mass we should pray for the grace to see through all the problems and duties of this life, to the person of Jesus who gives the promise of eternal life. Let us hail Jesus as our King and recognize that he is Lord of both the here and the hereafter.

O.J.M.

## Passion Sunday (B)

(Palm Sunday)

Mk 14 : 1-15,-47 ~ 15 : 1-39

## CHEERS AND BOOS

Professional ballplayers know what it is to hear both cheers and boos from a crowd. A shortstop may be hailed as a hero one day when he makes brilliant plays and goes three for four at the plate, and the next day he may be treated as a bum when he makes two crucial errors and fails to get even one hit. It is no surprise when a player complains that fans are fickle and have short memories. And of course he sees his opponents saddened by his success and delighted by his failure.

In his life, Jesus was playing no game. His work was supremely serious. During his public ministry he cured those with bodily ills, in anticipation of his sacrifice whereby he would heal people of the spiritual sickness of sin. He fed the hungry as a sign of the spiritual nourishment he would give in his own body and blood. These physical favors aroused the enthusiasm of the crowds, an enthusiasm which reached a fever pitch in the cheers and "hosannas" of Palm Sunday. His enemies were indeed saddened by his apparent success with the crowds, but Jesus knew that his hero's welcome would be short-lived. On Good Friday, the cheers and "hosannas" were changed to boos and taunts, to the delight of his opponents.

Jesus knew how people would react to his apparent failure on Good Friday. He tried to anticipate that reaction by teaching them that his death was a necessity for their salvation. During Lent in the gospels we have heard how he taught that he had to be lifted up on the cross, that he was to be like a grain of wheat buried in the earth, and that when the temple of his body was destroyed he would raise it up on the third day. To three of his apostles he gave the magnificent sign of his transfiguration. But the human memory is short, and the human heart is fickle. When Jesus was taken into custody, his apostles ran away in fear. When he was lifted up on the cross, the people jeered at him. When he was buried, his enemies thought it was the end of him. Admittedly Good Friday was a bleak day for anyone who had put his hope in Jesus.

Today we are asked to hail Christ as our King, our hero. But we must remember that Christ's victory came only through the cross. That is why on this day, even as we celebrate Christ's triumphant procession into Jerusalem, the Church gives us in this Mass the account of his passion and death. And in the reading from the letter to the Philippians, St. Paul summarizes the whole meaning of Holy Week and Easter: "He humbled himself, obediently accepting even death, death on a cross! Because of this, God highly exalted him. . . ."

St. Paul also gives a summary of Christian living: "Your attitude must be Christ's attitude." To be a follower of Christ we must accept with loving obedience whatever comes from the hand of God, including death itself. That is the only way to true happiness. Let us pray that our memories will not be so short that we forget this lesson when the time comes for us to share in the passion of Christ. Let us pray that we will not be so fickle as to accept Christ as our King when all is going well, only to reject him when we are faced with human suffering.

We do not read the account of the passion and death of Christ while forgetting how it all turns out in his resurrection from the dead. Nor should we forget that all of the bleak Good Fridays of our lives will lead to glorious resurrection in an eternal Easter Sunday.

C.E.M.

## Passion Sunday (C)
(Palm Sunday)

## *TRIUMPH THROUGH TRAGEDY*

Today in the procession of the palms we celebrate Christ as a King. It is a triumphant procession in anticipation of Easter Sunday, the Sunday of Christ's exaltation as King through his resurrection from the dead. Before we celebrate the resurrection, however, we recall the events of the passion and death of Jesus.

The death of Jesus has been referred to by some as a tragedy. In no sense was it such. In ancient Greek tragedy a man was thought of as being on a wheel of fortune. Once he had risen to the top, the gods spun the wheel to bring the man back to the bottom. The tragic hero was hurled to destruction by an inexorable fate. As presented by William Shakespeare, tragedy was also the fall of a hero, but his fall was brought about through his own fault, because of a flaw in his character—which critics have come to call the tragic flaw. For example, Macbeth's tragic flaw was his "vaulting ambition," a fault cleverly manipulated by Lady Macbeth, and which led to his destruction.

Jesus was certainly a hero, but his death was only an apparent fall. Moreover, his death was brought on neither by an inexorable fate nor by any flaw in his character. Rather, it was the result of a supreme virtue, his loving obedience to his Father. As we heard in St. Paul's letter to the Philippians, "Jesus was known to be of human estate, and it was thus that he humbled himself, obediently accepting even death, death on a cross!'' On Good Friday Jesus was in the eyes of men a failure, but in the eyes of God he had completed a life of perfect success because of his loving obedience. The death of Jesus was only an apparent tragedy.

On Easter Sunday, God the Father in raising Jesus from the dead manifested to the whole world the fact that the death of his Son was a great triumph. Again as we heard in the letter to the Philippians, "Because of this [that is, his loving obedience unto death], God highly exalted him and bestowed on him the name above every other name." It was precisely because of his obedient death that God the Father exalted Jesus. In other words, the triumph of Jesus came through his apparent tragedy. Through his death he rose to his throne in heaven as king.

In Christ's triumphal procession into Jerusalem on this day, the people hailed him as King, but they did so for the wrong reason. They were enthusiastic in their shouts of praise because they thought his reign would be nationalistic, political and within the immediate future. They wanted a king who would win an earthly kingdom through war, not a king who would gain a heavenly kingdom through death. And so on Good Friday the inscription on the Cross, "This is the King of the Jews," was one of mockery, not praise.

In the liturgy today we hail Christ as our King, but we must make sure that we do so for the right reason. He has not promised worldly peace that can be obtained from nationalistic security, but a spiritual peace which comes from imitating his loving obedience to God. He has proposed no political charter that would ensure material prosperity, but a way of living that guarantees eternal happiness in heaven.

We must accept Christ as King on his own terms; to wish to do otherwise would be a mockery. St. Paul warns us today: "Your attitude must be Christ's attitude." During these days of Holy Week we can obtain no greater grace than to share in the attitude of Christ, an attitude of loving obedience, which is the only way to turn apparent tragedy into triumph.

C.E.M.

# THE EASTER SEASON

**Easter Sunday (A)**

## *LORD OF LIFE*

On this Easter Sunday, people of faith throughout the world gather together because of the resurrection. On this day, in a sense, we follow Mary Magdalene in her search for the body of Jesus. She went to the tomb early in the morning. Hers had been a night of weeping for the loss of him who had reached out to her in mercy and hope. She would have followed him to the end of the world, but now she feared that for her the world itself was at an end.

She had responded to his loving forgiveness by a complete change of heart. Because of him, she had begun a new life. Perhaps on that Sunday morning, however, in the confusion of her sorrow she was wondering whether life itself was still worth living. Though she was looking for a dead body, not a very bright prospect, God was leading her to the light of a great truth. At first Mary thought she had found not even a dead body but only an empty tomb. She ran off in tears to tell Peter and John that the Lord had been taken away. Later, still not understanding, she returned to the tomb. Then it happened. She saw Jesus standing there. Through her tears she did not recognize him. He asked her, "Woman, why are you weeping? Who is it you are looking for?" She took him to be the gardener, and said, "Sir, if you are the one who carried him off, tell me where you have laid him and I will take him away." Jesus said one word, "Mary." With that, God's grace flooded her mind and she knew that Jesus had risen as the Lord of Life.

On this Easter Sunday, we are like Mary Magdalene in that we too are moving toward a tomb, our own! From the moment we began life in the darkness within our mother's body, we were on our way toward the darkness of the grave within mother earth. Death is inevitable. Since for many that is not a very bright prospect, our society is reluctant to admit the fact of death. We attempt to cover it over with euphemisms and pretense: no one ever dies; he "passes away." A corpse in the mortuary must be made to look, not dead, but only asleep. Still we cannot escape the reality of death. Face death we must, but we should do so in the light of Easter Sunday.

On this Easter Sunday, the empty tomb of Jesus tells us something about our own grave. There was a tomb for Jesus because he had really died. But that tomb was found empty on Easter morning because he had truly risen. What happened on Good Friday and Easter Sunday has great implication for us, because dying Jesus destroyed our death, and rising he restored our life. Death is not the end of the world for us. Jesus has gone before us in death to lead us to eternal life. We are going to die some day, but when Jesus comes again in glory our grave will be found empty, not because our body will have undergone the corruption of death, but because we will have risen with Christ to the glory of everlasting life.

When Christ our life appears, then we shall appear with him in glory. Easter asks us to make an act of faith in Christ rising from the tomb as the Lord of Life. It urges us to hope that we too shall some day rise with him. It promises us the complete fulfillment of our lives in eternal union with God.

An anonymous poet has summed up the meaning of Easter for us in these simple verses:

> In some future time,
>     maybe a thousand years,
>     maybe tomorrow,
> we will know a life sublime,
>     no more tears,
>     no more sorrow.
> We will stand on some high hill
> and see a world
> made beautiful by God,
> Who came to kill
> all hatred—sword and rod.
> And we will live
> accordingly.

O.J.M.
C.E.M.

**Easter Sunday (B)**

# A LIFE OF GLORY

Easter Sunday puts everything about Jesus into perspective and tells us what Good Friday was all about. It shows that what really happened on Good Friday was not an execution but a sacrifice, not a defeat but a triumph, not an end but a beginning. The death of Jesus was not an execution because no force, human or otherwise, had the power to kill Jesus. He freely accepted death in loving obedience to the will of his heavenly Father, as a sacrificial offering of himself for the salvation of the world. His death was not a defeat. Rather, it was a great triumph over the twin enemies of the human race, sin and death. His death was not an end, for Jesus made of death a passage to a higher, better life. He has gone before us in death to show us the way through the darkness of the tomb to the brilliant light of resurrection, the beginning of the fullness of life to which we are all called in the sacrament of baptism, which we will renew this day.

I believe that most of us tend to put Christmas and Easter together. We look upon these two days as the two feasts of the Church which mean the most to us. They are alike and yet different. At Christmas we celebrate a beginning in the birth of Jesus. Even though Jesus really began his human life nine months earlier at the time of his conception, we think of his birth as the beginning of his human life. In his birth, Jesus came to us, human like us in all things but sin. At Easter we also celebrate a beginning. It was the beginning of a fuller life, for Jesus did not rise from the dead merely to continue the life he had led on this earth for some thirty years. He rose to a glorified life of perfect happiness wherein he put behind him all the suffering and misery and tears that are our human lot. At Easter, in one sense, Jesus left us behind, but he wishes to draw us to himself so that we may share in his glorified life forever.

Christmas is of course much more appealing to us with all its decorations, its wonderful carols, and its spirit of gift-giving. Easter is almost stark in comparison. There is one simple symbol of Easter which we should think about, however, and that is the Easter egg. Originally when the Lenten fast was extremely strict in the early Church, eggs were forbidden food. It was only natural then that on Easter Sunday, people wanted to enjoy this food from which they had abstained during the long period of Lent. An egg, however, is an excellent symbol of the meaning of Easter for Jesus as well as for ourselves. Within a fertilized egg, life is slowly unfolding. When the time for hatching arrives, the chick emerges from the shell to begin a full, free life as Jesus emerged from the tomb to a glorified life. Right now we are living a very confined life, like that of a chick within its shell. We hope that one day we will break the shell of this life to be free to live with Jesus his glorified life. The bright colors with which we dye Easter eggs are a sign of our joy over Christ's resurrection and the expectation of our own.

Easter reverses the image of Good Friday. It shows that Jesus Christ is truly the one who will lead us to the happiness of eternal life in heaven.

C.E.M.

## Easter Sunday (C)

## *DAY OF HOPE*

Easter Sunday, like Christmas, is usually a very happy day. New clothes and bright hats, a good meal and a gathering of family and friends are all part of the day. It is different from the humdrum of daily existence which can discourage us with our problems, our sins, our lack of a sense of meaning and purpose in the routine of life.

And yet tomorrow will be blue Monday all over again. We will have to return to our ordinary lives with all our problems, frustrations and weaknesses. Today, however, should give us a vision, a goal that can give meaning and joy to our everyday lives. We should pray that this celebration of Easter will bring us the grace from God to see the meaning of the resurrection for Jesus and for ourselves.

When we reflect on the life of Jesus we can see that it was a very hard and difficult life, certainly more difficult and hard than ours will ever be. To begin with, Jesus was born poor, he lived poor, and he died poor. He knew the meaning of hard work and the squeeze of a tight budget as he grew up helping St. Joseph in his carpenter shop. When he was about thirty years of age he became a traveling missionary. He went about from town to town in the primitive society of Palestine as he preached to the people. Often he did not know where he would sleep at night or where his food would come from.

People came to Jesus with their problems, physical, mental and spiritual. Many seemed interested in him only for the sake of their own welfare. It is true that some people responded to Jesus, but more of them were either indifferent or positively hostile. During this past week we have reflected on how terrible were the final days of his life. All that Jesus did, he did out of love for his Father and for us, and today we celebrate the reward of that love in the resurrection. The resurrection brought fulfillment to the earthly life of Jesus; it was a new life of happiness and union with his Father in heaven.

And this new life through resurrection is our goal too. In fact, it is our hope in resurrection with Christ that should give meaning and purpose to our lives. We are meant for much more than this present life. We are destined to share not only in the suffering and the death of Jesus, but in his resurrection as well. That is why Easter Sunday is such an important feast for us. In fact, the resurrection is so important that in the mind of the Church every Sunday is like a little Easter. It is just too big a thing to celebrate and praise and thank God about only once a year. The Church calls us to Mass each Sunday to commemorate the fact that through death Jesus came to the glory of the resurrection, and we are invited in each Mass to praise and thank God for this great truth of our salvation. What Jesus did, he did for our benefit.

And every Sunday we are invited to receive the resurrected, glorified Christ in Holy Communion. Our Communion is a pledge and a promise that Christ will raise us from the dead if we are loyal and faithful to him.

Easter Sunday, then, should be a very happy day, like Christmas. But have you ever noticed how different Easter is from Christmas? Part of the difference is due, I suppose, to the unique atmosphere of Christmas with all its special decorations, its beautiful songs and carols, and its spirit of gift giving. And the Easter bunny is no match for Santa Claus. A more important reason for the difference is that at Christmas we celebrate a birth, and we all know what birth means because it is within our experience. Today we celebrate a resurrection from the dead, something we cannot know directly, something that is not yet within our experience. Resurrection is not something we look back upon, but which we look forward to in hope. And it is that hope which, even through all of our blue Mondays, should give joy and meaning to our lives.

C.E.M.

**Second Sunday of Easter (A)**

## *NOT SEEING, YET BELIEVING*

We have a saying that seeing is believing. It is an expression of our practical, hardheaded approach to life, the "show-me" attitude. It can also be a cruel saying, for it implies a lack of trust in another. At first glance, the doubting Thomas of today's gospel manifested a lack of trust. He wanted to see before he would believe.

And yet we should not be too hard on Thomas. At least he was doubtful about the right thing: whether Jesus had really risen from the dead and was actually alive. Everything that Jesus said and did centered around the fact of whether he could overcome death. If Jesus had not come back to life, despite all the wonderful things he had done while alive, he would not have been essentially different from any other man. All the miracles that Jesus worked were done ultimately to show his power over sin and its effect, which is death. He came to give life, but not just the human life that parents give their children. That kind of life has to end for all of us. He came to give a life that will never end, an eternal life of happiness and peace. Thomas was not willing to believe in Jesus as the eternal life-giver until he was sure that Jesus had overcome sin and death in his own person. He saw and touched the wounds; he knew by this that the person before him was really the Jesus who had been crucified. And by the signs of life he saw that Jesus was really alive again.

St. Peter says to us in his letter: "Although you have never seen him, you love him, and without seeing you believe in him. . . ." We live in an age of faith, a time of believing without seeing. As important as the resurrection appearances are as a testimony from the early Church, it all comes down to the fact that God has given us a gift of faith to respond to the truth of the gospels. Many people have read the gospels without receiving faith from them, but thanks be to God that we have received faith. And Jesus says in the gospel, "Blest are they who have not seen and have believed."

Faith is more than just accepting the truth of the resurrection. Through our faith we come into contact with Jesus. Our contact is not by touching the wounded hands and feet of Jesus, but by receiving from the wounded and risen Jesus the gift of divine life, especially in the sacraments. Easter, which we are still celebrating, centers around three sacraments. The first is Baptism. Again in his letter, St. Peter tells us that God "in his great mercy gave us a new birth unto hope which draws its life from the resurrection of Jesus Christ from the dead, a birth to an imperishable inheritance. . . ." Baptism is indeed the sacrament of Christian birth. By it we first received that divine life which is in Jesus. We received it as a seed, something that has to be nourished so that it may grow and develop. And so the second sacrament of Easter is the Holy Eucharist.

Holy Communion is meant to develop within us the seed of eternal life. In this Mass we will receive the resurrected, glorified Christ. His resurrected body is both a sign and a pledge of our own resurrection from death to eternal life.

The third sacrament of Easter is Penance. According to today's gospel, Jesus on the night of the resurrection breathed on the Apostles and said, "Receive the Holy Spirit. If you forgive men's sins, they are forgiven them." Catholic tradition (DB 920) has rightly seen in this occasion the origin of the sacrament of Penance. The sacrament of Penance restores within us the life of the resurrected Christ if we lose it by mortal sin, and heals the disease of venial sin which interferes with the growth of that life within us.

In these three Easter sacraments, we cannot see Jesus with our bodily eyes. We cannot touch Jesus with our bodily hands. Faith makes all the difference. We come to these sacraments without seeing and without feeling, and yet with faith we can cry out with Thomas, "My Lord and my God." And Jesus responds, "Blest are you who have not seen and have believed." Indeed we are blest, that is, are happy and fortunate, for our faith has put us into contact with the risen Jesus, the giver of eternal life.

C.E.M.

## Second Sunday of Easter (B)

# *FAITH POWER THROUGH FORGIVENESS*

Stories coming out of wartime concentration camps in Germany and Poland are full of insights of man at his best. St. Maximilian Kolbe turned a starvation block into a house of prayer. Sr. Benedicta (Edith

Stein) turned agnostics into believers. Common suffering seems to have forced common concern for each other. Sharing of food, caring for one another, forgiving offenses, occurred almost as Luke describes in the early Christian community.

But the most amazing aspect was the power some had to sustain their own life. Dr. Viktor Frankl suggests that certain "dying" victims had a vision of what they had to do when they got out. A child, husband, wife, parents, a neglected friend, someone—was waiting for them. They had faith that they were needed to settle a family feud, to apologize to a neighbor, and would get out. This faith to love and forgive was a power which enabled them to survive.

St. Luke suggests in the first reading that the apostles bore witness "with power." The power they had was their faith in the risen Christ and the power to forgive sins. It was this force that allowed the early Christians to become one, to have unity and to survive under persecution.

The Christian community and their Old Testament ancestors were impressed with the symbols of water and blood. Both are signs of life: water in the desert and the waters of Baptism; and the blood of Christ on the cross and the blood of the Eucharist giving life. Christ not only suffered the water bath of Baptism but came through the blood bath of the crucifixion.

We could apply this to ourselves and suggest that if we want to have unity and forgiveness, not only do we have to offer a cup of water to the least friend, but we have to be willing to offer our life. Christ has already given us "power" in Baptism and the Eucharist. He has shown us how to forgive in Confession. So why don't we believe strongly? Why don't we forgive freely?

Our problem is: we haven't seen, so we don't have a strong faith power. If Christ stood here before us and invited us by name to investigate his wounds, maybe we would have faith. But we haven't seen, so we can't be like the apostles; nor have we suffered together in persecution. We have no bond of concern for each other. We don't forgive. So when the risen Lord imparts his blessing of peace through the person next to us, we're not ready. We're suspicious of the others or we just don't care.

As bad as it sounds, there is room for a solution if we admit that we suffer from time to time, and recognize that everyone has problems. And if we can say we all are suffering together, and this has meaning in the light of Christ's suffering, we might be willing to forgive each other. After all, we're in the same boat and the same storm. Then we would be open to be "begotten by God" and to be given a stronger faith.

Recognizing that we suffer together leads to great forgiveness and concern. Being filled with caring allows God to be present and gives us stronger faith, which helps us to survive the suffering itself. "The power that has conquered the world [of problems and suffering] is this faith of ours."

We are blessed because even though we haven't seen the risen Christ, we have experienced his forgiveness in the sacrament of Penance and in the greeting of peace. His love flows through us in Baptism and the Eucharist (water and blood). The Lord knows we are not the greatest lovers and forgivers. We might not get close to being a Kolbe or Stein. But we have a lot to be proud of: we will try, and the Lord will call us blessed because we have not seen, but believe.

M.M.R.

## Second Sunday of Easter (C)
Suggested Use: Third Eucharistic Prayer

# WE'RE MAKING PROGRESS

Parents who see a child every day do not notice his growth, but others do. On Easter Sunday you probably got together with members of your family whom you hadn't seen since Christmas, and very possibly you observed how tall one or another of the children had grown. It is only after you have not been with a child for some time, that you can step back and notice his growth. Living things grow slowly, and that includes the world and the human race.

Sometimes we have the feeling that the world and the human race are not getting anywhere, not making any progress. Although it is true that the world is still full of hatred, poverty and unhappiness, it is false to maintain that nothing positive has been developing. One of our main problems is that we are too close to get a proper perspective. Today we should step back to get a better overall view of what has been going on. And this Sunday following Easter is a good day to do so, since Easter celebrates the victory of Christ over sin, and sin is the real cause of all sorrow and evil in the world.

Shortly after the ascension of Christ, his power was obvious in the many miracles performed by his apostles, such as we read about in the first lesson of this Mass. Although miracles do not seem to be in as much evidence these days, the power of the risen Jesus is still at work, slowly transforming our world. And miracles still happen. For instance, during this century some miraculous cures have been recorded at Lourdes, cures for which hundreds of pages of documents are available and for which the medical testimony is irrefutable. These events at Lourdes give witness to the power of the risen Christ. Moreover, modern medicine has made tremendous advances. We would be far from the truth if we were to think that such progress has been achieved without the power of the risen Christ, no matter what the faith or lack of faith of the scientists involved.

While we realize that we are still beset by many social ills in our country, progress has been made. We have only to think back to a time when some of our fellow human beings were slaves, mere chattel, in order to realize how far civil rights movements have come. Whether people recognize it or not, even social progress is due to the teaching as well as the power of the risen Savior of all men.

My point is not to inculcate complacency but to thwart a fear, born of pessimism, that our situation is hopeless. In his inaugural address on March 4, 1933, Franklin D. Roosevelt spoke these famous words: ". . . the only thing we have to fear is fear itself." This fear continually nips at the heels of our forward progress. Sometimes its attack is so vicious that its bite can paralyze all our efforts. No wonder Jesus was quick to calm the fears of his apostles in the two appearances recorded in today's gospel. "Peace be with you" was not only his greeting but his gift, the fruit of his resurrection from the dead.

The resurrection of Christ was both his own personal victory over sin with its consequences, and our victory as well. In fact the whole of creation has benefited from the resurrection. As the whole of creation was adversely affected by sin, so has it been bettered by him who overcame sin. Our difficulty is in seeing a progress which is gradual. The improvement of the world and the human race is part of the long process willed by God to reach its fulfillment in the person of his risen Son. This fulfillment will be realized only at the end of time.

Today, in order to encourage ourselves to work with Christ toward even greater progress, we should step back and get a better perspective on God's plan for the perfection of the human race and all of creation. Without fear we should make our own the words of the Third Eucharistic Prayer: "We hope to enjoy forever the vision of your glory through Christ our Lord from whom all good things come."

C.E.M.

### Third Sunday of Easter (A)
Suggested acclamation: "Lord, by your cross and resurrection you have set us free. You are the Savior of the world."

## WHILE ON THE JOURNEY HOME

Americans are probably among the most traveled people in the world. Most of us like to go places and see things. Possibly even now you are thinking about the summer and looking forward to some trip you would like to take. A trip helps us to get away from things and to forget our problems. But we really cannot afford to get too far from reality. We must return home to the business of everyday living, and get things back into perspective.

The engaging story we have just heard in today's gospel is about two men who had lost their perspective while on a journey. A good guess is that they had gone to Jerusalem from their home in Emmaus to celebrate the feast of the Passover. While in Jerusalem, they either witnessed or at least heard about the death of Jesus. It was a great blow to them. Despite the astonishing news that the tomb of Jesus was found empty, they failed somehow to put two and two together. Apparently all they could think of was that their hopes had been crushed with the death of Jesus on the cross. All of life was out of perspective for them.

Jesus seemed disappointed at their lack of sense. Then with supreme patience he explained the meaning of the scriptures, that the Messiah had to suffer die in order to enter into his glory, that his death was the means for achieving the salvation of the world. When Jesus broke the bread at table, they recognized him and saw that he was alive. They realized that Jesus had been raised, that their hope in him had not been ill-founded, that he was indeed the savior of the world. At Emmaus they got things straightened out; they regained their perspective on life and its meaning.

Some think that the bread Jesus broke in the home at Emmaus was the Eucharist, but it probably was not. After Jesus had instituted the Eucharist on the previous Thursday at the Last Supper, he left its celebration to his followers with the command, "Do this in memory of me." However, it does seem that the author of the gospel wanted his readers to think of the Eucharist when they read or heard this story, because by the time the gospel was written the expression, "the breaking of the bread," had become a Christian term to signify the Eucharistic celebration, and more importantly because at Mass much the same thing happens as occurred at Emmaus.

According to the gospel story, Jesus recounted what the scriptures had to say about himself. He then explained their meaning. In breaking bread he not only shared a meal with the two men, but also revealed himself to them. Here at Mass every Sunday we hear the scriptures read. They are explained in the homily. In our "breaking of the bread," our spiritual meal, Jesus presents himself to us as the one who passed through death to glory and thereby attained our salvation.

Like the men in today's gospel we too are on a journey. Our real home, our lasting home, is with our Father in heaven. Also like the two men we can lose our perspective while away from home; we can get out of touch with reality, lost in the distractions of everyday life, and become confused and discouraged. We need our own personal Emmaus, a place where we can get things straightened out again.

The Mass, the "breaking of the bread," is our personal Emmaus. We come here to church as we travel through life to heaven. In the scripture readings we learn many different things about Jesus, but they all really add up to what we have heard today in the first two lessons. The first lesson records a sermon of St. Peter wherein he proclaims: "God freed Jesus from death's bitter pangs and raised him up again." That idea St. Peter developed in his first letter, our second lesson today. He points out that the death of Jesus was our salvation: "Realize that you were delivered from the futile way of life your fathers handed on to you, not by any diminishable sum of silver or gold but by Christ's blood beyond all price . . . Your faith and hope, then, are centered on God."

After the consecration today you will be asked to make this acclamation: "Lord, by your cross and resurrection you have set us free. You are the Savior of the world." That acclamation will be your way of recognizing Jesus as did the two men at Emmaus.

As we journey through life with all of its problems and distractions we can certainly lose our perspective. Every Sunday Jesus invites us to Mass, wherein he speaks to us and reveals himself so that we can get things straight again. Indeed the Mass is our personal Emmaus.

C.E.M.


**Third Sunday of Easter (B)**

## *THE LEAST LIKELY IS THE BEST BET*

Just before the turn of the century, a train rumbled through a French province headed for Paris. Two men sat opposite each other: the one a young soldier obviously bored with the inactivity, the other an old man quite content to finger his rosary beads. As the monotonous miles bumped along, the soldier could restrain himself no longer. He blurted out in the direction of the old man: "God isn't going to save our world, science is!" The old man merely smiled and nodded, continuing to move the next bead through his fingers. The "put down" was too much of a challenge to avoid, so the young man launched into a tirade on the marvels of science in business and medicine. Declaring religion to be dying out as the light of science came in, he continued his attack until the train came into the Paris depot. As the youth stood up to get his bag, he felt sorry for the old man—silently taking the abuse for the past hour. Trying to sound a bit kinder, he introduced himself. The ancient one shook the soldier's hand and reached into his vest for a card. The youngster accepted the card and helped the old man down the step. Then he glanced at the card: "Dr. Louis Pasteur, Academy of Science, Paris."

All of us are surprised when the least expected person turns out to be the expert and produces the right answers. An inmate behind the fence of the mental institution watched a man outside standing by his car, after kids had run off with the bolts to one of his tires. "Take one bolt from each of the other tires and use them to hold that on until you get to a gas station." "That's a fine idea. What are you doing in there?" "Well, I may be insane, but I'm not stupid." We just don't have faith in certain people. We sell them short. The disciples on the road to Emmaus couldn't "see" Christ because they were convinced he was still dead.

Mary Magdalene was the same. She could not see Christ in the garden because she didn't look through the eyes of faith: faith in the risen Lord. And the disciples were terribly disturbed by a "ghost" because they were convinced Christ had died for good.

A lot of us suffer from this myopic vision. We fail to look for the right things in the right places. We don't believe what our eyes see. We have to gear our sights wider to the least expected carriers of grace, or continue to miss out. How many friends have we only superficially appreciated because we see no value in them? How often do we fail to read or study to find out about public issues, simply because we know we're right, or "all politicians speak the same way"? When is the last time you seriously listened to a "little kid"? How can we possibly grow wiser if we don't listen and search?

The same applies even more to our vision of Christ. If we only have faith in a remote god-creator who somehow keeps the world going, then we will not see and experience the God-man Christ who knows our problems, walks with us, accepts us for the way we are. We won't grow. To "experience" the divine presence of Jesus is just too emotional for us. If Jesus Christ asked for a bite of our fish—he couldn't be God. He's too common, too available.

As Peter suggests, we can "put to death the author of life" by our ignorance. If we don't have faith in the risen, loving Lord—he's as good as dead for us.

How do I know I have the right faith-vision of Christ? John answers: "The way we can be sure of our knowledge of him is to keep his commandments." Love others as I have loved you. At rock bottom this means appreciating those we think little of. Then we should start "acting" like Christ is right alongside of us. Talk to him during the day and share events. If we really get good at this practicing, soon the reality will dawn on us. The power of Christ will move over us with "sheer joy and wonder." And we will begin to know that "God raised him from the dead, and we are his witnesses." Then the peace and joy of the apostles will be ours. And we will want to spread the Good News. Maybe even begin when you turn to the one next to you and proclaim: "The Lord is risen, peace be with you."

M.M.R.

**Third Sunday of Easter (C)**

## *STUBBORNNESS AND STUBBORNNESS*

The world is always twenty minutes ahead of one man in Coventry, England. "In 1922," he said, "the clocks were changed twenty minutes. I never accepted that. Nobody was going to take twenty minutes out of my life." So he kept his watch set for the old time. He is twenty minutes late for every appointment. As a result, the determined man has been fired from half a dozen jobs. "They won't beat me," he declared. "I'm going to die twenty minutes late to show that I was right." Holding rigidly to one's outlook, even in a small matter such as twenty minutes of time, may bring a certain satisfaction, but it is terribly self-defeating. Before we are as stubborn as the man from Coventry, we had better make sure that we are right and that the matter is really worth while.

Stubbornness is a characteristic most of us have to claim as our own. And isn't it true that so often we are stubborn about things which really don't matter, or concerning which we are far from being experts? Most of us have gotten into heated arguments about sports or the hair style of the young, and probably our discussions about politics have at times become hot enough to start a fire in a rain-soaked forest. And it is very likely that after hours of talk we haven't budged an inch from our position, and neither has our opponent. Thousands of words exchanged with nothing accomplished.

Perhaps such "discussions" are actually a form of recreation with little harm done, but in some cases stubbornness can be very serious. Take the matter of changes in the Mass and in the discipline of our religion. I am not talking about changes arbitrarily invented by incompetent persons, but those introduced by the highest authority in the Church. Can we honestly pretend that we are virtuous when we obstinately refuse to participate fully in the Mass as it has been revised by the Church? Of course the opposite situation is equally wrong. A person who doggedly insists on freely improvising the prayer and ceremonies of the Mass with no regard for expert and well thought out directives of the Church, is way out of line.

When is stubbornness a virtue? Peter and the other apostles in the first reading are a good example. They were every bit as stubborn as the man from Coventry who would not change his watch, but there were two big differences. The apostles were absolutely correct and the matter was of supreme importance. They really had no choice but to refuse obedience to the Jewish authorities who had forbidden them to preach Jesus as the Messiah. Peter summed up the situation perfectly: "Better for us to obey God than men!" For him the issue was clear-cut and he was sure of his ground. He had enjoyed a direct experience of the risen Christ, as we read in today's gospel. He knew that Jesus is Lord. Peter and the other apostles were indeed stubborn, but their stubbornness was a virtue, not a foolish obstinacy.

We should be stubborn when it is a matter of conscience. Pressure from other people must not be allowed to move us from our convictions, whether it be a question of extra-marital sex or racial prejudice, abortion or social injustice. On the other hand, we cannot blithely use "conscience" as an excuse for abandoning a moral teaching of the Church which we find difficult to follow. Theologians have always taught that conscience is the supreme norm of moral activity, but they insist that conscience must be informed. We have to work from facts, not from feelings alone. We must have a firm, solid foundation for our stand, unlike the man who said, "I have my mind made up; don't confuse me with the facts."

From their contact with the risen Lord, Peter and the other apostles received both enlightenment to form convictions and strength to follow through with those convictions, even to death. Today as we receive the risen Lord in Communion we should pray for the same enlightenment and strength so that in following our consciences we may indeed be obeying God himself.

O.J.M.

## Fourth Sunday of Easter (A)

### *GOD COMMUNICATES*

Our first reading today is basically a sermon preached on the day of Pentecost. Peter stood up with the Eleven, raised his voice, and addressed the people. Peter proclaimed, "Let the whole house of Israel know beyond any doubt that God has made both Lord and Messiah this Jesus whom you crucified."

Most of the large crowd listening to Peter had seen Jesus or had at least heard about him. Some had even witnessed his miracles. But apparently they had failed to let God get through to them. Fortunately for them, God refused to give up, as he continued to communicate his truth through the words of Peter. When the people heard this preaching of Peter, they were deeply shaken. They asked Peter and the other apostles, "What are we to do, brothers?" When they finally realized the evil they had been responsible for, they sought forgiveness, and were willing to do whatever God asked of them. Some three thousand persons were baptized on that occasion.

God continues to break in on our lives. He never gives up on us. Remember the famous painting of Christ knocking at the door of a house with no latch or doorknob on the outside? When the artist was asked whether he had forgotten something in the painting, he replied that the door was the door of the human heart and could be opened only from the inside. God keeps knocking until we open.

One way in which God continues to communicate with us is through the pages of the Bible. Truths spoken by God and written down centuries ago are repeated in the Mass as being spoken to us for the very first time. In the Mass these truths are applied to our lives, and to them we must respond with an eager openness, as did the people on Pentecost. And God keeps working at it. He will never tire Sunday after Sunday of communicating his truth to us in the pages of sacred scripture.

There are other ways God uses to get through to us. Think about all the good things in your experience: life itself, your ancestors and family, the world in which you live, someone who loves and trusts you, and many other good things. All of these good things are God's communication. Think too about today's gospel presentation of Jesus as the Good Shepherd. Give a lot of thought to this figure of speech, "Christ the Good Shepherd," and try to realize the many wonderful things he does for you under this title, "the Good Shepherd."

Now turn to the things you consider evil in your life: suffering, sin, sickness, failure, and so forth. God permits these things to happen, but he never fails to draw good from them, if we give him the chance. The people whom Peter spoke to had missed their chance while Christ was on this earth among them, but God gave them the opportunity to grow from that experience through a profound repentance. God even allowed evil men to be the instruments of his son's death so that all of us could live, dead to sin, in accord with God's will. By his wounds we were healed. Many times, God breaks into our lives through the means of apparent evil since we will not always respond to him when we are not in trouble.

God is responsible for the good in your life, and he permits evil only that good may come from it. To the good you must respond with praise and thanks. And yet it is always right to give him thanks and praise, even for evil. The expression "Oh, my God!" uttered when we've heard some tragic news, can be turned into a prayer if we realize that God has only a good purpose in mind.

Through faith we must hear God's communication to us in the Mass as words addressed personally to us here and now. But our faith must go further. We must see God's communication to us in both the good and the bad in our lives. To all this communication we must respond with thanks and praise and with a willingness to change our lives as we ask, "What are we to do, Lord?" God will never give up on us. He will continue to knock at the door of our hearts until we open to him.

O.J.M.

### Fourth Sunday of Easter (B)

## *INVEST IN THIS STOCK*

Anyone who works for a living (unless he is self-employed) is very impressed with a kind employer. Most employees brag about it: "I have a tremendous boss. He only blows up when I make big mistakes." Or better, we brag about a superintendent who just happens to be a friend of ours.

The secret of Christ's early success was probably something like this. Simple people recognized Christ as a strong leader. But they also were flattered because this strong leader liked them, and he didn't get too upset when they missed the point. And we have a right to feel the same way. In spite of our frequent failings, Christ loves us. How much more flattering when we realize that Christ reflects the Father, the great God of thunderous creation who happens to like us. And more, he wants us not just to work for him but to join the family. Yet what else could we expect from a loving Father who calls us his children? The kinder that Christ was to his friends, the more they could marvel at and praise the Father: "our dear Abba."

This is probably the reason it's so hard to understand why the Jewish people of Christ's time rejected him. We can understand a stone being carelessly set aside by ignorant builders, but not the loving shepherd being rejected by his flock. It's like a doctor being dumped by his patients, or a mother abandoned by her children. Yet Christ didn't qualify for what the Jewish people felt they needed. His kindness as a leader was wasted on them. His death and resurrection were for nothing. They wanted a political-military leader who would give them back some civic and personal pride. Man is at his poorest when he seeks status above love. He is blindest when he seeks to dominate more than to be accepted.

But are we any different from the early Jews? What are we "out to get" for ourselves? Are we happy with love and acceptance, or do we long to "conquer" others: make them think we have all the answers; have a position in life to be envied by onlookers? This kind of striving lead to ulcers and frustration.

How wonderful it would be for us to admit we're loved by a Father beyond our wildest dreams. The Father doesn't give two hoots about the condition of the living room sofa or the latest model car. He was happy to give us his risen Son as a permanent gift. Yet we seem to be out for the wrong values. So our love of the things around us blinds us to the love of our shepherd and his Father.

And in our romance with glittering things that have no heart or smile, we turn around and become "hired hands" of Christ. Oh yes, we belong to the family business, but we have no love for the flock (our own brothers and sisters) and run out when it becomes difficult or demands are made on us. I'm not going to give up Monday night at the movies to attend the third grade school play. And if I do, I'm not stopping at the hospital to visit Harry's mother-in-law. Through our neglect we reject Christ the cornerstone. We proclaim that Christ is not the foundation of our values.

Like Peter, if we must give an answer today to why things are so bad in the world, it is that in practice many people have rejected the corner-stone of their lives. They refuse to follow the shepherd's lead. Money has become the main stone, and public opinion (What would the bridge club think? I couldn't skip bowling. What would the boys think?) has become our leader. Yet Peter warns us: there is no salvation in anyone else, for there is no other name in the whole world given to men by which we are to be saved.

We're totally free to follow the Lord. There's no pressure to sign up. The risen Christ turns to us and calls us by name as he did for Thomas in the upper room, and Mary in the garden. He asks us to trust him during this Mass. He has our welfare at heart. The Father worries more about us than a shepherd ever would over sheep, or a boss over his workers. And Christ offers us a greater profit sharing plan than any business has ever thought of. We become not only part of the Lord's work, but we become one of the family. "See what love the Father has bestowed on us in letting us be called children of God."

M.M.R.

## Fourth Sunday of Easter (C)
World Day of Prayer for Vocations

## *A UNIVERSAL SHEEPFOLD*

Early in his political career Senator Everett Dirksen of Illinois was verbally assailed by an Illinois voter who said, "I wouldn't vote for you, Senator, if you were St. Peter himself." Smiling benignly the Senator replied, "If I were St. Peter, sir, you wouldn't be in my district."

Fortunately each one of us has been invited to be a member of St. Peter's district. By our baptism we have been brought into the sheepfold of Christ, and we are called to belong to that large crowd which St. John saw in his vision as presented in the second reading today. What a beautiful picture he paints:

> He who sits on the throne will give them shelter.
> Never again shall they know hunger and thirst,
> Nor shall the sun or its heat beat down on them,
> For the Lamb on the throne will shepherd them.
> He will lead them to springs of life-giving water,
> And God will wipe away every tear from their eyes.

St. John's vision symbolically presents God's love for us as members of his Church. But in this Mass we should think not only of ourselves and our own welfare and security. We should also think of the needs of others, since the sheepfold of Christ is intended for all peoples of all places. Notice how Paul and Barnabas, in the first reading, travelled far from home to preach Christ. When some of their fellow Jews rejected their preaching, they were undaunted and turned to the Gentiles. They did so in order to follow out the instruction of the Lord: "I have made you a light to the nations, a means of salvation to the ends of the earth."

All Catholics, especially through the sacrament of confirmation, have the obligation of spreading the truth of Christ. And yet, in the Church some persons have been given a specific role in proclaiming Christ. They are priests and religious. There is such a manifest need for good priests and religious that the Pope has set this Sunday aside as a world day of prayer for priestly and religious vocations.

Perhaps you feel that praying for good priests and religious has little meaning, since God will always provide for his Church. It is true that God will provide, but he wishes to give vocations to young men and women in response to prayer. Take St. Paul for example. We observed him in the first reading as a dedicated preacher of Christ, but Paul was not always such. In fact, he persecuted the Church of Christ. When St. Stephen, the first Christian martyr, met his death, Paul stood by looking after the cloaks of those who were stoning Stephen, and Paul approved of his death (cf. Acts 7:58 ff). In his last moments Stephen prayed for his persecutors, and St. Augustine commented later on this incident: "If Stephen had not prayed, the Church would not have gained Paul" (*Sermon 315*). St. Augustine spoke of the power of prayer from his own experience. As a young man he led a dissolute, selfish life with no regard for the teachings of Christ. One person never gave up on him—his mother, St. Monica. Through her prayers, Augustine received the grace from God to become an outstanding bishop, a great theologian, and a saint.

That the Pope himself today asks for prayers from all Catholics is itself a sign of how valuable our prayers are. Join with me in this Mass, especially in the Prayer of the Faithful, in begging God for the grace of good vocations. You parents should be thinking of your children. Pray that God will direct them in their choice for a calling in life and that, if it be his will, they may respond to a priestly or religious vocation. Keeping a middle ground, do not try to push your children into a vocation and do not hold them back. You young people, a decision about your role in life lies before you. Leave open the possibility of a vocation as a priest or religious, and ask God to help you make the right decision.

May God grant, through the ministries in his Church, that all peoples may become members of the district of St. Peter in heaven.

O.J.M.

## Fifth Sunday of Easter (A)

### TAKE TIME

When do you get enough time to pray? Picking up after the children, getting the washing and ironing done, cooking the meals, cleaning the house—these things don't leave much time for prayer. Getting to work, doing the job, finishing up, getting home—these things don't leave much time for prayer. Each person, I am sure, has his or her own list of things that interfere with time for prayer. Yes, even priests and sisters and brothers have their lists. I have mine and you have yours. And the apostles had theirs. "It is not right for us to neglect the word of God in order to wait on tables." One would think that whatever the apostles were doing would be good and necessary. But they did not feel that way. From Christ they had learned the importance of prayer, of a life of prayer, and so they were able to see that when they did not pray enough, things did not go as they should. This has been our experience too.

So, the apostles proposed that several men be selected to assist them. "This will permit us," they argued, "to concentrate on prayer and the ministry of the word." A nice solution for them. But whom are we going to get to assist us, so that we can have some time for praying? This is a good question. I hope we don't turn it off because we believe that we do not have the obligation to pray as the apostles did. If we feel that we do not have as much reason for prayer as they did, then we missed the second reading of this Mass. Listen again. "You, however, are a chosen race, a royal priesthood, a consecrated nation, a people he claims for his own to proclaim the glorious works of the One who called you from darkness into his marvelous light." These qualifications are not those of the priesthood or religious life. They belong to each one of us by our baptism. Your proclaiming of the glorious works of God may be limited to your family, your school, the place where you live and work. But it is none the less real. You need the time to listen to God each day and to respond to the best of your ability. So, then, accepting the principle that prayer must be a part of our lives as Catholics, let us see what the possibilities are.

One of the first things about having time to pray, is to pray where you are and at what you are doing. It's not a question of words, but rather of an attitude of mind toward God. Just as God through Christ was present to the apostles in the gospel of this Mass, so is he present to us. We should make sure that we don't miss him present with us by looking for him someplace else. God is with you in the kitchen, in the office, on the street, with your friends, as you shop, when you dance. Yes, even when we sin. God is there. We don't have to look at him, merely turn our minds toward him.

Another thing about prayer: if we really want it, we'll have to give in time. We must slow down to a human tempo and we'll begin to have time to listen. As soon as we listen to what's going on, things will begin to take shape by themselves. The opening words of Jesus to the apostles as recorded in the gospel of this Mass are extremely important here. "Do not let your hearts be troubled. Have faith in God and faith in me. In my Father's house there are many dwelling places; otherwise, how could I have told you that I was going to prepare a place for you? I am indeed going to prepare a place for you, and then I will come back to take you with me, that where I am you also may be." If we really believed in this promise of Christ, made to us as well as to the apostles, a lot of the hustle and bustle would go out of our lives.

And that seems to be the point. It's the hustle and bustle mostly that interferes with our prayers. We must approach the whole idea of time in a new way. We live in the fullness of time. Every moment is God's own good time. We don't have to rush after what we seek. It is there all the time, and if we give it time it will make itself known to us. Much of our rushing around all day long and collapsing in a heap at night is due to our desire for personal fulfillment. This is not a bad desire in itself. Nor is it wrong for parents to have that wish for their children. It's how we go about it.

There is a kind of self-fulfillment that fulfills nothing but our illusory selves. What truly matters is not how to get the most out of life, but how to recollect yourself so that you can fully give yourself. It's something like living in a desert. The desert becomes a paradise when we accept it as a desert. The desert can never be anything but a desert if we are trying to escape it. But once we fully accept it in union with the passion of Christ, it becomes a paradise.

Idealistic? Yes. But unless we strive for time in which to communicate with God, we are never going to establish the lines of communication. Any attempt to renew our lives is going to have to include the element of sacrifice, uncompromising sacrifice. Many things that seem important in our society will have to be given up, if we are to slow the tempo of life sufficiently so that we can think, and observe, and listen, and pray. And that takes sacrifice. Maybe we can begin by uncluttering our minds and hearts in this Mass, the supreme sacrifice of Christ. It is through him that we come to the Father.

O.M.J.

**Fifth Sunday of Easter (B)**

# *HOW TO TRIM YOUR PRIDE*

In the late '50's all the home magazines began carrying supplements on the perfect diet. The energies of the '40's had faded away and we had become soft. Everything from grapefruit to bourbon was considered the missing element to burn away these calories. The '60's produced the cholesterol scare, canonizing the use of no-taste milk and the low cost table-spread that made you feel like a king and look like your children. And the '70's, not to be outdone, have deleted preservatives and harmful chemicals from diet food to keep us ecologically and naturally trim. And for some reason we instinctively go along with the high priests of advertising and the good advice of doctors. If you want to stay in shape, look younger and healthier, cut down on intake: life will mean much more.

It's too bad the mystics of the middle ages didn't patent their diets: fasting and self-denial. That was the perfect combination to keep you physically sharp and spiritually in tune. And in a way this is the analogy being used by Christ: a healthy tree, bush or vine has to be pruned.

We merely have to translate our Lord's example and our experiences from dieting into the "realer" world of problems and disappointments. If we look on worrying and suffering as a form of trimming or dieting, slimming down our selfishness to size, we might see value in being neglected once in a while by our friends. We might see some advantage in not getting higher grades or a raise. We might profit from a current sickness, or not crab too much about arthritis. If we're not trimmed down, our pride will grow, our selfishness will expand and become bloated, but we won't grow.

Our growth doesn't have to come through pain, but we can try to distract our self-intake by being concerned about others. Listening to and remembering someone else's current problems isn't too painful and it puts us in shape. We become more "beautiful," compassionate, patient and understanding.

And the best part of this struggle is that we are not alone. We may cut back sometimes but we're still part of the vine: Christ. Branches have certain advantages: they simply have to put to use the food and strength that come from the vine.

But we have obligations too. Christ doesn't expect miracles from us, but wants us to try with his help to reach out to others. The vine won't extend itself without the branches. And wherever the branches show up, the vine is appreciated or not according to the goodness of the branches. The Jewish Christians had a hard time deciding whether to accept Paul or not. But Paul proved he was joined to the vine by speaking out fearlessly in the name of Jesus, and worrying more about the gospel than his own welfare.

It's not that easy staying in shape as a Christian. We have to accept pain and disappointment. We have to listen more to others than we do to ourselves. We die a little each day to make room for the Risen life. And ultimately, as Christians we look forward to the final death, the last shedding of the human bulk. But death will be a real joy: the end of sin, the end of struggling, and the new permanently trim us. If we try to diet our selfishness, we learn in advance what it means to die: dying to self, but rising to Christ.

Christ died to give us life—not in small proportion, but life abundantly. For this I will praise you, Lord, in the assembly of your people.

M.M.R.

**Fifth Sunday of Easter (C)**

# THE PEOPLE OF GOD

The idea of oneness which is found in today's liturgy, is well expressed by the famous St. Augustine.

> The members of the Savior, numerous as they are, under the one head which is the Savior himself, united by the tie of charity and peace, make only one man. In the psalms their voices are often raised as that of one man; and there is heard only one voice, as if it were all, because all in one alone are one.

And another early teacher in the Church makes a practical application of this principle of unity. He is St. Ignatius of Antioch.

> Do not think that you can do anything good by yourself. The only good that you can do is done in common. A common prayer, a common petition, a single heart, a common hope, animated by charity in the joy of harmony: that is Jesus Christ, above whom there is nothing.

This sounds like a recipe for good family love and action. And this is pretty much the way the first Christians felt about themselves. We get some good insights in this morning's readings.

Paul and Barnabas, the first travelling missionaries, show the usual enthusiasm for the early successes of a new movement. First they encourage their converts who had been under pressure for becoming Christians. "We must undergo many trials if we are to enter into the reign of God." And St. John in the second reading has the same idea of encouragement for a persecuted people in mind. "He shall wipe away every tear from their eyes, and there shall be no more death or mourning, crying out or pain, for the former world has passed away." After Paul and Barnabas had given a new hope to their converts, "they called the congregation together and related all that God had helped them accomplish, and how he had opened the door of faith to the Gentiles." The enthusiasm with which they told what God had done was real and almost boundless. It's the kind of enthusiasm one hopes to hear when the congregation prays the responsorial psalm, especially the words, "I will praise your name forever, my king and my God."

Our enthusiastic participation at Mass depends in some degree on a realization of who we are. When we say we are the people of God, we mean just that. It might sound odd to some, but we must be a people who are in love, truly in love with one another as Christians, whether or not we happen to be members of the same blood family.

It is our mutual job to create the environment and the atmosphere in this church in which God can communicate to us and we can respond to him. This is my chief duty as the celebrant of this Mass, the leader of this assembly. Like Paul and Barnabas, I have called this congregation together to tell you of the wonderful works of God, especially that he has brought a people together in love. I, like John, must see a new heaven and a new earth, a new Jerusalem, which each parish ought to be: "A holy city, coming down out of heaven from God, beautiful as a bride prepared to meet her husband." It is my privilege at the lectern and at the altar to tell you, again in the words of John's revelation: "This is God's dwelling among men. He shall dwell with them and they shall be his people, and he shall be their God who is always with them."

But the creation of the parish environment and the atmosphere at Mass in which God and we can communicate, can result only from effort on the parts of all of us. The new liturgy is a good vehicle, not a perfect one, for creating such an atmosphere. But we must work at it. I must help you hear and understand God's revelation to us in the liturgy of the word. You must listen attentively and try to assimilate what you learn. The lesson today is an easy one to absorb—that is, the early Christians loved one another, at least in the sense that they were enthusiastic about the progress of this new way of life. Obviously, Christians, early and now, have to work at this business of loving one another.

This is not the time or place for a blueprint on how to create this environment and atmosphere in which communication with God occurs. Here we establish attitudes, which can help us rid ourselves of hatred and ill-will, ill-feelings and grievances. Here we celebrate the fact that God loves us enough to bring us together so that he can give his revelation to us. For example, today he tells us of the early Christians, of the great vision of future glory as seen by John, and of the chief characteristic of Christians, that they love one another. How we act toward one another in our homes, schools, rectories, at our work, in our recreations, all week, will determine in large measure what kind of true-love atmosphere we have created for our Sunday worship. We are at a certain level at this time. During this week we will grow, so that next Sunday we will be able to create just a little higher level of environment for our communication with God. For all that we are at this moment, let us enter as enthusiastically as possible into this Mass, celebrating the wonderful fact that God has first loved us, so that we can love him and our fellow man in return.

O.J.M.

## Sixth Sunday of Easter (A)

## *SIMPLE PRAYER*

In the gospel, we saw Jesus taking the apostles as they were and where they were. They were mixed up, puzzled, confused and frustrated. They were particularly concerned and distraught because Jesus had said that he would have to leave them. They were suffering the terrifying human fear of being left to face life all alone. There is scarcely anything more frightening than the thought of having to grapple with the problems of human existence all by yourself, with no help, no guidance, no consolation from anyone else. It is the fear felt by the widow without her husband, as her children have gone from home to live their own lives. It is that terrible illness, called "homesickness," experienced by the young person who has left home for a strange, new school. It is the terror of the small child lost on a camping trip.

Jesus understood how his apostles felt. He wished to make it clear that their fear was groundless as he said, "I will ask the Father and he will give you another Paraclete—to be with you always . . . I will not leave you orphaned; I will come back to you." We can see one example of the fulfillment of Jesus' promise in today's first lesson. Even after his ascension Jesus did not abandon the people of Samaria, in whose region he had worked miracles during his public ministry. His help to them came from Philip the deacon, who was acting on the impulse of the Holy Spirit, as he responded to Christ's command to preach the gospel. Philip left Jerusalem for Samaria. There his preaching met with immediate success. When further spiritual help beyond baptism was needed—that is, the giving of the Holy Spirit by the laying on of hands—Philip and

Peter and John came to Samaria and confirmed the new converts.

What happened in Samaria has continued down through the centuries. The promise of Jesus has also been fulfilled in us. We too have received the Holy Spirit, and because of him we are not left alone. Through the power of the Holy Spirit, the Father and the Son are present within us. But we have to find God even within ourselves. We have to search him out. We must respond to his presence within us. In a word, we must pray.

If we have the idea that real prayer is only for mystics, or that prayer must be a very complicated formulary with just the right words of theological precision, we should rid ourselves of that notion. Simple prayers are good prayers. Exalted through the Mass truly is, even here we find simple prayers and we learn just what earnest, sincere prayer should be.

We begin the Mass with the sign of the cross, "in the name of the Father and of the Son and of the Holy Spirit." Prayer begins with a recognition of God, and should include an awareness of his presence within us. Most assuredly we stand unworthy before God because of sin. At the very outset of each Mass we are asked to realize our sinfulness. At my invitation we all bowed our heads and tried to prepare ourselves to celebrate the sacred mysteries. As a group of people trying to offer God suitable worship, we humbly asked forgiveness of our sins. That is a theme which continues as we pray "Lord, I am not worthy to receive you, but only say the word and I shall be healed."

Throughout the Mass we turn to God for help in all the many prayers of petition, especially the Prayer of the Faithful as well as in the presidential prayers at the end of the entrance rite, the preparation of the gifts, and the Communion rite. Each Mass itself is a total prayer of praise and thanksgiving, as the very word "eucharist" signifies.

Even this sketchy survey of the Mass should help you to see that the prayer of the Mass is basically very simple. "God help me . . . forgive me . . . thank you"—in essence that is our prayer. They help us to be ourselves before God, and they have the advantage of beginning right where we are with God. Simple prayer will help us to find God, so that we need not be left alone in the struggle of life. Our prayer at Mass must carry over into the other activities of our lives. Take the time and make the effort to continue prayer through the week right where you are at any time. In your mind and heart, if not on your lips, say "God help me . . .

forgive me . . . thank you.'' Of course your own words are best, but these three simple ideas are what make up good prayer.

It is indeed a terrifying experience to be left all alone in life. Because of God's presence within us, we need not have that experience if we learn to turn to God with simple, earnest prayer in all the aspects of our lives.

O.J.M.<br>C.E.M.

## Sixth Sunday of Easter (B)

### *OH YES, HE'S A PERSONAL FRIEND OF MINE*

Have you ever had the experience of feeling talented and clever in some groups, and with others you feel you have very little to offer? Like the young father who is a champion athlete with his son around, but comes in last with his friends on the golf course. It's so much easier to share a good story with your fellow workers than it is with the supervisor. And if we look closely at this Jekyll and Hyde situation, most of the time our ''success'' depends on just how much ''acceptance'' we enjoy from the group we're with. Without ever hearing it, we know by instinct when we are appreciated and we respond. A smile or nod is like a roar of applause or hugs and kisses. We are encouraged and made confident. With this support we are good at what we're doing.

But strangely for all our eagerness to have a good reception, we miss our best fans: God our Father and Christ our Brother. ''Love then consists in this: not that we have loved God, but that he has loved us.'' Christ knows us at our best and appreciates our efforts to try harder. How much confidence would you have if you experienced Christ as your happiest listener, your best audience? And praise the Lord, he is your best friend. Christ has laid down his life for us, made himself available at all times, and solemnly calls us friends.

To show our appreciation, we simply have to extend the call we've experienced to those around us. ''I choose you. I call you friend.'' It's simply a matter of sharing the wealth. Or better, as Christ spoke to us last week, we are the branches of Christ reaching out to support those who haven't experienced the richness of the vine. This acceptance can't stop with those immediately around us. Like the proverbial pebble in the brook, the circle has to widen if Christianity is to keep its slogan: look how they love one another. Peter had to be told by the Holy Spirit to open the circle of the Church wider to take in Cornelius.

And how much sooner might there be a unity of churches if we Catholics were simply to convince other Christians of our acceptance of them? No suspicions, no better-than-thou notions would be the way to start. We would still be painfully aware of differences in doctrines. But we easily allow our friends to have different opinions and continue fully to accept them. Why not treat other Christian assemblies the same way?

Christ has certainly set the pace. The Easter joy of the apostles was based on the risen Lord's re-establishing the bond of friendship. After all, the apostles had run out on Christ during the crucifixion. But peace-be-with-you wiped away fear and guilt and their joy was made complete.

If you don't think you have much skill in bringing Christians together, try short steps. Watch for occasions just to compliment those around you at work or school. This mild acceptance they experience will make them more responsive to your friendship. Your love will grow and the Lord will make you bolder to share deeper values about your God and your Church.

At this Mass there are friends around you ready to support you, to wish you peace. And don't forget. You have a very influential friend upstairs. He'll back you up all the way.

M.M.R.

## Sixth Sunday of Easter (C)

## *AUTHORITY, FREEDOM, AND LOVE*

In the early Church there arose a problem about transferring Jewish regulations into the new Christian community. Gentile converts to the Church could not see why they had to be coerced into following practices which had nothing to do with the Church founded by Jesus Christ. The matter of circumcision was particularly controversial.

When this problem came to the attention of the apostles and elders in Jerusalem, they discussed the issue at length and came to a conclusion. Their proposal was: "It is the decision of the Holy Spirit, and ours too,

not to lay on you any burden beyond that which is strictly necessary . . . ''
And the burden that was laid upon them was a disciplinary thing because
of the culture of the time. It was customary for those who offered
sacrifice to the Roman or Greek gods to eat of the sacrifice, thereby
showing that they agreed to this particular form of worship. Since one
cannot worship the true God and profess worship of idols at the same
time, the decision was that Christians must abstain from meat that had
been sacrificed to idols. But the idea that circumcision was necessary
was definitely rejected.

This episode in the early Church involved the importance of freedom which human dignity demands. No one in authority should lay on
others a burden beyond that which is strictly necessary. We find that
many times in life, in our care and concern for those who are under our
authority, there is a tendency to exaggerate the kinds of decisions that
must be made to help others grow and develop in a way most beneficial to
them and those with whom they live. This exaggeration tends to be found
among parents with their children, pastors with their parishioners, and
heads of institutions and schools with their students and pupils. There is
real tension between the exercise of authority and the expression of
freedom.

Today we celebrate God's goodness in giving us enlightenment in
this troublesome problem. In the gospel we heard the words of Jesus:
''Anyone who loves me will be true to my word, and my Father will love
him, and we will come and make our dwelling place with him always.''
Love is the crucial point in regard to the exercise of authority, as well as
to the submission to authority. Parents, for example, must have a true
love for their children if they are going to exercise their authority in such
a way as to help them grow and develop. And children must submit with
love, whereby they show that they understand that parents intend only
good for them.

Of course it is easy to talk about such love, and very difficult to put
it into practice. But difficulty is no excuse for not trying, since love is the
only answer. Everyone with any kind of authority must ask himself:
''Why do I lay down laws and rules—what is my motive?'' Is authority
used as a nourishment for one's ego, a selfish expression of power?
Whose welfare do we have in mind? Would we want others to use their
authority as we use ours? Honest answers to such questions are a big step
forward.

On the other hand, when we are subject to authority we must also ask ourselves questions. When we insist on our freedom, do we have in mind only our own convenience, our whims, our self-indulgence? Are we simply too proud to give in? Do we refuse to see the good intentions of one in authority because of our own stubbornness? If we were in authority, how would we want those subject to us to react? Again, honest answers to such questions are a big step forward.

These days we are suffering turmoil and conflicts in society, in the Church, in our schools, and in our homes. In trying to solve our problems of authority and freedom, let's do so with a hopeful attitude. Through the Holy Spirit we can be as successful with the problem of authority and freedom as were the apostles and the early Christians. Then we will know the meaning of the words of Jesus: "Peace is my farewell to you, peace is my gift to you."

O.J.M.


**Solemnity of the Ascension (A)**

## *AN INFLUENTIAL INTERCESSOR*

If today's feast of the Ascension were in a popularity contest with the other feasts of our Lord, I am afraid that it would probably come out last. And this is really a shame because, in a certain sense, the Ascension could be called the greatest feast of our Lord since it is his supreme glorification.

God the Father responded to the magnificent act of love of Jesus in dying on the cross by restoring his life in the resurrection, but that life was brought to the full in the ascension. Jesus rose from the dead, not to continue the earthly existence which began in Mary's womb, but to receive a new, heavenly existence in the place of honor at his Father's right hand. The ascension completed the resurrection. It exalted Jesus as Head of the Church and bestowed on him the title of "Lord." By means of the ascension, God the Father confirmed the meaning of his words spoken at the time of the transfiguration: "This is my beloved Son on whom my favor rests. Listen to him."

The ascension, however, was not a retirement ceremony for Jesus, as if with all his work done he could sit back and relax, far removed from the turmoil and anxieties of our life in this world. The Lord Jesus is still active and very much concerned with us, his people. He has not lost that sense of compassion and love which he beautifully manifested while on this earth. We are constantly in his thoughts. In the "Gloria" of the Mass, we rightly say to Jesus: "You are seated at the right hand of the Father: receive our prayer." And in his place of influence with the Father, Jesus responds by making our prayers and our sacrifice his own. The Mass we offer is a reality because Jesus in heaven unceasingly offers to his Father the sacrifice of the cross as he shows him the wounds he accepted out of love for us. Jesus can save us who approach him, since he forever lives to make intercession for us (Cf. Heb 7:25). Whenever we pray, but especially when we offer the Mass, Jesus stands before the Father and says: "These are my people. From them I have been taken. Like them I was born of a woman, and I have suffered and died as they must suffer and die. These are my beloved people on whom my favor rests. Listen to them."

And Jesus is always heard by his Father. Do you think that the Father could possibly turn a deaf ear to the Son whom he has exalted and glorified in the place of honor at his right hand? Never! And because of Jesus, God the Father listens to us. If we had to pray alone on our own merits, we would have reason to despair. But because we have Jesus always living to make intercession for us, we should have the greatest confidence. Even in the darkest days of our lives when we are sunk in the deepest depression, we would firmly trust that God will raise and exalt us just as surely as he did his own Son.

                                                                    C.E.M.

## Solemnity of the Ascension (B)
Suggested Use: First Eucharistic Prayer with Special Communicantes

# THE FLOWER OF THE RESURRECTION

The Ascension tends to be neglected among the great mysteries of the life of Jesus Christ. We commemorate the birth of Jesus in the joy of Christmas. We appreciate the magnitude of his death as the sacrifice of the cross. We celebrate his resurrection in the glory of Easter. But the Ascension? It is tucked away in the quiet of a middle-of-the-week observance, almost as if we are not quite sure what to do with it.

We can understand the place of the Ascension only if we see it in relationship to the other central events in the life of Jesus. Jesus was born as one of us, so that he could enter into the human situation as our Savior. He came to rescue us from our twin enemies, sin and eternal death. By his sacrificial death Jesus won the victory over sin and death, and that victory was manifested in his resurrection. Jesus made the passage through the darkness of death and emerged triumphant in the light of his resurrection. But Jesus did not rise merely to take up again the earthly existence that he had begun at the moment of his incarnation. The ascension shows that he rose from the dead to a new, heavenly life. His ascension was his return to the Father, his glorification in heaven at God's right hand, his exaltation as the Lord of Life. The ascension is an integral part of the resurrection itself, as the fruit is part of the tree, or better, as a full-blown flower is the purpose of stem and bud. The ascension indicates the newness and fullness of the risen life of Jesus Christ. We really cannot imagine what this life is like. In fact we don't even have a good word to describe it, but there is one word you will hear repeated in the Mass—an inadequate word, the only word we have, and that word is "glory." Jesus ascended to a life of glory.

The ascension of Jesus is important to us because life is precious. We cling to life in this world, despite all the sorrow, all the pain, all the frustration of human existence. We cling to this life because it is the only life we know. And yet we really do not want this kind of life forever. We yearn for the perfect life that will never end, the life of glory.

In times past, men searched for the fountain of youth so that they might always be young and never have to die. Their searching strikes us as a little naive. But some scientists today are almost as naive, as they probe into the aging process in the hope of finding a way to prolong life and eventually prevent death itself. Such searching and probing misses the point. The life we are made for is not found in this world, but in heaven—and to find it we must, like Christ, pass through death to a sharing in his resurrection and ascension.

We have been called to a great hope in Christ. In him our frail human nature has been raised to glory. One day his glorious heritage will be ours. We do not have to fear a physical aging process that will lead to death; we need fear only the disruptive power of sin, which alone can destroy us. Jesus has given us the victory over sin. Today as we look toward heaven, toward Jesus in glory at the right hand of the Father, we do so with the belief that he will come again to raise us to a sharing in the fullness of life, the life of glory.

C.E.M.

## Solemnity of the Ascension (C)

# A SIGN OF HOPE

The celebration of the Ascension of Jesus Christ into heaven is not only an important event for us, but a very practical one as well. It occurs not on a Sunday, but almost in the middle of the week when we are very busy with the ordinary necessities of our everyday lives. The Church calls us away for a moment from the duties which occupy most of our time, so that we may lift our eyes to heaven and be reassured about our eternal destiny in God's plan.

We celebrate the fact that Jesus, the Lord, has been taken up into heaven. Through his obedient suffering and death Jesus has been raised from the dead, and in his ascension he enjoys the fullness of life. On this feast, God wishes to enlighten our innermost vision so that we may know the great hope to which he has called us (second reading). We are destined to follow Jesus where he has gone before us (preface). Our glorious heritage is to share in his spiritual wealth forever. Most of us desperately need this sign of hope.

In this life we are much like a farmer who goes about the business of preparing the soil, planting the seed and cultivating a crop. A dry spell prevails. There is a danger, a nagging fear, that the crop will fail, that all the work has been in vain. Then one day the farmer looks to the sky. He sees dark clouds, heavy with moisture, slowly gathering over his farm. The sun is obscured, but the darkness is not a sign of despair; it is filled with hope. He begins to pray that the clouds will bring much-needed moisture to his parched crops. He waits patiently. Then with a flash of lightning and a roll of thunder, the clouds pour down their life-giving rain. The storm passes and the warm, cheerful rays of the sun break through.

Whatever occupies our time—working at a job, being a homemaker, going to school—we are probably like the farmer who first looked only at the soil. We have a "downward" vision. That can be very discouraging because we run the risk of becoming bored or frustrated with life, fearing that it is not worth the trouble or that everything we do has very little meaning. From time to time we need to look, not downward, but upward toward heaven where Jesus has gone before us. Our vision is obscured now by the dark clouds of the problems we face in life, but we must never despair. We must believe that, as suffering and death led to fullness of life for Jesus, so the clouds of this life will bring the life-giving waters of God's grace to us. In death, filled with greater awesomeness than a flash of lightning and a clap of thunder, the clouds will part for us and we will see the Son of God in all his glorious radiance coming for us.

The celebration is one of hope as we look toward heaven. When we leave this Mass, however, we should hear a voice within us saying: "Why do you stand here looking up at the skies? This Jesus who has been taken from you will return." From this Mass we go back to looking "downward" as we again take up our everyday lives. But we should do so with a great optimism and a firm hope.

C.E.M.

**Seventh Sunday of Easter (A)**

## *REJOICING, WITH A DIFFERENCE*

On Easter and the following Sundays we hear a lot about rejoicing in the liturgy, and the Masses of the season are characterized by an expression of joy—the one word, "Alleluia." What is the jubilation all about? Why, the resurrection of Christ, of course! The resurrection of Christ should fill our hearts with joyful "Alleluias" because it is the cause of Christian hope and confidence about our own future. We have the belief that as Christ was raised from the dead to the fullness of glorified life, so we too will be raised.

But if the truth were to be told, for many of us the "Alleluias" have a slightly hollow ring, and the joy we hear about is something we don't always feel. It isn't that we don't have faith or hope. It's just that the resurrection of Christ seems so far in the past and our own resurrection so far in the future. And the joyful "Alleluias" in church are often drowned out by the dissonant clangor of our everyday world.

Today in the second reading we hear that familiar word, "rejoice," once again. But wait a minute. There was a difference. Let's go back and look at that reading again. "Rejoice insofar as you share in Christ's suffering." That really is rejoicing with a difference, a difference so great that it seems a little crazy. Who wants to be happy about suffering? Yes, St. Peter insists, "Happy are you when you are insulted for the sake of Christ." And he goes on to say, "If anyone suffers for being a Christian, he ought not to be ashamed. Rather he should glorify God. . . ."

St. Peter's idea of rejoicing over suffering deserves reflection on our part.* To begin with, there was a time when Peter held just the opposite view. When Jesus said one day that he had to go to Jerusalem to suffer greatly and be put to death, Peter judged suffering and death to be so undesirable that he blurted out: "May you be spared, Master! God forbid that any such thing ever happen to you!" Later when a servant girl questioned him about his being an associate of Jesus, he was so unhappy with the implied insult that he denied even knowing Jesus. On Good Friday he was so afraid of undergoing the same fate as Jesus, that he made sure he was not even around to see what was going on.

Something happened to Peter after the death and resurrection of Jesus that changed his outlook completely. That something we are going to celebrate next Sunday on the feast of Pentecost, the coming of the Holy Spirit. It was a real happening for Peter and the other apostles. The Holy Spirit, with his gift of wisdom, penetrated their minds so that they could clearly see a truth that Jesus had been telling them all along. That great truth was the Paschal Mystery, the fact that the passion and death of Jesus led directly to the glory of his resurrection. It was not that Jesus suffered patiently because he knew his passion would last only for a while and would soon be over. Rather, it was that he knew his obedient acceptance of suffering and death would be the cause of his glorious resurrection to the fullness of life. "For the sake of the joy which lay before him he endured the cross, heedless of its shame" (Heb 12:2). In other words, Jesus was happy to suffer because he knew what the result of his loving obedience would be.

---

*That St. Peter was the author of this epistle was not called into question until the 19th century. However, arguments against Petrine authorship are by no means conclusive. In either case, since the epistle certainly reflects the teaching of the apostles, including that of Peter, it seems homiletically valid to speak of Peter as the author.

Peter and the others were also given to understand that the Paschal Mystery applied to Christians as well as to Christ—that for us too, obedient acceptance of suffering will lead to the fullness of life as we share eventually in the resurrection of Christ. This was a truth they practiced as well as preached, for all of them happily suffered much for the sake of Jesus. I think that all of us know that our suffering takes many forms, physical and emotional. It is not only illness that we must accept, but all the loneliness and frustration of human existence.

The important thing is that we have the Christian outlook on suffering, which is ours through the Holy Spirit's gift of wisdom. It is not like the attitude of the man we joke about who beats himself over the head because it feels so good when he stops. Rather, it is more like the attitude of the student who is happy to take the pains to study because he knows it will win his degree; or like that of the man who is happy to work hard because he knows his efforts earn a living for his loved ones; or like that of the woman who is happy to get out of bed at night to care for her sick baby, because she knows her sacrifice is necessary for his health. This happiness is not the glee of a little child without worry or concern; it is the satisfaction of a mature adult who knows that it is all worthwhile.

Let us ask the Holy Spirit to give us his gift of wisdom so that we may have the right sense of values in our outlook on life. With that outlook, our "Alleluias" need not be hollow, and we may even feel a little of the Christian joy that should be ours as followers of Christ.

C.E.M.

## Seventh Sunday of Easter (B)

### *JUMP, I'LL CATCH YOU*

It's amazing how the problem of faith is so similar for people at any age. College students, housewives all speak the same: "If I could only see and experience Jesus as the apostles or as the saints did, then I could easily believe."

And just as amazing, the problem seems to have been the same for the apostles: if only they could see God the Father, then they could believe. "Lord, when will you show us the Father?" Our Lord opens his arms and simply asks them to make the jump of faith: when you see me, you see the Father. And evidently they jumped.

This means that our faith begins with faith in the testimony of those who first believed in Christ. We accept their impression, their convictions that Jesus is Lord, Christ is God. We place our natural trust first in their faith, their acceptance of Christ. Then our accepting this "second hand" faith, thanks to wonderful grace, becomes "first hand" faith and even leads to the real experience of Christ.

But we shouldn't think this two-step process puts Christ at a distance from us. Our faith is a response to a personal call. The choice of Matthias in the first reading is one of the most un-celebrated yet significant steps in the early Church. Matthias is the second generation of believers along with Titus, Timothy, Barsabbas, Barnabas and us. Christ choosing Matthias through the other apostles is as good as Christ choosing us through the Church today. "You have not chosen me, I have chosen you."

We have been hand-picked just to experience God. And John describes this process of discovering God. No one has ever seen God. Right. Even Moses on Mt. Sinai had his face shielded from the vision of God. But John tells us that God is love. And any of the chosen who abide in love, abide in God already. Second step: any of the chosen who acknowledge that Jesus is the son of God, God dwells in him and he in God.

The Father is with us, ready to be experienced, if we can only wake up. If only we can dislodge ourselves from our "world" of hurry-up, quadrasonic purple frozen foods, new cans and new duds, we will be free to see. If we recognize that we don't belong to radios and TVs, we're not cousins of the freeways, we're not owned by the world—then the joy of Christ can be made complete in us. Faith helps us recognize that our Father is God, our Brother is Christ and our name is "Christian," not "Worldling."

And Christ has worked hard to keep us together. He reminds us of his death for us through the marks in his hands and feet. He has transcended all limitations through his resurrection to be with us this morning at Mass. He is here to protect and guard us from our goofy world. The Risen Lord reminds us that we have been chosen to succeed the apostles; to spread the presence of God through our love for each other and to realize that we don't need to depend on things that rust for complete joy.

Maybe we spend too much time and energy reaching out for the

Lord. Too bad. He is right next to us, and we're too exhausted to experience him and too afraid to make a tiny jump.

M.M.R.

### Seventh Sunday of Easter (C)

## *UNITY AMONG CHRISTIANS*

Stephen's prayer in the first reading of this Mass is for the same purpose as that of Christ's prayer in the gospel—that is, unity among all Christians, among all peoples for that matter. The reason for his stoning was the same as the belief expressed by John in the second reading. Stephen had just finished declaring that Jesus Christ is the one in whom we are to be saved. John's language in his book of Revelation is something like the symbolism in some of our modern movies. But underlying the symbolism of a tree, a city with gates, of offspring, of a morning star, of a bridegroom and bride, there is the basic truth that Christ is the Alpha and the Omega, the Beginning and the End, the First and the Last. Our common bond among all men is Christ. And it is this Christ who prays that our unity will be complete.

The Christian community, as we find it in the United States today, has certainly produced much good fruit. As we look around our parish groups gathered throughout the various dioceses of this country, we note many fine parochial plants. Even though we have felt the financial pinch because of changing neighborhoods, nevertheless our parish systems are some of the best in the world. And when you couple with this the great effort that is put forth in the conscientious education of so many hundreds of thousands who are not in our parochial schools, but are in our CCD programs, you get a good idea of the efforts that are being put forth to dispel religious ignorance. Our children still come out of our Catholic homes to become priests, sisters and brothers, even if not in the larger numbers of some years ago. These are very tangible and worthwhile fruits produced by reason of Christian solidarity. Furthermore, we pray and worship together and we realize the fruitfulness of Christ's words, "I pray that they may be one in us, that the world may believe that you sent me." Under the direction of the Pope, our bishops, and our pastors we know that we are trying to reveal Christ to the world in which we live, so that the love of Christ may live in us, and we may live in the love of Christ.

Part of the reason for the lack of more evidence of the vigor of Christianity in our times is due to the fact that the good which does come about is the result of mostly individual effort. Much more could be accomplished through the collective effort of the entire Christian community. It might be a parish effort, or that of a diocese, or the united action of all of us in the country. With cooperative effort, how many more people could be brought back to the sacraments—if so much of the effort to help them was not left in the hands of the Legion of Mary members only. How many more persons could be truly helped, not just have their hunger temporarily alleviated, if so much of this kind of Christian charity were not left to members of the St. Vincent de Paul Society only. What a great boon it would be for our youngsters if the work of imparting the basic principles of the life of Christ and his teachings were done by the entire parish, instead of by the few members who devote themselves in some way or another to Confraternity of Christian Doctrine work. Just think of the extent of the influence of Christian charity that could be exercised by a total parochial effort to visit the sick in the hospitals, rather than have this work of mercy limited to visiting those who belong to the same society as you do, or perhaps members of your own family, or business associates.

The evils that we are confronted with today in our society have been sufficiently pictured for us in all sorts of studies in magazines, on television, in special movies, in daily newspaper accounts and radio reports. And many worthwhile solutions have been offered by our bishops, by the government, the executive officers of many associations, and the leaders of social reforms. However, the good influence of the Church is not going to be offered to society with sufficient extension until there is a truly cooperative action that involves almost everyone who professes to be a follower of Christ. Not until we operate on a wide enough scale, where the large majority of our people are engaged in bringing Christ to the world in which we live, will large numbers of people know that the Father has sent his Son, and that the Father loves everyone even as he loves his Son, Jesus Christ.

O.J.M.

**Pentecost Sunday (A)**

# ONE BODY, ONE SPIRIT

When the day of Pentecost came, it found the apostles and other disciples of Jesus in one place. Although they were physically together, they were far from united in their minds and hearts. After Jesus had left them for heaven, they felt like orphans, abandoned and confused. Doubts filled their minds and fear tugged at their hearts. What was to become of them? Would they undergo a fate like that of Jesus on the cross? Feeling abandoned and confused, each one could think only of himself—for in time of fear our worst inclination toward selfishness becomes manifest and our instinct for self-preservation becomes all-pervading.

Then an amazing thing happened. With a great rush of wind the Holy Spirit came upon them, that same Holy Spirit who had sanctified Mary. Doubts and fears were blown away. The apostles and disciples stood up together like one man and boldly went forth to proclaim the marvels God had accomplished in Jesus Christ. They had become like Mary in their dedication to Christ. All thoughts of selfishness and disunity had been left behind in the upper room. The Church, born from the side of the Savior on the cross, had now been formed by the Spirit into a unity and manifested to the world.* From all eternity the Holy Spirit unites the Father and the Son in an unchanging embrace of love. After Jesus had ascended into heaven and returned to his Father, he sent forth the Spirit from himself and his Father upon the Church to unite all its members in love as one body.

The Church of Jesus Christ is like a human body in which there are many parts: arms, legs, eyes and ears. Despite its many parts the human body is a whole, a unity, with all the parts working together harmoniously for the good of the one body (second reading). Informing and uniting all the parts is the life-giving principle, the soul. Look around you

---

*It is a poor analogy to speak of Pentecost as the birthday of the Church. Pentecost is more properly termed the epiphany of the Church, for the Church was born with the death of Christ and manifested on the day of Pentecost. See the encyclical of Pope Pius XII, *Mystici Corporis Christi*, nos. 27-29. The idea of Pentecost as the birthday of the Church is a popularization without foundation in the writings of the Fathers or the official documents of the Church.

C.E.M.

today. You see the universal Church in microcosm. You see men, women and children of every age, background and culture. Throughout the world the Church embraces all peoples of all places. It is a true melting pot. Uniting all the people of the Church is its life-giving principle, its soul, the Holy Spirit (cf. Pius XII, *Mystici Corporis Christi*, 60f).

Look around this church again. We are all gathered together in one place, like the apostles and disciples on Pentecost. Today on this Pentecost Sunday, the Father and the Son wish to renew and intensify their sending of the Spirit upon us, the Church. We are called to stand as one man to profess one faith with one voice (Preface). Putting aside all selfishness and individualism, we must open ourselves to the power of the Spirit who can blow away all fear and doubt. How earnest and sincere should be our prayer in this Mass: "Grant that we, who are nourished by his body and blood, may be filled with his Holy Spirit and become one body, one spirit in Christ" (Third Eucharistic Prayer). Young or old, white or black, rich or poor, each one of us has been called to be a member of the one body of Christ. Like Jesus Christ himself, the head of the body, filled with the Holy Spirit we are to look to heaven and call God our Father.

When Jesus promised the Spirit, he first said to his apostles: "Peace be with you." Peace is the fruit of unity and harmony. When we offer each other the sign of peace in this Mass, we are actually praying that we will be open to the Spirit of love who unites us as one in Christ. This Pentecost today can have real meaning in our lives if, filled with the Holy Spirit, we leave this Church determined to be instruments of peace and harmony to others. Only our own selfishness can inhibit the beautiful movement of the Spirit. Worshipping God as one people in this Mass, we can also lead lives in accord with who we truly are: one body, one spirit in Christ.

C.E.M.

**Pentecost Sunday (B)**

## THE GIFT OF WISDOM

It is not difficult to imagine the condition of the apostles after Jesus had ascended to heaven. They felt alone and scared, like so many little children lost in a big city among unfriendly people. They huddled together in the upper room, confused and frightened, not knowing what to do or where to turn, or what was to become of them. They had indeed heard Jesus proclaim that he would not leave them alone, that he would send the Holy Spirit, but the meaning of his promise had not penetrated their befuddled minds.

Then on the day of Pentecost, Jesus fulfilled his promise. In a marvelous manifestation he sent the Holy Spirit to his apostles. They were changed in an instant. They went forth before the crowds gathered for the feast of Pentecost and preached Christ with boldness and almost careless abandon. And remember that these were the same men who had run away in fear when Jesus was arrested. Among them was Peter, who during the passion had been afraid to admit to a young servant girl that he even knew Jesus.

Obviously Peter and the other apostles enjoyed a newfound courage. The change within them, however, was more fundamental than a transformation of cowardice into bravery. They now experienced a completely different outlook on life. They no longer felt alone and confused. They knew what was really important: not whether they were safe or not, or even whether they lived or died; what was really important was that they be on Christ's side and do his will. In an instant it was perfectly clear to them that Jesus really mattered. They had a new, incisive sense of values. In a word, they had received the gift of wisdom.

The gift of wisdom which transformed the apostles is a gift that we possess too. We experienced our own personal Pentecost when we were confirmed. There was no marvelous manifestation, only the simple sacramental ceremony. But in the sacrament of confirmation, Jesus truly sent his Holy Spirit to us with all his gifts, including the gift of wisdom. Why is it then that we are often confused and befuddled? Why are we seemingly so different from the transformed apostles? One reason is that we sometimes put obstacles in the way of our wisdom. We let our sense of values get mixed up.

It is not surprising that we become confused about real values. It is very likely that we find this day of Pentecost a time for paying bills without money, a time for trying to make ends meet when the ends seem miles apart. We are pressured by advertising which attempts to create a feeling of need within us for unnecessary items, and which tries to stimulate desires for the bigger and the better. We live in a society wherein the yardstick of success is financial gain, a criterion which induces tensions and anxieties.

Even children become victims of false pressures. A young boy must be a star on the little league baseball team, and to strike out with the bases loaded becomes a tragedy both for him and his parents. A little girl must be cute and attractive and wear the latest little girl styles, or she is a failure in her own eyes and a disappointment to her father and mother. Teenagers sense the pressures to be popular, to go along with what is the "in" thing, not to be a drag or a prude. Some college students feel impelled to get a degree, no matter what may be the value of the courses they are taking.

It is not surprising that we find ourselves so different from the apostles on the day of Pentecost. This feast of Pentecost has always been looked upon as a celebration to stimulate our apostolic spirit so that we may live the Christian life with courage, and proclaim the truth of Christ with boldness both by words and actions. But there is something more fundamental than courage and boldness, and that something is the gift of wisdom. That wisdom we all desperately need.

Today on this feast of Pentecost, we have the opportunity to renew our gifts of wisdom, our sense of values. In this Mass we should pray that we may see what is really important—not whether we are rich or popular or whatever, but whether we are on Christ's side, whether we are really trying to live according to the teachings of Jesus. We should pray that we may be able to see clearly what is really important in life. The gift of wisdom is indeed a great gift from God, because it can give us a true sense of values.

                                                              C.E.M.


**Pentecost Sunday (C)**

## *RENEWAL IN THE SPIRIT*

Just before his ascension into heaven, Jesus said to his apostles: "You will receive power when the Holy Spirit comes upon you, and you are to be my witnesses in Jerusalem, throughout Judea and Samaria—yes, even to the ends of the earth." Today we are celebrating the fulfillment of those words. It was by the power of the Holy Spirit that the apostles proclaimed the good news of Jesus, a proclamation that has come through the apostles even to us living today.

Just what was the effect the Holy Spirit had on the apostles? Was it courage? Yes, it was, as we see in St. Peter who before Pentecost had been afraid even to admit that he knew Christ. Was it strength? Yes, it was that too, as we see in the other apostles who before Pentecost had run away in terror when Jesus was arrested. But the effect was much more than courage or strength. In one word, it was love. The Holy Spirit gave to the apostles the love that exists between the Father and the Son. He gave them himself, for the Holy Spirit is love.

In a way, the Holy Spirit is the most difficult person of the Trinity for us to know. We are taught that the first person is the Father. We have some idea of what that means. The majority of us have known a person whom we have called "father." That experience helps us to know something about God the Father. We are taught that the second person is the Son. All of us are the children of our parents, and that fact helps us to know something about God the Son. In other words, we know persons who are fathers and we know persons who are sons. But the Holy Spirit is love itself. Just what is love? It is a relationship with another, a feeling, a commitment. Love is many things. But a person? We simply do not have the experience of a person who is love itself. And yet that is exactly what the Holy Spirit is. We know that love is the "cement" of all happy family life, the bond that keeps a family together. But with God, the love between Father and Son is so perfect that it is a person, the Holy Spirit.

And so when the Holy Spirit came upon the apostles, he united them and filled them with love which was the motive, the moving power, behind what they did. And this same Holy Spirit is at work in the Church among us today. The Vatican Council states in its *Constitution on the Church*: "The Holy Spirit gives the body [of the Church] unity through himself, through his power, and through the internal cohesion of its members, and he produces and urges love among the believers" (par. 7).

No one who has eyes to see or ears to hear can doubt that we need the unifying power of the Holy Spirit in the Church today. The work of Christ is not done among disharmony, discord and dissension. Certainly there will be disagreements, but we must never let such disagreements split the Church into factions. We cannot go our separate ways, believing what we choose and doing what we wish. The work of Christ, the work of salvation, can be accomplished only by what we do together within the

Church. The Vatican Council, in its same *Constitution on the Church*, says: "It has pleased God to make men holy and save them not merely as individuals without any mutual bonds, but by making them into a single people, a people which acknowledges him in truth and serves him in holiness" (par. 9).

Our times must see a renewal of the Holy Spirit. We will have a new Pentecost in the Church only if we open our lives to the power of the Holy Spirit. In the Eucharistic Prayers, the Church has been inspired to place the Holy Spirit in great prominence once again. Each of the new prayers has two invocations of the Holy Spirit. The first is a prayer that the bread and wine may become the body and blood of Christ by the power of the Holy Spirit. The second is a prayer that all who receive the body and blood of Christ may be brought together in unity by the Holy Spirit.

As we receive Christ today, we should do so realizing that all our fellow Catholics throughout our parish, our country, and even to the ends of the earth are sharing in this same Holy Communion. Let us pray that we who are nourished by the body and blood of Christ may be filled with his Holy Spirit so that we may become one body, one spirit in Christ (cf. Eucharistic Prayer No. 3).

C.E.M.

**Trinity Sunday (A)**

## OUR RELATIONS

As we draw closer to summer time, some of us are beginning to think about vacations. Our plans may include visiting relatives. We hope for pleasant times, since our relatives are people to whom we have ties either because of blood or marriage. Relatives, together with our friends, make us aware of the fact that we are not alone in this world and that our lives are led, not as rugged individuals, but in relationships to other people. Our closest relatives are those within the immediate family which is formed by the relationship of parents and children. The human family is a reflection of God himself.

Our faith teaches us that in God there are three persons. We call the first person "Father." When we speak of God as "Father" we could just as easily say "Mother" or, better still, "Parent," for in God there is no sex. Nonetheless, when you say the word "father," you necessarily imply the existence of another person, the child. A person becomes a father when he gives life to his child. Fatherhood is a quality which is then added to his person. A father is a man, a person, long before he becomes a father.

God is a Father, and this name necessarily implies another person, the Son. But God did not become a Father. In fact, there was no time when he was not Father, for fatherhood is not a quality which is added to God. God the Father is fatherhood personified. Remember that being a father means giving life to another. From all eternity God the Father gives life to his Son, and the only thing that makes him a distinct person is the fact that he gives life to his Son. God the Father does not have a relationship to his Son. He is that relationship itself.

God is also a Son, a Child. A child is one who receives life from another. We are children of our parents, but being a child does not exhaust our personhood. We are persons in our own right, which we can see from the fact that when our parents die we continue to exist. But the only thing that makes God the Son a person is the fact that he receives life from his Father. God the Son does not *have* a relationship to the Father. He *is* that relationship.

Between parents and their children, in a good home, there is a bond which we call "love." Love is difficult to describe. It is a warmth, an affection, a feeling—and most important of all it is a bond which unites people. Love is many things, but the only thing that love is not, in our experience, is a person. In God love is a person. Between God the Father and God the Son there is a bond of union, uniting them in love. In God this bond is the Holy Spirit. The Holy Spirit does not *give* a relationship of love to Father and Son. He *is* love personified.

The truth of the Trinity has an important bearing on how we should live. Some people wonder why in church, where we come to worship God, we hear so much about how we are to treat people. But think about it for a moment. We believe that we are made in the image and likeness of God. We are called to become like God himself. The Trinity shows us three persons, each of whom is entirely unselfish and each of whom is a real person only in relationship to another. The Father gives himself completely to his Son. The Son is concerned only with looking to the first person as his Father. The Spirit exists only to unite Father and Son in an eternal embrace of love.

Our fulfillment as human beings comes about only in our relationships with God and other people, and not in being turned inward upon ourselves. Our greatest happiness comes from being generous and unselfish. Reflect on people who think only of themselves—people who are so wealthy, for example, that their whole lives are taken up with pleasure and play. We may be tempted to envy such people until we hear that their marriage has ended in divorce, or that they have turned to drugs in an attempt to alleviate boredom, or worse still that in complete despair they have taken their own lives. On the other hand, the happiest and most fulfilled human beings are the saints, men like St. Vincent de Paul who devoted himself to the salvation of the destitute people of France, and women like Mother Cabrini who dedicated her life to the sick and suffering in our own country.

I am convinced that upon reflection we can see that our own greatest happiness has come when we have tried to get out of ourselves, when we have made the effort to be unselfish and generous toward someone else, whether a member of our family or otherwise. God's revelation of himself as three persons tells us that we find fulfillment not as rugged individuals but in relationships to other people, and that we come to happiness not in selfishness but in genuine concern and love for those around us. In being generous and loving we begin to match the image according to which we are made, a God in whom there are three persons whose whole being consists in unselfishness.

C.E.M.

## Trinity Sunday (B)

## *IT'S ALL VERY PERSONAL*

It is a great sign of friendship to tell someone a secret about yourself. And the more personal and intimate the secret, the more personal and intimate is the friendship. In fact, you tell the secret not only as a sign of friendship but also as a way of getting closer to your friend, for your secret is part of yourself.

Jesus has a great love of friendship for us. It is not surprising then, that he has revealed secrets to us about himself. Because his love is so personal and intimate, the secrets are personal and intimate.

The mystery of the Trinity is the secret concerning the inmost private life of God. The Jews, chosen people though they were, did not know that there are three persons in God. As we read in the first lesson, God revealed himself to Moses as "Lord," the one great God, creator and master of the whole world. We are privileged through Jesus to know about the great truth of the Trinity.

Because of the revelation of Jesus, we as Catholics believe that in the one God there are three persons. The first person is the Father. He is called "Father" because he is the source of life for the Son. The second person is called "Son" because he receives his life from the Father. Father and Son love each other with a love more complete and perfect than we can imagine. Their love is so perfect that it is a person, the Holy Spirit. This third person, as the personal love between Father and Son, is the bond of union or oneness between Father and Son.

Maybe we too often think of God as just God, some indefinite, nebulous blur in our minds, not as three real persons. Even when we pray, perhaps we do so with a word on our lips, such as "God" or "Jesus," but without any deep realization that prayer is a very personal matter. God has called us to enter into a personal relationship with himself, and the relationship that we have to each person is different.

We are the children of God the Father, and we must think of him as a Father when we pray to him. We are his children because we have become like the second person, his Son. Never, of course, can we be equal to the Son, but we do stand in somewhat the same relationship as he does to the Father. The Holy Spirit has been given us to make us children of the Father. He is the bond of union that makes us one with God the Son.

Without a realization of our relationship to the three persons, we may find the liturgical way of praying a bit strange. Notice that almost all the prayers of the Mass are addressed to the Father through, with, and in the Son. They are done so in union with the Holy Spirit. We find this attitude of prayer all through the Mass, but there is one classic example. That example is called the great doxology, and it comes at the conclusion of the Eucharistic Prayer. The priest holding up the body and blood of Jesus, the Son, looks to heaven and says to God the Father: "Through him, with him, in him, in the unity of the Holy Spirit all glory and honor is yours, almighty Father, for ever and ever." That magnificent prayer reflects our relationships with the three persons. Our prayer of praise is directed to the Father because everything, even life itself, comes from him. We pray through, with, and in Jesus because we share in his sonship. We pray in the unity of the Holy Spirit because he unites us to the Son.

All this is not to say that we must not pray to God the Son or to the Holy Spirit. We should. In fact, before we can pray in the liturgical way we must develop a real devotion to both God the Son and the Holy Spirit. But we must come to appreciate the value of praying to the Father through the Son in the Holy Spirit. After all, when Jesus taught us to pray he said, "When you pray, say 'Our Father.' " It has been observed that Christianity is not so much looking at Jesus as it is looking in the same direction with him, that is, to the Father.

And so the Trinity is indeed a very important mystery for us, not just something to believe and then forget about. This great truth should shape our attitude toward the three persons in God and influence our prayer. Indeed, the mystery of the Trinity is a very personal matter.

C.E.M.

## Trinity Sunday (C)

# *WE ARE OF GOD'S FAMILY*

One of the most amazing accomplishments of our times is what we have been doing in space. The thing that is most intriguing to me is what they call "extra vehicular activity"—walking in space. It is fascinating to think about what it must be like to be way out there among the stars and planets, just floating around like a human balloon set free from its moorings. Imagine for a little while that you have been selected by NASA to walk in space. You go through all the training and preparations. On the appointed day you have a perfect liftoff into orbit. Then the great moment you have prepared for arrives. You open the hatch of your space capsule and slowly venture forth into the unknown vastness of space. You float away from home base, the space capsule. A strange, exhilarating feeling that you have never experienced comes over you. It is a wonderful feeling of freedom. But then suddenly something goes wrong. You are free, but too free, because your tie with the capsule has inexplicably been broken. By some freak you remain alive, as you see the capsule with your fellow astronauts moving away from you at tremendous speed. A terrifying experience.

When you stop and think about it, nothing can be more terrifying than being all alone. It is really the one great thing that we dread: being all alone, with no one, absolutely no other person. We all want to belong, to have a happy, warm relationship with other persons. This is fundamentally the reason why we have such a strong instinct to found a family. And everyone somehow wants to belong to that safe, secure inner circle of persons that we call a family. But every human family is imperfect in one way or another. There is, however, one family that is perfect in every way, and that family is God.

Today is the feast of the Blessed Trinity, the day on which we celebrate the magnificent truth that God is a family of persons. God is not some awesome, nebulous power that created the universe and floats around out there somewhere in outer space. God is three persons. The first person is the Father; the second person is the Son. It is by means of these family names that God has revealed himself to us, because his life is essentially one of family-type relationships. Between Father and Son there is of course a bond, a bond of love. In God this bond is so perfect and complete that it is a person, the Holy Spirit. God the Father and God the Son from all eternity are locked in personal, perfect love and companionship through the love that is the Holy Spirit.

God has not merely revealed this truth to us. He has also invited us to share in this family life. The inner circle of God's family is not closed; it has been opened to us, and we have been called into it.

By our baptism we were born of God the Father. He really and truly became our Father on that day, because he gave us a share in his own divine life. God the Son became our brother, because we became like him. And the Father and the Son gave us a share in their love by giving us the Holy Spirit, the bond of love that brings us into the inner family circle. In today's epistle, St. Paul gives witness to our share in God's family: "the love of God has been poured out in our hearts through the Holy Spirit who has been given to us."

All through his life Jesus, the Son of God, addressed God as "my Father." But when he taught us to pray, he instructed us to pray by saying "Our Father." His Father has become our Father as well. Today in this Mass we are gathered as the family of God in his home, the Church. We are one with Christ, our brother, and the Holy Spirit is within us so that we may love our Father as we should. In this Mass, as taught by our Lord, we will say "Our Father who art in heaven." Then God will invite us to his family table for the family banquet in Holy Communion.

Sometimes we may feel that we want to be free of God and his fatherly commands and directions, as a child sometimes yearns for independence from parental control. As with the astronaut walking in space, the first moments of freedom are exhilarating. But deep down, that is not what we really want. We want and need to belong, to have a deep personal relationship with others. Our human families are only the reflection of our eternal destiny which begins now in the Church. For God has called us into the inner circle of his own family life, the Blessed Trinity.

C.E.M.

## Solemnity of Corpus Christi (A)

(Sunday after Trinity Sunday)

# *POWER AND LOVE*

Imagine that you are a peasant working in a paddy in Red China. An old man cautiously approaches you and bends to whisper a single word in your ear, "Come." You look up and notice that several of the workers are slowly moving as unobtrusively as possible toward a secluded edge of the paddy. You follow. You arrive at a thicket and see that the people are lying down among the bushes in the high weeds, and you join them. The old man lies down too, and props himself slightly on his elbows. Before him are a small, dark loaf of bread and a battered tin cup. In scarcely audible tones he begins to recite familiar words. They are the words of Jesus at the Last Supper, and this is the Mass. Despite the misery of your existence and a terrifying fear of discovery, you are filled with the happiness of anticipation that a long-held wish is about to be fulfilled. For the first time in nearly three years, you are going to receive Jesus in Holy Communion.

Such is the condition of the Church in Red China today. The story is a true one, related by a missionary expelled from that communist country. More than anything else about China he had remembered how much those oppressed people, deprived of the Mass for so long, appreciated the value of Holy Communion. Frequently we do not appreciate something that is easily accessible to us. We take it for granted. Sometimes only deprivation can restore our sense of values. A woman had been away from the sacraments for almost twenty years. Her family and friends were overjoyed when she finally went to Confession on the day before Easter. They asked her what it was that finally induced her to return to the Church. She answered, "You cannot imagine how much I missed Holy Communion; I couldn't stand to remain away any longer."

Today's celebration of Corpus Christi is an opportunity to renew our appreciation of the Eucharist, not by depriving ourselves of Holy Communion, but by trying to realize just one truth among many about the Eucharist. That one truth is that the Eucharist manifests the power and the love of God in a most extraordinary manner.

God's power and love have always been manifest in the world, sometimes in special ways. For example, in the first reading we recalled the power of God that fed the people of the exodus miraculously with the manna from heaven. He fed them in this way because he loved them. But how much greater is the power and love that God shows us in the Eucharist. The Eucharist is not merely a miraculous bread, but truly the body and blood of Jesus Christ. And it is not a bread that will nourish us only for a while, as did the manna, but a divine food that will bring us to eternal life. The Eucharist is a reality only through the almighty power of God, and it is a gift to us because of the supreme love of God. Only God's almighty power can change bread and wine into the body and blood of Christ. Only his love is so strong that it moves him to give so tremendous a gift.

Today's gospel contains the first promise of the Eucharist. Jesus said, "The bread that I will give is my flesh for the life of the world." St. John records that the people quarreled among themselves and protested, "How can he give us his flesh to eat?" It is really little wonder that the people balked at the idea. As they looked up at Jesus, they saw only a man. Without faith, they could not know that the words on his lips were no empty words. Without faith, they could not realize that his hands were full of power and his heart was full of love.

All through his life, Jesus used his power as a sign of love as he went about doing good, curing the sick, cleansing the lepers, and feeding the poor and hungry. When the time came for him to pass from this world, he showed the extent of his power and the depth of his love. At the Last Supper he took bread and said, "This is my body." He took the cup of wine and said, "This is the cup of my blood." He gave us his body and blood to cure us of the sickness of sin and to be a spiritual food that would give us everlasting life.

Today in this Mass, Jesus says to us, "Come—come to the altar to receive me in Holy Communion." Happy are we who are called to his supper. No matter how frequently we receive Jesus, we must never fail to appreciate what a great gift the Eucharist is. The priest holds the host before us to see and says simply "The Body of Christ." As we look upon the Eucharistic body of Christ, our "Amen" should express our faith in the truth that his hands are full of power and his heart is full of love.

C.E.M.

## Solemnity of Corpus Christi (B)
(Sunday after Trinity Sunday)

# *THE BODY AND BLOOD OF CHRIST*

The hallmark of Catholic piety is belief in the Real Presence of Christ in the Eucharist. This belief is so fundamental a part of our faith that one simply cannot be a Catholic without it. It is very appropriate, then, that we celebrate each year this feast of Corpus Christi, the feast of the holy Eucharist.

And yet we must not concentrate so much on the fact that Christ is present in the Eucharist, that we fail to see why he is present. We should not think that Christ becomes present solely so that we may receive him in Communion, nor should we confuse the Mass with a eucharistic devotion such as a holy hour. In other words, we need a larger view of the Eucharist.

In the early days of the Church, the Eucharist was reserved after Mass only for the purpose of giving Communion to the sick and dying who could not come to Mass. Our own devotion helps us to see that there are other reasons for reserving the Blessed Sacrament in our churches. But we need not fear that the early Catholics doubted in any way what we call "the Real Presence." The Real Presence was, you might say, taken for granted as only the starting point for the profound meaning of the

Eucharist, which was celebrated as an event, a happening, making real on the altar the one sacrificial death and resurrection of Jesus Christ as the supreme worship of the Father.

The Mass is the unbloody sacrifice of the cross. Jesus died once; he cannot die again. But through the consecration, Jesus is shown forth to us in the state of victimhood. In the words of the late Pope Pius XII: ''The Eucharistic Sacrifice is the unbloody immolation of the divine victim, which is made manifest in a sacramental manner by the separation of the sacred species and by their offering to the Father.''

Christ is present, then, in the Eucharist not as we are to one another: sometimes loving, sometimes not; sometimes interested, sometimes indifferent. Rather, he is present precisely in the highest expression of his identity as the loving Son of God the Father, who offered himself for our sake in sacrifice. Christ is present in the reality of his death and resurrection.

In a little more than a month we will again celebrate the Fourth of July. Think about a sky rocket on the Fourth, shot into the air. As it reaches the highest point of its trajectory it explodes, revealing all the beautiful colors contained within. Now imagine that this supreme moment of beauty is freed from the limits of time and space—it does not end, but remains without fading in all its brilliance. Returning to Jesus Christ, let us remember that every moment of his life was lived as God's loving Son and our Savior. But in his death and resurrection this beautiful life bursts forth in a brilliant expression of devotion and concern. This expression, through the power of the Eucharist, does not end but remains without fading, freed from the limits of time and space.

Jesus is present in the Mass in the one, unique act of dying and rising as the exalted victim of sacrifice. He is present in his body, given up for us. He is present in his blood, shed for us. Under the sign of spiritual nourishment, he is the source and pledge of our resurrection from the dead. To put it another way, Jesus comes among us not in a static fashion, as is a person asleep in his bed. Rather, he is present dynamically in the great event of his dying as the victim of sacrifice and in his rising to glory.

The wonder of the Mass is that, even though we live centuries after the sacrifice of Christ, we share in his offering of himself in perfect love to the Father. With Mary, we too in a certain sense stand at the foot of the cross. This truth is proclaimed in all of the Eucharistic Prayers following the consecration. Notice particularly the words of the Third Eucharistic Prayer: "Father, calling to mind the death your Son endured for our salvation, his glorious resurrection and ascension into heaven, and ready to greet him when he comes again, we offer you in thanksgiving this holy and living sacrifice." The Mass is our expression with Christ of complete love for God the Father.

And the Father responds in love by giving us in Communion his Son, the Resurrection and the Life, who proclaims in today's gospel: "He who feeds on my flesh and drinks my blood has life eternal and I will raise him up on the last day." This gift is God's sign of his magnificent love for us.

To sum up, Jesus is present on our altar so that through him, with him, and in him we may give all glory and honor to the Father in union with the Holy Spirit. He is still our great high priest, our mediator with the Father. The Eucharist is the sacramental reality of his death and resurrection, our offering to the Father, and the Father's pledge that we are his children who will share his life forever as his resurrected sons and daughters. How right it is that we celebrate this feast of the body and the blood of the Lord!

C.E.M.

## Solemnity of Corpus Christi (C)
(Sunday after Trinity Sunday)

# *IN MEMORY OF ME*

The '60s saw the violent death of three prominent Americans: John Kennedy, Robert Kennedy and Martin Luther King, Jr. Each year on the anniversary of their deaths, memorial services have been held throughout the country. These services all have had one thing in common: they have been sad and somber. The reason is that the death of each one of these men seemed so pointless. They were all cut off in the full flowering of manhood from a life of promise and purpose. For each of them, most of their life's work still lay before them when the moment of death came abruptly and without warning, to the shock, dismay and horrible surprise of their fellow Americans. No wonder then, that the yearly memorial services have been overclouded with sadness and sorrow.

How different was the death of Jesus. His death, rather than being pointless, was the most significant act that has ever taken place in the history of mankind. Nor was Jesus abruptly cut off from his life's work, despite his youth when he died. He had done all that he had come to do. In fact, the whole meaning of his life reached its climax in the moment of its end. Jesus had come principally as a Savior, to destroy death and sin by his own death on the cross. And because of his resurrection from the dead we know that his death, far from being a defeat imposed by his enemies, was a glorious and happy victory.

Moreover, Jesus' death did not come without design on his part. His death was something that he freely accepted. Mere men, no matter how deep their hatred or how powerful their means, did not have the ability to put him to death. On several occasions his enemies had tried to kill him, but since the hour willed by the Father was not at hand, they were powerless.

On Holy Thursday, the night before he was to die, Jesus knew with certainty that he would soon be dead. He had waited and prepared well for this moment. During his public ministry, he had even given signs of what he would do. Today's gospel episode, the feeding of the five thousand, was one of those signs. At the Last Supper, thinking of his followers who would come after him, he took bread and wine and pronounced those words reminiscent of the creative words of God at the beginning of time itself: "This is my body. . . . This is my blood." Then he spoke words rich in meaning for us: "Do this in memory of me."

Jesus had given to his apostles and to all of his followers for all time, his body and blood as a memorial of his triumphant death. In today's epistle of St. Paul, we have our most ancient record of the Last Supper, one even older than that found in the gospels. After giving his account of the institution of the Eucharist, St. Paul added these words: "Every time, then, when you eat this bread and drink this cup, you *proclaim* the death of the Lord until he comes." We *proclaim* his death. The Greek word used by St. Paul means "to announce," "to herald," almost "to shout about." We are ashamed of the deaths of the Kennedys and Dr. King. As Americans, we would wish that peoples of other nations might have been kept from the tragic truth. But not so with the death of Jesus. In our memorial service of the death of Jesus in the Mass, we proclaim it, we shout it out—for his death is the good news of our salvation. The Eucharist is our means of celebrating that death with all the overtones of joy and happiness which the word "celebrate" suggests. The death of

Jesus was a beginning, not an end. His earthly life was changed into glorious life through his resurrection.

This feast of Corpus Christi used to be celebrated on a Thursday, because the Last Supper was on a Thursday. But now, because the Eucharist is so important to us, this celebration has been changed to a Sunday so that more people may take part in it. Every Mass is a celebration of the death of Christ, but on this feast of the Blessed Sacrament in a special way we wish to proclaim, to shout with joy, about the death of Jesus as we wait for him to come in glory.

C.E.M.

# SEASON OF THE YEAR

## Second Sunday of the Year (A)

Suggested Use: Fourth Eucharistic Prayer

## *THE PRISM*

Less than a month ago, we celebrated the magnificent event of the birth of Jesus Christ. In the fullness of time, God the Father sent his only Son to be our Savior. All of the previous history of the world centered on that moment, and in a certain sense time stopped, and we started counting time all over again from that great moment in history.

God made long and elaborate preparations for the sending of his Son. That preparation was largely a series of selections of people who would lead to the coming of Christ. It was a narrowing-down process. In Adam, God had called the whole human race to be his chosen ones. After sin, God set apart a man, Abraham, to be the father of his chosen people. Abraham was followed by Isaac, and he in turn was followed by Jacob, who had twelve sons, the progenitors of the twelve tribes of Israel. From among those twelve tribes, God selected one, the tribe of Judah, to be his specially favored people. From within that tribe he consecrated one family, the house of David, as the source of the Savior. Finally, God chose an offspring of David, Mary, as the person to give birth to Jesus. With the coming of Jesus, God's action began to broaden, for Jesus came to be the Savior not only of the Jews, but of the whole world.

Even during the period of selection in the Old Testament era, God was gradually making it clear that the Savior would be for all men. The first reading of this Mass was composed as the Jews were being freed from their captivity in Babylon. It indicates that they would be a source of salvation for the whole world: "I will make you a light to the nations, that my salvation may reach to the ends of the earth."

When John the Baptist saw Jesus, as we read in today's gospel, he realized that he was the fulfillment of all the centuries of preparation in the Old Testament. John proclaimed, "Look there! The Lamb of God who takes away the sin of the world!'' Jesus was indeed the Lamb of God, but as such he was much more than the paschal lamb, whose blood saved the Israelites alone in Egypt. He was the Lamb whose blood would wipe away the sin of all people of all time. John was the last of the prophets of the Old Testament, and in one sense he was speaking in the person of all of the prophets before him when he said, ''After me is to come a man who ranks ahead of me.''

Jesus is like a prism. All of the light of God's truth and grace through the history of the Old Testament, narrowed down to focus on his person. That truth and grace passed through Jesus to be diffused now to everyone, for all people of every nation are called to be God's new chosen ones. As St. Paul in the second reading wrote to his converts at Corinth, ''You have been consecrated in Christ Jesus and called to be a holy people, as are all those who, wherever they may be, call on the name of our Lord Jesus Christ. . . .''

We too have been consecrated in Jesus Christ. We have been baptized with the Holy Spirit, the Gift of God, who has brought us the fullness of grace. By no means should we have to suffer any kind of ''identity crisis.'' We are the new chosen people of God, his spiritual children. Coming after Christ as we do, we stand at a vantage point of time through God's favor. All of the centuries of preparation by God for the sending of the Savior, all that Christ did in his earthly ministry, have been diffused through Christ to us.

As we progress through the liturgical year, we will hear recounted at Mass the wonderful works God did in the Old Testament. We will also witness Jesus going about proclaiming the good news of salvation. Then in Holy Week, we will once more see him as the Lamb of God who shed his blood for our salvation. We will celebrate his resurrection in the hope that we too will share in that resurrection. Today, our use of the Fourth Eucharistic Prayer will give us a summary of all of these things.

The preface will remind us once again that it is right that we should give thanks and praise to God for all that he has done for us. An attitude of thanks and praise should set the tone of our worship here at Mass throughout the entire year. We will have that attitude if we remember who we are as the new chosen people of God, the people who now enjoy the benefit of all that God has done in the history of salvation.

C.E.M.

**Second Sunday of the Year (B)**

## CHRIST AND HIS PEOPLE

Two weeks ago we celebrated the epiphany of our Lord, his manifestation to the Magi. A star pointed out the infant Jesus as the Savior of the world. Today we celebrate a manifestation of the adult Jesus as Savior of the world. This time he is pointed out, not by a star, but by the prophet, John the Baptist. As Jesus walked by, John said to two of his own disciples, "Look! There is the Lamb of God!"

The title, "Lamb of God," seems at first a strange designation for John to use. Actually, the phrase is rich in biblical connotation. It recalls the exodus of the Israelites from slavery in Egypt. When God sent his avenging angel to kill all the first-born of the Egyptians, the Israelites sprinkled the blood of a sacrificial lamb on their doorposts. The angel, seeing the blood, passed over the homes of the Israelites. They were saved by the blood of the lamb. Then the Israelites were led by Moses through the waters of the Red Sea out of the slavery of Egypt and to freedom. The exodus formed the Israelites into the people of God. It was the great saving event of the Old Testament, comparable to the death and resurrection of Jesus in the New Testament.

We have no idea of how fully John the Baptist understood the phrase, "Lamb of God," but when John the Evangelist wrote his gospel in the light of full revelation, he saw the implications of that title. We have been saved from the slavery of sin through the blood of Jesus Christ shed on the cross; and we have become members of his Church, the new people of God, by passing through the waters of baptism. Though our vocation has been less dramatic, we have been called as definitely as was Samuel, who heard God speak his name in the night (first reading). God spoke our name through the priest who baptized us. We have been chosen just as surely as were those men who left the Baptist to become apostles of Christ. With Andrew we can say, "We have found the Messiah."

The effect of our Christian call is almost staggering. To begin with, Jesus Christ is not some figure of ancient history lost within the pages of the New Testament. Jesus lives today! And we are really much more than his followers. We have become part of him, part of his mystical body. Yes, Jesus lives today—in heaven, in the eucharist, and in us!

I believe that most Catholics are familiar with the teaching of Jesus that whatever we do to his brethren, good or bad, we do to him, good or bad. Because Jesus really lives in his followers, what is done to them is done to Jesus. We must also recognize that the converse is equally true. Jesus wants to act in and through us. We take him with us wherever we go, for good or bad. Listen again to these emphatic words of St. Paul in today's second reading: "Do you not see that your bodies are members of Christ? Whoever is joined to the Lord becomes one spirit with him."

For St. Paul, the presence of Jesus within a Christian was the motive for avoiding sin as well as for doing good. When we are petty and mean; when we spread slander or detraction; when we are hateful and envious; Jesus is with us and we drag him through the filth of our sins. It is a chilling thought, but it is true.

A very practical approach is to ask ourselves, "Would Jesus do what I am about to do, or say what I am about to say, or even think what I am now tempted to think?" We should not make Jesus a part of something we know he would never do, or say, or think himself. More positively we should ask ourselves, "What would Jesus do in this situation?" The answer should help us decide what our conduct should be.

Jesus will come again today in Holy Communion. Through the Eucharist he wants to transform us into himself, so that we may become more and more a part of the mystical body. We must cooperate by promising him that we will try to act only as we know he would act, so that his presence in this world may continue through us. When Jesus was an infant, the star pointed him out to the Magi. When Jesus was an adult, the Baptist pointed him out to the apostles. Now we can point to heaven or to the Eucharist and say to others, "There is Jesus." But Jesus wants more. He wants us to be able to point to ourselves and say, "Here is Jesus living and acting within me."

C.E.M.

**Second Sunday of the Year (C)**

## *THE CHURCH AT CANA*

Today's gospel about the marriage feast at Cana is one of the most humanly appealing stories about Jesus. To see his interest and concern for the young married couple is something I believe we all appreciate. There is also a warm humanness about the fact that Mary, his mother, apparently refused to take "no" for an answer from Jesus. And yet there seems to be something deeper about the gospel, something very significant underlying the charming narrative.

We have a hint that there is something more here than just a story, for St. John apparently takes it for granted that his readers know that the water became wine. He really does not emphasize the miracle at all. Everyone knew, in John's estimation, that Jesus had worked a miracle. John's point was that the whole episode was a sign, a sign of the Church. John's thinking is a little complex, but it is worth going into.

It is noteworthy that the event takes place at a wedding feast. The Old Testament pictured the people of Israel as the spouse of God, and saw in a wedding feast a symbol of the Messianic age. We heard an example of this imagery in the first reading of today's Mass, from Isaiah: "As a bridegroom rejoices in his bride, so shall God rejoice in you." St. Paul, in accord with this same symbol, spoke of the Church, the new Israel, as the bride of Christ. And so, it appears that St. John used the wedding feast to show that he wished to say something about the Church.

Next, we must notice the prominence of Mary in the story. The Vatican Council has reemphasized an old, favorite idea of the early writers that Mary is a sign of the people in the Church. In a sense, she sums up in her person the whole human race as called to follow Christ. This is why Jesus addressed her with a term that strikes us as strange for a son to use, "Woman." That word is rich in biblical connotation. It recalls the first woman, Eve, whose name means "mother of all the living." Mary as the new Eve is the new mother of all the living, and so represents all of mankind. At Cana, Jesus stated that his hour had not yet come. Mary in effect told him that we wanted his hour to come. The word "hour" meant his death and resurrection, the great mystery whereby he would gain our salvation. When Jesus worked his first miracle at the implicit request of Mary, he was beginning that whole series of events that would inevitably lead to his death and resurrection.

By his death and resurrection, Jesus was to form the new people of God, the Church. As Jesus changed the water into a fuller and richer liquid, that of wine, so he was going to change the old Jewish religion into the fuller and richer religion of Christianity. The choice wine kept until later in the history of the human race is Christianity, and we are the ones who enjoy it.

Yes, we are the ones who benefit by the Church, but the Church is not something we simply enjoy. It is not merely a source of goodness for us, as we sit back and drink its pleasant wine. Notice in the gospel story that, though Jesus worked the miracle by his power alone, he did so in cooperation with others: with Mary, the headwaiter, and his assistants. And so in the Church, each one of us has his job to do in cooperation with Christ.

St. Paul, in the second reading of today's Mass, is also talking about the Church. He tells us that in the Church there are many and varied functions which different people perform. The Church is not just the Pope and the bishops. All of us together make up the Church, and each one of us must do his share for the good of the whole Church.

Today there is a lot of criticism of the Church. Some people are disillusioned and unhappy, because they feel that the Church is not helping them. Others say that the Church does not have any impact on society. Still others maintain that the Church has lost its character of holiness. We certainly have the right to criticize the Church. However, if we choose to complain we had better remember whom we are complaining about. We are complaining about ourselves, for we are the Church. It is not honest or valid to step back and look at the Church as something apart from ourselves, any more than we can step back from and complain about an infected finger as if it were not part of us. We are the Church. What the Church is today largely depends on what kind of people we are.

Some time after their wedding day, a young couple comes to realize that marriage is more than something you enjoy. It is something that both husband and wife have to work at, because marriage is what they make it. And so with the Church. The Church today will largely be what we make it. Christ is doing his part. Are we doing ours?

C.E.M.

## Third Sunday of the Year (A)

# *NO FACTIONS*

After Pope Pius XII died, his successor was a little-known Cardinal by the name of Angelo Roncalli. Almost everyone asked, "Who is he?"

or "What will he be like?" Some even referred to him with a certain disdain as merely a "transitional pope." Soon, however, the human warmth, simplicity and good humor of Pope John XXIII won the favor of Catholics, those of other religions, and even those of no religion at all. Anecdotes about him appeared in the secular press; he was good copy.

It was certainly a wonderful thing that Pope John had such an appealing human nature. That appeal made it a lot easier to respond to him, especially considering that many felt he had a "hard act to follow." The engaging virtues of Pope John are ones that every bishop and priest could do well to emulate, and yet the essential quality of Pope John was not his warmth, or his simplicity, or his good humor, but rather that he was the vicar of Jesus Christ. There is only one Savior, Jesus Christ, and he is the one to whom we owe complete devotion and attachment.

In today's gospel we saw the Savior call Peter and Andrew, and James and John, so that they might become fishers of men. Jesus knew that in the plan of his Father, he was to spend only a limited period of time on this earth. And part of that plan was that after Jesus had ascended into heaven, other human beings like ourselves would continue his saving work in this world. Of course the human qualities of Jesus' ministers make a difference, but true faith will help us see through these qualities, whether good or bad, to the person of Jesus acting through his bishops and priests.

Sometimes undesirable qualities in a bishop or priest can turn a person away from religion. Perhaps it is even worse when appealing characteristics attract people not to Christ, but solely to the person of the bishop or priest himself. Such was the case at Corinth when St. Paul wrote the letter we heard in the second reading today. Some people said that they belonged to Apollos. Apparently they were attracted by the fact that he was an eloquent speaker, well versed in the scriptures (cf. Ac 18:24). For different reasons others professed allegiance to Cephas, another name for Peter, and still others to Paul. Such human allegiances produced factions and dissensions among the Christians at Corinth. Paul indicated that quarrels and factions based on attachment to the ministers of Christ were as absurd as thinking that Christ himself had been divided into several parts.

Despite Paul's vehement denunciation of factions at Corinth, there is no doubt that human qualities do affect our religious reactions. For example, when the changes in the Mass were introduced, some people thought that Pope Paul had gone too far, that he had destroyed the grand and beautiful dignity of the old Latin Mass. They objected that they could not pray at Mass any more, because of all the noise people were making with their responses and hymns. Though they were not exactly attached to a person in the Church, they were attached to an old way of doing things which the supreme authority of the Church, acting in the name of Jesus Christ, had changed for good and solid reasons. Though they did not profess allegiance to Apollos or Cephas or Paul as did the Corinthians, they were tied to a mistaken notion of tradition instead of being loyal to Jesus Christ, guiding his Church in the world today.

Looking at the other side of the problem, some people refuse to participate in Mass unless it is accompanied by a certain musical setting and enhanced by an intense feeling of community and led by a celebrant who freely improvises in a highly personal fashion. Certainly, the Mass should be meaningful in a contemporary atmosphere—and there is no excuse for a careless, sloppy and impersonal celebration of Mass—but no one should be so attached even to legitimate attempts to make the Mass significant in our own day that he fails to see the value and worth of the Mass, no matter what its manner of celebration may be. The balanced Catholic saw a person like Pope John XXIII in his essential role—that is, as vicar of Jesus Christ. And in the same way, we must appreciate the Mass in its essential quality as the celebration of Christ and his people in our communal worship of the Father.

Of course, this whole question of human qualities is complicated. We are not disembodied spirits without emotions and feelings. Personalities of priests and bishops, as well as styles of celebrating the Mass, do make a difference. In this whole problem, however, we should not put Jesus in the position of the fisherman who tried four varieties of bait with no success. In frustration he threw some coins into the stream and muttered, "All right, go and buy yourselves something you do like." As St. Paul pointed out, Christ is the one who died for us as our Savior, and it was in his name that we were baptized. To him alone must we be attached with an unshakable allegiance.

C.E.M.

## Third Sunday of the Year (B)
### FAITH AND REPENTANCE

When we hear of Jonah in the Bible, most of us think of the incident in which he was swallowed by the great fish. Actually, that story was but a prelude to today's first reading. God wanted Jonah to preach to the pagan city of Nineveh, but Jonah felt that only Jews should hear the word of God, and so he tried to run away. In a storm at sea, brought on by God's anger, he was cast into the water only to be swallowed by the fish and then vomited on the shore. He received a second command from God, to preach to the pagans of Nineveh. That time he obeyed, and much to his surprise the people heeded the word of God and repented.

So-called fire and brimstone sermons of the type preached by Jonah are no longer popular. Nor would such a sermon be appropriate for you, since your very presence at Mass is a sign of your good will. You would probably be shocked and dismayed to hear me stand in the pulpit and shout out like a modern-day Jonah: "Repent! The end is coming." And yet in today's gospel we hear Jesus himself proclaim: "This is the time of fulfillment. The reign of God is at hand! Reform your lives and believe in the good news."

Shortly after he appeared in Galilee preaching the need for repentance and faith, Jesus called Andrew and Peter and James and John away from their work as fishermen to make them fishers of men. That same call Jesus continues to extend to bishops and priests down through the centuries. The reason is that his message of faith and repentance is a message for people of all times and all places. And so it is that the Vatican Council in its *Constitution on the Liturgy* stated: "The Church announces the good tidings of salvation to those who do not believe, so that all men may know the true God and Jesus Christ whom he has sent, and may be converted from their ways, doing penance" (9). Then, perhaps to your surprise, the Council said in the same document: "To believers also the Church must ever preach faith and penance" (*ibid*).

Yes, even to believers the Church must constantly preach faith and penance. The penance referred to is perhaps better termed "repentance." Repentance means a turning away from sin and a turning toward God, a true change of heart necessary for all of us. To begin with, we are all really converts to the faith. No one can be born a Catholic in the way which we can be born an American citizen. Even if we were baptized as infants, at some time we must make for ourselves a profession of faith and a decision to follow Christ. Perhaps you are one of those persons who has taken your religion for granted—you are a Catholic simply because that is the way you were brought up. Today Jesus says to you:

"Reform your life and believe in the good news!" Now is the time to realize that Jesus is the only way to salvation, and that your whole life must be based on his teachings. Money cannot save you, nor friends, nor society, nor the state. Only Jesus can make your life a success.

A middle-aged man had been what is sometimes called a "Sunday" Catholic. His religion had meant little more than going to Mass once a week. Then he was informed that his wife was to undergo surgery because of cancer. The doctors promised no hope. Suddenly he felt all alone and helpless. On the morning of the operation, he decided to go to Mass to pray for his wife. By sheer coincidence it was Ash Wednesday. He followed the crowd of people toward the altar to receive the ashes. As they were placed on his forehead he heard the priest say, "Remember, man, that you are dust and unto dust you shall return." In that very instant he was struck with the shortness of life, and he realized that not only was his wife close to death but that he himself was inevitably going to die at a time he knew not. That night his wife was dead. Through his grief he could see that even the longest life is short, and that time is precious.

Yes, time is precious. It is so precious that God gives it to us only moment by moment, and he never gives us a single moment without taking the previous one away. If we have squandered or abused a moment of time, we can do nothing to change it. All that is left is for us to work harder in the future. The earliest Christians believed that the entire world as we know it would soon pass away in the second coming of Christ. That was one of their motives for taking their religion seriously. As a matter of fact we simply do not know when Christ will come again, but we do know the world will end in effect for each one of us the day we die. Now is the time to repent, to have a change of heart, to "re-form" our lives in accord with the teachings of Christ. Every one of us can stand some soul-searching to determine what is holding us back from following Jesus completely. This is a very personal, individual matter. The answer will be different for each one. But an answer we must find, if we are to heed the words of Jesus: "Reform your lives and believe in the good news."

C.E.M.

### Third Sunday of the Year (C)
Suggested Preface: Sundays of the Year I

## THE FULFILLMENT

It seems that God likes to do big things in a little way. At Christmas time, we saw the Savior of the whole world born in a simple, humble cave in a small, unimportant town. Today in the gospel, we see the fulfillment of centuries of promises and waiting come to pass in the unpretentious synagogue of the virtually unknown village of Nazareth.

It was the practice in synagogue worship to have a reading from the Law and another from the Prophets of the Old Testament, followed by a sermon. In today's event, Jesus was invited to act as both reader and preacher. It was really as if the eyes of all the people of God who had ever lived were looking upon Jesus at that moment. Century upon century of promises from God and of waiting by the people focused upon that moment in time. Jesus read a passage from the book of Isaiah. Then he spoke simple, but momentous words—words beyond the comprehension of his listeners: "Today the Scripture passage is fulfilled in your hearing." Jesus was the perfect fulfillment of everything ever written in the Old Testament; he embodied and completed in his one person the whole destiny and purpose of the chosen people.

In the first reading of this Mass, we heard Ezra reminding the people of their destiny. In reading the word of God to them, he was reminding them that they were a chosen race, a royal priesthood, a holy nation, a people set apart. God had set apart his chosen people so that they could preserve his truth, his law and his worship, and mediate God's blessings to all men.

People's minds had been darkened because of sin; it was difficult for them to know God. But from the chosen people God raised up great prophets, teachers of the people, like Moses, Isaiah, Jeremiah and many others. These men taught the people what God was like. By means of the prophets, the judges and the kings, God pointed out the way of life that his people were to follow. God made of his chosen ones a priestly people. They were set apart to offer pleasing worship to the one true God and to receive his favors in return.

But the whole destiny of the chosen people was in the future, in a great day of the Lord when the Messiah would come. The Messiah was not just to fulfill some prophecies made about his coming; he would perfect and complete the whole purpose of the chosen people.

Then on that apparently ordinary day in the humble synagogue of Nazareth, the big thing happened in a little way. Jesus in simple words spoke tremendous truth. In effect he said: "I am the one you have been waiting for. All the centuries of promise and waiting have become reality in me." With his pronouncement another great truth began to unfold. Jesus as Messiah was also God himself, a fact that was never clear in the Old Testament. Because Jesus was God, he was more than a prophet or a teacher. A teacher says, "This is the law; follow it and you will be on the way to happiness." Jesus being God could say, "I am the way; follow me." A priest of the Old Testament offered worship in the name of the people and prayed that God would grant his favor of eternal life. Jesus as God was the perfect priest who offered himself as victim of sacrifice and won for us eternal life with absolute certainty. Jesus gives us himself and says, "I am the life."

We are the new chosen people of God. We are people, however, not of promise but of fulfillment. Jesus is alive and active among us, the people of the Church. To fulfill our destiny, we must be committed to Christ. He is the person we must know, because he is the truth. His way of living we must follow and imitate, because he is the way to true happiness. His grace we must strive to preserve and increase within ourselves, because he is the life, and that grace must flow out to the whole world through us.

Our commitment to Christ should be strengthened by our celebration of the Mass. It is here that we hear the truth of Christ proclaimed. It is here that we see how Christ lived. It is here that we receive Christ as our spiritual life. Christ is our truth, our way and our life. It is here in the Mass that we are pre-eminently in contact with Christ. From what we do here, we should derive the power to fulfill our destiny as the chosen people of God.

What we do may appear simple, and perhaps to some even shallow. But God seems to like to do big things in a little way. Big things happen in this Church every time we celebrate Mass.

C.E.M.

**Fourth Sunday of the Year (A)**

## *UPSIDE DOWN IS RIGHT*

When Thomas Jefferson wrote the Declaration of Independence, he stated that "man has been endowed by the Creator with certain inalienable rights. . . ." He specified three of these rights. The first was the right to life. The second was the right to liberty. The third he listed, not simply as happiness, but as the *pursuit* of happiness.

Everybody wants happiness, but it is the most elusive of all human pursuits. Perhaps one reason is that we do not all agree on what makes for happiness. Some say you have to be rich to be happy. Others agree with the idea behind the beer slogan, "Live with gusto; after all, you only go around once in life." Some insist, "Look after number one; take care of yourself." Others protest, "I want to be free to do what I want, when I want, and the way I want." And of course there is the cliché, followed by not a few, "Eat, drink and be merry for tomorrow you die."

Jesus disagreed with all these ideas. In fact in his proclamation of the beatitudes read to you a few moments ago in the gospel, Jesus took all these ideas and turned them upside down. He said to be happy is to be poor, to be sorrowing, to be lowly, to be merciful, to suffer persecution. That sounds crazy to most people. The precise meaning of each of the beatitudes is not easy to explain—scholars have written many long commentaries on them. This is no wonder, because though the beatitudes do not exhaust all of Christian teaching, they do capture much of the heart and spirit of Christianity. Perhaps today, in thinking further about only the first of these beatitudes, we can appreciate better what it means to be a Christian and in the process discover how the upside down ideas of Jesus lead to true happiness.

What does it mean to be poor in spirit? Many Christians, throughout the centuries since the day Jesus proclaimed this beatitude, have found happiness in embracing voluntary poverty out of love for God, but the primary concern of Jesus was not with how much people do or do not have. Surely, Jesus had no illusions that destitution and happiness go together. Actually, Jesus urged his followers to help overcome the destitution of others. When Jesus used the word, "poor," he did so against a whole background of Old Testament theology. The poor of the Lord in the Old Testament, the *anawim*, were those people who did not rely on any worldly means to fight the battle of life. They did not trust in wealth, or military power, or political shrewdness. They depended completely on God to protect them and lead them successfully through life. They stood before God, helpless and defenseless, trusting in him and him alone. They were the humble and lowly spoken of in the first reading today. They took refuge in the Lord. They were the poor in spirit.

Does all this sound unrealistic? Many would say that it does. After all, you can't look after number one or live with gusto if you don't depend on money. You can't be free to do whatever you want if you rely on God for help, because his help comes only to those who keep his commandments. And yet we have the word of Jesus that poverty of spirit is happiness. That happiness begins even now, as we see in the serene peace of the saints, who lived according to the beatitudes. In another way, the words of Jesus look forward to a happiness that is to come in heaven, but that is realism. Even those who live only to eat and drink know that tomorrow they die. And then what? Is the pursuit of happiness so ephemeral that it must end with death? Eat and drink today and die tomorrow—what a bleak, depressing outlook on life!

Others protest that to be happy you have to be self-made and self-reliant—the old rugged individualism idea. That is why they say you have to look after number one. They judge religion to be a crutch, a means of strength for a weak personality, a form of psychological support. But again, where does realism lie? The realistic, mature person faces the truth. If a man is crippled, he must use crutches. To look upon his crutches with disdain, or in a moment of supreme foolishness to throw them away with the protest that he can be independent of them, is the height of unrealism and stupidity. The truth is that we are the creatures of God, the Supreme Being. We depend on him for our existence, as well as for all the means of survival both in this world and in the next. You may call religion a crutch, if you like, but you must also be prepared to recognize that as human beings we are spiritually cripples. That is a harsh way to put it, I admit. But I hope that it brings out the truth that to be realistic and mature, as well as psychologically healthy, we must admit our complete dependence on God.

St. Paul in the second reading recalled how God chose from among the Corinthians the weak, the lowborn, the despised, and those who counted for nothing to be his people, the new *anawim*. We must realize that we too are called to be the new *anawim*, the people who are poor in spirit. In this Mass we should stand before God, conscious of the fact that we are helpless and defenseless, and that we must put our whole reliance on him.

As far as many are concerned, the beatitudes are an upside down view of life. An upside down cake, when it comes out of the oven, looks very plain and unattractive. But when it is cut and served, the appetizing part is then on top. At present the beatitudes of Jesus may not appear attractive, but when he comes in judgment Jesus will show that beneath the surface appearance his teaching contains both truth and beauty, leading to lasting happiness.

C.E.M.

### Fourth Sunday of the Year (B)

## *JESUS, LORD AND SAVIOR*

The chosen people all through their history had sought communication from God. In his concern for them, God raised up prophets like Moses and Isaiah and Jeremiah. A prophet was a spokesman, a "mouthpiece" for God, one who spoke on his behalf to the people. Frequently a prophet prefaced his words with the phrase, "Thus says the Lord God." This phrase indicated that the prophet was speaking not on his own authority, but solely on God's authority, according as God had manifested his will to him. God promised through Moses that one day he would send a great prophet, as we heard in the first reading. After the resurrection, the Church understood that this promise was eminently fulfilled in Jesus Christ (cf. Ac 3:22ff and 7:37ff). Actually, Jesus was much more than a prophet. He spoke on his own authority. Not once did he preface his remarks with the usual phrase, "Thus says the Lord God." Rather he proclaimed, "*I* say to you. . . ." It was a bold departure, one which did not go unnoticed.

The people also observed that Jesus taught differently from the scribes, the official experts in written law and oral tradition. The scribes instructed the people by quoting the famous teachers of the past, somewhat in the manner in which a contemporary lawyer refers to previous court decisions. But Jesus spoke on his own, and never made appeals to the testimony of others. His way of teaching was so different that he held the people spellbound.

If Jesus held the people spellbound with the authority of his words, he amazed them with the power of his deeds. Jesus freed possessed persons from the presence of evil spirits. He did so simply, sometimes with a single word. These miracles signified in action what he preached in words. He proclaimed that in himself the kingdom of God had come, a divine kingdom that would be victorious over the forces of evil. When the people saw what Jesus did, they exclaimed, "He gives orders to unclean spirits and they obey him!"

We may think that we are more sophisticated than the people of Jesus' time. What they attributed to the presence of unclean spirits, we would perhaps classify as epilepsy or some form of psychosis, such as schizophrenia. And yet, we would be unfair to today's gospel if we were to pretend that it does not describe the real exorcism of real devils.* After all, modern psychiatry does not satisfactorily indicate the origin of all disturbances, especially those particular cases in which there are no organic causes. We would be naive indeed if we were to think that a psychiatric description explains away the power of the devil in all instances. We need modern psychiatry, but we must not be so gullible or fatuous as to think that it alone, or any other human force, can be the savior of the world. We need both the teaching and the power of Jesus.

Human intelligence and natural resources have come under the saving power of Jesus Christ. That is why we can and should use them for the good of the human race—but if we think that we can rely on human or earthly means alone, we will find that we are pitted against a foe too powerful for us to overcome. Our faith, in the light of the resurrection of Jesus from the dead, tells us that he is Lord and Savior. That is why his words had such authority and his deeds such power. Those words and deeds are still a living reality among us, for Jesus is not dead. He is alive and waiting for us to turn to him with confidence as our Lord and Savior.

C.E.M.

*Cf. *The Four Gospels* by Bruce Vawter, C.M., p. 101.

**Fourth Sunday of the Year (C)**

## *TAKING GOD AS HE IS*

In today's gospel we see an amazing reaction on the part of the people. In the synagogue of Nazareth, Jesus proclaimed that he was the one the people had been waiting for, the fulfillment of all their hopes. But when he spoke the plain truth to them, they became upset. In fact, they worked themselves into such a frenzy that they drove Jesus out of the synagogue and tried to kill him.

It does not seem that the people merely *failed* to recognize Jesus for who he was. Rather, they *refused* to recognize him. To some extent they could not bring themselves to believe that this hometown boy, for Nazareth was where Jesus grew up, was the Messiah. More precisely, they had their own ideas of what they wanted the Messiah to be. They expected him to be a political leader, a military conqueror, a social reformer—one who would set right all the political, military and economic wrongs of the day. They rejected Jesus because he did not fit their notion of what he should be.

It was not the first time in Jewish history that such a rejection had taken place. Our first reading in this Mass was from the prophet Jeremiah, who was born some 650 years before Christ. When he was sent by God to speak the plain truth to his contemporaries, he met stern opposition from the people, the priests and the king himself. The people were guilty of idolatry, and refused to accept the God preached by Jeremiah. He was imprisoned, humiliated and finally died in exile.

Have times changed very much? Do we as Catholics really accept God as he is? It is a real temptation to try to fashion a God who meets our wants instead of our needs. It is not always easy to accept God as he is. Maybe a key to the problem can be found in what we hope for in life.

We want nice things: a comfortable home, a nice car, color television, good food. It is perfectly all right to pray for these things, but if we do not get them we must not be distressed. We must remember that Jesus was born poor, lived poor and died poor. Mary and Joseph did not arrive in Bethlehem in a ten thousand dollar car, nor did they have a mansion in the suburbs to offer Jesus. We all want comfort, but Jesus showed us that money is not what life is really all about. And Jesus is our God.

We all want to get along with other people. We don't like it when people disagree with us or make things unpleasant. But Jesus spent almost all his public life in a confrontation with the scribes and the Pharisees, who fought him every inch of the way. And Jesus is our God.

We like to have our leisure and our comfort. Children can be a real bother. They take a lot of time. They get on your nerves. Maybe you have older parents for whom you are responsible. They can be very unreasonable in their demands. It would be great to be free of the burden. Maybe that freedom is what we want from God, instead of praying for the love and patience that St. Paul speaks of in today's epistle Jesus was always at pains to be of service to others, to give of his time and effort to help others. And Jesus is our God.

When there are tragedies—a sudden, unexpected death; a tremendous financial loss; a severe disappointment by children—we wonder why God has abandoned us. We don't want God to treat us badly. But Jesus saw St. Joseph, his foster father, die at an early age. He saw his mother going it alone as a widow—and that without any government aid. And Jesus is our God.

We should pray that God will help us. But we cannot fashion a God of our own choosing. We cannot think of God as nothing more than a supreme "Mr. Fixit" or a glorified government welfare agency. God is good and God will help us, but he will not always give us what we want. He will give us what we need. He gives us our faith. He gives us the opportunity to grow spiritually by being generous and loving with him and with our fellow human beings, in the way St. Paul has urged in today's epistle. And these are things that will lead to our true happiness, our eternal salvation.

We cannot afford to drive God out of our lives as the people of today's gospel drove Jesus out of their synagogue, and we have no right to try to fashion a God according to our own plan.

C.E.M.

## Fifth Sunday of the Year (A)
Suggested Use: Third Eucharistic Prayer

## SHARING WITH OTHERS

Some time ago a man moved to a small Southern town, where he lived in a large house all alone. Little was known about him, but it was said that he had an extraordinary talent for playing the piano. In a short time an almost mystic legend grew up about his abilities in every form of music from the most intricate of classical compositions to the wildest of modern styles. There was one strange thing about the whole situation: he refused to play in the company of anyone. Despite the urging and sometimes the pleading of those who had come to know him, he consistently stuck to his refusal. One day a woman, perhaps playfully, challenged him by saying, ''I don't believe all this I hear about how you can play the piano. Give me a demonstration.'' The man answered, ''What you have heard about me is true. I used to play for others, but no more. Now I play only for myself.'' The woman asked, ''But why play only for yourself?'' After a moment of silence the man responded, ''I learned music by myself. I practiced long hours by myself. Now I choose to entertain only myself.''

Perhaps your first reaction is to say that this story is unrealistic. You are amazed that someone with such talent could be ignorant of the fact that he had actually done little by himself, that he needed a piano which someone else had invented and others had skillfully produced, that he needed music which someone else had composed and others had printed, and so on in a long list of persons upon whom he depended. Most important of all he was dependent on God, who had given him his musical talent to begin with. You may also think the story is unrealistic because you wonder how anyone could be so selfish; talent is given to us to be used. Then too, you may be questioning how anyone could possibly impose upon himself what was obviously a deep unhappiness and loneliness. And yet the story is true. The story is so true that it is repeated in different ways by many people, perhaps even by ourselves.

Are we really generous in the use of our God-given talents? Today in the gospel, Jesus tells us, ''Your light must shine before men so that they may see goodness in your acts and give praise to your heavenly Father.'' That is saying a lot. To begin with, we must be honest about admitting that God has given us gifts and talents—in fact, everything that we have. We will profess this fact at the beginning of today's Eucharistic Prayer when we pray, ''All life, all holiness comes from you,'' and we conclude the Prayer with the same sentiment by saying, ''We hope to enjoy forever the vision of your glory, through Christ our Lord, from whom all good things come.''

Once we recognize God as the source of all that we have, we must then realize that our gifts are to be used for the benefit of others so that they may see God's goodness in us. Today's first reading gave us a few practical suggestions about sharing what we have with others: to feed the hungry and to give clothing and shelter for those in need. It goes without saying that we hear a lot of appeals both in church and outside church, but maybe we dismiss these appeals too readily. Perhaps we feel, as did the man in the story I told, that we have worked hard for what we have and now we deserve to enjoy it all ourselves. But that attitude is a contradiction of the truth that all we have comes from God, including the abilities we use in earning money as well as the energy we expend.

Money, however, is not the only thing we should be willing to share with others. There are things which cost more than money, such as our time and our convenience. For some people, writing a check for a charitable cause or dropping an extra dollar in the collection on Sunday is the easiest thing they can do, and that they are willing to do. But it may well be that someone you know needs, not your money, but a willing ear to listen to his sorrows and troubles. You parents may, after a hard day, be settling down to relax and watch TV when one of the kids comes in, bursting at the seams, to tell you about what happened in school. Or you kids: perhaps there is someone in your class that nobody seems to like, someone who never gets any attention. In all these and like circumstances, we must be willing to share our time and our kindness with others.

What is really needed, what Jesus is talking about in today's gospel, is an attitude of mind: a realization that God has given us all that we have, our abilities and even our personalities. God does not want us to hide our talents selfishly or to hoard our goods. He wants us to share what we have and what we are with others, so that seeing his goodness in us they may learn to praise God, the source of all goodness.

C.E.M.

**Fifth Sunday of the Year (B)**

## *HAPPILY FOREVER AFTER*

A certain man of more than comfortable means was highly respected in his community. He had acquired his considerable wealth quite honestly, and he enjoyed the reputation of being a person of integrity and deep religious convictions. He doted on his seven sons and three daughters, though he sometimes worried about spoiling them with his generosity. In the eyes of his friends and neighbors, as we say, he had it made. Then suddenly everything went wrong. His business failed and he was left a pauper. During a party at his oldest son's house, the roof collapsed in a violent windstorm, killing all ten of his children. He himself was stricken with a strange disease, which his doctors could not diagnose or cure. And his wife was on the verge of leaving him.

This account was not found in a recent newspaper or magazine, though it could have been. It is the story of Job, from a book of the Bible written about four hundred years before Christ.* That book tackles the perennial problem of why good people must suffer instead of being rewarded in this life by the God they faithfully serve.** It is a problem we face every day—not that we believe we are as virtuous as Job, but we do get to wondering why some people who seem to care nothing at all about God and religion apparently do so well in life, while we must struggle with many forms of human suffering. Job wondered about that, too. His "friends" tried to convince him that he had to be guilty of some heinous sin that had brought on God's punishments. Job examined his conscience, but could not honestly admit to any such sin. And yet his suffering continued to the point that he cried out, as we heard in the first reading, "I shall not see happiness again." Job pulled himself together and remained patient with God. In a sense, he wanted to give God a chance. He was rewarded with a profound insight. Through God's grace he suddenly realized that no mere human being, with his inadequate notions of good and evil, reward and punishment, can possibly probe the depths of God's wisdom and justice in the handling of human affairs. A man is presumptuous indeed to criticize God's guidance of life.

Jesus, too, was concerned with the problem of human suffering in all its forms. We saw him in today's gospel curing people who were afflicted in various ways, ranging from the simple fever of Peter's mother-in-law to diabolical possession. When he rose early the next

---

* Modern scholars differ widely in their dating of the Book of Job, placing it anywhere between 600 and 300 B.C., but at a time when people expected reward or punishment only in this life.

** In the famous dialogue section Job and his friends never use the proper name of Israel's God, Yahweh (except for 12:9, probably a copyist's addition). One theory is that the author apparently wished to say that Job was not necessarily an Israelite, that the problem of the suffering just man is common to all humanity.

morning, he sought a quiet place to pray. During his prayer he possibly spoke with his Father about human suffering, for the misery of the people must have still occupied his mind. Soon, however, his prayer was interrupted by Peter and his companions, who informed him that everybody was looking for him. We can only surmise that the people wanted more favors from him. Though Jesus made no comment, he seemed to rise from prayer with a renewed sense of purpose. He said: "Let us move on to the neighboring villages so that I may proclaim the good news there also. That is what I have come to do."

At first glance, it appears that Jesus ignored the continued pleas of the people for help. If more cures were needed where he already was, why did he decide to move on? The reason is that he had not come to free people from all suffering in this life. He had come to preach that God's love is present and active in this world in the midst of even the worst adversity, that there is hope for eternal salvation and lasting happiness, and that somehow in God's plan suffering obediently accepted leads to that salvation and happiness. He used his power to cure in order to confirm his message and to give a hint, a kind of preview, of the perfect healing of human ills that would come only in heaven. He did not use his power to prevent his own suffering and death. Rather, he freely embraced the cross because he knew the value of human suffering accepted in loving obedience to God. In the Mass we joyfully celebrate the sacrifice of the cross, because of the glory to which it led Jesus and will one day lead us too.

With Jesus, the answer to human suffering—an answer sought by Job, by ourselves, by everyone—takes on a new dimension. With Job, we must still realize that we cannot begin to understand the wisdom and justice of God, and that we are in no position to criticize God's guidance of the universe—but in the preaching and actions of Jesus we can see suffering in a new light. Suffering is not to be endured in some stoic fashion because we can do nothing about it, or because we dare not revolt against God, or because if we wait long enough we will have relief in this life as did Job, who lived happily ever after—until his death. The ultimate value of human suffering is to be found only after death—or better, through death. If we suffer and die in union with Jesus, we will also rise with him to a new life wherein we will indeed live happily *forever* after.

C.E.M.

**Fifth Sunday of the Year (C)**

## *STICKING TO IT*

This day in the liturgy could well be called "Vocation Sunday." In the first reading, Isaiah described his call by God. In the second reading, St. Paul spoke of his own vocation to be an apostle by the grace of God. Finally, in the gospel we saw St. Peter's call to be a "fisher of men." All three of these men left one form of life for another that God had chosen for them. The new life was more demanding, and required both sacrifice and perseverance. And each of the three stuck to the new life chosen by God.

Strangely enough these days, some priests are going in the opposite direction. They are leaving the priesthood to which they have been called for other vocations. They are not persevering; they are not sticking to the job. But this lack of perseverance is not confined to the priesthood or religious life; it is a syndrome of a society. Divorce is becoming more frequent, and laws are being changed to make divorce even easier. It used to be that people pretty much settled down in one community for almost all of their lives, but moving from place to place has become almost a characteristic of our society. College deans report that students in greater numbers than ever before are changing their majors. You probably know many people who are dissatisfied with their jobs, and are constantly looking for something else. Even with all the changes in the Mass, some people seem to become quickly bored and want something new and different. Perhaps with all the bombardment of our senses through the entertainment media and the many experiences that are open to people today, we have become jaded. Perhaps with the great amount of leisure that modern gadgets afford us, we have become bored. Jaded and bored, we easily become dissatisfied.

The problem, no doubt, is much more complicated than I have pictured. In fact, I cannot even begin to know what all the problems are—they are different for each person. But with regard to priests, one of the problems is that "in the old days" the *last* thing a priest thought about was leaving the priesthood for something else. Certainly priests had problems then, but somehow the vast majority simply felt that the problems had to be worked out within the priesthood. These days, leaving seems to be the first thing thought of. And the same was true of

Catholic couples. Of course, there were divorces between Catholics. But for most Catholic couples, divorce was the last thing they thought of. These days, it seems with some to be one of the first things that occurs to them. And so with other areas of life, whether it be school or jobs or home: the attitude of mind seems to have changed.

I believe that the attitude of mind we have makes a big difference. We are bound to have failures and discouragement. We always get a little bored doing the same things over and over again, especially the older we get. Yet one of the greatest graces God gives us is the grace of a new beginning every day. No matter how many mistakes we make, no matter how we may botch up our lives, we can always begin again. Here is an outlook on life that may help: each day is like a whole new lifetime.

When you awake in the morning, you are bleary-eyed and a little groggy. As we say, you are not operating on all cylinders. You are somewhat like a new baby just being born. With the first cup of coffee, you begin to wake up and gradually come to full vigor, like a person in his youth. Then the work of the day begins. As the day wears on, you begin to wear out. You start to get tired and weary, like a person in old age. Finally the day is over and it is time for welcome rest and sleep. Sleep is a biblical symbol of death, as it is in much poetry, and so when you go to sleep it is like dying, like ending your life. But you wake the next morning, and a whole new life lies before you. You can forget the past with all of its frustrations and boredom, and start to make the most of the new life that God has given you.

In today's gospel, our Lord asked Peter to do something that at first looked pretty stupid. Every good fisherman knows that the best time for fishing is during the cool darkness of the early hours of the morning. But here was Jesus the carpenter telling Peter the professional fisherman to start fishing during the worst time of the day. The results were not just good; they were amazing. Of course, the only reason that Peter succeeded was that he had our Lord's help.

We too have that help, even in the apparently stupid things we sometimes have to do. We receive that help especially here in the Mass. It is a help to persevere, to stick to it in whatever our vocation in life may be.

C.E.M.

## Sixth Sunday of the Year (A)

Suggested Use: Long Form of the Gospel

# *MORE THAN JUST GETTING BY*

When you go to a doctor, you want to have the assurance that the man is medically well-educated, that he has kept up on recent developments, that he is competent and experienced. You want a doctor who is conscientious—not one who will be satisfied with doing the bare minimum for you, just so that he won't become involved in a malpractice suit. You rightly feel that your health is too important to entrust it to a charlatan, a quack.

Your spiritual well-being is much more important than your physical health. What is at stake is not good health which at best can last only seventy years or so for most people, but eternal happiness and the fulfillment of the whole purpose of human existence. From time to time we all need a good spiritual check-up, a thorough examination. In one sense we are our own spiritual physicians, because under God we ourselves determine what our spiritual health will be. Maybe we are not spiritually well-educated. More importantly, perhaps we have not kept up on recent developments in the Church's thinking. As a result we may even be spiritual charlatans, spiritual quacks.

Let me explain what I mean. We have all learned somewhere along the line that to commit a serious sin, three things are required: grave matter, sufficient reflection, and full consent of the will. If one of the three conditions is not met, then there is no serious sin. But if we are only concerned with avoiding sin, especially by means of a strictly legalistic approach of looking for loopholes, then we are like the doctor who does the bare minimum so that he won't become involved in a malpractice suit. Our lives then are based on fear lest we find ourselves accused of a capital crime in God's court of law. Just getting by within the law is not what Jesus had in mind for the Christian.

Today's gospel is part of our Lord's Sermon on the Mount. In that sermon Jesus set forth, among other things, basic principles of Christian conduct. He said that he had not come to abolish the law found in the Old Testament. That law was an expression of God's will for his people, but because it was necessarily put in human words it was an imperfect expression of God's will. Jesus wanted to show that it was the spirit behind the law that really counts, and that spirit is found in a responsible, generous love of God and our fellow human beings. Jesus fulfilled the law first by his more complete teaching on love, some instances of which you have heard in today's gospel, and secondly by his own supreme example of love. Jesus did not ask his Father, ''What is the very least that I must do in order to save the world, what is the bare minimum needed to get by?'' No, Jesus responsibly and generously went all the way, even to death on a cross.

The Church wants us to follow the spirit of the law as we see it in the person of Jesus. As the Church tries to guide us in the spirit, some people have become disturbed. They think the authorities have gone soft. Here is one example: it used to be that the Church forbade the eating of meat on Friday under pain of serious sin. We know that law has been changed, but does it mean that the Church believes that things should be easier for us? Not at all. The whole idea behind the old law was to make us aware of the need to do penance for our sins, and to offer a specific means for practicing that penance. It was a way of telling God that because we loved him we were sorry for our sins. And yet, as a matter of fact some people were just keeping the letter of the law to avoid serious sin. They were not eating meat, it is true, but they were dining on delicious lobster or other meatless delicacies. The whole spirit behind the law of Friday abstinence was forgotten. Now the Church says to us: Do more than just avoid sin. The Church challenges us as adults to adopt our own means of penance. Today is a good time to examine yourself on what you have done for penance since the law of Friday abstinence was changed.

We also know that we must go to Mass on Sunday. But there is a spirit involved in this law too. Jesus says that if our brother has anything against us, we should leave our gift at the altar and first go and be reconciled with our brother. In other words, we must celebrate the Mass as responsible, generous people. Our worship of God our Father is pleasing to him only if it overflows into love for all his children. To tell God in the Mass that we love him, while we despise or even ignore him in his children, is a contradiction and certainly not the spirit of the law. Going to Mass on Sunday only to avoid a sin won't do.

Jesus tells us today that just getting by is not enough. We are not satisfied with a doctor who does the bare minimum for us, and we should not be satisifed with doing the bare minimum in order to avoid serious sin.

C.E.M.

## Sixth Sunday of the Year (B)

Suggested Use: Penitential Rite A; Preface for Sundays of the Year I

# A PEOPLE SET APART

People these days probably look upon cancer as the most frightening of human afflictions. Among the contemporaries of our Lord, leprosy held the first place. Undoubtedly people at that time also died of cancer, but no one really understood it as a cause of death since it was internal and therefore invisible. Leprosy, though lacking the devastating effects of cancer, was external and loathsome to look upon. Because the disease was considered to be highly contagious, the leper was forced to live in isolation, away from his family and friends. More distressing for a devout Jew, however, was the fact that he was considered levitically unclean, and as such unfit to share in the public worship of God. The Jews were a royal priesthood, a holy nation, a people set apart for the authentic worship of the one true God. The leper was cut off from this worshipping community.

The leper in today's gospel revealed how desperate he had become, by entering a town in order to seek out Jesus. Jesus was moved to pity, rather than horror, at the sight of the man and cured him. It is worth noticing that the gospel says that Jesus *touched* the man, something all others would have been afraid to do, not only because they feared contagion but because touching a leper rendered one also levitically unclean. Jesus manifested that he was compassionate, but more importantly he showed that, as the source of all spiritual cleanness, he himself could not be made unclean.

Jesus then sent the man to the Jewish priest. It was the prerogative of the priest to decide whether the man was now fit to undergo the purification rites which would join him once more to the worshipping community.

As we will acknowledge in today's preface, we are the new chosen race, a royal priesthood, a holy nation, a people set apart. Back in 1947, Pope Pius XII wrote, ''All the faithful should be aware that to participate in the Eucharistic Sacrifice is their chief duty and supreme dignity.''* In order to fulfill this chief duty with supreme dignity we too should be

* *Mediator Dei*, 80.

clean. There is, however, no levitical law in the Catholic Church; nothing external can make us unfit to worship God. Only sin, like an invisible cancer, can make us unworthy to celebrate the Eucharist in the company of the worshipping community. Our first cleansing was at baptism. Confession is a sacramental cleansing, necessary in the case of serious sin. The penitential rite at the beginning of Mass is intended to make us realize that we must be sorry for all sins, even little ones. We confess first to God, because every sin offends him directly. We also confess to one another, to our spiritual brothers and sisters, because sin hurts others and lessens our bond of oneness with all of God's people. If we are sincere in our sorrow, we are touched by the forgiving hand of Jesus, the source of all cleanness.

This penitential rite has a positive purpose. Once we have asked forgiveness, we should then with a sense of freedom from the disease of sin enter wholeheartedly into the celebration of Mass. To complete the quotation from Pope Pius XII, "All the faithful should be aware that to participate in the Eucharistic Sacrifice is their chief duty and supreme dignity, *and that not in an inert and negligent fashion, giving way to distractions and daydreamings; but with earnestness and concentration.*"

After the liturgy of the word, and before we move to the liturgy of the Eucharist, we have a further reminder of our vocation as a chosen race, a royal priesthood, a people set apart. Several persons, representing the entire community, bring bread and wine to the altar. This bread and wine, fruit of the earth and the work of human hands have been given to us by the Lord of creation as our food and drink. Bringing this food and drink to the altar is a sign that we are now setting them apart from ordinary, daily use for a very special purpose, the worship of God. That action should remind us that we must now set ourselves apart from all our ordinary, everyday activities to do something special, to celebrate the Eucharist.** This does not mean that we should not offer our daily lives in worship to God. We should, for as St. Paul has already reminded us in this Mass, "Whether you eat or drink—whatever you do—you should do all for the glory of God." Every aspect of our lives should be sacred as done for God, but the point is that in the Mass we are engaging in the

---

** Cf. "Explaining the New Offertory Rite" by Charles E. Miller, C.M. in *The Homiletic and Pastoral Review* for September 1969, pp. 924-927.

most significant action of life itself, an act of worship in union with Christ, the purpose of which is to give meaning and value to all the little things we do every day. In the Mass we fulfill our chief duty and express our supreme dignity as a chosen race, a royal priesthood.

The old levitical laws of the Jews concerning ritual uncleanness strike us as odd and unreasonable. Their purpose, however, was to emphasize the sacredness of worship. We should approach the Mass with an awareness of its sacredness, and we should try to enter into its celebration with as much attention and devotion as possible.

C.E.M.

**Sixth Sunday of the Year (C)**

## THE GREAT ISSUE OF LIFE

We are now well into the last third of the twentieth century. History will no doubt record that this century was one of amazing progress, a time of incredibly rapid advances in almost every area of human endeavor. We are moving so fast that our latest productions are almost obsolete the minute they roll off the assembly line. And all our progress is due to one thing: our scientific knowledge. Travel, communications, medicine, agriculture, entertainment—almost every phase of our lives has been improved by science. It is science that has lifted us far above the primitive conditions of our ancestors.

Yet, despite our advances, there is a problem which our ancestors faced and which is still a problem for us today. There is one reality which has plagued the human race from its beginning, and will continue to plague the human race until time is no more. This ever-present problem, this inescapable reality, is the fact of death.

If you stop and think about it, in life the greatest issue is death. The life of each one of us must end in death. It is true that we have to work to improve the world we live in; we must try to overcome the blight of poverty, the idiocy of war, the injustice of racial inequality. But even if all these problems were to be solved in a flash tomorrow, we would still have to face death. Now our medical men are making great strides against disease and all forms of illness; life is being extended by means of heart transplants and other amazing operations. But no matter how great the medical advance, death will still await us. And even though our scientists may soon make space travel a commonplace occurrence, we will still find that we cannot fly away from the awesome fact of death.

Where shall we turn for a solution to this inevitable fact of death? To science, medicine, or what? Listen again to the blunt but truthful words of Jeremiah from the first reading of this Mass: "Cursed is the man who trusts in human beings, who seeks his strength in flesh, whose heart turns away from the Lord." Such a man, says Jeremiah, is like a *dead* bush—yes, *dead*. Pessimistic? No, just factual. And then follow his optimistic and equally factual words: "Blessed is the man who trusts in the Lord, whose hope is the Lord." Such a man is like a vigorous, sturdy tree, which is *alive*.

Jesus is the solution to the problem of death. As we heard today in St. Paul's epistle, "Christ has been raised from the dead, the first fruits of those who have fallen asleep." The first fruits of the harvest were an indication of what could be expected from a later harvest. Christ's resurrection from the dead is a sign of our own resurrection. Christ has made the successful passage through death before us, and has come out alive. By his death he destroyed the power of death to destroy us. By his resurrection he has won for us a new life. In this Mass, following the consecration you will be asked to make this acclamation of faith: "Dying you destroyed our death; rising you restored our life; Lord Jesus, come in glory."

Our trust is not in any human means; our hope is not in science; our reliance is not upon medical research. It is Jesus who will raise us from the dead to a new life. He will not effect an organ transplant to prolong our earthly life; rather, he will give a share in his own glorified life. What we all yearn for is not merely the continuation of this present life; we want the perfect life, the full life, which is found only in God.

And in this Mass we have a pledge that Jesus will raise us from the dead. This pledge is the risen, glorified body of Jesus that we will receive in Holy Communion. Jesus said, "He who eats my flesh . . . I will raise him up on the last day."

It is no wonder that in the gospel today Jesus said, "Blest are you poor, you who hunger, you who are weeping." He could say these words with serene calm, because he knew that what he had to offer was much more valuable and desirable than riches, or plenty to eat, or temporary happiness. He came to offer eternal life. He had the solution to the great issue of life, death itself.

And happy are we to have Jesus, because dying he has destroyed our death and rising he has restored our life.

C.E.M.

## Seventh Sunday of the Year (A)

## *ONE TRACK WITH A TWIST*

Sometimes we say of a person who keeps insisting on the same idea that he has a one track mind. Even though the comment is usually not a favorable one, I must admit that Jesus was a person who had a one track mind. The idea which he kept insisting on was love of God and love of neighbor. The emphasis in today's readings is on love of neighbor, even though the two commands cannot really be separated.

It seems to me that there are two reasons why Jesus was almost always talking about love. The first is that God himself is love, and to be loving is to become more God-like. Jesus says that we must be perfect as our heavenly Father is perfect. The second reason for Jesus' insistence on love is that, even though we can glibly talk about love, it is very difficult to practice. Jesus wanted us to know that he was very serious about the command of love.

I do not know of anyone who does not think that this commandment is a beautiful one. I cannot imagine any normal or sane person saying that this commandment is really a very bad idea. Anyone who has ever lived within a loving environment has experienced the beauty, the warmth and the comfort of love. Our problem with this commandment is not that we do not agree with it, but only that it is indeed difficult and demanding in practice.

But it is very important that we attend closely to the gospel today. Jesus, it is true, is on his usual track about love but today he adds an important twist, one which is not easy to agree with. He goes beyond the Old Testament book of Leviticus with its familiar commandment, "You shall love your neighbor as yourself." Jesus wants us to love our neighbor, but today he does not have in mind the kind of neighbor from whom you borrow a cup of sugar or the friendly neighbor with whom you have a cup of coffee every day. He is talking about the neighbor who lets his kids break your windows, who plays incredibly loud music until two in the morning, who in short drives you crazy. Jesus wants us to love people who have hurt us deeply, who have lied about us behind our backs, and who actually do not care whether we live or die.

It is not Christian to hate communists, to disdain Iranians, or to hold in contempt any ethnic group. Jesus' command is, "Love your enemies pray for your persecutors, offer no resistance to injury." A pagan society thinks that this way of living makes no sense; in fact, many people would go so far as to say that today's gospel is insane.

But Jesus means what he says. Nor are his words glibly spoken. He does not ask of his followers anything which he himself has not practiced. It should not be hard for us to realize that Jesus loved his enemies. The crucifix is a constant reminder that Jesus died for sinners, that he prayed for those who were putting him to death, and that he offered no resistance to injury.

Even if we agree with Jesus, his commandment with a twist is not easy to practice. In fact, it is impossible except with special help. That special help is given us in the Holy Eucharist. This sacrament, if we are open to its effects, will gradually transform us to make us more like Jesus himself. And to be like Jesus is to be a loving person, one who loves generously and without making exceptions. It may take a lifetime to get to the point of truly loving even our enemies, but Jesus is serious about his commandment. He is so serious that he gives his own body and blood in the Eucharist so that we may become more like him in his way of loving.

C.E.M.

## Seventh Sunday of the Year (B)

# *WORDS OF FORGIVENESS STILL*

We take words for granted. We speak hundreds, perhaps thousands, of words every day without giving very much thought to this human activity. And with our multi-media communications we seem to have accepted the Chinese proverb that one picture is worth a thousand words, but at least in one instance that proverb must be turned around. One word from God is worth more than a thousand pictures. God's word is powerful. It is creative. In the beginning God said, "Let there be light," and there was light. In today's gospel Jesus said, "Your sins are forgiven," and they were forgiven.

The setting for the words of Jesus is a memorable scene. When the four friends of the paralytic found it impossible to get through the door to see Jesus, they climbed to the roof with the paralytic on his mat. The roof of this Palestinian house was constructed of beaten earth and twigs or loose flat stones, easily displaced. When the young men had made a large enough hole, they lowered their friend into the room where Jesus stood. Immediately Jesus realized what was expected of him, but he decided first to give the man not what he wanted but what he needed— not a physical cure but a spiritual one. He said simply, "Your sins are forgiven." The scribes were horrified, and their unspoken objection was a good one: "Who can forgive sins except God alone?"

Because Jesus realized what they were thinking, he decided to give a proof of the effectiveness of his words. He posed the question, "Which is easier to say, 'Your sins are forgiven'? or to say, 'Stand up and walk'?" The idea is that you can get away with saying, "Your sins are forgiven." There is no test of whether the words have done anything, since no one can see sins in a man's heart. But if you say to a man who cannot walk, "You're cured," everybody can tell in an instant whether the words have produced any result. Jesus did not need to wait for an answer to his question. He declared, "That you may know that the Son of Man has authority on earth to forgive sins" (he said to the paralyzed man), "I command you: Stand up! Pick up your mat and go home." All eyes turned from Jesus to the man lying on his mat. There was a moment of supreme suspense: would he really get up? No doubt bewildered, yet responsive to the words of Jesus, the man rose to his feet, picked up his mat and went outside in the sight of everyone. The people quite understandably were awestruck. Jesus had made his point: his words were powerful; they accomplished what they signified. With his words he had forgiven the man's sins just as surely as he had cured him of paralysis.

Jesus forgave the paralytic's sins by his own authority because he was divine. But he did so in a human way, using his voice and tongue and lips to pronounce the words of forgiveness. Those words of forgiveness are with us still, especially in the sacrament of Penance. The priest does not forgive sins by his own authority. Were the Church to maintain that he does so, all could reasonably object, "Who can forgive except God alone?" Jesus takes over the voice and tongue and lips of the priest to pronounce the words of absolution. Continuing and extending his incarnation through the priest, Jesus is the one who forgives our sins in Confession. He is as present to us as he was to the paralytic.

The gospel points out that Jesus was moved by the faith of the paralytic and his friends. Climbing the roof indicated that they were determined to let nothing keep them from seeking the help of Jesus in a great need, even if they did not understand what the primary need was. We could do well to imitate their strong faith in our attitude toward Confession. Nothing should keep us from seeking the forgiveness of Jesus in this sacrament—not inconvenience, or embarrassment, or dissatisfaction with the minister. Inconvenience? Should we not be willing to climb over every obstacle to seek the forgiveness of Jesus? Embarrassment? How absurd it would have been if the paralytic had objected to his friends, "Don't take me over to that house where Jesus is; everybody will see that I can't walk." All of us are crippled by some sins—that is only human—but how foolish we would be to remain spiritually paralyzed through serious sin only because we are embarrassed at what the priest or others may think of us. Dissatisfaction with the minister? As a priest I am certainly at fault if I am impatient or perfunctory in Confession, but remember that in this sacrament you can always receive what you really need: the forgiveness of Jesus Christ.

I think we would all appreciate Confession a lot more if the effects of sin and forgiveness were not both internal. If the effects of sin were as visible as paralysis and if forgiveness were as obvious as picking up a mat and walking, we very likely would have little trouble placing a great value on the sacrament of Penance. Be that as it may, we should seize the opportunity of this Mass to renew our faith in the forgiveness of Jesus Christ and to give praise and thanks to God for a truly wonderful sacrament.

C.E.M.

## Seventh Sunday of the Year (C)

## *FIRE AND WATER*

There is an old saying that you have to fight fire with fire. Frankly, I have never quite understood this saying. In the literal sense it is obviously false; you have to fight fire with water. I suppose that in the figurative sense it is supposed to mean that you cannot let people take advantage of you. If people cheat you, you have to cheat them back. If people malign and vilify you, you have to treat them in kind.

How different from this approach is the teaching of Jesus. In effect, he says that we must fight the fire of hatred with the quenching water of love. Jesus tells us to love our enemies, to do good to those who hate us, and to bless those who curse us. The scholars point out that the word "curse," used in the original Greek, implies spite, jealousy, bad will. Jesus, then, is not talking about a situation in which someone may unintentionally hurt us, as for instance when someone says something that wounds our feelings without his realizing it. No, Jesus is talking about even those circumstances in which someone deliberately and maliciously offends us.

It is easy for us to profess that we love all mankind—all mankind, that nebulous something which we never encounter except in the abstract. It is an altogether different matter to love an individual in the concrete who is, from the natural point of view, entirely unlovable as far as we are concerned. Jesus refuses to allow us the complacency of professing a love for mankind in general. He has deliberately put his teaching about love as the greatest commandment within the context of its severest test and proof. Christianity is not supposed to be easy. It is a demanding religion that is intended to bring out the highest qualities of the human spirit, as elevated and assisted by God's grace. In fact, it is only by God's grace that we can live the Christian life. The teaching of Jesus in today's gospel, viewed humanly, is difficult in an extreme degree.

Jesus did not merely mouth this doctrine. He practiced what he taught. In his passion and death, Jesus put his teaching into practice. Even though the human race had disobeyed God and lost his friendship, Jesus did not abandon us. Even though we had offended God, Jesus did not decide to have nothing to do with us. He gave the supreme expression of love by dying on the Cross. And his love and his forgiveness were not just for some nebulous abstraction known as "sinful mankind." His love and forgiveness were for each of us as individuals. When he was dying on the Cross, he looked down on those individuals who had maligned and vilified him and conspired to put him to death, and said, "Father, forgive them." Jesus at that moment showed that he loved his enemies.

He was doing good to those who hated him. He was blessing those who had cursed him.

Each one of us has to think about putting this teaching into practice. Look at David in the first reading. He had no doubt about the enemy he was required to love. Saul hated David, he had become insanely jealous of him, and had tried to kill him. When David had the opportunity to assassinate Saul, he refused to do so despite the prodding of Abishai. And so with us. We have to get out of the abstract idea of loving our enemies. We have to put the teaching of Jesus into practice with those individuals who have hurt us in any way. It is not so much that we have to think about loving the enemies of our country. The kind of forgiveness we need is not the kind that we can theoretically extend to the almost anonymous man we read about in the papers who raped and murdered three teenage girls. It is the individual who is part of our lives that we have to be concerned about—the relative, the friend, the associate who has hurt us deeply.

The love taught by Jesus is a demand that unaided human nature cannot meet. But St. Paul reminds us in today's epistle that we are new, spiritual men. We have been made like the glorified Christ and have a share in his life, by means of the waters of baptism. The fact of our baptism into Christ should remind us that we cannot fight fire with fire. We must put out the fire of hatred by means of the quenching waters of Christian love.

C.E.M.

**Eighth Sunday of the Year (A)**

## *GROWING DOWN IS GROWING UP*

Today we benefit from a situation with God's people which occurred before the coming of Christ. The people had returned from exile in Babylon. All the work needed to rebuild Jerusalem and re-establish their religion had discouraged them. They felt forsaken and forgotten by God. Through his prophet, God offered a beautiful image of consolation and assurance: "Can a mother forget her infant, or be without tenderness for the child of her womb?"

It is a moving experience to think of God as a tender, loving mother. But there is something wrong with the image. As a matter of fact, some mothers do forget their infants. Some mothers are without tenderness for the children of their wombs. Every day, mothers destroy unborn infants through abortion. And all too often we hear of a mother who has abandoned a child, and occasionally we learn of a mother who has killed her child. God is never like a bad mother. The truth is that no human example can adequately represent God. God is far above our way of thinking. He is more loving than we can ever imagine. We are always reaching to find a way of understanding him.

In the gospel we also find beautiful images of wild flowers and the birds of the air. Because God is so loving and provident, God wants us to be as free of care and anxiety as are flowers and birds. But there is something wrong with this image too. The flowers we see in church have been picked, taken from their natural habitat, and they will inevitably wither and die. We have all probably come across a little bird who has fallen from a tree. He lies dead at our feet. These experiences may lead us to think that what Jesus has to say really isn't very practical. What would happen to us if we actually tried to live as do the birds of the air and the lilies of the fields? Parents have to earn a livelihood. They have to have the means to take care of themselves and their families. People who do not work for a living, people who do not try to take care of themselves, people who do not worry over money and the necessities of life are, in our society, called bums. They exist on skid row in a state which is below human dignity and they are rather generally held in contempt. Being like the birds of the air or the lilies of the fields is a nice thought, but it isn't a very realistic one.

Even Jesus had to reach to find examples of how we should live, just as the prophet had to reach to find an example of what God is like. The problem is not found in the prophet nor in Jesus. The problem lies within us. God is so far above us, so far beyond human experience that it is difficult for us to grasp what God is like. Sometimes his ways are the opposite of our ways. His values are the opposite of our values.

We can help ourselves understand a little better by thinking about the process of growing up. A newly born human infant is the most helpless of all species. Some animals are virtually independent the moment they are born, but a human infant cannot survive. As we grow, we gradually start to do things for ourselves. Our parents are still needed, but we learn to do things for ourselves. Then we start to think for ourselves and to ask questions. We go to school and for the first time we have experiences in which we are free from our parents. As we become adolescents, we yearn for even greater freedom. And when we become adults, we have to take care of ourselves and others. That is when we begin to worry about our livelihood, what we are to eat or drink or use for clothing.

In our relationship with God, the opposite is true. We begin our relationship with God by being independent of him, so independent that we are separated from him by sin. When we first realize what our union with God through baptism means, we are just beginning. We are still filled with anxiety and worry. We are still living what we think is freedom. We even believe we are responsible people. If we continue to grow in union with God, we start to let go. We gradually give up power over our own lives. Not all of our time is spent away from God. We yearn for more time in prayer. Then God wants to move us to a point where we learn to depend completely on him, as an infant does on his parents. Today in the gospel, Jesus used images which have the same message as his command that we become like little children. And we should become like little children because God is more loving and caring than we can ever imagine.

In the Mass, we have a sign of what God is like and what our relationship with him should be. His love and care are shown in the gift of the Eucharist, the precious body and blood of his Son, as our nourishment. This gift is something we cannot earn. There is no way of paying for it. How much should the Eucharist cost? What have we done to merit it? The truth is that God feeds us even though we do not sow or gather into barns.

Most important of all, we should not become discouraged if we still find the gospel message of complete dependence on God a little impractical. We have to grow in that dependence. Growing is a long, hard process. Life is really concerned not with growing up, but with growing down—back to the state of a little child, even of an infant. That is true, spiritual maturity, for it is only in growing down that we will grow up toward heaven to be embraced by an all-loving Father.

C.E.M.

**Eighth Sunday of the Year (B)**

## *THE JOY OF CHRISTIANS*

Jesus disturbed people because he was different. He was different from John the Baptist, whom the people had come to respect. John was austere and aloof, but Jesus was relaxed and at ease with every type of person. John preached a fire and brimstone type of sermon, but Jesus preached sermons that were simple and homey, drawn from everyday experiences to which his listeners could easily relate. Jesus was also different from the Pharisees, the religious leaders of the day. The Pharisees had taken all the joy and spirit out of religion by their legalistic approach to man's relationship with God, but Jesus taught a religion of happiness and love.

It is not surprising that one day some people objected to Jesus that his disciples did not fast, as did the disciples of John and the Pharisees. Jesus answered in a manner typical of him, with a reference to human experience. He said that for his disciples to fast while he was still with them would make as much sense as mourning at a wedding banquet in the presence of the groom. A Jewish wedding banquet was quite a jubilant affair. Remember how important the wine was at the wedding feast of Cana. At a wedding feast, the Jews apparently kept in mind one of the psalms which praises God for producing wine from the earth "to gladden men's hearts" (Ps 104:15). Then Jesus admitted that the time would come for fasting when he would be taken away, an allusion to his death.*

Where does that leave us? Is Jesus still with us so that we should not fast, or has he been taken away so that we should fast? The more obvious answer is that Jesus is not with us; he has died and has been taken away into heaven. In a sense that is correct, and so fasting is in order. There will always be a time in the Church for fasting as a sharing in the suffering of Christ until he comes again in glory. Fasting, however, has been de-emphasized in the modern Church partly because of the renewed realization that the resurrected Jesus is indeed still with us, not only in the Eucharist, but in ourselves as members of his Church through baptism. That is why our religion should be one of happiness. It was a jovial

---

* Many scholars maintain that this verse is an addition of the early Church to justify its practice of fasting, which found its motivation in the mystery of the cross.

monk, Abbot Marmion, the son of an Irish father and a French mother, who wrote, "Joy is the echo of God's life within us."

Moreover, Jesus has entered into a union of deep love with us, not unlike the marriage union. Jesus eminently fulfilled the words of God to his people in our first reading today: "I will espouse you to myself forever; I will espouse you in love and mercy; I will espouse you in fidelity." It was not without reason that Jesus referred to himself as the bridegroom, a man who wants to share a life of happiness and love with his bride. Of course every marriage has its ups and downs, but in a good marriage there is even happiness in having someone to share the downs with. And the spiritual marriage of Jesus and his people is a good marriage. He is ready to share everything with us because of his deep love, a love of fidelity forever.

Because of this union of love, our lives should be characterized by a spirit, not of mourning or sadness, but of joyful and generous love which overflows to others. Maybe you know a couple obviously in love—if you are married, God grant that you are that couple—whose home is always open to anyone. Their mutual love is so great that they seem to have a lot of love left over to share with others. Not only do the parents and the children have many friends, but the whole family without fail is ready and eager to help other people. We as members of the Church must try to realize that the love Christ has given us must overflow, like the miraculous wine at the wedding feast of Cana.

Our spirit of joy and love should begin right here in Church. The Mass is not a somber memorial service, conducted by a sorrowful widow. It is a *celebration* of the death of Christ, with all the spirit of jubilation which the word "celebration" suggests. We do not mourn over the death of Christ, for we see it in the light of his resurrection and with a realization that it was through his death that Jesus espoused us to himself. Our celebration is enhanced, not with food and wine, however elegant and exquisite, but with the body and blood of Christ. Jesus again proclaims: "This is my body which is given up for you. This is my blood, the blood of the new and everlasting covenant." That covenant is the marriage covenant, effecting our union with Jesus.

Yes, Jesus is still with us and he wants his joy and love to spread from our hearts and through our hands. Let all the world look at us and see that we are different as Jesus was, and let all the world say, "Those Catholics are a happy and joyful lot."

C.E.M.

**Eighth Sunday of the Year (C)**

## *ON THE WAY*

If a physician had to wait until he was in perfect health before he could practice medicine, he would not be of much service to his patients. If a counselor had to wait until he was free of all emotional imbalance before he could counsel others, he would be out of work. And if a priest could not preach morality until he was the equivalent of a saint, he would be the most silent of all men.

None of us is perfect. Each one of us has his own particular faults and failings. And yet Jesus in the gospel today seems to be stating rather categorically that we must be perfect before we may correct others. Such a teaching makes things virtually impossible for anyone who is charged with responsibility over others. How can a foreman or supervisor on the job ever give directions to the other workers? How can a manager or coach of a ball team presume to train his players? How can parents discipline their children and how can teachers correct their students?

What does Jesus mean by his apparently harsh statement, "Remove the plank from your own eye first; then you will see clearly enough to remove the speck from your brother's eye"? Jesus understands our human nature very well. He recognizes our weaknesses. He knows full well that no one with authority or responsibility, be he pope or president, parent or priest, is perfect. Perfection is not what Jesus expects.

By the extraordinary figure of speech, the plank in the eye, Jesus had in mind an attitude of smugness, a superiority complex, a holier-than-thou outlook. The person with the plank in his eye is the one who thinks he is better than everyone else. He is his own greatest admirer. He attributes all his accomplishments, which may be real enough, to himself and forgets all about God. Pride is a vice which makes us pleasing neither to God nor our fellow human beings. As would a plank in the eye, pride induces blindness. This spiritually blind person fails to see his own sins or the virtues of others. Worst of all, he fails to see the goodness of God.

Where does that leave us? It is not prideful for us to say that we are trying with God's grace to be the kind of people he has called us to be. Our very presence here at Mass indicates, until the contrary is proven, that we want to hear the word of God and to follow it. We want to be the good tree that produces good fruit in God's vineyard.

No, we are not perfect. And yet we ought not to use the excuse of human weakness for doing nothing. St. Paul in the second reading today urged us to be steadfast and persevering, fully engaged in the work of the Lord. We should never have a negative attitude which says, "Oh well, we are only human," as if being human were some kind of disgrace. We are called to great things by God. Death is not the end of us. Jesus has overcome death by his own death, and given us the victory by his resurrection. Our humanity may be frail and weak now, but this corruptible frame, says St. Paul, will take on incorruptibility and immortality.

The gospel today concludes by saying that each man speaks from his heart's abundance. Our hearts should be filled with thanks to God for his goodness to us in calling us to a high destiny, and for his patience with us as we struggle on our way to our heavenly home. Let our voices in this Mass speak the praises of God, for it is good to give thanks to our God.

C.E.M.

## Ninth Sunday of the Year (A)

## *THE TWO HOUSES*

Jesus told the parable of the two houses against the background of simple Palestinian living. A water supply was indeed precious, and the temptation was to build on level, sandy ground near a wady, one of the water courses which for most of the year was a trickling stream at best. In the dry season, the house was secure enough. In the rainy season, however, the wady could become a torrent overflowing its banks and causing a flash flood. The simple, mud-brick dwelling built near the wady would collapse under the pressure of both water and wind in the rain storm.

A prudent man sought the higher rocky ground for building his home. Though the location was inconvenient because it was somewhat removed from a water supply, in the rainy season it proved to be safe and sound. The man who built on sandy ground was thinking only of present convenience, whereas the man who built on solid rock was preparing for future security.

The meaning of the parable is clear. It is easy to give shallow assent to the beautiful teaching of Jesus about love of God and our brothers, about generosity, sacrifice and service. Even unbelievers have done that. It is quite another thing to take his words into our hearts and make faith in them the firm foundation of our lives. Every Sunday we hear the words of Jesus, and we profess our faith in him. But we must not let his words be something we hear only with our ears, or our faith be something that we merely express with our lips.

Moses, as we heard in the first reading, told the people to take God's words to heart, to wear them on their wrist and on their foreheads. Some of the Jews took him literally. They made small boxes, called phylacteries, and placed within them a parchment on which certain key texts from the books of Exodus and Deuteronomy were written.* They wore these phylacteries on the left wrist and on the forehead. The trouble with some of these people was that God's word stopped right there; it remained external and did not penetrate their heart and soul. To wear the phylacteries was easy; to live by the words they contained was not. Those who did not live by the word of God were indeed like the foolish man who built his house on sand.

St. Paul in the second reading was complaining about the same problem. His point was that a mere external observance of law, without the firm foundation of faith, was no security for salvation. The faith he was speaking of was more than intellectual assent. It involved the total commitment of the person to Christ in trust and obedience. In his own way he was saying, the same as Jesus in the gospel, "None of those who cry out, 'Lord, Lord,' will enter the kingdom of God but only the one who does the will of my Father in heaven."

Today, we are challenged by Jesus to make faith in him the firm foundation of our lives. We are being asked to live not a convenient life but a secure one. It is convenient to build our lives on the soft, shifting sands of compromise, excuse and pretense. We can easily compromise with the philosophy that says the good life is secured by money, position or power. We can find an excuse for anything we want to do by adjusting our consciences to suit our actions, rather than directing our actions according to what we know is right. We can pretend that we will accept any sacrifice God demands of us, provided the demand is not a present reality.

But if our lives are without a firm foundation, how will we stand

* The usual texts were Ex 13:1-6 and Dt 6:4-9 and 11:13-21.

against the storm that God may allow to buffet us? What will be our attitude on a rainy day when we have lost our job and are faced with a huge hospital bill? How firm will we be when the winds of temptation are driving us to abandon our responsibility of love and loyalty to spouse and children? How will we accept the sacrifice when our lives seem to be crumbling because of the sudden death of a loved one, or the unexpected accident which debilitates us or one of our children? Will our foundation of faith be strong enough to say to God, "Your will be done"?

The time to prepare for a storm is not during the height of its ferocity but in the calm before the storm. That time is now within this very Mass. It is not enough to hear the word of God. We have to pray that his word will penetrate our hearts and souls. It is insufficient to have the name of God on our lips. We must make God's will the directing force of all we do. We cannot afford to live according to present convenience. Now is the time to prepare for future security by making real faith in God the firm foundation of our lives.

C.E.M.


## Ninth Sunday of the Year (B)
Suggested Use: Third Eucharistic Prayer

## *"I DON'T GO TO CHURCH ANY MORE"*

What do you do when your son stops going to Mass? Or your daughter? Or both? Do you simply put your foot down and say, "As long as you're under our roof you are going to Mass"? But does that really answer the question your son or daughter is silently asking? Or you may take another route: "After all the money we've spent on your Catholic education, and all the other sacrifices we've made for you, this is what we get out of it, an irreligious child?" Again, no one in his right mind can deny the sacrifices Catholic parents have made to support our parochial grade and high schools as well as C.C.D. programs, but does your statement about sacrifices answer the unspoken question in your child's mind? And even if you decide that it's up to your boy or girl to make his or her own decision about going to church, your position still does not answer the question that is troubling them.

The question that needs answering is not from parents to children:

"Why don't you go to Mass any more?" Rather, it is from child to parent, "Why do you go to Mass every Sunday?" You may think that your answer is obvious, that your good example over all these years should be sufficient answer in itself. Obviously if you did not think it important, you would not have made the effort to get yourself and your family to Sunday Mass. After all, there have been many days when you did not feel like going, but you went anyway. And what about those days during vacation when you went miles out of your way to find a church? Don't these efforts say anything at all about why you go to Mass? Don't they shout out that Sunday Mass is the most important thing in the week? But the gnawing question is still there, "Why?"

The readings in today's Mass give us some clues for answering the question. At first glance, the reading from the Old Testament seems to reinforce the statement, "You go to Mass because I tell you to go." "Take care to keep holy the sabbath day as the Lord, your God, commanded you." However, as we read at the end of the section we find that God gives not only the command, but also a reason for it. God recalls to the minds of the people for whom this law was written, that they were once slaves and he brought them out of captivity. "This is why the Lord, your God, has commanded you to observe the sabbath day." The release from the slavery of the Egyptians was not a negative gift, but God's positive way of establishing the Israelites as the chosen people. Because their freedom from the Egyptians was such a grand thing, the Hebrew people were commanded by God not to forget it. And the remembrance was to be kept alive by setting aside one day each week to recall such a magnificent benefit.

We go to Mass because God tells us to go, but there is a reason behind the commandment—a reason we can see only if we have faith. It all really comes down to that—faith that because God has created us, we belong entirely to him; faith that Jesus has saved us from the eternal death of sin; faith that in our baptism, God granted us freedom from the slavery of sin and made us his new chosen people.

The second reading today can give us some good insights into the significance of our baptism. By baptism, such a close relationship with God was established that we can act in the person of his Son, Jesus Christ. In fact, it is true to say that Christ does not fulfill his redemption of mankind except through us. Nowhere is this more perfectly accomplished than in the Mass. If we are going to be true to our heritage in baptism, then the Mass becomes an integral part of our lives. We are the people about whom the Third Eucharistic Prayer is speaking when it says, "From age to age you gather a people to yourself, so that from east to west a perfect offering may be made to the glory of your name."

Parents who realize the necessity for harmonious action among all the members of the family if all are going to benefit, should be able to see also the necessity for God to gather his people to himself, at least once a week. It is when we come together as a group of people who believe in the same God, who have each benefited by the redemption of his Son, who are all inspired by the Holy Spirit, that we can fulfill the words we proclaim in the preface: "It is right to give him thanks and praise." We should not come to church out of fear that something terrible will happen to us if we don't; rather, we should wish to join with Christ and all those called together here to praise God our Father for his wonderful benefits to us.

When we have struggled sufficiently with the question, "Why go to Mass?", we will find that it really does all come down to a question of faith. In the final analysis, we go to Mass because we believe in God and in what he has done for us. We believe in Jesus Christ, who in the gospel for today proclaims himself "Lord of the sabbath." We believe in his words, "This is my body . . . this is my blood . . . do this in memory of me."

O.J.M.

## Ninth Sunday of the Year (C)

### *UNWORTHY BUT WELCOME*

St. Luke, whose gospel we are reading during this liturgical year, is the kind of person I am sure we would all like. From his writings one gets the impression that he was a broad-minded, congenial and happy person. He had a great affection for the stories told by Jesus, and he knew how to put them down in writing in a way which was interesting and provocative. Because his stories are interesting, they catch our attention. Because they are provocative, we can through prayerful thought delve through several layers of meaning within them.

On one level of today's gospel is a fulfillment of the prayer which we heard in the first reading. That prayer asked that all people, and not just the chosen people, might receive God's favor through their faith. The centurion was not a Jew but a Roman, and represented all those people who would be called to the Church after the death and resurrection of Jesus.

The Church, reading this gospel story on another level, has adopted the words of the centurion as a preparation for Communion. Just before Communion the priest says, ''This is the Lamb of God who takes away the sins of the world. Happy are those who are called to his supper.'' To these words we all respond, ''Lord, I am not worthy to receive you, but only say the word and I shall be healed.''

The Church finds that these words are suitable before Communion because of the dispositions manifested by the centurion when he came face to face with Jesus.

The centurion displayed a remarkable humility. He was an officer in the army of the Roman Empire which had conquered the Jews. He had to swallow his pride to come before Jesus, a Jew, to ask a favor. He had to admit that he, a Roman, could do nothing to help his servant, that he needed Jesus. He also manifested a great faith that Jesus possessed the power to cure his paralyzed servant. Perhaps most important of all, he was confident that Jesus had enough concern, even enough love for him, to grant this extraordinary petition.

The humility, faith and trust of this man serve to remind us of what our attitude should be as we receive Holy Communion. Jesus came into our world to cure the human race paralyzed by sin and near death. He wanted to free us of the spiritual crippling disease, so that we could live a full, human life as children of God. His mission was to give us the means to live in such a way that we could join him in the everlasting wedding supper in heaven.

Jesus does not force his loving power on anyone, and he does not pressure anyone to receive him in the Eucharist. We are called to respond freely to him through faith, humility and trust. We must have faith that Jesus, and Jesus alone, has the power to help us. We must have the humility to admit that we need Jesus, that of ourselves we can do nothing, that all human resources are insufficient to make us spiritually sound. And we must trust that Jesus loves us, that he welcomes us, that he is eager to help us.

In the strict sense, no one is really worthy to receive Jesus in Holy

Communion. In fact, we are not worthy of any of God's favors. Every-thing from God is a gift. But as we respond to God's invitation to receive Communion, we should indeed be happy that through the power of the Eucharist we are benefiting from the healing and strengthening power of Jesus, our Savior.

C.E.M.

## Tenth Sunday of the Year (A)

Suggested Use: First Eucharistic Prayer

## *SINCERITY*

When the first reading of today's Mass was composed, Israel had sought help during time of trouble by means of political alliances with foreign nations. She had made the mistake of relying on human forces rather than on God. Then through the preaching of the prophet, Hosea, she realized that her suffering was a punishment from God for sin, and once again she turned to him in repentance. But her repentance was both insincere and presumptuous. It was insincere because the people thought that repentance for sin could be expressed in merely external aspects of religion, such as the offering of sacrifice, without any real change of heart. It was presumptuous because the people thought that God's punishment would last only for a while no matter what they did, and that eventually he would relent. They took the weather conditions of their country as a symbol of God's actions toward them. They knew that the dry season (a symbol of God's punishment) was inevitably followed by the spring rain (a symbol of God's forgiveness).

Hosea, the prophet, was called by God to bring the people to their senses. He too used the weather as a symbol, but in a different way. Speaking for God, he accused the people of being fickle by telling them that their piety was but a passing thing, like the clouds and the dew which are present in the morning but by afternoon have dissipated in the warmth of the sun. That kind of piety, expressed in merely external worship, would simply not do. God demanded that his people persevere in their faithfulness to him, no matter what their pressures or temptations might be. They were to rely on him and not on any merely human powers. But the people were insincere.

How different was Abraham, about whom we heard in the second reading, from the people of Hosea's time. Abraham was given an almost incredible promise by God, that he would be the father of many nations, despite the fact that he was very old and his wife far beyond the age of bearing children. He did not protest that God's promise was impossible. He refused to be persuaded that he had to look elsewhere for help. "He never questioned or doubted God's promise" because he was sincere in his love and piety toward God.

The same kind of sincerity was manifested by Matthew, described in today's gospel. Matthew as a tax collector enjoyed a lucrative position; his job insured a regular and handsome income. The sincerity of his devotion to Jesus was measured by how much he was willing to give up to follow him. The Pharisees, who complained that Jesus had accepted Matthew, were not unlike the people in today's first reading. Their religion was hollow because it was based on externals only. That is why Jesus quoted to them the words of Hosea, "It is mercy I desire and not sacrifice." The word "mercy" does not mean "pity." It could just as well have been translated as "love" or "piety." Jesus wanted the sincere devotion which he saw in Matthew, and not the shallowness which he saw in the Pharisees.

The question is: what does Jesus see in us? Does he see sincerity? Some maintain that the word "sincerity" comes from two Latin words, "sine" and "cera," which literally mean "without wax."* It is said that ancient Roman sculptors tried to conceal surface cracks in a statue with wax. Of course, as soon as the statue was exposed to heat the wax melted away and the cracks were exposed. The sculptor had failed to work sincerely, that is, without wax. Is our piety sincere, or are its cracks covered over with wax which melts away in the heat of temptation? It is easy to put faith in God while everything is going well for us. The real test comes when God demands absolute trust, as he did with his promise to Abraham. Are we willing to let our piety be tested by how much we are willing to give up for God, as Matthew did?

I have no idea of what God may ask of you as a test of your piety and devotion to him. But you will know when the time comes. You will find yourself saying things like, "God, why did you do that?" or even worse, "God can't love me because if he did, he would never have let this

---

* Though the *Oxford English Dictionary* states that this etymology is not probable, it does not seem devoid of all possibility.

happen to me.'' Perhaps you have already had this experience. In either case, this Mass is your opportunity to renew your absolute faith and trust in God. Try to mean the words we will say to God in the First Eucharistic Prayer: ''You know how firmly we believe in you and dedicate ourselves to you.''

Even as I speak to you, the wax of the candles on the altar is slowly melting away, a reminder to us of what our piety should not be. Together, let us pray that our piety will be without wax, that is, really sincere.

C.E.M.

### Tenth Sunday of the Year (B)

## *A HOUSEHOLD DIVIDED*

The first reading today is typically human. Adam and Eve are much like two children, neither of whom is willing to accept responsibility for having done wrong. The scene is similar to that in which a father comes home to find the television set broken. He says to his young son, ''Didn't I tell you not to fool around with the television?'' The boy replies, pointing to his little sister, ''Don't blame me; she made me turn it on.'' And the little girl explains, ''My friend came over and wanted to watch TV.''

Adam, like the little boy, refused to accept responsibility and blamed the woman. More seriously, he even implied that God was somewhat at fault as he said, ''The woman whom *you* put here with me—she gave me fruit from the tree.'' The woman in her turn also implicitly involved God as she blamed the serpent, for the serpent was likewise a creature of God. Dissension and division were the result of sin, but they were also its occasion. If Adam and his wife had stuck together, unified by their loyalty to God, they could have overcome the temptation to evil. The words of Jesus in the gospel, though spoken of the forces of evil, apply equally to mankind: ''If a household is divided according to its loyalties, that household will not survive.''

We simply cannot afford dissension and division among ourselves, since we are engaged in a bitter war against evil. God proclaimed, speaking to the serpent as the symbol of the forces of evil, ''I will put enmity between you and the woman, between your offspring and hers.'' Enmity means all-out conflict to the end with no truce, no compromise, until one force emerges as the victor. Jesus through his cross and resurrection has won the victory in himself. If we are going to share in that victory, we have to stick together, united through our unswerving loyalty to him.

In the Eucharistic Prayer, we beg God to grant us unity. That must not be an idle prayer. Together, we receive Jesus in Holy Communion as our bond of union with each other. That reception of the body of Christ must not be an empty ritual. Before Communion we are urged to exchange a sign of peace, but true peace can come only through our victory over sin and evil. Our sign of peace, then, can be offered with sincerity and effectiveness only if we come forward to receive Jesus with eagerness to share his love with everyone without exception, for only the union of Christian love can lead us to victory over sin and evil.

Our enmity with the forces of evil will last until Christ comes again in glory. If we, as the brothers and sisters of Christ, as the household of God, remain united in our loyalty to our heavenly Father, we can have the firm confidence of sharing in Christ's final victory.

C.E.M.

## Tenth Sunday of the Year (C)

## *DEATH TO LIFE—WITH COMPASSION*

The great issue of life is death. Face death we must, but as people of faith we believe that Jesus is the Lord of life and death, and by his own death and resurrection he has destroyed death and restored life.

It is helpful for us to note the contrast between the first reading and the gospel. In the first reading, we have heard how Elijah did indeed raise the son of the widow from death to life. He did so, however, not in his own name or by his own power. Rather, he called upon the Lord to let the life-breath return to the body of the child. Jesus on the other hand, stood before the dead man and spoke a command filled with power and authority: "Young man, I bid you get up." The dead man immediately sat up and began to speak. Jesus showed that he himself is indeed the Lord of Life. Our eucharistic acclamation will be most appropriate for today's liturgy: "Dying you destroyed our death, rising you restored our life. Lord Jesus, come in glory."

The title, "Lord of Life," may have a ring of aloofness about it. Pehaps this expression suggests that the Lord is far above us, removed from our simple and ordinary human lives. Although St. Luke is eager to proclaim clearly and forcefully that Jesus is the Lord of Life, he does so within the context of the story, which is full of feeling and compassion. By means of this story he gives us a picture of the loving heart of Jesus, our Savior.

The funeral scene upon which Jesus came was one which would induce pity from any sensitive person. The dead man who was being carried out to burial was the only son of a widowed mother. Jesus himself was moved to compassion, not for the boy, but for the mother. He realized that the most difficult time for her was still in the future when, after the burial of her only son, she would have to return home to an empty house all alone. She would have no idea of what might lie ahead for her, how she would support herself, or who would take care of her. Jesus quickly grasped the full meaning of the sad scene before him.

It is not unthinkable that Jesus, in his imagination, looked to a day yet to come when another widow would be following the dead body of her only son to the grave. Jesus loved his own mother dearly, and in the moment of today's gospel that love rushed through his spirit and over-flowed in tenderness for the confused and distraught woman who stood beside the lifeless body of her son. The high point of the gospel was not the moment when Jesus restored life to the dead man. The high point was that moment indicated by St. Luke, when Jesus gave him back to his mother.

Jesus is indeed the Lord of Life, but he is not distant from us or unaware of our feelings and needs. He is a compassionate and loving Lord who invites us to receive his body and blood as the means of our strength in our needs and as the pledge of everlasting life. Jesus will indeed raise us from death to life, but even as we move toward that great moment, he continues to treat us with love and compassion.

C.E.M.

**Eleventh Sunday of the Year (A)**

Suggested Use: Fourth Eucharistic Prayer

## *GOD'S LOVE IS FOREVER*

If you have ever wondered whether God loves you, you are not without company. People of all times and places, even those of the most primitive and unenlightened conditions, have believed in some kind of God. It is obvious that this world—the universe—had to be made by someone, and that someone we call God. But people have not always been certain as to what kind of God, God is. Does he really care about his creation, or has he walked away, letting the universe shift for itself? Even if he does have concern for his creation, does he love *me*—personally, as an individual? That is a question even believers wonder about. And a vital question it is.

Much of the Bible has been written with the express purpose of showing that God is indeed a loving God. For example, the first reading today was addressed to the Jews as a reminder that God loved them so much that he freed them from the slavery of the Egyptians and made them his special people, a kingdom of priests, a holy nation. In the gospel we saw the God-man, Jesus, his heart moved with pity for the people who were like sheep without a shepherd. He sent his apostles out to do good things for them for one reason: he loved them. In fact, Sunday after Sunday we see God's love in Jesus.

Of course, the greatest sign we have of God's love for us is the death of Jesus on the cross. God's love is so great that he gave his own Son to us, and that Son loved us so much that he gave his life for our salvation. You just cannot have a greater sign of love than that.

People of primitive religions felt that they had to placate a god who was about to hurl vindictive lightning bolts upon their heads because of their wickedness. They offered sacrifices to their god, sometimes even human sacrifice, in order to appease him in his outraged sense of justice. It just never occurred to them that there was a God who loved people so much that he would give his own Son to be a victim of sacrifice.

In meditating on this Christian revelation concerning the sacrifice of Jesus, St. Paul was overwhelmed by the realization of how much greater divine love is than human love (second reading). Only in extraordinary circumstances is a human being willing to die for someone else.

A good father and mother will indeed protect their child from a threat to his life at the expense of their own life, but they will not be willing to do the same for a stranger, much less for an enemy. Imagine that you arrive home one day to find that a thief has broken into your home, taken all your valuables, and murdered your spouse and children. Meanwhile near your home, the police have engaged the thief and murderer in a gun battle. You arrive on the scene and deliberately intercept with your own body a police bullet intended for the outlaw, because you want to die in his place. Impossible to imagine? Of course it is. Such an action is asking too much of human nature, but it was not too much for God. St. Paul in the second reading proclaims, ''It is precisely in this that God proves his love for us: that while we were still sinners, Christ died for us.'' It is something to think about: Christ died for us when we were his enemies because of sin.

So that we would never forget his love, Jesus gave us the Eucharist on the night before he died. ''Do this in memory of me,'' he said. In every Mass, Jesus is made present as a victim, for the Eucharistic species under which he is present are a sacred sign of the actual separation of his body and blood (cf. *Mediator Dei*, 70). Pope Pius XII wrote, ''It cannot be over-emphasized that the Eucharistic Sacrifice of its very nature is the unbloody immolation of the divine victim, which is made manifest in a mystical manner by the separation of the sacred species and by their offering to the Eternal Father'' (*Mediator Dei*, 115).

The Mass should be a constant reminder of how great God's love really is. And God's love does not change. He still has that kind of love for us. At times, we may wonder if that is really true. We may feel that God has turned his back on us, that he has changed. That is precisely when we have to remember that the Mass means that God does indeed still love each one of us.

There is a verse in today's responsorial psalm which we should allow to penetrate our minds and our hearts. That verse is: ''The Lord is good; his kindness endures forever and his faithfulness to all generations.'' God's love is not only great. It is forever.

C.E.M.

**Eleventh Sunday of the Year (B)**

# A GROWING ORGANISM

No one has actually seen a tree grow. Its growth is too slow for the human eye to perceive. Nor, for that matter, has anyone ever seen a child grow. It is only after you have not been with a child for some time, that you notice how tall he has become. Living things grow slowly.

The Church, too, grows slowly because it is a living organism. It is made up of human beings who, like the cells of the human body, form the mystical body of Jesus Christ. Growth is what our Lord is talking about in today's gospel. He started with the twelve apostles, a very small group of men. Those men after Pentecost went out and began the conversion of the whole world, so that today the Church has more than half a billion people as its members. About one in every six persons is a Catholic. When Pope John summoned the Second Vatican Council, more than two thousand bishops from every nation responded to his call. If the apostles could come back to earth today, they would be amazed at the growth of the Church.

The growth of the Church is of course due to the power of God, and God's power cannot be frustrated by either the evil or the incompetence of men. As a seed planted in the earth has an almost mysterious ability to develop while the farmer sleeps, so the Church has an inner divinely given dynamism which ensures its continuing and spreading from age to age. And yet the role of the members of the Church is far from passive in God's plan. What God could do all by himself, he has decided to do with and through the members of the Church.

Back in 1943 when he wrote his encyclical on the Church as the Mystical Body of Christ, Pope Pius XII put it this way: ''Dying on the cross Christ left to his Church the immense treasury of the redemption; towards this she contributed nothing. But when those graces come to be distributed, not only does he share this task of sanctification with his Church, but he wants it in a way to be due to her action'' (46). That you and I are Catholics today is traceable to the action of those who have preceded us in the faith. That the Church spread from Palestine over the centuries to all the countries of the world is due, under God, to the goodness and holiness of the members of the Church.

When we think of how the Church began with such a small group and see what it is today we are indeed amazed, but we must never become complacent. Now it is our turn to do something, for we bear the responsibility for continuing the spread of Christ's Church. We know that we should give good example and try to talk to people about the Church. Today, however, let's try to focus on something very important, something that may escape our realization.

The Church is like a human body. As the vitality of the body depends on the health of its cells, so the vitality of the Church depends on the holiness of its members. We may think that the sins we commit offend God alone and harm only ourselves. That is not true. Sin damages the whole Church, just as an infection in any part of the body affects the whole body. On the other hand, we may feel that we are not very important, that our prayers and penances cannot accomplish very much. That too is not true. When we try to live good lives as Jesus has taught us, we are very instrumental in the building up of the whole Church.

Listen to these words of Pope Pius XII from the same encyclical on the Mystical Body: "Deep mystery this, subject of inexhaustible meditation, that the salvation of many depends on the prayers and voluntary penances which the members of the Mystical Body of Jesus Christ offer for this intention . . ." (*ibid.*). Deep mystery indeed: God wills that the salvation of others should come about through our prayers and penances. Subject of inexhaustible meditation, something we must never forget, that the goodness of our lives can really benefit others.

C.E.M.

## Eleventh Sunday of the Year (C)

### *FORGIVENESS AND LOVE*

(Note:    This gospel poses a problem in translation. The NAB version is impossible to reconcile with the context: ". . . Her many sins are forgiven because of her great love." Most commentators insist that the translation should reflect the idea that the woman loved Jesus much because he had forgiven her. It is this latter understanding which is followed in this homily.)

It is extremely difficult for us to form an accurate picture of God. We have been taught that God is all-knowing, all-powerful and all-wise. Today's readings suggest a somewhat less awesome and much more touching picture of God. They seem to indicate that God is eager for our love, that he has an urgent desire and ardent hope that we will respond freely to his goodness.

The background of today's first reading is that King David, even though he had many wives, lusted after Bathsheba. When she became pregnant, David saw to it that Uriah was placed at such a position during one of the battles that he would be surely killed. In effect, David compounded adultery with the crime of murder.

God could have struck down David on the spot. He could have allowed Uriah's fellow soldiers to rise and revolt against David for such a terrible injustice. God could have done any number of things to punish David, but God wanted his love. And so God sent Nathan the prophet to David to arouse his conscience and to make him aware of his terrible sins. God also gave David the grace of repentance. God was so eager to forgive, because he was eager for a return of love from David.

Jesus himself exemplified his Father's ardent desire for our love, in the gospel scene today. The woman who washed and perfumed the feet of Jesus, as a sign of reverence and love for him, was a well-known sinner. She had experienced the merciful compassion in the teaching and actions of Jesus. She knew in her heart that he was her Savior bringing her mercy and forgiveness. Her response of love was so great that she could not restrain herself even in the presence of Simon the Pharisee. Simon was abashed as well as indignant. He could not understand how Jesus, acknowledged to be a prophet and a Rabbi, could tolerate even the presence of the woman, let alone her touch. Jesus attempted to explain to Simon what he had failed to grasp about God. Jesus made it clear that the woman was so responsive in love because her many sins had been forgiven her. Simon was apparently smug and complacent. He saw himself as superior to the woman, and not in need of forgiveness. He wanted no part of a God who would be quick to forgive in order to be loved.

We ourselves are weak and we are sinners. The woman shed her tears as a sign of love for Jesus, but we must remember that Jesus shed his blood for the forgiveness of our sins. That great act of love on our behalf should beget love in us for God.

The Mass is our constant reminder that God is eager for our love and that he seeks to draw us by the grace of forgiveness. Every Mass is the living memorial of the death and resurrection of Jesus, and in every Mass we hear his words proclaimed, "This is the cup of my blood . . . shed for you and for all for the forgiveness of sins.'' God is the Father of forgiveness, and his forgiveness should lead us to love him completely.

C.E.M.

## Twelfth Sunday of the Year (A)

# *NO INTIMIDATION*

Our first reading in this Mass was from the prophet Jeremiah, who was born some 650 years before Christ. That reading merely hints at all the painful experiences Jeremiah had to endure as God's prophet. When he was sent by God to speak the plain truth to his contemporaries, he met with stern opposition—to put it mildly—from the people, the priests, and the king himself. They were all guilty of abandoning the true God in favor of the practice of idolatry, and they refused to accept the God preached by Jeremiah. He was imprisoned, humiliated and finally died in exile from the land he loved.

Jesus did not minimize the dangers that would await his own disciples. In effect, he warned them that their fate could be similar to that of Jeremiah: disdain, torture, even death itself. He told them that, no matter what people might do to them, they should not really be worried. Of course such an exhortation may at first sound glib, but Jesus had a good point. To die, after all, is the common lot of everyone. No human power can do more to a man than nature itself will eventually accomplish. So why fear death for a good cause?

Then Jesus, after telling his disciples not to be afraid of death, told them to be afraid of God. It was an unusual motive for Jesus to use, but he realized that the time would come when things would get so rough for his followers that they would need every possible motive to persevere. So he did not hesitate to warn them that the only person they should fear is God, who has the power to bury both body and soul in the eternal death of hell. He warned them not to abandon God in the face of human threats, because only God has the power of eternal damnation.

But Jesus could not bring himself to leave his disciples with that image of his Father. As he had done on many occasions, he reminded them that God really loved them. To do so he used the commonest, most valueless creature he could name in Palestine: the sparrow, two of which sold for next to nothing. Not even a sparrow dies without God's consent, he told them. How much more precious were they in the eyes of God, whose concern extended to the numbering of the hairs on their heads. And another motive for perseverance appears: that kind of God is worth anything that may be demanded, and he is a God who will help people meet his demands.

Difficulties for God's followers have not changed. They were real for Jeremiah 650 years before Christ, and they are real for us two thousand years after Christ. We need and will continue to need every possible motive to persevere. Jeremiah and the apostles suffered ridicule and disdain. Perhaps you have suffered the same because in your business you have stuck by Christian principles in refusing to cut corners, not to mention the throats of your competitors, with financial loss to yourself. Maybe you have been accused of ''polluting the environment'' because you have brought four or five children into the world in a spirit of generosity and love. It may be that you are undergoing real torture in trying to keep your marriage and home together, because you believe that Jesus meant it when he said, ''What God has joined together, let no man put asunder.'' Almost everyone has felt the influence of the playboy philosophy which treats sex as a toy, rather than as a sacred power entrusted to us by God who demands responsibility and maturity in its use.

Every day, our lives bring pressures to abandon our Christian principles: the conversation we are expected to join which drags someone's name through the mud; the attitude others want us to share that says that you should not get involved when someone needs help; the opinion some people think we dare not contradict which maintains that our religion is irrelevant and useless in this modern world. No, we don't have to search for challenges to our loyalty to the teachings of Jesus Christ. They are all around us.

Remember the words of Jesus: ''Do not let men intimidate you.'' That means: don't follow their opinions and their slogans, and don't imitate their example. Don't be afraid of their ridicule and their disdain. The very worst that any human can do is to kill you; he cannot condemn you to hell. If you are going to be afraid, at least be afraid of the right person. Fear God! Yes, fear him—but also remember that he loves you. The God whom we worship in this Mass has the power to destroy us in hell, but he is also the God who has such care and concern for us that he will give us the strength to persevere in all that he demands of us.

C.E.M.

## Twelfth Sunday of the Year (B)

## *STORMS AND TRUST*

One evening, after preaching to the people all day long, Jesus asked his disciples to take him by boat across the Sea of Galilee. Jesus was worn out from his labors, and was apparently looking for a little rest and relaxation. He was so exhausted, in fact, that he fell asleep in the stern even as strong winds began to buffet the light fishing craft. Sudden squalls on the Sea of Galilee are not extraordinary. The Sea, about 685 feet below sea level, is surrounded by mountains on almost all sides. As the warm air rises in the evening, cool air rushes down from the mountains and in a short time can transform the calm water into danger-ous waves of seven or eight feet. Jesus was sleeping serenely during just such a violent disturbance. In panic, the disciples woke Jesus with pleas for help.

Jesus then did exactly what we would expect him to do. He rebuked the wind and said to the sea, "Quiet! Be still!" Immediately there came a great calm. Then Jesus did something unexpected. He rebuked the disciples just as he had rebuked the wind. In effect, he said to them as he did to the sea, "Quiet! Be still!" Jesus appeared annoyed that they had become terrified, but who wouldn't be terrified in such a situation? What had the disciples done wrong? In a time of crisis, they turned to Jesus for much-needed help—it seemed the only thing to do. And yet Jesus complained, "Why are you lacking in faith?"

Jesus' point was that the disciples should have had more confidence in him. Jesus knew what he was doing when he told them to cross the Sea. He put them into the dangerous situation, and they should have had complete trust that he would take care of them. It was only after they had exhausted all human means to save themselves as they bailed water and adjusted the rudder to bring the ship to, that they *finally* thought to wake Jesus. In other words, they looked to Jesus for help only as a last resort when all else had failed—whereas, though still using human means, their very first thought should have been of Jesus. They had not yet come to the realization that Jesus, whom they called "Teacher," was actually the Lord and Master of all creation (cf. first reading).

What about our faith and trust in God? Imagine this scene which takes place somewhere every day. A person surrounded by his family lies dying in a hospital bed. The doctors have admitted that the case is medically hopeless. A member of the family, out of the hearing of the sick man, murmurs, "I guess all we can do now is pray." All we can do now is pray. . . . Such a statement betrays a lack of real faith, an attitude that turning to God in prayer is but a last resort in dire circumstances. It resembles that lack of trust found in the disciples during the storm on the Sea. Jesus wishes to teach us today that our attitude must be different, that our prayer of trust as we turn to God for help must be a habitual part of our life in all its circumstances. We must use human means to help ourselves, but not with the idea that we will turn to God only after all our own efforts have failed.

God should not be the last person we think of, as we are buffeted by the storms of life. We should not wait until the violent winds blow before we pray to God. A little child does not turn to his parents only when he is in serious trouble. He is completely dependent on them, and somehow feels that all good things come from them. He looks to his parents for food when he is hungry; he runs to them for comfort when he has skinned his knee or had his feelings hurt; he seeks solace from them when he is lonely and blue. Above all, he wants to feel that he belongs, that he has their love and interest all the time.

No matter how young or old we may be, in relation to God we are like little children, and God is a Father more loving and interested than even the best of human parents. He wants us to look to him in all the circumstances of our lives, not merely when we are in serious trouble. God is Lord and Master not only of the universe, but of our individual lives as well. He has placed us in this world, he knew what he was doing, and he will take care of us if we have real faith and trust in him.

The prayer of trust, then, is not some last-ditch effort to ward off impending disaster, as suggested in the words heard so often, "All we can do now is pray." It should instead be a child's confident turning to God as a loving Father. In all the circumstances of our lives, we should pray with confidence in the words our Savior gave us: "Our Father."

C.E.M.

**Twelfth Sunday of the Year (C)**

## *THE MYSTERY OF SUFFERING*

There is a great mystery in human suffering. The father of three children lies on what will soon be his deathbed. He is forty-seven years of age, a devoted husband and father, a respected doctor in the community, an active member of his parish. Cancer has spread from his pancreas throughout his abdomen. There is one unanswered question in his mind and in the minds of his family and friends. That one question is "Why?"

It is not an easy question to answer. There is indeed a great mystery in human suffering. The mystery is that somehow there can be a tremendous value in human suffering. Just how, it is impossible to say with complete satisfaction; but that there can be value in it is beyond doubt. Jesus himself has shown us the great value of suffering.

In today's gospel we heard Jesus say, "The Son of Man *must* endure many sufferings." He *must* suffer because such was the plan of God for the salvation of the world. It is not that God in heaven looked down upon his suffering Son, and took some kind of twisted pleasure in what he saw. Nor was it really a question of some type of payment for sin in the old idea of a tooth for a tooth and an eye for an eye. Perhaps we get closer to the truth when we realize that suffering is the measure of a man. It shows how big a person he is. It can also be the test of love, because we are willing to suffer for a person to the extent that we love him. As Jesus himself said at the Last Supper, "There is no greater love than this: to lay down one's life for one's friends." Still, even these ideas leave us unsatisfied. There is obviously a mystery about suffering.

And yet, the value of suffering is undeniable. Thomas a Kempis, who lived some 1300 years after Christ, wrote these words: "If anything had been better and more beneficial for man's salvation than suffering, Christ would have shown it by word and by example." The word of Christ we heard in today's gospel: "If anyone wishes to come after me, let him deny himself, and take up his cross daily, and follow me." The example of Christ we know full well: not only did he take up his cross, but he died upon it.

St. Peter warns in his first epistle: "Since Christ has suffered in the flesh, do you also arm yourselves with the same intent" (1 P 4:1). St.

Peter is telling us that since Christ has suffered, we must suffer too. The reason for this is given by St. Paul in today's epistle: "All of you who have been baptized into Christ, have clothed yourselves with him." To be a Christian means to be like Christ. We are called to continue his way of life in the world, and that way of life includes suffering as an indispensable ingredient.

Our Christ-like suffering takes many forms. It is found in the anguish of parents who care for a paralyzed son who they know will never walk again. It shows itself in the humiliation of a man who cannot provide for his family, and who must turn to others or to the state for help. It is the boring monotony of a housewife and the poignant loneliness of a widow. The list of human suffering is almost without end.

If we were to go through the New Testament page by page, we would find many passages dealing with Christ's suffering and our suffering. More importantly, we would also find that not once does the New Testament touch on the suffering and death of Christ without also speaking of the glory of his resurrection. Not once does the New Testament bring up the necessity of our own suffering, without emphasizing the happiness that will come from that suffering. In today's gospel, Jesus said that he had to suffer, that he would be put to death. In the same breath, he also stated that on the third day he would rise again.

And so with us. Somehow in God's plan, suffering is good for us. It will lead to our final glory and happiness just as surely as it did for Christ. In God's plan, suffering and true happiness cannot be separated. In the Mass, we celebrate both the death and the resurrection of Jesus. We do not separate suffering and happiness in the Mass any more than we can separate them in our lives.

C.E.M.

**Thirteenth Sunday of the Year (A)**

## A CHRISTIAN WELCOME

One thought in our minds at this time of the year is the commemoration of the birth of our country with the signing of the Declaration of Independence on July 4, 1776. Since 1886, one hundred and ten years after the signing of the Declaration of Independence, the Statue of

Liberty has stood on Liberty Island in New York harbor as a symbol of our country. Graven on a tablet within the pedestal upon which the statue stands, is a poem written by Emma Lazarus, which reads in part: "Give me your tired, your poor, your huddled masses yearning to breathe free, the wretched refuse of your teeming shore. Send these, the homeless, tempest-tost to me. . . ." Today let us reflect on whether we, not only as Americans but especially as Catholics, have continued to extend this invitation to those with whom we now share this country.

In a sprawling suburban area of one of our largest cities there are over three hundred thousand homes, yet social workers have been able to find only thirteen homes there willing to offer shelter and care to retarded foster children.* From among three hundred thousand homes, only thirteen willing to say: "Send these homeless, tempest-tost children to me." Social workers admit that the reasons for their failure to place these children are many: a lack of communication as to the need, misunderstanding or even prejudice, and fear of inability to cope with the problems. But only thirteen homes from among three hundred thousand willing to welcome a retarded child! Something is wrong.

Perhaps your reaction is that expecting people to take that kind of a child into their homes is asking too much. People have their own children to worry about; they have their own lives to lead. And maybe your reaction is such, because you know in your own heart that you do not have the heroic generosity required to accept a retarded child. If you are feeling a little uncomfortable in this realization about yourself, that is a good thing. I know that in thinking about this whole matter I feel a little uncomfortable myself, and it is a feeling I need very much to shake me up a little bit.

St. Paul reminded us in the second reading today that by our baptism we died a death to sin. It was meant to be an end to the pride and selfishness which is our common inheritance as human beings, and a beginning of a new life of love and generosity like that of Jesus himself.

And so we must come to grips with what Jesus told us in the gospel: "He who seeks only himself brings himself to ruin." Selfishness is the direct opposite of the true Christian spirit to which we pledged ourselves at our baptism. Selfishness, in fact, will lead us right back to the death from which Jesus wished to free us in that sacrament. It is no wonder,

* Reported in the *Los Angeles Times* for Feb. 7, 1971.

then, that Jesus begs us to open our hearts and our lives to others, to crack open the hard shell of indifference with which we have surrounded ourselves. We don't dare to get involved. We are afraid that we may lose our much-desired serenity. But the plea of Jesus continues to sound in our ears: "Welcome the lowly, the poor, the despised of this world." To this plea we must not remain deaf.

Perhaps the problem of the retarded children is not a very practical one, because its demands are too great and the situation too unusual. Let's get practical, then! How generous are we? I don't mean now with reference to the seemingly endless collections for the foreign missions and for the poor to which we are asked to contribute in church. Real generosity and unselfishness are required when people put demands on our time and our convenience. Reflect on your reactions. One day, you are especially busy. You are about to leave on an important point of business, when the doorbell rings. It is a neighbor who is depressed and lonely. That neighbor needs you, your time, your sympathetic ear. Perhaps someone else keeps you on the phone for a long time with what seems to you to be petty problems, but which are making him depressed and weary of life itself. That person needs your patience and understanding. Maybe a man stops you on the street. His hair is disheveled, his grey trousers stiff with grime, his shoes shabby with wear. As he asks for a handout, he needs to be given not only money but also respect and a sense of dignity as a human being. If we cannot meet these simple demands with unselfishness, if we cannot give a Christian welcome to those who need our time and interest, then we will never grow toward the mature generosity required by our baptismal commitment.

Would that we could make our own the words inscribed on the pedestal of the Statue of Liberty, and address them to Jesus: "Give me your tired, your poor, your huddled masses yearning to breathe free, the wretched refuse of your teeming shore. Send these, the homeless, tempest-tost to me. . . ."

C.E.M.

### Thirteenth Sunday of the Year (B)

## GOD HAS TIME FOR PEOPLE

What is God really like? Did he create the world and then send it spinning into space with little concern, or is he still interested in the welfare of his creatures? Is he so busy looking after the big, important people of the world who shape history itself, that he has no time to look after all the little people like you and me? Is he patient with our foibles, tolerant of our failures, understanding toward our pettiness? What indeed is God really like? Actually, we can come to know what God the Father is like by coming to know Jesus, his Son, as he is set forth in the pages of the gospels.

There are two facts about Jesus which we must constantly keep balanced in our minds. The first is that he is truly divine, the Son of God, the perfect image of his Father. The second is that he is truly human, just as human as we are in everything except sin. Since Jesus is truly God, the image of his Father, we can know what God is like by knowing Jesus. Since Jesus is truly human, through him we can get to know God in a human way. In other words, Jesus reveals God to us through his humanity. As Jesus said to Philip the apostle at the Last Supper, "Whoever has seen me has seen the Father" (Jn 14:9).

Today's gospel contains an important revelation about God as seen through the humanity of Jesus. As the narrative begins, a large crowd had gathered around Jesus. It was an excellent opportunity for him to communicate his message to a considerable number of people. Like a good teacher, Jesus no doubt had a "lesson plan," a well-thought-out instruction he wished to impart that day. He had scarcely begun when Jairus, one of the officials of the synagogue, interrupted him with an earnest appeal for his critically ill daughter. Seeing the distress of the father, Jesus was willing to abandon his own plans in order to meet the needs of the man kneeling before him, and prepared to follow him home. Though he uttered no word of complaint, Jesus must have been wondering where the man lived, how long it would take to get to his home and return, and whether all his potential hearers would still be waiting for him when he got back.

At that moment, with all these thoughts running through his mind, Jesus felt someone touch him, the woman with the hemorrhage. It would have been very understandable if Jesus had become impatient, if he had said something like, "Woman, don't bother me now. Can't you see that this important man wants me to save his daughter from death? You and your problem can wait!" Instead, Jesus realized that this poor woman was important too, and that her problem, though not nearly as great as that of Jairus, was big to her. With compassion in his eyes and sympathy in his voice, he said gently, "Daughter, it is your faith that has cured you. Go in peace and be free of this illness." But before he could finish speaking with the woman, he was interrupted again by the friends of the official who arrived to say that the girl was dead. Undaunted by this information, Jesus turned his attention back to Jairus, followed him home, and raised the girl to life.

Let me tell you what this gospel says to me about God. It says that God is not too busy running the universe—that he really does have time for people, big people like Jairus and little people like the unnamed woman. When I talk to God about my difficulties, I am not afraid that he will reply, "I would really like to help you, but I just don't have time; I am too busy looking after important people like the Pope and the President." This gospel says that God understands human nature and realizes that my problems are very relative—relative to me! I think we have all been struck by the statement of the man who said, "I complained because I had no shoes until I met a man who had no feet." Though that encounter helped to put poverty in perspective, it did not really solve the man's problem—for it failed to put shoes on his feet, and that is what he needed. My problems, though perhaps small in comparison with those of others, are big to me simply because they are my problems. God recognizes this fact. I am confident that he will never turn away from my prayers for help, and protest, "Look, I have bigger things to worry about."

Finally, this gospel says that God finds no problem too little to bother with or too big to solve, not a non-fatal hemorrhage nor death itself. My faith is that God will see me through *all* the difficulties of this life and will finally lead me successfully through death to eternal life.

I for one am very grateful that the events described in today's gospel were so vividly remembered by the early Christians and recorded with such detail by the evangelist, for this gospel tells me that God does indeed have time for people. God has time for you and me.

C.E.M.

## Thirteenth Sunday of the Year (C)

# DEMANDS OF DISCIPLESHIP

I think that we all admire a man who sees a job that has to be done, and goes ahead and does it despite opposition and difficulties. To say that a man has the courage of his convictions, is to imply that he is worthy of esteem and praise.

Jesus was a man who had the courage of his convictions. It was his appointed task to effect the salvation of the world, and he allowed nothing, absolutely nothing, to stand in his way. In today's gospel, we saw Jesus on a journey from Galilee to Jerusalem. His journey necessarily took him through the territory of the hostile Samaritans. He made no attempt to conceal from them that his destination was Jerusalem. To admit to being a Jew among the Samaritans was bad enough, but to let it be known openly that one was headed for Jerusalem was extremely risky. Jerusalem represented all that the Samaritans hated and despised about the Jews. It was not unknown that pilgrims headed for Jerusalem were ambushed by Samaritans and murdered on the road. But Jesus refused to be deterred even by such a threat. He had a job to do.

In St. Luke's gospel, it is clear that when he speaks of Jesus going up to Jerusalem, he wishes to indicate more than the destination of a journey. He intends that we understand that Jesus was living through all those events that would bring about our salvation, events that would have their climax in Jerusalem in his death and resurrection.

After Jesus had proclaimed his own determination to fulfill his mission, a series of events occured that allowed Jesus to teach an important lesson. That lesson was the fact that Jesus demanded from his disciples the same kind of determination that he himself manifested. Apparently after he had left the region of the Samaritans, three men met him and expressed their wish to be among his disciples. What Jesus said to each of the men contains a vital teaching for us as modern-day disciples of Jesus.

To the first man, Jesus made it clear that discipleship involves extreme economic uncertainty. A disciple has to be prepared to undergo a renunciation similar to that of Jesus, who did not enjoy the ordered and serene existence of even vagrant animals. Christianity is not a form of social security. We cannot think that a comfortable economic status is one of the rewards of being faithful to God. Perhaps the opposite will be required of us.

The second man wanted to go first and bury his father—a reasonable request. Jesus told the man to let the dead bury their own dead. Precisely what Jesus meant by these words is by no means clear. They appear to be harsh and unreasonable. Probably the meaning is that for the disciple of Jesus, everything and everyone that could interfere with his call must be considered as dead, even his own parents. In other words, we cannot allow anyone or any consideration to stand in the way of fulfilling what Jesus asks of us.

To the third man, Jesus said that "whoever puts his hand to the plow but keeps looking back, is unfit for the reign of God." Jesus requires our undivided attention. Once we have declared our willingness to be his disciples, we must not turn aside to any other way of life.

Jesus wanted to make it clear that he was demanding even more than was asked of the people of the Old Testament. In the first reading today we saw that Elijah, though reluctantly, did allow his disciple, Elisha, to go back and take care of some of his affairs before following him. That kind of turning back, Jesus will not allow.

At first hearing, the words of Jesus are enigmatic. Jesus does not ask us to abandon our natural obligations, such as those we have toward parents or children. In other places, he clearly teaches that we must fulfill these obligations; in fact, he emphasized the need to love our neighbor. Even in today's epistle St. Paul reminds us: "The whole law has found its fulfillment in this one saying: you shall love your neighbor as yourself." Jesus knows that we have to earn a living, that we have to be concerned about many things of the world. He does not expect us to live in a kind of vacuum, cut off from the world of reality around us.

On the other hand, we must not water down the teaching of Jesus. We cannot live in such a way that we are really not any different from those people who profess no religion at all. Maybe we need to examine our consciences, to see what are those things that are keeping us back from being perfect disciples of Christ. Maybe we all need some thorough soul-searching, to determine what are the excuses we offer to Jesus for not following him completely. Let us hope that we can determine why it is that we do not always have the courage of our convictions.

This is a very personal, individual matter. The answer will be different for each one of us. But an answer we must find, since Jesus has called us to be his disciples without any looking back.

C.E.M.

**Fourteenth Sunday of the Year (A)**

## *"COME TO ME"* *

During these summer months, some of us travel great distances to be with friends whom we have not seen in some time. We do so because friendship is very precious and valuable. The Bible says in the Book of Sirach: "A faithful friend is a sturdy shelter; he who finds one finds a treasure; a faithful friend is beyond price; no sum can balance his worth" (Si 6:14f). Yes, friendship is very precious and valuable, but also how fragile. Perhaps we find when we visit someone who once was a very close friend that there is now little to say, when before no conversation seemed too long. Where we were always at ease, we feel awkward and uncomfortable. The old sparkle is gone forever. How seldom a friendship lasts a lifetime, or anything like a lifetime. More and more as we grow older, we tend to forget people who used to be so very important to us. We may send them a card at Christmas, if we can succeed in finding the address, and that is the extent of our contact. How good we were at making friends when we were young, but how bad at keeping them.

There is one friend who is always constant, always there when we need him, a friend who never fails us. That friend is Jesus. We think of Jesus in many ways, each with its value but also its limitation. Jesus is the Good Shepherd who has loving concern, but a shepherd has many sheep to look after. Jesus is the divine physician who can cure us of our spiritual ills, but a physician always has a large number of people waiting to see him in his office. Think now of Jesus as a friend, a personal friend, especially in the Eucharist. After all, he claimed that title for himself at the Last Supper when he instituted the Eucharist. He said, "You are my friends" (Jn 15:14). Today he asks us to accept his friendship with the beautiful invitation: "Come to me, all you who are weary and find life burdensome, and I will refresh you."

With a close friend you feel free to just drop in, for your friend is always available to you. Jesus wants us to think of him that way. Jesus with his infinite power and infinite love, makes himself infinitely available to us. Go to Communion during a Mass in a private home with only a few present, or go to midnight Mass in a huge cathedral with almost

---

* Based on a sermon by Msgr. Ronald A. Knox, "Jesus My Friend."

endless lines of people slowly moving toward the Communion stations—it makes no difference. In either case it is the same Jesus who says to you eagerly and lovingly, ''Come to me.'' He is there waiting for you like a person who has come to meet you at a crowded bus terminal, looking for that particular gait, that special way of holding yourself, which will single you out at a distance.

And do not complain that the friendship of Jesus feels unreal to you or impersonal, because he is hidden under the sacramental veils of the Eucharist. After all, what a sense of intimacy you feel from a friend's handwriting in a letter. You readily see through the veil of words on a page to the person of your friend. Even when you are with a friend, you are only hearing his voice and seeing his face. Voice and face are veils that hide the real person, and yet how easily you see behind those veils. In any true friendship it is the person you love, not external appearances. Though the veils change as the hair grows thin and grey and the face becomes lined and wrinkled, the real person is still the same—the person who is your friend.

If we had faith, real faith, the sacramental veils under which Jesus comes to us in Communion would lift and part; we would get a much greater sense of nearness to him under the appearance of bread than we get when we are with a friend under the token of voice and face. Nor need we feel that Jesus is but a distant friend, since he almost always remains silent. With a true friend, even silence can be filled with meaning and warmth.

In the responsorial psalm today, we reflected on what a good friend Jesus is: ''The Lord is gracious and merciful, slow to anger and of great kindness; the Lord is good to all and compassionate . . .; the Lord lifts up all who are falling and raises up all who are bowed down.'' And that same Lord says to us, ''Come to me, all you who are weary and find life burdensome, and I will refresh you.'' May our faith make us realize what a treasure we have in the Eucharist, for there waiting for us under the sacramental veils is Jesus, our friend.

C.E.M.

**Fourteenth Sunday of the Year (B)**

## A PROPHET WITHOUT HONOR ?

One of the most common failures of our human condition is that we tend to take things and people for granted, especially if they have become very familiar to us. A college professor once observed that students soon become bored with their regular instructors and fail to appreciate their scholarship. They either doze through their classes or skip them altogether, but flock with eagerness to hear the special lecture of an "expert." The expert need not be better informed or more astute than the members of the faculty. His appealing mark of distinction is that he is different.

One time when Jesus returned to his home town of Nazareth, he stood up to preach on the sabbath in the synagogue. He met with opposition because he failed to manifest any mark of distinction. The people did not complain that his message was shallow or inane. Actually, they were openly amazed at what he had to say. Their objection was based on the fact that he was too familiar to them. They could not accept this hometown boy turned prophet. They knew him as the village carpenter, the son of Mary, a woman they had seen coming and going like all the other women of the area. And now they heard Jesus speaking in their local synagogue with the Galilean accent which was characteristic of their own speech. Jesus perceived their negative reaction and summed it up by saying, "No prophet is without honor except in his native place, among his own kindred, and in his own house."

Is Jesus without honor, or at least proper honor, here in his own house, this church? We have heard the gospel so many times, we have become so familiar with the discourses, parables and miracles of Jesus that we run the risk of failing to appreciate it all. Sometimes we may even put more faith in the words of some magazine author or commentator on television, than we do in the words of Jesus Christ.

There is a real danger that we may take the entire Mass for granted. Even though the Mass in recent years has undergone a marvelous restoration through changes suggested by the profound scholarship of liturgical experts and introduced by the supreme authority of the Church, the "new" Mass is already becoming "old" and familiar to us. Actually the Mass should be a wonderful experience for us, but in order to make it such we need more than all the externals of celebration which may now surround it. We need individual, personal reflection. Let me offer a few suggestions, which I hope you will think about very carefully.

As you drive or walk to church, or in the few moments you may have before Mass begins, make the effort to impress on yourself what is about to happen. Say to yourself: "God is about to speak to me in the scriptures, and I will reply to God in the prayers and hymns. Jesus will make the great sacrifice of the cross truly present on the altar and he will give me the opportunity, with my fellow Catholics, to join with him in this offering to our Father. Then I will receive Jesus in Holy Communion as a pledge of my own resurrection as well as a means of strength to carry on until the day when he comes again." It will take you even less time to make this reflection than it takes me to say it now.

Then during Communion or when the Mass is over, spend a moment or two in thinking about what has happened, trying to realize that you must strive to live a life in accord with the teaching you have heard and in fulfillment of the offering you have made of yourself to God.

You may be thinking that it is easy for me as a priest to do all these things, because I live next door to the church and can get here in a matter of seconds, and because I don't have to get a whole family ready to come to Mass. That's all true. My point is that if you want to appreciate the Mass, you have to make an extra effort to do so. If you find you are always late for the 10:45 Mass, pretend that the Mass begins at 10:30. That will give you an extra fifteen minutes for the unexpected. While driving to church, instead of discussing what you are going to do *after* Mass, try to talk about what you are going to do *during* Mass. When you get to church a few moments early, having benefited from the extra fifteen minutes you allowed, you parents could remind the kids to settle back and think about the Mass—which can serve as a reminder to yourselves. And rather than being the first ones out of church, take just a little time to think about what has happened and how you should try to live through the day and the week coming up. And it would be a great idea to talk about that on the way home in the car.

The Mass, however simple and familiar it may be, is just too important to take for granted. Jesus and his Mass should not be without honor either here in his house, the church, or in our minds and hearts.

C.E.M.

**Fourteenth Sunday of the Year (C)**
Suggested use: Fourth Eucharistic Prayer

# THE WORK OF DISCIPLES

Last Sunday in the gospel, we heard Jesus tell us that he expects much from his followers. He told us that we must be prepared to undergo economic uncertainty and that we cannot let any consideration stand in the way of our Christian duties. In today's gospel we saw Jesus sending the seventy-two disciples to carry out his work.

There is a sense of urgency in the words of Jesus, "The harvest is rich, but the workers are few." Jesus knew at that moment that in the plan of the Father he was to have a limited amount of time on this earth. He knew that his followers would have to carry on his work after his death and ascension into heaven. He yearned to have all men come into his kingdom. He saw how much work remained to be done, and he realized that too few people would be willing to take up the work. When he said that the harvest was indeed great, he was thinking not only of the people of Palestine in his own time, but of people of all times and places. Yes, there is a certain urgency in the words of Jesus: "The harvest is rich." There is also in his words an implicit plea: "The workers are few." He is today asking all of us to be his workers.

Too often in the past, lay people have been willing to leave to priests and sisters the work of spreading the good news of Jesus. Of course it is true that priests and sisters have a special obligation, but lay people are to be among the laborers of Christ.

Let me call your attention to these words of the Vatican II *Decree on the Laity:* "Incorporated into Christ's Mystical Body through baptism and strengthened by the power of the Holy Spirit through confirmation, the laity are assigned to the apostolate by the Lord himself" (3). The day you were baptized, you became part of the family of God, the Church. As you know, in a family everyone has to work together. It is true that a baby is pretty much on the receiving end. But as children grow older, they should learn to take upon themselves some of the responsibility for the smooth, happy running of the home. Older brothers and sisters should help their parents, and should even look after the younger members of the family. A time comes when children can really cooperate with their parents. And it is a beautiful thing to see adult brothers and sisters helping one another. Your baptism brought you into God's family; you must take up serious responsibilities in the Church.

A mature person does not think only of himself. You received the Holy Spirit at confirmation so that you could be concerned with the spiritual good of others. Today in the Eucharistic Prayer, you will hear these words: "And that we might live no longer for ourselves but for him, he sent the Holy Spirit from you, Father, as his first gift to those who believe, to complete his work on earth. . . ." Yes, in confirmation you received the Holy Spirit to help to complete the work of Christ on this earth.

The Vatican Council, in its document on the laity, has given some general directives as to how you are to carry on the work of Christ. Please listen carefully to these words which are addressed to you: "There are innumerable opportunities open to the laity for the exercise of their apostolate of making the gospel known and men holy. The very testimony of their Christian life, and good works done in a supernatural spirit, have the power to draw men to belief and to God" (6). No one can deny the power of good example. Just the way you live can do more good than many sermons and many books.

But good example, however powerful, is not enough. The Council document goes on to say, "An apostolate of this kind does not consist only in the witness of one's way of life; a true apostle looks for opportunities to announce Christ by words addressed either to non-believers with a view of leading them to faith, or to believers with a view to instructing and strengthening them and motivating them toward a more fervent life" (6). For some reason, a lot of Catholics seem reluctant to talk about their faith. How different are others, such as Jehovah's Witnesses, who appear to have such a burning zeal as to be offensive to some people. Of course, we do not want to be obnoxious zealots, but I do think we could borrow a little of their enthusiasm.

Today you, as a baptized and confirmed Catholic, should give serious consideration to what you can and should be doing to help spread and solidify the religion of Jesus Christ. And you should pray that you may respond to the strength of the Holy Spirit given to you in your confirmation. Jesus says to you, "The harvest is rich, but the workers are few." Will you respond to his plea for help?

C.E.M.

**Fifteenth Sunday of the Year (A)**

## *HEED WHAT YOU HEAR*

Today's gospel is unusual in that Jesus is presented as giving his own explanation of the parable—something we ordinarily have to figure out for ourselves. Following this lead, let us together try to heed what he has said by reflecting on the implication of his teaching for us today.

Jesus says that the seed is the word of God. What is this word of God? You hear it every Sunday during Mass—in the lessons, the gospel, and even in the homily. This word of God is like the rain which falls from heaven; it is meant to produce fruit, to have an effect. God's word is not mere entertainment or diversion. If you watch a program on TV, there is nothing you have to do about it—just sit back passively and enjoy the program or flip the channel button until you find something you like. To God's word, however, we must respond and we must never "turn it off."

Jesus visualizes several different forms of response to God's word. First are those people who let the devil take the word of God out of their hearts. They give in to his temptation to think that the Church is out of date, old-fashioned, irrelevant—that what the Church teaches no longer applies to us today. Then there are people who hear something at Mass and they say, "Now that really is a good idea. I certainly ought to do that." But as soon as they walk out the front door of the church, they forget all about the good idea they heard. Next are people who get so caught up in the cares and riches and pleasures of this life, that deep down they prefer all these things to God. They want their heaven on earth: no suffering, no mortification, no trouble, no pain. Finally, there are those who listen to God's word and respond by applying it to themselves in an effort to lead a life like that of Jesus. A good example of a man who listened to God's word and responded to it is St. Paul. God's word changed his whole life, shaped his outlook and influenced his behavior. It gave him a profound view of life, as we heard in the second reading when he said, "I consider the sufferings of the present to be as nothing compared with the glory to be revealed in us."

What must you do to hear God's word with profit? To put it simply, the first thing you must do is to be in church on time for the liturgy of the word, the first half of the Mass. In fact, the *Constitution on the Sacred*

*Liturgy* of Vatican II strongly urges priests "that when instructing the faithful they insistently teach them to take their part in the entire Mass" (56). Secondly, you should realize the value and importance of God's work. As Jesus said in the gospel, "I assure you, many a prophet and many a saint longed to hear what you hear but did not hear it." Your appreciation of God's word should move you to try to see how the word of God applies to you personally, and what you can do about it. As the homilist, I am supposed to help you to do this, but all I can do is help. You must take responsibility yourself. Please let me be plain and blunt about this matter. You should not sit here in church and apply what you hear to others, rather than to yourself. If, for example, you hear something about the need for patience, don't nudge your spouse to imply that what is being said applies to him or her and not to you. And please do not protest that a priest certainly has a lot of gall talking about something when he is just as guilty as anybody else. No priest in his right mind pretends that he is perfect, or that he has no need to practice what he preaches. If a priest happens to touch some nerve of prejudice, especially in the area of war or race relations or social justice, try not to get your defenses up. If you do honestly feel that the priest is preaching merely his own opinions and not the word of God, do not complain to someone else about him. Take the trouble to go to the priest himself and try to get things clarified. Above all, remember that the word of God is intended to produce fruit in your life.

Actually, your response should begin right here at Mass. The *Constitution on the Sacred Liturgy* states that "the two parts which, in a certain sense, go to make up the Mass, namely the liturgy of the word and the eucharistic liturgy, are so closely connected with each other that they form but one single act of worship" (56). What you hear in the word should become a motive for your worship of God. When the word shows how good God is, you should want to express your love for him. When the word shows that God is our Savior, you should want to thank and praise him. When the word reminds you that you must keep God's commandments, you should want to express your sorrow for having failed. When the word reveals that God has love and concern, you should want to turn to him in confidence to ask for what you need.

Jesus concluded his parable about the seed with an exhortation that applies to us today, especially within the context of the Mass: "Let everyone heed what he hears."

C.E.M.

**Fifteenth Sunday of the Year (B)**

## *CHANGE AND PERMANENCE*

Within the past thirty years or so, more profound changes have occurred than in all of previous recorded history. These changes have affected people's way of living, moral and social values, education, communications—virtually every phase of human existence. Even our language changes radically because of the constant introduction of new words as well as a new meaning given to old words. If William Shakespeare were to come to the United States today, he would be able to understand only five out of every nine words in our vocabulary. The greatest writer of the English language would be semi-illiterate.

The speed of change is so great that nothing in our society seems stable or reliable. This modern phenomenon takes its toll on all but the young. The constant need to adjust and keep up with the times taxes the mind as well as the body, with the result that many people live in an unrelenting state of anxiety and confusion.

Perhaps without realizing it, we look for something that has not changed, something familiar and comforting. For many of us that means our faith, our religion. One thing we always used to hear about the Catholic Church was that it could not change. And yet in the Church too, we have seen a lot of changes in recent times—in the Mass for example, and even in some of our practices, such as Friday abstinence. How can the supposedly unchangeable Church be changing so much? The explanation lies in the fact that the Church remains the same in essentials and changes only in incidentals. Though some people easily confuse incidentals with essentials, we can readily see that there is a real difference between them. We ourselves throughout life remain the same essentially and change incidentally. When we were conceived in our mother's womb, we were only a tiny, single cell. That cell began to divide and multiply, and then one day we were born. We began to grow and to develop, so that today we are very different from what we were the day we were born. Through all these incidental, though rather significant changes, we each remain the same person. There is something about a person which makes him who he is, and it is that essential something which cannot change.

The same is true of the Church. It changes in incidentals and remains the same in essentials. For instance, in today's gospel we saw Jesus send the apostles out to preach the need for repentance. Today the Church still preaches that need for repentance. Repentance means a turning away from sin and turning toward God. The Church no longer commands Friday abstinence as an expression of repentance, because the form is incidental. Rather, she encourages greater charity and prayer as a form of repentance, because that seems better suited to our times and needs.

The Church continues to proclaim the essential message we heard in today's second reading. God the Father has chosen us to become his children, freed from sin by the blood of Jesus Christ and sealed by the power of the Holy Spirit, who is our bond of union with the Father and each other. As the family of God, we are called to praise and thank God by means of the Eucharistic Sacrifice for all his wonderful goodness towards us. That sacrifice was first offered by Jesus himself at the Last Supper in Aramaic. Then it was offered in Greek, later in Latin and other languages. Today we offer the very same sacrifice in English. The language of the Mass is incidental. It is what *happens* at Mass that is essential, and that has remained the same down through the centuries.

In a sense, the Church is like an old home in which a family has lived for generations. One day, the head of the family decides that the old home needs a little updating. He begins to paint the whole house, put in electricity and install modern plumbing. During the renovation the family continues to live in the home, and it proves to be a trying time. Everybody is disturbed by the inconvenience, and some think it was all a big mistake. It would have been better, they feel, to have left the old house the way it was, or even to have abandoned it and moved to a new place. Then one day the renovation is complete. Only then is every member of the family convinced that the father had the right idea, that all the inconvenience was more than worth it. The Second Vatican Council initiated a renovation in the Church which is still going on, and will continue. Some people persist in saying that it was all a mistake, that they should have left the Church the way it was, even if it was old-fashioned. Still others have abandoned the Church entirely. But it was the Holy Spirit himself who actually made the decision to update the Church in incidentals while keeping it the same in essentials.

Amid all the uncertainties and anxieties brought on by a too rapidly changing world, we have something that is truly stable and reliable;

something that can continue to give meaning and purpose to life; something which is essentially the same as it was almost two thousand years ago when it came from Jesus Christ himself, and will remain essentially the same until Jesus Christ comes again in glory. That something is our Catholic religion.

C.E.M.

**Fifteenth Sunday of the Year (C)**

# THE GOOD SAMARITAN

The parable of the good Samaritan breathes forth a spirit of bigness, and yet it was occasioned by a question that betrayed a certain pettiness. The lawyer asked Christ, "Teacher, what must I do to inherit everlasting life?"

If the lawyer had heard very much of our Lord's preaching, he had certainly missed the point. Apparently, the lawyer hoped that salvation could be achieved once and for all by doing some single thing. Jesus' preaching had been an effort to overcome a naïve legalistic approach to religious life. He emphasized that one's whole life in every aspect had to be tuned to God, that one's attitude was more important than any single act. And so in the answer Jesus gave, derived indeed from the Old Testament, we hear an epitome of the *spirit* of the law that should color everything that one does: love God completely and love your neighbor as yourself. Jesus' point was that a person does prepare himself for eternal life by performing any single work, great or small, but that he does so by living his whole life in accord with the law of love.

The lawyer was not satisfied with the answer, which he seemed to consider as too general. He wanted to get down to specifics. He wanted a nice, neat limit within which he would fulfill his obligations. His question, "And who is my neighbor?" was petty, small. The answer in the parable demanded bigness, generosity.

The parable meant to say that everyone is our neighbor, not just the people we live with, not just the people we like. Jews and Samaritans hated each other. The lawyer was a Jew, and so he thought of Samaritans as heretics, traitors, worthless scum, incapable of doing any good at all. The fact that the Samaritan was the hero of the story, and not the Jew, gave a special bite to it as far as the lawyer was concerned. It was a story of the least likely person showing love to someone he was supposed to despise. The point was painfully clear: there are no limits as to whom the law of love must be applied. The teaching is easy to understand, but hard to put into practice.

Maybe we have some subconscious objections to taking the parable of the good Samaritan in a literal way. In these days if you come across a person in apparent distress on a highway, you think twice before you stop. After all, it might be a plot by robbers to get you to stop so that they can take you for all you have, and leave you as the one beaten and bleeding along the road. Law enforcement officers have warned people not to pick up hitchhikers; you never know what they may turn out to be. We live in an age of violence. Besides violence at home, there is war and the threat of war abroad. What can we do about it?

Maybe, like the lawyer, we would like a nice, neat answer: some one specific thing we can do. But the attitude, the atmosphere that each one of us can create by the way in which we try to live the law of love, can make the difference. One time I asked a professor of history why it was that war has always been a part of human history, and why today especially there seems to be so much violence in our society. I expected some profound explanation that might involve complicated economic and political factors, or something like that. All he said was that I was asking the wrong question. The real question is why are there squabbles even within a family. He seemed to be implying that it all starts with something like the Cain and Abel incident in the Bible, brother against brother.

And so, it gets down to something we have heard before: charity begins at home. As individuals, each one of us can feel pretty helpless in the face of violence, hate, racism, prejudice and war itself. What can one person do? We must begin at home, not in the sense that we limit our love to those near and dear to us—that would be contrary to the parable today. Rather, charity begins at home in the sense that thereby we can hope to create a better climate all around us. I firmly believe that we will never have true thoughtfulness and kindness outside the home, until there is thoughtfulness and kindness within the home. This may seem a small way of coping with a big problem of hatred in our world, but if everyone thinks that what he does means nothing, then indeed nothing will be done.

Someone has commented that the good Samaritan in the parable represents Christ himself. Whether that be correct or not, it is true that Jesus found the human race in bad shape, like a man beaten and lying on the roadside near death. He came to our rescue, and gave the supreme example of love, an example we are celebrating in this Mass. That is the example we are all called to imitate.

C.E.M.

**Sixteenth Sunday of the Year (A)**

## *WHITE HATS AND BLACK HATS*

The old-fashioned Western movies have always enjoyed popularity; and despite the realistic trend in films, I suppose their popularity will continue as the old Westerns reappear on television's early or late show. One thing you have to say for the old Westerns, is that they were nice and simple in their approach to life. You knew just where everybody stood. The good guy always wore a white hat, rode a beautiful white horse, and sported two pearl-handled six-shooters which never seemed to need reloading. The bad guy always wore a black hat, rode a scraggly black horse, and had to struggle along with a single, dirty-looking gun which always ran out of bullets just in time to save the good guy.

Though the apostles obviously never saw an American-made cowboy movie, they wanted the same simplistic approach to life. They thought of Jesus and themselves as the good guys, and the scribes and Pharisees as the bad guys. They wanted Jesus to ride up on his white horse and wipe out all the scribes and Pharisees in one great burst of righteousness. Jesus in his wisdom had a completely different outlook, and in today's parable he tried to move his apostles to share that outlook. The wheat represented good people, and the weeds, bad people. The weeds to which Jesus referred were of a species that was indistinguishable from wheat until both were full grown. A farmer who tried to rid his field of wheat before harvest time ran the serious risk of destroying some of the wheat along with the weeds. A prudent man waited until harvest time. The point was clear. The apostles were not to make judgments about the goodness or badness of people, not even about the scribes and the Pharisees. A very important point too, which the parable cannot exemplify, is that whereas weeds can never become wheat, bad people can become good. And as a matter of fact, one Pharisee that we know of, Nicodemus, became a follower of Christ. The apostles, like Jesus himself, were to be concerned not with the destruction of people but with their conversion.

As we study the gospels, it becomes very clear that Jesus was intolerant of intolerance. He forgave the woman taken in adultery; he accepted the repentance of Mary Magdalene; and he made an apostle of Matthew, who had been a religious outcast because of his profession as a tax collector. But he excoriated the self-righteous, who thought of themselves as just and despised others. Even in this parable of the weeds and the wheat, addressed though it is to the apostles themselves, there is an undertone of rebuke, for Jesus implies that to judge others before God does so is foolish, as foolish as trying to pull up the weeds before the day of harvest.

I don't think it unnecessary to say that this parable applies to us as well as to the apostles. For example, one of the most diabolically inspired movements in our day is the one which pretends that there is nothing wrong with abortion. The Vatican Council in one of its rare condemnations spoke of abortion as an "unspeakable crime" (*The Church in the Modern World*, 51). We cannot condone the taking of innocent human life simply because it has not yet been born, and we must oppose abortion as we would any other form of murder. Despite all this, we have no right to judge the consciences of the pro-abortionists, nor must we ask God to destroy these people in order to rid the world of the evil of abortion. God wills to let these people continue in the world "until the harvest time"—to give them a chance.

Getting perhaps closer to home, it may be that a close friend or a member of the family or a priest we have known has left the Church. It is not our business to conclude that such people are weeds in the sight of God. We just can't be sure. And looking at the same problem from another angle, can we say that we ourselves always have the certain, evident sign of being wheat? Is it not true that we begin every Mass with an admission that we are sinners, that we have failed in our thoughts and in our words, in what we have done and in what we have failed to do? I don't know how you feel about it, but I for one am very glad that I will be judged, not by my fellow men, but by the God described in the second reading, a God who judges with clemency and who permits repentance for sins.

It would be nice if life were as simple as the old Western movies made it out to be, but it is not. There is some good and some bad in all of us, something to make us look like wheat and something to make us look like weeds. Judgment we must leave to God, when he comes for his harvest at the end of the world.

C.E.M.

## Sixteenth Sunday of the Year (B)

## *COME AND REST*

Modern day means of communication are nothing short of fabulous. In a matter of seconds we can know not only what is happening on the other side of the world, but even on the moon itself. It is almost impossible to realize that we have actually seen live television pictures from so far out in space. Yes, modern means of communication are fabulous, and yet they pose a threat to each one of us. With their ever-present stimuli through sight and sound, they can be detrimental to much-needed peace and quiet.

The result is that while we are rushing to keep up with a world moving at terrific speed, we may in our haste just pass by the whole meaning and purpose of life because we have almost no time to think. We may look back with smiles on another, simpler generation of Americans who had little better to do on a hot, July evening than sit on the front porch, rocking back and forth in a favorite chair, trying to catch a breath of fresh air outside a stuffy, un-air-conditioned house. Whether the people of that never-to-return era used their time well, we do not know, but at least they had the opportunity for a little peace and quiet, a precious opportunity which we all need desperately to create for ourselves.

The communications media can do more than simply destroy an opportunity to think. They can and often do exercise a tremendous influence over our value judgments. Consider for a moment the many commercials to which we are exposed and which are so much a part of contemporary life. It is generally agreed that advertising is a necessary element in a competitive economy. Its honest purpose is to supply a choice among products, but many commercials are unabashedly designed to create desire rather than satisfy needs. In their pitch, they frequently rely on base human motivation, as we see sex exploited, social status exalted, and economic advancement canonized. The average American is exposed to about 560 commercial messages every day, most of which are calculated to make him dissatisfied with what he has, and to induce him to want the new, the bigger, the better product. To be open about it, most commercials cater to gross selfishness.

Consider now in contrast, how little time is dedicated to God here in church. Sunday Mass absorbs about fifty minutes once a week—less time than most of us spend in listening to the radio each day and vastly less time than most of us consume in front of the television set every evening. Is it any wonder that we don't remember from week to week what we have heard in the scriptures at Mass? Should we be surprised if even an occasionally good homily has little or no effect on our lives? The word of God faces unfair competition for our attention.

The communications media have a potential for good. We can and should derive benefit from them by way of entertainment and information. The point is, we need an antidote to counteract their potential poison. Today's gospel is not without a suggestion. We saw Jesus, surrounded by a large crowd of people, say to his apostles, "Come by yourselves to an out-of-the-way place and rest a little." No one had a more important and urgent mission than did Jesus, and yet he knew that important things cannot be accomplished without peace of mind, that even urgent matters cannot be handled properly without reflection.

Battered as we are by almost ceaseless noise and distraction, we run the risk of wandering aimlessly through life like sheep without a shepherd. Subtly influenced by commercials, to which we would like to think we pay but scarce attention, we may be nurturing selfishness rather than rooting it out. We need to de-stimulate our senses, to lessen the constant flow of sound and images into a weary brain. We must not be afraid of silence, as we force ourselves to turn off the radio, the stereo, the television, and put down our newspapers and magazines—at least during *some* time of the day. We don't have to play the radio *every* time we get into the car. We don't have to have the TV on *all* evening. We must search for solitude and an opportunity to think and pray. Alone with God, we should ask ourselves where we are going, what we are trying to accomplish, whether we are using the principles taught by Jesus to solve our problems and shape our opinions. Life is too short to live so much of it in a state of distraction.

The Lord is our Shepherd who wishes to lead us in right paths (responsorial psalm). To follow the Lord, we have to be able to hear him. From time to time at least, we have to deliberately and of set purpose tune out the noise and distractions of our communications media so that we can tune in to the voice of the Good Shepherd.

C.E.M.

### Sixteenth Sunday of the Year (C)

## *JESUS SANCTIFIED HUMAN LIFE*

When Angelo Roncalli became Pope John XXIII, an amazing thing took place. His delightful humor, his obvious affection for people of all ages and cultures, his dignified yet earthy humanity won not only the respect but the love of Catholics and non-Catholics alike. Stories that indicated his humor and humanity circulated rapidly. Maybe you remember that he was supposed to have been asked, "How many people are working in the Vatican?" and he answered with a twinkle in his eye, "About half of them."

Pope John showed the whole world that being Pope had not divorced him from everyday-type living. It may surprise you to hear that in being so very human, the Pope was only imitating his master, Jesus Christ. Maybe our image of Jesus is of an awesome man, somewhat aloof, and with perhaps a distant, idealistic look in his eyes. We must remember that the Son of God became a true human being, like us in everything but sin. As a true human being, he entered into all the aspects of daily living and made them holy. Jesus showed us that holiness has to do with *everything* in life.

Wishing to emphasize the true humanity of Jesus, the Fathers of the Vatican Council stated, "By his incarnation the Son of God has united himself in some fashion with every man. He worked with human hands, he thought with a human mind, acted by human choice, and loved with a human heart. . . . He blazed a trail, and if we follow it, life and death are made holy and take on a new meaning" (*The Church in the Modern World*, 22).

The gospel today highlights a Jesus who is friendly, charming and witty, a Jesus with a human heart. Jesus had become a very close friend of Lazarus and his two sisters, Martha and Mary. Their home in Bethany was a place where Jesus went with apparent frequency to relax from the ardors of his ministry and the vile attacks of the scribes and Pharisees. Jesus had dropped by one evening. Martha got a little excited because she wanted to fix a nice dinner for Jesus. Mary, the younger sister, was so happy to see Jesus that all she wanted to do was sit and talk. Martha probably shot some mean looks at Mary to make her realize that she should be helping in the kitchen. When Mary refused to take the hint, Martha spoke up, "Lord, are you not concerned that my sister has left me all alone to do the household tasks? Tell her to help me." Martha's words indicate that she was on very friendly terms with Jesus. Suppose you had some mere acquaintance to your home for dinner. Could you imagine yourself talking to him the way Martha spoke to Jesus? You would speak that way only to a close friend.

The response of Jesus shows that he knew Martha very well. Actually he chided her for being something of a fuss-budget, like Lucy in the *Peanuts* comic strip, but he did so with perfect good humor. The way he repeated her name, "Martha, Martha," tells us that he was smiling at a friend whose excesses and little failings were known to him. Jesus told her that he was more interested in their company than in having a fine dinner, and that even one dish would be sufficient.

St. Luke, more than the other evangelists, shows us a Jesus full of human feeling and understanding. He shows us a Jesus who, in the words of the Fathers of the Vatican Council, "worked with human hands, thought with a human mind, acted by human choice, and loved with a human heart."

On a more profound level, this gospel reveals an even deeper appreciation of the human. In the Jewish society of the day, women had but little to do with religion. A woman could not be the disciple of a rabbi, since only men were considered intelligent enough to understand the law. Jesus put the lie to that outlook by inviting Martha to be what Mary already recognized she could be, his disciple. Jesus treasured both Martha and Mary as he did Lazarus, for all were called equally to be children of God.

We know that here at Mass, we are to offer ourselves with Jesus in sacrifice to the Father. It is easy to remember to offer the big things, the difficult things. Today we are reminded that we must also offer the simple, even pleasant, things to God. We must not put religion into one little isolated compartment, having to do merely with duties and obligations and formal prayer. If we try to live every moment of our lives in imitation of Jesus and in union with him, then "life and death will be made holy and will take on a new meaning."

C.E.M.

**Seventeenth Sunday of the Year (A)**

## *PROSPECTING, CHRISTIAN STYLE*

Many prospectors came to California in the gold rush of 1849. Any one of them could have related to today's parable of the treasure in the field. The prospector was a man who had reached an important decision which influenced his whole life. He was willing to risk everything on the possibility of hitting a gold strike which would make him a wealthy man. It was a decision that required sacrifice and steadfastness.

Let's trace in imagination the history of one of these prospectors. The first thing he did was to decide that he was going to base his whole future on the hope of finding gold in California. He sold his farm in the midwest and began the long journey across the Great Plains, through the tortuous passes of the Rocky Mountains, and over the Sierra Madre range into the Sacramento Valley. It was a difficult journey, with dangers from climate and hostile tribes. Many times, the prospector became discouraged and was tempted to turn back, especially as he came across the corpses of those who had succumbed to the weather or who had died in a gun battle along the way. But his hope of finding gold moved him to press on.

When he finally arrived in California, he had to spend long hours each day mining and panning for gold. From time to time he grew so tired and weary, that he would squander his meager earnings on a wild evening in the local tavern. The next morning, however, his terrible hangover convinced him of his foolishness and he realized that he had much work to do before he could really relax. On one occasion he became so disappointed by continued failure, that he went into town and spent several weeks in drinking and card playing. All the while he failed to work his claim. Eventually he remembered his yearning for gold, and he started all over again. After more years of many disappointments, he struck a rich vein. His dream became a reality because ultimately he stuck to his fundamental decision.

Our lives as Catholics are not unlike that of the prospector. God has called us to share in the divine life of his Son (second reading), a calling given us in our Baptism. Our aim is to find the gold of eternal life. Somewhere in life, however, we must make a firm decision that we are going to work toward the complete fulfillment of God's call, so that we may indeed enjoy eternal life with him in heaven. Our purpose is to achieve something much more precious and lasting than even the finest gold. We really have to make up our minds about that. It is a long, difficult journey through life until we reach our goal. We may become discouraged along the way. From time to time, we will grow tired and weary and squander our spiritual strength on foolish things—nothing too serious perhaps—small sins of selfishness, impatience, laziness. Maybe one day we even go so far as to begin to give up on God. We may be led to such a state because of a sudden death of a loved one, a severe financial setback, or perhaps a strong temptation to violate our sexual commitment as married people or our status as single people. A serious sin for us is doing what the prospector did as he failed to work his claim for several weeks. But deep down the prospector did not really want to abandon his desire to find gold, as was shown by the fact that he did start all over again—just as we, despite serious failures at times, do not really want to abandon God. After serious sin we have to start all over again.

All sin gets in the way of fulfilling our real purpose in life. Small sins waste our time and inhibit our progress. Because of our weakness as human beings, some small sins are inevitable, but we must still work with God's help to eliminate them. Serious sin should not be a part of our lives at all, because serious sin not only prevents us from going forward but also points us in a false direction. It clouds our vision and may one day turn us completely away from the treasure we are seeking. Most important of all, we must let nothing, absolutely nothing, change our purpose in life. Because sin is a reality, we must make sure that our commitment to God is firm. Solomon, as we read in the first lesson, prayed for an understanding heart so that he could fulfill his call from God to govern his people. We must pray for a realization of our true end in life, and for the help we need to persevere in reaching that end.

Today's responsorial psalm gave us the right attitude. We prayed these words: "I have said, O Lord, that my part is to keep your words. The law of your mouth is to me more precious than thousands of gold and silver pieces. . . . For I love your command more than gold, however fine. For in all your precepts I go forward; every false way I hate." Jesus did not hesitate to present our final reward as a motive for perseverance, as he spoke of the treasure in the field for which a man was willing to sell everything. We are prospectors, Christian style. If we keep our faith and hope in eternal life, more precious than the finest gold, we will find no sacrifice too great. And one day, our dream will become a reality as we strike the rich vein of eternal life.

C.E.M.

**Seventeenth Sunday of the Year (B)**

## SIGNS AND THE EUCHARIST

Today, we began the reading of the sixth chapter of the gospel according to St. John. Since the chapter is very long, seventy-one verses to be exact, the Church has divided it over five successive Sundays. Lengthy though the chapter is, it forms a whole, its theme being the need for faith in Jesus and in his promise of the Eucharist.

As the story begins, we see that Jesus was followed by a very large crowd as he came to the shore of the Sea of Galilee. Jesus had attracted the people because of the miracles he had been working for the sick—but as evening grew on, Jesus became aware of a very ordinary, practical problem. The people had nothing to eat, and for most of them a long journey back home still lay before them. Jesus took upon himself the responsibility of feeding the people. He did so in a miraculous way.

We should not get all involved in just how Jesus worked the miracle. Speculation on the manner of the miracle takes up where the gospel leaves off, for the gospel tells us what happened, not how. Moreover, though it is true that Jesus worked the miracle out of a motive of compassion for the crowd, his concern went deeper than their need for physical nourishment. Rather, he speaks of the miracle as a sign, something intended to make his readers think of a reality other than ordinary bread and physical nourishment. That something is the

Eucharist. St. John says that Jesus took the loaves of bread and "gave thanks." The Greek word he used for "gave thanks" was the very word which, even when he wrote the gospel, was already the name used for the Blessed Sacrament, "Eucharist." Also, St. John noted that the feast of the Passover was near. The notation is more than an indication of the time of the year, for the Passover feast was celebrated with a liturgical meal which was the memorial of the salvation of the Jews from slavery in Egypt. That liturgical meal was a prefigurement, a kind of preview, of the Eucharist. St. John presented the feeding of the five thousand, then, as a sign that Jesus wanted to feed his countless followers with a spiritual food in a memorial meal by means of the Eucharist.

On the day following the feeding of the five thousand, Jesus would make his first promise of the Eucharist. That promise would indeed be extraordinary, a real test of faith in Jesus. The miracle of the loaves was a sign well suited to prepare the people to hear these words of Jesus: "The bread that I will give is my flesh for the life of the world." As he used his power to feed five thousand people with only five loaves of bread, so he would use his power to change bread into his body to feed multitudes spiritually throughout the ages.

There was still another sign to follow. When the people realized what Jesus had done for them, they wanted to make him king—with the idea that with Jesus as their leader, they would never have to do a day's work again. He could go on feeding them miraculously. Jesus of course did not want to be that kind of a king, and so he hid from the people. His disciples guessed that he would eventually show up in Capernaum on the other side of the lake, his headquarters at the time, and so they got into their boat and started across the lake. When they had rowed three or four miles, to their utter amazement they sighted Jesus approaching the boat, walking on the water.

Walking on the water was another sign in preparation for the promise of the Eucharist, for Jesus showed that he had power over his own body, a power that he would use in making his body truly present under the appearances of bread. The next day, the people found out what had happened, because they knew that there was only one boat and that Jesus did not get into that boat, and yet had reached the other side. Undoubtedly they made inquiries, and it was then that they heard what Jesus had done.

As we shall see on a later Sunday, even these tremendous signs were not enough for most of the people to respond with assent to the promise of the Eucharist. Why they failed to accept the truth that Jesus would give his flesh to eat, we simply do not know. But the account of these two signs, the feeding of the five thousand and the walking on the water, has been recorded in the gospel to bolster our faith in this great mystery of our religion. But their proclamation in the gospel today should serve as an occasion for us to renew our faith in the Eucharist. We can make the words of today's responsorial psalm a beautiful expression of that faith: ''The hand of the Lord feeds us; he answers all our needs.'' The eyes of the faithful look hopefully to the Lord, and he gives the spiritual food of the Eucharist.

C.E.M.

## Seventeenth Sunday of the Year (C)

## *''TEACH US TO PRAY''*

During our Lord's life, one of his favorite spots for prayer was the Mount of Olives. On that site a Church has been erected called ''Pater Noster Church'' or simply ''The Church of the Our Father.'' In the arcade of the Church are thirty-two stone tablets upon which the words of the Our Father have been inscribed in thirty-two languages. It was possibly on the Mount of Olives that Jesus had been praying when his apostles came and asked him to teach them how to pray.

The apostles were perhaps looking for a precise formula to use in prayer, but it was not Jesus' intention to give them such. Rather, he wished to indicate to them the manner, the spirit, and the feeling they should have in prayer. The early Christians understood that it was the idea of the prayer that was important, and not the precise words.

The apostles were both surprised and amazed at Jesus' answer. They were surprised at the brevity of the prayer. They had observed how Jesus himself spent very long periods in private prayer. Naturally, they expected that he would possibly recite for them what he said in those extended periods of prayer. Also, at that time daily Jewish prayers were long and involved, comprising as many as eighteen benedictions. The apostles were amazed at the familiar term ''Father'' with which they were told to address God. It is true that the Jews thought of God as their

Father; but in the entire Old Testament, God is referred to as a Father on only fourteen occasions, and the Jews never dared to address him as such in prayer. In the first reading today, we saw how careful even Abraham was in pleading with God to spare Sodom and Gomorrah. Though he was bold in his approach to God, he was cautious not to appear brazen or impudent. Abraham did not use the term "Father" but only "Lord." You can imagine how the apostles must have felt when they were told that they were to be more familiar with God than even the great Abraham was!

Jesus used the Aramaic word *"Abba"* for "father." The English word simply does not have the same connotation. *"Abba"* was the word a little child used in speaking to his father. It was a homey, family-word. "Dear Father" comes close to the meaning, but perhaps our word "Dad" or even "Daddy" is closer. Jesus meant to show us the childlike trust we should have in prayer, no matter how old or sophisticated we may be. No wonder Jesus had such concern for little children. Only they can teach us the complete trust we must have in God; the absolute reliance on him; the tender, loving affection that should be ours.

The word, however, has more than a psychological implication. It expresses a great truth that God as our Father is the source of all our life, spiritual as well as physical. St. Paul, in the second reading today, speaking of baptism, wrote, "God gave you new life in company with Christ." In baptism, God truly became our Father. He gave us a share in the same life that his divine Son possesses in fullness from all eternity. And so when we pray, God sees in us the person of Jesus, and he can say of us, "This is my beloved Son in whom I am well pleased."

Whenever we pray, but especially here at Mass, we should realize that we are not praying alone—that Jesus is living and praying within us and that it is he who makes our prayer so pleasing and so effective.

The Church has used the "Our Father" in the Mass for a very long time. Its use is recorded in the *Didache*, a Christian book written before the year 100, but it was probably used in the liturgy even before the gospels themselves were written. A very ancient custom places the "Our Father" at the beginning of the Communion rite. This use was no doubt inspired by the petition, "Give us this day our daily bread." "Bread" is meant to include all of our necessities, but it signifies even more. Scripture scholars say that the word usually translated as "daily" really means "tomorrow." We are saying "Give us tomorrow's bread." But the word "tomorrow" among the Jews did not mean merely the next day, but also the "Great Tomorrow," the final consummation of God's plan for salvation.

In a Christian sense, the petition is a prayer for that divine food, the bread of life, that will bring us to eternal life. That bread of life is the Eucharist. It is the divine food which nourishes and increases the life of Jesus within us. It is the great gift from our loving Father in heaven, a gift which on the "Great Tomorrow" will bring us to the fullness of our union with Jesus in heaven as true children of God our Father.

How fortunate we are that we can "pray with confidence to the Father in the words our Savior gave us."

C.E.M.

## Eighteenth Sunday of the Year (A)

### SHADOWS AND REALITY

The story of how Jesus fed over five thousand people with five loaves and two fish is very familiar to all of us. Despite its familiarity, we may easily miss the point behind it. We can get all involved in just how Jesus worked the miracle, but speculation on the manner of the miracle takes up where the gospel leaves off—for the gospel tells us what happened, not how. Moreover, though it is true that Jesus worked the miracle out of a motive of pity for the crowds, his concern went deeper than their need for physical nourishment.

We have a key to how the early Church viewed the miracle, for St. Matthew describes Jesus' actions in terms which allude to the institution of the Eucharist: "He looked up to heaven, blessed, and broke the loaves." Even as we hear the words of the gospel, our minds should easily turn to the words of the consecration in the Mass. The point behind the gospel story, then, is that the feeding of the five thousand was a sign that Jesus wanted to feed his followers in a spiritual manner by means of the Eucharist.

Jesus is concerned with the totality of our lives, but his main objective is to direct us toward our spiritual destiny. That is what is uppermost in his mind for us. For example, we would be inclined to think that Jesus used bread and wine when he instituted the Eucharist, because bread and wine reminded him of that grace which he intended the Eucharist to give us. But, if you think about it, it was just the other way around. When God created the world, he gave common bread and wine, food and drink, for our use so that we might understand something of the Eucharist when it was instituted. God did not design the Eucharist to be something like bread, simply because bread came first in time. He designed bread to be something like the Eucharist, because the Eucharist came first in his intention.*

God knew what he was doing when he created. The end that he had in mind was our spiritual destiny, and it was that end which shaped his plans. What is true of bread and the Eucharist is true of our lives as a whole. As material bread is but a shadow of the real, spiritual food in the Eucharist, so our earthly lives are but a shadow of the real, spiritual life that God has called us to. Unfortunately, too often we view things the other way around. Those things which we can see and touch and weigh and measure appear to be real, whereas they are only shadows of what our lives are actually all about.

The deepest yearnings of the human heart can find fulfillment only in God. If we fail to have this spiritual perspective on life, we are bound to suffer the frustration of disillusionment. For example, some people just expect too much from love and marriage. Every marriage begins with the thrill of discovery. To love another person deeply and intimately, and to be loved in return, becomes an overwhelming preoccupation. But the ardent affection and strong personal attachment cannot last, for no human person, however wonderful, can fill up our intense need and longing for love. Human love is but a shadow of the reality of loving God and being loved by him. Indeed, human love can be a beautiful thing—but even its beauty is but a reflection of what can be with God. There is no need to be disappointed with the inevitable cooling of human emotion, or to think of marriage as a failure when the honeymoon does not last forever—provided we can keep in mind that everything human is but a shadow of spiritual destiny.

Think of what you will—the greatest accomplishment, the most exquisite pleasure, the highest honor—nothing human can really satisfy us. Only God can do that, and the sooner we realize it the happier and more purposeful our lives will become.

* From an idea by Msgr. Ronald A. Knox in his sermon, "Real Bread"—an idea which, I suppose, can neither be proved nor disproved.

Sin blocks our vision. It is like a huge black curtain before our eyes, hiding the bright spiritual meaning of life. Faith can lift that curtain. One reason we are here today is to pray for this faith, as we celebrate the Eucharist. God is patiently directing us through the shadows of this life toward the glowing reality of eternal life with him in heaven. How ardently we should pray for the faith to see the end which God himself has had in mind all along!

C.E.M.

## Eighteenth Sunday of the Year (B)

# *FAITH COMES FROM A HEARTY APPETITE*

Appetite has always been a barometer of health. When someone is "off his feed," he is not feeling too well. And more seriously, we worry when an elderly person or someone suffering from alcoholism doesn't feel like eating. Strength diminishes as the appetite does. But in a happier sense, picture the traditional joy of a mother feeding the "lumberjack" pangs of her growing children. And more than one bride (sharing a recipe with her mother-in-law) has become convinced that the way to a man's heart is through his stomach.

It's easy to suspect that the way to the Jewish hearts of the first century seems to have been through their stomachs. After multiplying bread, our Lord had an eager audience. But it was the kind of audience that's grabbing but not listening. And so our Lord gave the rebuff: have faith not in manna (which is looking to the past), nor in the luncheon loaves (with minimum strength for the present), but have faith in me, the Bread of Life.

The kindness of Christ's admonition for us today is that, in spite of our being somewhat unworthy, he trusts our motives and gives himself to us in Communion. He gives the gift that improves our motives and expands our appetite for him. Most of us are hungry for Christ and want what he has to offer. And this appetite for Christ is as good a way as any to describe faith. In the divine circle, the more we are hungry for Christ, the more fulfilling is the Eucharistic Bread. And the more satisfying our experience of Christ in Communion, the stronger our faith becomes, and the more frequently and fervently we seek Christ.

The saints with their hunger for Christ are much more satisfied and filled with the Eucharistic Lord than we are. We're not saints. We may even be at the zero point. We really need more faith, and are starving for it. Lost pilgrims or campers start out looking for directions, friends, and home. But as things get worse, their longing is simply for food. So after a while, if we're really bad off, our longing for identity, success and acceptance gives way to a simple longing for some permanent food: Christ. But we have to allow our hunger-faith appetite to grow. If we're not faith-hungry, then like a sick person we won't find Christ very appealing.

But how can we acquire a greater appetite for Christ? "Lay aside your former way of life and the old self which deteriorates through illusion and desire, and acquire a fresh, spiritual way of thinking. You must put on the new man. . . ." And put on the new man by having "faith in the one God has sent." We know faith in a friend comes and grows through experience together. We lean on him for support, share our problems—and in time, faith is there. It's the same with Christ. We ought to lean on him, share our burdens, communicate with him. Bad day at the office, noisy kids, uninterested parents ought to be shared. What better time than when we have co-union with Christ in the Eucharist? Our new man has burdens, and longs for Christ. So we share the load at Communion time with the Lord, and satisfy the longing for Christ by receiving the Eucharistic Bread. The more we share, the better the friendship. The more we eat, the greater the fulfillment of his presence. More friendship and greater fulfillment bring stronger faith.

The problem for many early listeners and prospective believers of Christ was that they had faith only in bread, not in him—just as their ancestors had faith in manna and quail, but not in the Father who provided the nourishment. Our Bread is bound to evoke stronger feelings of faith for us, since it is Christ himself. Better than discovering a diamond in a piece of rock, better than money found in a tin can, we find in the Eucharistic Bread Jesus Christ, God himself. And more than being an "eternal meal ticket," Christ is the friend to share the journey, remove hunger and thirst, and fulfill the appetite's wildest fancies. Give the Eucharist a try. The taste is divine.

M.M.R.

**Eighteenth Sunday of the Year (C)**

## *RICH IN THE SIGHT OF GOD*

One of the greatest longings each one of us feels is the desire for security. To look to the future and see old age coming inevitably, and to fear that perhaps there will be no security for that old age is indeed a frightening thought. It is not surprising that sooner or later we face the need of planning for the future, of trying to make sure that security will be ours, especially when we have passed the age of being able to hold a job and make a living. Advertisements for insurance, savings accounts and the like, all appeal to our deep instinct for security.

Jesus understood our yearning for security, and in today's parable he wished to put that yearning in proper perspective. The rich farmer of the parable could today be growing wheat in Kansas or corn in Iowa. A bumper crop forces him to tear down his available barns and build even larger ones. With all his possessions snugly laid away, he congratulates himself on a job well done. He has security. He has proved himself to be a prudent organizer, a good planner, a man respected in the community. And yet God calls him a fool.

What did the farmer do wrong? There is no sign that he was dishonest or that he cheated anyone or deprived them of what was rightfully theirs. What then was his mistake? He was greedy. Just before telling the parable, Jesus warned, ''Avoid greed in all its forms. A man may be wealthy, but his possessions do not guarantee him life.'' Greed leads a person to rely solely on material possessions for his security. It is the fault of the ''self-made'' man who thinks he holds his future in his own hands. He depends only on himself for his security, and that leads to a practical forgetfulness of God even though he may go to church regularly. He wants security in the future, but he does not look far enough into the future beyond the inevitable fact of death, to a security that only God can guarantee.

This kind of greed is not confined to the wealthy by any means. All of us can be guilty of it. Our society is such that it almost forces us to be preoccupied with the need for money and material possessions, no matter how we may fight its influence. The day-to-day struggle for survival in a competitive society can become all-absorbing. Certainly we have to work and to save, but we are sadly mistaken if we think that possessions will give us the kind of security we really need. No matter how much money we may have saved up, the time will come for God to say to us, "This very night your life shall be required of you." What of our security then?

The words of St. Paul in the second reading fill out the teaching of the gospel. St. Paul says, "Set your heart on what pertains to higher realms. . . . Be intent on things above rather than things of earth." Sound advice, but how do we put it into practice in the face of daily needs? Are we supposed to stop earning money and saving for the future? No, that is not the answer. Rather, it is the way we go about things, our attitude of mind, which makes the difference. Remember that the rich farmer in the parable had forgotten all about God and the real meaning of life. The only thing he was working for was security in this life. He did not look far enough into the future for his security.

Jesus wants us to respond to our instinct for security. He wants us to use it, however, to work for eternal life by becoming "rich in the sight of God." He wants us to stand before God and acknowledge that we are poor in the sense that every good thing comes from him, that without God we are spiritually bankrupt. One of the most important things about prayer is to say to God, "I can't go it alone. Without you, I can't do a thing. Help me." This is the very sentiment with which we will begin today's Eucharistic Prayer: "Father, you are holy indeed, and all creation rightly gives you praise. All life, all holiness comes from you. . . ." We must all mean the words of that prayer. We must beg God to lead us through this temporal life to eternal life. Then we can have the confidence that when we die, God will say, "You were wise indeed, for you grew rich in my sight." And that is eternal security.

C.E.M.

## Nineteenth Sunday of the Year (A)

### *A TINY WHISPER*

Shortly after six o'clock on the morning of Tuesday, February 9, 1971, all of Los Angeles awoke at the same time. It started with a slight, ominous rumble, followed by a terrifying rocking of the earth as if monstrous buffalo were stampeding across the land. The earthquake lasted less than a minute, but in an instant sixty-two persons were dead and millions of dollars of damage had been done. Two hospitals collapsed, and a freeway was tossed about like a plastic toy. That morning, many more prayers than usual were directed to heaven. There are no atheists in foxholes, and there are none in earthquakes, either. As Johnny Carson quipped on his show that night, "The meeting of the God-Is-Dead Society has been cancelled."

Of all natural calamities, earthquakes are probably the most terrifying. If there is a flood, you can get to higher ground. If a hurricane is coming, you can be warned to evacuate. But with an earthquake, when the very ground gives way beneath you, you feel completely helpless. It is not surprising to us if people turn to God during an earthquake, but it may be disappointing to God—if that is virtually the only time they pray. Prayer is not some last-ditch effort to ward off an impending evil. Prayer should be a seeking for God in all the circumstances of our lives, even the ordinary, simple ones.

This was a lesson that Elijah the prophet had to learn. Elijah thought of himself as a failure because he could not convert his people from idolatry. In his disappointment, he yearned to die because God seemed far from him. Then the Lord told him to go to the mountain because he, the Lord, would pass by. Seemingly, Elijah expected a marvelous manifestation. But he did not find God in a mighty wind, or a great fire, or even an earthquake. To his amazement, Elijah felt the divine presence in a breeze so gentle that it was like a whisper. Nothing could have been more simple and ordinary.

Peter had to learn much the same lesson. When he asked Jesus to let him walk on the water, he wanted him to suspend the laws of nature. He wanted a miracle as a sign that it was really Jesus whom he saw on the lake. But because his faith was not solid, neither was the water beneath his feet. He began to sink. Then he really prayed. Peter had made two mistakes. The first was to think that he could find Jesus only in a miracle. The second was to turn to Jesus in real prayer only when his life was threatened. Jesus did not commend Peter. Rather, he pointed out that his faith was very weak, so weak that he thought to turn to Jesus only in what was truly an extraordinary situation.

Do we need to learn this lesson about prayer? Isn't it true that when everything is going well for us, it is easy to forget about God? But just let some big problem arise—the grave illness of a loved one or a natural disaster like an earthquake—then we get serious about prayer. We have the feeling, "All we can do now is pray." That feeling betrays an attitude that prayer is but a last resort.

Jesus teaches us that prayer must be a habitual part of our life in all of its circumstances. A little child does not turn to his parents only when he is in big trouble. He is completely dependent on them and somehow knows that all good things come from them. He looks to his parents for food when he is hungry; he runs to them for comfort when he has skinned his knee or had his feelings hurt; he seeks solace from them when he is lonely and blue. Above all, he wants to feel that he belongs, that he has their love and interest all the time.

No matter how young or old we may be, in relation to God we are like little children, and God is a Father more loving and interested than even the best of human parents. He wants us to turn to him in prayer in all the circumstances of our lives, not merely when we are in big trouble.

In this Mass, as in every Mass, we pray to God for our needs. We express those needs especially in the Prayer of the Faithful. That is good, but it is not enough. Despite the greatness of the Mass, it does not exhaust our need for prayer. Every day must be filled with prayer, not memorized formulas or set phrases, but our own personal words—words like, "Father, help me to do your will, give me courage and strength, don't abandon me, protect me, lift me out of my depression and sadness." We don't even have to say the words out loud; a tiny whisper within our hearts will do.

Above all, we should not need something like an earthquake to shake us into a realization of our need for prayer. If we remember that God is our Father and we are his children, we will turn to him in prayer in all the circumstances of our lives.

C.E.M.

## Nineteenth Sunday of the Year (B)

### *FOOD FOR TRAVELING*

Funerals are obviously difficult times in anyone's life. Especially so for a priest or minister who hopes in some way to console the family of the deceased. Psychologists try to soften the professional burden by suggesting that it doesn't matter too much what you say to the family. Their shock doesn't allow much listening. What does help is that the concerned priest is present to share some of the grief. But while this may be true of a shocked family (not hearing specific words), a counselor wants to be saying something, not just at a funeral, but whenever death comes up.

Fortunately and blessedly, a priest can simply say "Christ is life." Death is the lonely step seen from our end of the dark valley. But for the dead person, this is the grandest step of his life. And the ease of counselling almost doubles, if the person has been able to attend Mass regularly and has received the Eucharist. "I am the bread from heaven. If anyone eats this bread he shall live forever."

Our Lord's listeners certainly understood the literalness of his words. What they questioned was how could such claims be made by a hometown boy. Many men have dreamed of immortality, but no one before or after Christ claimed to be food for eternal life.

A short time ago, two seventh grade CCD students were asked to "role play" the following situation. "John, your best friend Mark was absent from school. A few days later, someone says that Mark was killed in an auto accident in the north. That afternoon you're walking around the shopping center, sad over the loss of your friend, when suddenly you see him—live as can be, standing by a counter. The real story is that Mark went to see his grandmother. The family had a car accident. No one was hurt. All are home now. But you don't know this. All you know is that Mark is dead, but you see him standing there. Now, what do you say to him?"

After stammering and smiling, each of the boys found it very hard to play the role. The whole class found it too hard to do realistically: meeting someone you thought had died. It is hard to imagine life after death. This explains why faith in the resurrection is somewhat difficult. But taking another approach, science tells us that energy can't be annihilated. Its form may change, but it is still around. The human body and personality, with its detectable electrical and chemical energy, when it faces death faces a change in its form, but not a destruction of its energy. Christ simply frees us from chemical terms, and suggests to us what this life is about.

The Lord knew what he was talking about. In his own death and resurrection, Christ demonstrates the power of the Eucharist to carry us through life and death to our resurrection. With the real presence of Christ, the Eucharist contains the God of Ages, the Lord of Life. And in receiving Communion early in life, we receive the seed of immortality. Through the years we begin to live the resurrection, growing day by day, year by year until its full unfolding at our death.

But this process of eternal life isn't automatic. Paul tells us we can slow down this ascent to life. Bitterness, passion, anger, harsh words, not only ''kill'' others but stunt our growing and can even suffocate the life within us. So we have to be careful to feed this life with the Eucharistic Bread and keep a road map in mind for where this life is taking us. Fortunately, we're not looking for broom trees and death; we're traveling to find the Father. And no one has seen the Father except Christ. So our Lord knows what we need. He eagerly gives us the bread to carry on our journey to the Father. And happily, the Eucharist carries us far beyond forty days. It carries us on to the end and the beginning beyond. Taste, and with the coming of death, see the goodness of the Lord.

M.M.R.

## Nineteenth Sunday of the Year (C)

Suggested Use: Long Form of the Letter to the Hebrews; First Eucharistic Prayer.

## *A LEAP INTO THE ARMS OF GOD*

Flames from his burning house prevented a father from entering. Then he saw his son in the bedroom window. He cupped his hands to his mouth and yelled, ''Jump, son, jump!'' The boy in terror shouted back, ''Daddy, I can't see you, I can't see you!'' The father called again in desperation, ''Jump, son! Daddy will catch you!'' Trembling with fear, the boy stood poised at the window. Then he jumped. That little boy, unable to see and thoroughly frightened, made the leap into his father's arms. He did so because of the great trust he naturally put in his father. With his father there, he knew nothing could harm him.

Faith for us is a blind leap into the arms of God. It is a firm conviction, a gift from God himself, which is our only answer to the terrible, dark mystery of where we came from and where we are going. It is a child's trust in the hand that will lead us through the terrors that reach out to us from the dark. There is no faith needed to walk into a brightly lighted room in which we clearly see that there are no dangers, no uncertainties. "Faith is confident assurance concerning what we hope for, and conviction about things we do not see."

In today's Eucharistic Prayer, we will refer to Abraham as "our father in faith." He is our father in faith because we are all his spiritual descendants as the people of God, but also because he is clearly a genuine example of what our faith should be. God had made extraordinary promises to Abraham. He told him: "This is my covenant with you: You shall be the father of a multitude of nations; I will establish my covenant between you and me and your descendants after you throughout their generations, as a perpetual covenant, that I may be a God to you and to your descendants after you" (Gn 17:4, 7). Though Abraham and his wife, Sarah, grew old with no legitimate heir, Abraham kept his confidence in God. Then when Sarah was beyond the natural age of childbearing, she had a son, Isaac.

After Isaac had become a young boy, just when Abraham was content to feel that all of God's promise would be fulfilled in Isaac, God commanded him to give up his son's life in sacrifice. Abraham was in tremendous mental turmoil. It was terrible enough to be asked to sacrifice his son. The thing that disturbed him the more was that the death of his son would seem to make God's promises about descendants impossible of fulfillment. When Abraham led Isaac to the place of sacrifice on the mountain top, he could not see the bright sunshine of hope about to be fulfilled, but only the dark clouds of confusion which faith alone could penetrate.

Abraham's faith was being put to its supreme test. He saw in Isaac all his hopes and dreams. He saw in Isaac the person through whom God would fulfill his promises. As the old man stood with the knife clutched in his trembling hand, he was in mental anguish over how this sacrifice could make sense. Yet he was willing to reach out his free hand to God, to be led through the darkness of confusion and fear. That was enough for God. Abraham's faith was firm and unwavering, and so God sent his angel to stay the hand of sacrifice. Isaac's life was spared, and a ram was substituted in his place.

It is no surprise, then, that today's Eucharistic Prayer will refer to Abraham as "our father in faith." Abraham was a man approved by God because of his faith. That kind of faith must be ours, too. It is a faith that is more than an intellectual assent to truths revealed by God. It is a faith that involves the commitment of our entire selves to God. It is trust, reliance, a confident assurance, a firm conviction that God is good, that he is a true Father to us in every circumstance of our lives. It is the faith we express also in today's Eucharistic Prayer in these words of the priest: "Remember all of us gathered here before you. You know how firmly we believe in you and dedicate ourselves to you." Yes, that is the idea: to be dedicated to God because we know that he is dedicated to us.

God calls us to make the leap into the mysterious darkness of life. We must make that leap with the confident assurance that the arms of God our Father will be there to catch us.

C.E.M.

## Twentieth Sunday of the Year (A)

# *NOT AN EXCLUSIVE CLUB*

Probably you can remember that when you were a kid, you formed a club with other kids in your neighborhood. You may even have had a clubhouse of sorts where you held meetings. There really wasn't much of a purpose or goal to the club, but there was one quality that gave it value in your·eyes: not everyone could belong. Membership was selective. The fact that some kids were excluded made belonging mean all the more to you. There are people who continue this childish game even after they have grown up. They form clubs with selective membership, with undesirables excluded on the basis of financial status, color, or even religion.

The first Christians were of course Jews. Some of them believed that only Jews could be Christians, while others protested that to be a follower of Christ, a non-Jew had to be circumcised and follow the law of Moses. This was the situation despite the teaching of our first reading today from the Old Testament, which states that messianic salvation is offered to all who believe in the Lord and keep his commandments, regardless of origin or social condition.

The story in today's gospel was preached in the early Church to correct an attitude of exclusiveness. The Canaanite woman was non-

Jewish. When she asked a favor of Jesus, he insisted that his mission was to the chosen people, the house of Israel. When she refused to accept "no" for an answer, there followed a painful scene. Apparently, the poor woman trailed after Jesus, wailing and crying. Apparently too, she attached herself to various disciples who looked deceptively sympathetic for a moment, which prompted them to complain to Jesus, "Get rid of her. She keeps shouting after us." Jesus remained unperturbed by this feminine storm, and resorted to one of his favorite devices. He told a parable, but with quite a sting to it: "It is not right to take the food of sons and daughters and throw it to the dogs." But the woman had the last word, and that in an argument with the Son of God himself. With quick wit, she turned the parable to her own purpose as she observed, "Even the dogs eat the leavings that fall from their masters' tables." She refused to be daunted by the harsh words of Jesus. With a womanly instinct, she seemed to realize that he was being "cruel only to be kind," for his harsh words elicited from the lady a tremendous expression of faith. She became a living fulfillment of today's first reading, that salvation would come to all who believed in the Lord. And the point behind this unusual gospel story was that even non-Jews would share in the blessings which Jesus came to bring.

It was a hard lesson for the early Christians to learn, but before long the shoe was on the other foot. St. Paul had to write to the non-Jewish Christians at Rome to remind them that they must not boast that they had taken the place of the chosen people of God (second reading).

I suppose that people will protest that they have a perfect right to form exclusive clubs; but when they want their religion to be little more than an exclusive club, we have a situation that is intolerable in the sight of God. God does not discriminate against anyone. He welcomes all who believe in him and wish to do his will. And so the Church of Jesus Christ calls everyone. It is indeed a sad, scandalous situation when the members of any parish refuse to welcome someone warmly into their number, whether it be because of his low economic or social status or because of his poor reputation. It is your business to make everyone feel welcome in this church, no matter how he may be dressed, or how unappealing he may appear, or what others may say of him. The fact that he comes to church must be taken as a sign that he wishes to respond to Jesus; and, who knows, his faith may be greater than even that of the Canaanite woman.

Jesus invites us to receive him in Holy Communion. He yearns to unite to himself all who will accept him in faith. If others are good enough for Jesus, they should be good enough for us. Before receiving Jesus together, you will be invited to offer each other the sign of peace. You should offer this sign with sincerity, even if you do not know the person next to you. This sign of peace is a seal and pledge of the fellowship and unity which are found in our common reception of the body of Christ.

It is understandable that children would wish to form an exclusive club, but that is not the kind of Church which Jesus Christ founded and to which we belong.

C.E.M.

## Twentieth Sunday of the Year (B)

### IT'S WISE TO EAT

When I was in the seminary and a fine fellow student would "drop out," deciding not to continue to study for the priesthood, I would begin a long process of evaluation. "He's a better student than I am—gets all A's. He's a fine speaker, has a great personality. He'd really wow the people as a priest. Why did he drop out?" I never came up with very good answers. And the passage of years hasn't helped the questioning. Even today, the same twinge of examination pops up when a priest I know decides not to remain in the priesthood. And this situation isn't unique to the priesthood. How many married couples—so ideally suited (we thought) are having trouble staying together, while the mixed-matched defy all predictions and are happily married? How many "bad" kids grow up and become great people, while their talented peers can't find a place in life?

It all would be baffling, except that through these experiences an awareness evolves. You become aware that there is a subtle wisdom guiding events in the world. It obviously isn't my wisdom. All my "winners" seem to be walking out. Word gets around about a priest who is marvelous with the sick, or small children, and his classmates remember what a poor student he was in the seminary. The unsuited couple become wonderful parents. Or the child who wouldn't amount to much goes off to join VISTA. The book of Proverbs gently gives us clues for these events. "Let whoever is simple turn in here." God's wisdom has all things worked out. And he generally uses the simple to confound the wise.

And the confrontation of human and divine wisdom can be best seen in the Eucharist. Human judgment declares it only bread. After all, be reasonable. How could it be anything else? Divine judgment declares: the bread that I give is my flesh for the life of the world.

The extension of God among men is called wisdom throughout the Old Testament. One could almost substitute "Christ" in the first reading today for the word "wisdom." Christ in the first reading does invite us: "Come eat my food and drink the wine I have mixed: forsake foolishness that you may live, advance in the way of understanding." Paul is just as insistent: "Do not act like fools, but like thoughtful men. Make the most of the present opportunity."

And this is where the nonchristian listeners of the Lord went astray. They understood clearly Christ's offer of flesh to eat. But their "profound" human wisdom told them this could not be. So they were foolish enough to pass up life itself.

If your faith is confused these days, listen to Christ: to him who lacks understanding, I say, come eat my food. If you have worries about the Church, the vocation crisis, the condition of the world today, come eat my food. If your problems and disappointments make little sense, come eat my food. Don't rely on your own wisdom to save the world; try to discern the will of the Lord. And come eat my food, and drink the wine I have mixed. Forsake foolishness that you may live; advance in the way of understanding. Then real wisdom will come to you: Christ himself.

M.M.R.

## Twentieth Sunday of the Year (C)

## *DIVISION AND PEACE*

I think we can all agree that human slavery in our country, which is dedicated to personal freedom, is an anomaly beyond our powers to understand. Whether the slaves were treated well or poorly is not the point. It is simply abhorrent that one human being would be actually owned by another human being. As I look back on that era, I cannot imagine how slavery could have been tolerated, not to mention actually justified in the minds of the people.

I suspect, however, that another generation, more enlightened than our own, will look back upon our times and ask: "How could they have tolerated it? How could they have possibly justified it?" The "it" that I am referring to is abortion. Abortion is the direct killing of an innocent human being, an aberration far worse than owning a fellow human being. The Catholic Church stands virtually alone in its opposition to this horrible killing of defenseless babies. We, as individual Catholics, must never weaken in our efforts to protect the unborn by every available means.

But abortion is one example among many immoralities in our society. Others are attacks upon the sacredness of marriage and sex. Racial and ethnic prejudice as well as injustice to minority workers are still others. Some people, even some Catholics, say that the Church ought to stay in the sanctuary and out of the social arena. Usually, such opposition comes only when consciences have been goaded from complacency, when people have been disturbed in their peace of mind because of latent guilt.

Think back to the era of slavery. Do you think that the Church should have said nothing against this immoral institution? Imagine, however, the effect of a sermon condemning slavery given to a congregation of slave owners. Don't you think that some would have walked out, that others would have protested that the priest had no business sticking his nose into their business, or even that the Church ought to restrict itself to praying?

Hindsight is easy. We easily condemn slavery today, as we easily condemn Nazism and the horrors of the concentration camps. In fact, today there are still some who say that Pope Pius XII should have been more active in opposing Hitler and his crazy ideologies. Let's profit from that kind of hindsight and recognize that the Church must not be silent regarding social matters in our own time. Nor should we as individuals become defensive if a social teaching of the Church hits home.

The gospel you heard a few moments ago is a strange paradox. Jesus, the Prince of Peace, proclaims that he has come not for peace but to light a fire on earth, a fire to purify human life of injustice and hatred. And if such purification demands division even within families, then remember that Jesus says: "I have come for division." The message of Jesus is not all milk and honey, or sweetness and light. Jesus was no Casper Milquetoast, mouthing platitudes that could be turned into bumper stickers. Rather, he was forceful and uncompromising when the truth had to be proclaimed, no matter what the consequences. Our second reading in this Mass exhorts us to "remember how he endured the opposition of sinners." The Old Testament prophet, Jeremiah, similarly refused to compromise with the evils of his day. For his efforts he was accused of treason, thrown into a cistern and left to die.

Jesus came to bring peace, but not a false peace which is the spoiled fruit of the attitude which favors peace at any price, a price which is a compromise of moral principles: a giving-in to wrong when it is convenient, a willingness to go along with evil when it is profitable. True peace does not come from selfishness and greed.

In every Mass just before Communion, we pray for peace. True peace comes only from union with Jesus Christ. Let us understand that our sacramental union is a sham, if we are not willing to follow all the teachings of Christ and his Church. And conversely, through our union with Christ we can overcome all reluctance to accept his teachings, and so find that peace of mind and heart for which we all yearn.

C.E.M.

## Twenty-First Sunday of the Year (A)

# *THE ROCK*

Whenever we speak of St. Peter we do not ordinarily pay much attention to his name, but his name is unusual. As a matter of fact, there is no evidence that anyone had the name "Peter" before Christian times. Peter, you see, is actually a nickname; the apostle's real name was Simon. Since there is frequently a playful irreverence in the giving of a nickname, we may be surprised to find Jesus himself giving Simon his nickname of Peter, which means "rock." Jesus, however, was not playful; he was extremely serious. The moment was a solemn one and very momentous indeed.

Unfortunately, in English the full impact of the name is lost on us. Jesus used the Aramaic word for "rock," and that word was translated in the gospels by the Greek word, "petros," from which we have derived the name "Peter." But we have also kept in our language the Anglo-Saxon word "rock" to refer to a mass of stony material. In French the idea comes across clearly, since French has only one word for the man's name and for "rock": *pierre*. To put it awkwardly, Jesus was saying, "You are *Pierre* and on this *pierre* I will build my church."

Nicknames are given to people to describe one of their characteristics. That's why we call some people "Shorty" or "Speedy," or something like that. When Jesus called Simon, "Rock," he was implying that he was solid and firm, like something suitable for a foundation. Remember that Jesus himself said in a parable that the wise man built his house on rock, so that when the torrents came and the winds blew the house did not collapse (Mt 7:25). Actually, it is a little surprising that Jesus gave this unlikely nickname to Simon. After all, Simon seemed to be a person who was anything but solid and firm. He was so weak that he denied he knew Jesus. Even after the day of Pentecost, he was so unstable in the question of whether converts to Christianity had to follow the law of Moses or not, that St. Paul had to withstand him to his face and remind him to follow the correct teaching (Gal 2:11-14).

And yet Jesus clearly chose Simon to be the solid, firm foundation of his Church. As our new translation has it, he said to Simon: "You are Rock, and upon this rock I will build my Church." Jesus was sure of his choice, for he went on to promise, "And the jaws of death shall not prevail against it." Jesus was confident that when the torrents would come and the winds blow, his Church would stand firm because it was solidly set on Simon, the Rock.

Despite the apparent ineptitude of Peter, Jesus was proven to be wise. His plan worked. When the torrents of persecution came pouring down on the early Church, it stood firm. When the winds of internal dissent and confusion buffeted the early Church, it did not collapse. And what was true of the early Church has been true of the Church all through the centuries, right down to our own times, as the authority of Peter has been passed from pope to pope. Some of the popes have been great men, men not only of piety but also of vision; but others have been, humanly speaking, almost totally devoid of any qualifications to lead and strengthen the Church. There have been eras of serenity in the history of the Church, but there have also been times of violent storms. Through it all, the good and the bad, the Church has escaped from the jaws of death.

Why has the plan of Jesus worked? The reason is that Jesus is still with his Church, especially in the person of the pope, no matter who he may be. Peter and the other popes are not the successors of Jesus, but only his vicars. A vicar is a substitute, a deputy. He exercises authority only in the name of another person—the person to whom the authority really belongs. And so the authority of the pope is really the authority of Jesus Christ. To put it another way, Jesus is the real rock of the Church. Ultimately he is its firm, solid foundation. Jesus, by means of the Holy Spirit, continues to lead and strengthen his Church through his vicar on earth, the pope.

These days, some people seem to think that the Church has become pretty shaky, but it has definitely not collapsed under the torrents and winds of modern problems, nor will it do so. The plan of Jesus will continue to work until he comes again in glory. No matter what you may think of the present pope, either favorably or unfavorably, no matter who the next pope will be or what he will be like, the Church of Jesus Christ stands on the pope as on a rock. Make no mistake about that. You have the guarantee of Jesus Christ himself that no torrent, no wind will destroy his Church, firmly set on its foundation, the "Rock."

C.E.M.

## Twenty-First Sunday of the Year (B)

### *WILL YOU STAY ?*

On a number of Sundays now, Christ has been speaking about giving himself to us in the Eucharist. And today he finally asks: Do you accept this? Do you really appreciate what I have been telling you about Communion, or have you considered me like a car salesman on TV: it's too much to take seriously? Would it be easier to leave politely rather than have to give an answer, rather than have to live up to the reality of the Eucharist?

To live up to the Eucharist means, among other things, seeing that through the Eucharist people become one with Christ. Paul gives us one fine example, or application, and he isn't speaking mere poetry. He's talking about some of the effects of seeing others as one with Christ through the Eucharist. If a wife sees her husband as "eucharistic," she will offer respect to him. If a husband sees his wife as "eucharistic," he will give himself for her. They will do this totally, caring for each other as they do their own bodies. "This sort of talk is hard to endure; how can anyone take it seriously?" Remember when you used to hear that "marriages are made in heaven"? Maybe the saying should be: no one comes to union with another except through Christ, and no one comes to Christ unless brought by the heavenly Father.

Husbands and wives are the Church in miniature, an expression of the "eucharistic" people of God. They can give a sample of how we should care for each other, and can remind us that Christ's deep love for us is best seen in this total kind of love. Love is caring, protection, respect and growth.

To accept the fact that we are all bound to this type of love is difficult, but we must do so if we really want to accept the Eucharist. The teachings of Christ through the Church on divorce or abortion are easily digested when they don't apply to us. But for the poor parent and three children abandoned by the spouse, for the young girl discovering pregnancy outside marriage, the talk of the Church is hard to endure—especially when not too many today are taking these words seriously.

Would even the experience of seeing Christ in his glory, a vision of heaven, make some life situations any easier? Probably not. A strong spirit has to fill us, the spirit of Christ that comes to us through the Eucharist. It is a spirit which gives strength to a married person to live singly, for a young girl to have her child and then offer it for adoption.

Christ gives us the Eucharistic food, the strength to make difficult decisions. He gives us his presence as a friend. The Lord is close to the brokenhearted. He gives us his Spirit as counselor to see wisdom. But all this helps only if we believe. Some of the Jews left Christ because they could not believe in the Eucharist. But husbands and wives and families with faith can stay together and remain in the Church because of the Eucharist as well. Each of us can find help to cope with problems, even be heroic. And we ought to turn to assist those around us who have still greater problems.

Let Joshua ask the question during this Mass, "If it does not please you to serve the Lord, decide today whom you will serve." Beg Christ to help you with your answer. "Lord, there may be days when I'm tempted to walk out, but to whom shall I go? You have the words of eternal life. We have come to believe, we are convinced that you are God's Holy One."

M.M.B.

**Twenty-First Sunday of the Year (C)**

## *ARE A FEW TO BE SAVED ?*

One of the strongest instincts of a human being is the desire to belong, to be included in a group, and even to be part of the "in" crowd. It is not without reason that people of all ages tend to form clubs and organizations. There is a feeling of security that comes from the sense of belonging. Always to be left out, always to be excluded is a cause for sadness; but on the other hand always to be counted in, always to be sought after, can be an excuse for complacency.

It was this instinctive desire to belong that prompted someone from the crowd listening to Jesus to ask, "Lord, are they few in number who are to be saved?" Jesus was probably asked this same question countless times during his preaching about the kingdom. Among many of the Jews, the question of whether the Gentiles would be saved as part of the kingdom was generally not even considered. They believed that descent from Abraham, together with the faithful observance of the Law, was what counted. The question asked of Jesus, therefore, referred only to the Jews. Apparently, the man who asked the question expected Jesus to give him a guarantee that he would be saved simply because he was a descendant of Abraham.

First, Jesus refused to answer the question about numbers as irrelevant. He insisted that the people should not be concerned about how many are saved, but rather that people should work to make sure of their own salvation, regardless of what others may do. Secondly, he shook the man out of his complacency by declaring that blood descent from Israel's ancestry is no guarantee of entrance into the kingdom. Salvation is not automatic for anybody. Jesus condemned the smugness that lay behind the man's question, and added a stern warning that one must work hard to gain entrance through the narrow door that leads into the kingdom.

That the words of Jesus apply to us as Catholics is obvious. We were incorporated into the new people of God, the Church, not through physical descent from Abraham, but through the spiritual generation of baptism. Just being a Catholic, however, is no guarantee of salvation. Nor is it proper for us to sit back and ask a lot of irrelevant questions about the salvation of those who are not Catholics. First, such questions often imply that since we as Catholics will be saved, it is only natural to wonder how people who are not Catholics can possibly be saved. Secondly, the asking of such questions expends energy on something that is entirely up to God in his wisdom and mercy. This is not to say that we are not to work for the salvation of all men or try to win converts to the Church. Our Lord's point simply is that we cannot take our own salvation as a matter of course. It is something we must work at, and work hard. There is no room in God's kingdom for the smug or complacent person.

To gain entrance into God's kingdom, more is required than mere membership in the Church. We must try to do God's will in every aspect of our lives. Today's second reading from the letter to the Hebrews emphasizes one particular aspect of God's will: his wish to discipline us as his children, so that we may be worthy members of his spiritual family. Good parents know that children need discipline if they are to mature, but a child of any age can resist discipline and thwart the most conscientious efforts of his parents. A child who rejects discipline and training wants to derive benefits from his family in an automatic fashion, without any cooperation on his part. Often, too, you hear a child complain about his own discipline when his friends seem to be getting away with murder. He fails to see that his parents are doing him a favor.

Today's second reading correctly states: "At the time it is administered, all discipline seems a cause for grief and not for joy, but later it brings forth the fruit of peace and justice to those who are trained in its school." One of the worst things we can do is to revolt against the trials that God sends us. We don't have to pretend that God's discipline is fun, but we do have to see that it is necessary to make us worthy of his kingdom. And it is very childish of us to complain that those who are not Catholics seem to get away with murder. God is doing us a favor by the discipline he imposes on us.

So we have no answer to the question of whether many or few will be saved. What we do know is that we cannot afford to be smug or complacent about our own salvation. We must work to do God's will and to cooperate with his fatherly discipline, so that we can squeeze through the narrow door that leads into his eternal kingdom.

C.E.M.

**Twenty-Second Sunday of the Year (A)**
Suggested Use: Third Eucharistic Prayer

## *DIVINE STANDARDS*

Whenever you love somebody, you don't want anything bad to happen to him, any more than you want something bad to happen to yourself. However, when you take it upon yourself to decide what is good and what is bad for another person, your judgment just may not agree with his.

Such was the situation in today's gospel. Jesus clearly told his apostles that he had to go to Jerusalem to suffer greatly and be put to death, and be raised up on the third day. The prediction of his death was such a surprise and a disappointment to the apostles that they scarcely even heard the words about resurrection. They were downcast and dejected. Then Peter decided that suffering and death were bad for Jesus, and he took it upon himself to lift what he thought were the sagging spirits of Jesus by saying, "May you be spared, Master! God forbid that any such thing ever happen to you." To Peter's utter astonishment, Jesus exploded with a violence rarely seen in him: "Get out of my sight, you Satan! You are trying to make me trip and fall." Can you imagine how poor Peter must have felt, how shocked he must have been?

Without realizing it, Peter was playing the role of Satan, tempting Jesus to follow the easy, human path of an earthly messiah rather than adhere to the plan of his Father. It was not an easy plan for Jesus to accept, this plan of suffering and death, and Peter was not making it any easier by his well-intentioned comments. Later, in the garden of Gethsemani, Jesus struggled to accept this will of his Father, and Peter even then failed to understand what was going on as he slept through the whole ordeal.

Jesus summarized Peter's whole problem in one sentence: "You are not judging by God's standards but by man's." Man's standards say: "Be comfortable; seek security; take care of yourself; don't overdo it." How different are God's standards! God shows in Jesus that real happiness comes through suffering, true joy through sorrow, and everlasting life through death. Jesus said that he *must* suffer and die in order to be raised up. That was the will of his Father.

Peter did not want what he judged as bad things to happen to his

Master, nor did he want them to happen to himself. So, after his rebuke, he was in for more amazement and shock as Jesus went on to say: "If a man wishes to come after me, he must deny his very self, take up his cross, and begin to follow in my footsteps." The plan of the Father applied not only to Jesus, but to his disciples as well. And that means us, too.

Just *why* God demands suffering is a mystery, something that even Jesus did not explain. It is not that God in heaven looks down upon our suffering and takes some kind of twisted pleasure in what he sees. Nor is it really a question of some kind of payment for sin, in the old idea of an eye for an eye and a tooth for a tooth. Perhaps we get closer to the truth when we realize that suffering is the measure of a person. It shows how big he is. It can also be the test of love, because we are willing to suffer for another if we love him enough. But when all is said that can be said about it, we simply must accept suffering in trust and confidence as Jesus did. That involves every form of suffering, not just the physical kind, but all the mental and emotional anguish, the frustrations, the loneliness, the boredom of human existence. Accept it all we must, but we should not be surprised if our acceptance is a struggle. It was a struggle for Jesus. And as we look up at the crucifix and remember that Jesus tells us to take up our cross, we may be tempted to say, "May we be spared! God forbid that any such thing ever happen to us!"

When we feel that way, we must remember that Jesus not only said that he had to suffer and die, but also that he would be raised on the third day. If we share in the cross of Christ, we will share in his resurrection as well. St. Paul, therefore, reminds us today not to conform ourselves to this age, but to offer our bodies as a living sacrifice to God (second reading). We are here to follow that advice, to offer ourselves with Jesus in the Mass. We will pray after the consecration that Jesus "may make us an everlasting gift" to the Father (Third Eucharistic Prayer). God will accept the gift of ourselves in union with Jesus, if we willingly embrace suffering and even death as Jesus did. Then we can expect to "share in the inheritance of the saints," those people who heeded the word of Jesus and took up their crosses and followed him.

In our lives we must judge by God's standards, not by man's. If we can learn that lesson today, then we will see that God loves us and does not want bad things to happen to us. Suffering is not bad, because in

God's plan it will lead us to happiness. God's ways are not our ways, but God's ways are best.

C.E.M.

## Twenty-Second Sunday of the Year (B)

### *OF LIPS AND HEARTS*

At first hearing, today's gospel sounds like a scene from a family dinner table. How many parents have asked their children as they sat down to eat, "Did you wash your hands?" The Pharisees had observed some of the disciples of Jesus eating meals without having washed their hands. Their concern, however, was not with hygiene but with religious practice. Originally, symbolic purification had been connected with the Jewish liturgy, somewhat after the present practice of the priest washing his hands during the Mass. By custom over the centuries, that ritual washing was extended to circumstances of everyday life, and in the minds of people like the Pharisees had taken on an importance out of all proportion to the value of the act.

Jesus objected strenuously to the attitude of the Pharisees. It was not that the washing was a bad thing. What was bad was the notion that such formal and merely external actions constituted a person's religion, to the exclusion of what was really important as an expression of piety. Insistence on such actions had taken all the heart out of religion. The people had received God's commandments through Moses and had been told to observe them carefully (first reading), but it was a lot easier and less demanding for a Jew to wash his hands than it was to love God with his whole being and his neighbor as himself. Perhaps a parallel situation is the fact that it is a lot easier for us to say grace before meals than it is to be kind and considerate, without bickering or arguing, during the meal. Saying grace is good, but to think that it alone, with no attempt to show love for those with whom we eat, makes us religious is to fall into the error of the Pharisees.

Perhaps we have been more Pharisaical in some of our Catholic practices than we would like to admit. In recent times, a lot of our customs have become little more than history. Most of us can recall that a "practicing" Catholic was one who was at Mass every Sunday, went to confession and Communion at least once a month, never ate meat on Friday and wore a medal. These criteria, these norms for being a "good" Catholic, were not bad. They were, however, dangerous because they could, and sometimes did, lead to complacency in religion. Some people regret that the old external signs of piety are being lost, but let's try to be honest about this problem without putting up our defenses. Isn't it true that it has been relatively easy to get to Mass every Sunday? There was sometimes a pride in refusing to eat meat on a Friday in the company of non-Catholics, but the sacrifice involved was really not very much. Getting to confession regularly involved more effort—an effort which, incidentally, some of us should be using again—but perhaps our confessions were vague and more a case of routine than an expression of true sorrow with sincere repentance. And the wearing of a medal did not make us a good Catholic, any more than putting a patriotic bumper sticker on a car makes the driver a good American.

Please do not misunderstand me. I am not saying that you should not come to Mass every Sunday or wear a medal. My point—the point of Jesus in the gospel—is that merely external practices do not make us religious. We can never overemphasize this truth. In fact, we are even now in danger of falling into another form of externalism in our manner of celebrating the Mass. This is what I mean. Singing the hymns and saying the prayers aloud within the Mass are important. Anyone who does not think so has not been listening to the official teaching of the Church. But if we do these things without attention and devotion and a sincere attempt to express real love for God, we may very well hear God say: "This people pays me lip service, but their heart is far from me." Much more of the Bible is being read as part of the Mass, and yet hearing the word of God is not enough. As St. James tells us in the second reading: "Act on this word. If all you do is listen to it, you are deceiving yourselves." Most Catholics these days are receiving Holy Communion every Sunday, and that is a very good thing; but if we are not making an effort to grow more like Christ in our lives, we are neglecting one of the purposes of Communion. Moreover, if we think that we can express love for God here at Mass, and then go out and make no attempt to show love for his children by trying to overcome the misery and injustices which are part of our society, we are modern-day Pharisees.

The Pharisees had missed the meaning of religion. There is no easy, external thing we can do to guarantee our being devout. God asks for a devotion which involves our whole being. In the words of today's responsorial psalm, God wants us to walk blamelessly and do justice, to think the truth in our hearts and slander not with our tongue, to harm not our fellow man. He requires a piety which involves not only our prayers but also our actions, not only our lips but also our hearts.

C.E.M.

## Twenty-Second Sunday of the Year (C)
Suggested Use: Third Eucharistic Prayer

# *HUMILITY, PROFOUND REALISM*

The protocol, which is the background of our Lord's teaching in today's gospel, may strike us as rather stiff and stuffy. A precise seating arrangement is something we would reserve for only the most formal dinners, but among the people of our Lord's day it was almost a part of daily routine. To receive a place of honor at the dinner table was for them a mark of great personal distinction. Everyone hoped to be given the highest place possible. Jesus neither approved nor condemned the social etiquette of his day, but he took the occasion of this dinner to teach an important lesson: pride has no place in the kingdom of God. Humility is necessary if we wish to be pleasing to God and to be accepted into his kingdom. This humility taught by Jesus is one of the characteristics of the saints.

Saints are, of course, extraordinary people, but one of the most extraordinary things about them is their humility. Frankly, their humility at times seems to border on the unreal. Take St. Paul the Apostle, for example. His writings make up a large portion of the New Testament, and we frequently hear his letters read here at Mass. He was indeed a great man, full of love for Christ and his fellow human beings, a man of wisdom and zeal. And yet he spoke of himself as the worst of sinners (1 Tm 1:15). St. Vincent de Paul is famous the world over for his wonderful works of charity. He spent a lifetime in the service of others. When he died at the age of eighty, it was more from exhaustion than old age. But this magnificent saint referred to himself as "a miserable wretch" and declared that he was unworthy of even the simple food he consumed. These saints are but two examples among many.

Were the saints a little psychotic on this point of humility, or were they actually in touch with reality in a deeper way than the so-called "normal" person? Let it be understood that the saints were not psychotic, that they were in profound touch with the Great Reality, God himself. The reason they could sincerely feel such deep humility was that they compared themselves with God, and not with their fellow men. Their faults, their failures, their weaknesses were manifestly clear to themselves in the brilliant light of God's perfection.

If we could only learn to compare ourselves with God, how could we feel anything but humility? Pride comes from a false point of comparison. These days, it is commonplace to read in the papers or hear on television about people whose lack of morals is notorious. The mafia don makes a fortune in a narcotics racket, the effect of which reduces people to a state that is lower than that of the animals; and he compounds his gross disrespect for the dignity of human beings by coldly decreeing the murder of competitors who get in his way. Some movie stars, whom we idolize at the box office, produce only disgust in us by their apparent disregard for the permanence and sacredness of marriage. The man who murders one of his children and abandons two others on a Los Angeles freeway shocks us almost to disbelief.

It is easy to feel pretty proud of ourselves in comparison with this type of person. The comparison makes us feel complacent, and the desire for such a comfortable feeling is behind a lot of prejudice, racial and otherwise. Looking down on others gives us a sense of personal elevation. If you are under six feet, you are short by today's standards; but if you could manage to live among pygmies, you would think of yourself as a giant.

A pride that is produced by comparing ourselves with despicable people, or with people that we may consider as despicable, is condemned by Jesus. The complacency it begets inhibits our spiritual growth, and even from a natural point of view puts us in an unhealthy state of mind. God's own perfection is the ideal toward which we must strive. We will never reach this ideal—but keeping the ideal, this proper perspective on life, should be a healthy incentive to keep on trying to improve ourselves.

By our own unaided powers, we can't even begin to be more God-like. That is one reason we are here at Mass today. We are here to say to God: "You have given us a high goal, your own holiness. Of ourselves we can do nothing. Only you can help us. Please give us the help we need to better ourselves.''

The saints in their humility were profound realists. Because of their humility, God has exalted them in his heavenly kingdom. We too, with God's help, must work toward that same exaltation by trying to practice the humility taught us by Jesus today.

C.E.M.

## Twenty-Third Sunday of the Year (A)

## *LOVE AND CORRECTION*

You can probably remember a television commercial for a certain mouthwash. The scene opens with a young man trying to get up enough courage to tell his boss the terrible truth that he has (what could be worse?) bad breath. He rehearses the little speech he plans to give, in which he will advise his boss to use this certain mouthwash. Then with fear and trembling he approaches the boss and begins his carefully prepared speech, with a bottle of the mouthwash in his hand. Before he can get to the point, the boss sees the bottle and with a burst of jubilant enthusiasm exclaims, "Ah yes, I use that every morning now." End scene, no more problem about bad breath.

The only realistic aspect of this commercial is that you would probably find it very difficult to come out and tell someone that he has bad breath. And if it were a question of something really serious or important, you would find it almost impossible to tell a person about his fault. Would that bad breath were the only objectionable fault people have! The world would indeed be a simple and easy place in which to live. As a matter of fact, human beings come up with some pretty big failings, failings that can frustrate the purpose of their own existence and make life miserable for others. Should it be any concern of ours, or should we just live and let live? Who is going to appreciate it when you bring up his faults? Well, St. Paul tells us today: "Owe no debt to anyone except the debt that binds us to love one another." That is a pretty big debt, because "love is the fulfillment of the law" of God. It includes everything, and Jesus teaches us in the gospel that part of love is to correct the faults of others.

In some situations we have a grave obligation simply because of our relationship with others. The most obvious example is that of you parents with your children. It has always been hard to get a happy medium between absolute tyranny and downright permissiveness. You have to decide in this very complicated matter what you must do to create the proper atmosphere in which your child can grow toward mature responsibility, but you should never think that no discipline and no correction will accomplish this goal. Children, like the rest of us, are affected by original sin. They need guidance and direction—more when they are younger and less as they grow older. Psychologists also remind us that a child who is never guided or directed feels abandoned by his parents, even as he delights in his unwarranted freedom. Some gross misbehavior by a child is nothing more than a pitiful attempt to win a little attention from his neglectful parents. No child enjoys discipline, even well-motivated discipline, but deep down he recognizes that it is a sign of love and concern. It probably will be only later in life that he will look back and appreciate what you as parents have tried to do for him.

You husbands and wives have an obligation to correct each other's faults; not in a spirit of nagging pettiness or faultfinding, but in a spirit of loving communication. And as Jesus says, ''Keep it between the two of you.'' If you really think that your husband does not spend enough time at home, tell him, not your girl friend next door over a cup of coffee. If you think your wife is a sloppy housekeeper, tell her, not the boys you bowl with. Sure it's a touchy thing; sure it has to be handled delicately. But it is usually better to risk having a little fur fly and perhaps solve a problem, than to let it drag on indefinitely and grow into something that pushes you farther and farther apart.

Moreover, you husbands and wives who are here together are both hearing what Jesus is saying about pointing out faults. You know that his words should not be taken as an excuse for a gripe session. On the other hand, when your spouse tries to talk about something wrong, don't fly off the handle. Remember that he or she is just trying to be a good Catholic and follow the teaching of Jesus. And of course, it has to be a two-way street: when you point out the other's faults, you should be prepared to hear about your own, because none of us is perfect.

This teaching abut correcting the faults of others applies to all our human associations, both in and outside the family. Maybe you know that a friend of yours is drifting into an affair. Don't just gossip about that person until he or she has wrecked a marriage, and then sit back and say, "Boy, I could see it coming for a long time." Perhaps someone you work with has been hitting the bottle, and as a consequence is not on the job the way he should be. Don't wait until the boss has to fire him, and then complacently observe, "Well, it's no surprise to me; the only wonder is that the boss didn't get on to him sooner."

In the first reading, we heard how God made Ezekiel watchman over Israel, to warn his people about dangerous conduct. God said, "I hold you responsible." We too are responsible, not only for ourselves but also for others. In this delicate matter of correction, we need courage—courage both to give correction and to take it.

C.E.M.

## Twenty-Third Sunday of the Year (B)

# *TO HEAR AND TO SPEAK*

After a very long illness, a woman completely lost her hearing. Apparently a virus had destroyed the auditory nerve in both ears. It was like cutting the wire on a telephone; she was totally deaf. She went from specialist to specialist in search of a cure, but she always received the same answer: medical science had not yet found a way to replace the damaged nerve. Finally, a man posing as a doctor promised that he could cure her by means of hypnosis, and the woman paid him ten thousand dollars, every penny she owned. Unfortunately the man was a charlatan, a quack. He took her money and that was the last she ever saw of him.

The fact that the woman was willing to pay so much money to regain her hearing points up how much we value our human faculties—once we have lost them. If we try to put ourselves in the place of the man in today's gospel, I think we can begin to appreciate his predicament. The man was deaf. Try to imagine what that means: to be cut off entirely from the whole world of sound. In a moment of danger, a human voice could not warn him. In a time of sorrow, a human voice could not console him. The laughter of children, the conversation of friends, the joy of music—these were not a reality for him. And as a consequence of his deafness he could not speak plainly, for he could not hear himself. He found it almost impossible to let others know how he felt or what he wanted. He could not express his emotions or his feelings. He lived in a world almost completely cut off from the people with whom he lived.

You can understand, then, his joy and enthusiasm when Jesus cured him. What a great day that was for him! Do you think he ever forgot it as long as he lived? Engraven on his memory was every detail: the time of day, the place, the weather, everything. Even the bystanders were so impressed that, as the gospel says, "Their amazement knew no bounds."

It is only natural that we should take for granted our ability to hear and our ability to speak. It is natural, but it is not right. These are great powers for which we must be grateful, and the best way to be grateful is by using these powers as God intended. The power to speak is one of the faculties which separates us from animals. We abuse this power when we use it to tell an untruth, to spread ugly rumors or demeaning gossip. Speech is intended to communicate truth and goodness, not lies and hatred. Our hearing too is to be used judiciously, not as an encouragement to another's abuse of his speech by lending our willing ear. Moreover, both our speech and our hearing are meant for something even higher than human communication. They are also our means of communicating with God. The rite of baptism brings out this higher use.

When we were baptized the priest touched our ears, saying the very word used by Jesus to cure the deaf man: "Ephphatha!" This was a sign that our ears should be opened not merely to the words of our fellow men, but also to the word of God. It meant that we should hear the word of God in faith. Faith opens our ears spiritually. Other people may hear the word of God in a physical way; that is, they may listen to the reading of the Bible, but without faith they do not hear that word as God's communication. They are, for one reason or another, spiritually deaf, as we ourselves were without the gift of faith received in baptism.

In the Mass, we hear the word of God in the scriptures and in the homily. We must try to open our ears in faith and listen attentively. Once we hear the word of God in faith, we must then respond by means of our power of speech. Once we believe in God, we must praise him, thank him, ask him for what we need, and express our sorrow for our sins. We must make a real effort to participate with intelligence and devotion in the prayers and hymns.

I am sure that the deaf man in the gospel really appreciated his powers after he had been cured. Today we should pray God to give us an appreciation of what we have: first, for our power to speak to each other, as well as for our power to speak to God in prayer; secondly, for our ability to hear each other, as well as for our ability to hear the word of God in faith.

The woman who had lost her hearing because of a virus was willing to pay ten thousand dollars for a cure. God cured our spiritual deafness by means of baptism, and it was a gift. It is a gift we should never forget or take for granted.

C.E.M.


## Twenty-Third Sunday of the Year (C)

## *DEDICATION*

Living the Christian life does not demand the impossible. On the other hand, it does not present us a course of life that is easy. Luke seems to present Christ in this gospel as speaking to somewhat of a large crowd, many of whom were probably thinking of becoming disciples. Jesus lets them understand that they must renounce anything that could stand in the way of following him completely, whether this be father or mother or even their own life. "Count the cost," he says, "before you make the decision to follow me." Don't try to put up a building unless you know you can finish it. Don't go to war unless you are sure you are going to win. These are illustrations of the type of previous consideration recommended in the first reading from the book of Wisdom. "What man knows God's counsel, or who can conceive what the Lord intends?" And the answer comes back a few verses later. "Who ever knew your counsel, except you had given Wisdom and sent your holy spirit from on high? And thus were the paths of those on earth made straight."

Usually when we talk of something or someone interfering with our fulfilling our dedication to Christ, we think of some sinful attachment. And this, where it is true, has to go. But for these few moments, let us look into the lack of effective fulfillment of our commitment to Christ because we adhere too closely to our own pet ideas. That is, we fail to communicate. Give up your unwillingness to hear and to truly listen to others; pastors and parishioners, teacher and pupil, parents and children, employer and employee. I think that when we give up our anxieties, our defenses, our stubbornness, we will find that we work together better with others to bring Christ into our own lives and those of others.

Crisis in dialogue occurs when the participants fail to speak and respond to each other, but turn away defensively for the purposes of self-justification. To establish good communication, selfishness must be replaced by a willingness to try to see the other person's point of view. Only then will the truth begin to come through. Being a Catholic must mean more to us from what we can give, rather than what we can receive. The parents who say they are too tired to listen to their children or they cannot understand them, or children who don't appreciate what parents do for them, are shutting off the lines of communication.

The second element that must be present for good communication is mutual trust. The first reading from the book of Wisdom touches on this point. ''For the deliberations of mortals are timid, and unsure are our plans.'' Without mutual trust each person has to be on his guard against the other, almost as if he were dealing with an enemy. Even our words have to be weighed, not in the interest of wisdom, but for the sake of safety. How much greater progress is made where there is a mutual trust and respect. A quotation from St. Augustine is applicable here: ''The members of the Savior, numerous as they are, under the one head which is the Savior himself, united by the tie of charity and peace, make only one man. In the psalms their voices are often raised as that of one man and there is heard only one voice, as if it were all, because all, in one alone, are one.''

We all must be willing to face up to discussion and fruitful action concerning the problems that confront us. If we are not to remain a Church obsolete and irrelevant to the difficulties of our human existence today, then each of us has to be willing first to talk seriously about these things. Are there not better solutions to overpopulation than the pill, abortion, euthanasia? How assist senior citizens fulfill a useful function in their community? What constructive suggestions can be offered to movie and television producers to improve programs? What can we do to have a more effective parochial liturgy? These are sample questions that we as a group of people dedicated to Christ ought to be tackling, and tackling together in harmonious dialogue.

Christ asks much of us as his disciples. One thing he wishes from us is that we make the honest effort to communicate with each other in mutual trust, so that together we may do his work in this world of ours.  O.J.M.

**Twenty-Fourth Sunday of the Year (A)**

## *SPIRITUAL AMNESIA*

In these days of credit cards and loan companies, almost every week means more bills in the mail, frequently without the money to pay them. Suppose that you receive a big bill in the mail, with payment long overdue. You sit down and write a nice letter, asking for an extension. Can you imagine your amazement if you were to get a letter by return mail stating that your debt had been completely cancelled? After you had overcome your shock, you would say, "There must be a catch to this."

We are in deep spiritual debt to God because of sin, a really big debt. Every sin is a terrible evil because it offends God. We cannot even begin to imagine how bad sin is, because we cannot appreciate how good God is. And yet we know that when we have sinned we can go to confession and have our sins forgiven, no matter how serious or frequent the sins may be. The infinite, forgiving God is represented by the king in today's parable. The official, who owed a huge amount, pleaded with the king only for a delay. Notice an important detail of the parable. The king not only heeded the plea of the official, but granted even more than he dared ask for. "Moved with pity, the king let the official go and *wrote off his debt.*"

God does indeed wish to write off our debt of sin completely, but there is a catch. Jesus tells us what the catch is: if we want God's forgiveness—and we all need that badly—then we must forgive injuries done to us. This point was so important in the mind of Jesus, that when he taught us to pray he gave us these words: "Forgive us our trespasses as we forgive those who trespass against us"—words we will pray once again in this very Mass. We have to take these words and the teaching of Jesus seriously. We must be like the official in the way he sought forgiveness, but unlike him in the way he refused forgiveness.

Jesus never tired of teaching the need to forgive others, because he realized how difficult a virtue it is for us. Someone says something behind your back. You find out about it. Your indignation grows and the hurt festers in your heart. The more you think about it, the less inclined you are to forgive this "enemy" of yours. Or someone insults you in front of others, or ignores you, or stands you up for an appointment. It may not seem important to anyone else, but it is important to you and you find the offense hard to forgive.

It is not surprising that we find it hard to forgive. That is the way human nature is. You see, it takes bigness to forgive. That is why it is easy for God to forgive, difficult for us. Even when we think we are very good about forgiving others, it may not be enough. Peter thought he was being very big about the whole thing, when he put it this way to Jesus: "When my brother wrongs me, how often must I forgive him? Seven times?" Perhaps Jesus chuckled to himself about Peter's supposed generosity, but he made it clear that seven times was not even close to being enough. His reply, "seventy times seven times," meant "without limit"—as often as you are wronged, that is how often you must forgive.

A real test of our bigness is not only how frequently we forgive, but how completely. Haven't you heard someone say, "I forgive, but I just can't forget"? Maybe you have said it yourself. That attitude—forgiving but not forgetting—is in reality far from the ideal that Jesus had in mind. To nurse hurt feelings, while mouthing words of pardon, is not really Christian forgiveness at all. We say, "I just don't want to get burned again," and what we actually mean is that we now wish to alter our relationship with the person who has hurt us.

Jesus wants us to practice his kind of forgiveness, the kind he not only preached but also practiced. After any injury, for which a person is sorry, nothing changes. Remember what Peter did to Jesus at the time of his passion. Not once, but three times he denied that he even knew Jesus. Before that denial Jesus had promised Peter that he would be the head of the Church, and despite Peter's denials during the Passion, Jesus stuck to his promise. Jesus didn't say, "All right, Peter, I forgive you, but I just can't forget your disloyalty and so someone else will have to take your place." True forgiveness involves a kind of spiritual amnesia.

Any offense against us is a mere fraction of what we are guilty of by sin before God. God will indeed write off our debt, but there is a catch. If we want forgiveness from God, we must forgive those who have offended us—with no limit on the number of times and with a generous act that not only forgives but also forgets.

C.E.M.

**Twenty-Fourth Sunday of the Year (B)**
Suggested Use: Fourth Eucharistic Prayer

## MAKE UP YOUR MIND

Richard Cardinal Cushing is credited with the following recipe for renewal.

> If all the sleeping folks will wake up,
> And all the lukewarm folks will fire up,
> And all the dishonest folks will confess up,
> And all the disgruntled folks will sweeten up,
> And all the discouraged folks will cheer up,
> And all the depressed folks will look up,
> And all the estranged folks will make up,
> And all the gossipers will shut up,
> And all the dry bones will shake up,
> And all the true soldiers will stand up,
> And all the Church members will pray up—
> THEN you can have the world's greatest renewal.

Since Vatican II, we have been moving in the direction of bringing the lay apostolate "to a boil." The readings in this Mass urge us to continue working in this direction. For "the renewal of the Church depends in great part on a laity that fully understands . . . their own co-responsibility for the mission of Christ in the Church and in the world" (Martin Work).

The question Jesus addressed to his disciples is the same one he addresses to us. Our baptism brought us into contact with Christ and his saving grace. As we grow up and come to the maturity that allows us to make responsible decisions, it is necessary to make up our minds about Jesus Christ. "If a man wishes to come after me, he must deny his very self, take up his cross, and follow in my steps." This is a decision that must reflect what Isaiah prophesies of Christ as we have it in the first reading. "I have not rebelled, have not turned back." Our response to this first reading, "I will walk in the presence of the Lord," is a further affirmation of our decision to go with Christ. When we seek for solutions to the problems of our society, we must say with Peter, "You are the

Messiah.'' It is foolish to look for salvation for ourselves or society in general, in anyone except Christ.

Our decision to follow Christ is only half fulfilled when we live our lives only according to ''don'ts.'' Eddie observed all the ''don'ts,'' but he gave very little attention to the ''do's.'' He never stole from anyone, but neither did he go out of his way to contribute to those who are hungry. Eddie could not be accused of cheating the other fellow, and yet you couldn't say that Eddie was generous in lending a helping hand. And that's the whole way Eddie's life went—a person living his life in only half measure. St. James, in the second reading today, is rather forceful on the minimum value of living your life on the negative side. ''If a brother or sister has nothing to wear and no food for the day, and you say to them, 'Good-bye and good luck! Keep warm and well fed,' but do not meet their bodily needs, what good is that?'' Incidentally, Eddie never misses Mass, but, then, he never participates either.

The following of Christ demands positive action. We have to make up our minds to let his words and actions have a definite influence in all the decisions we make. We must show positive works, and the faith that underlies those works. It will cost us sufferings of various kinds to be a full Christian. ''Christ began to teach his disciples that the Son of Man had to suffer much.'' If we will be Christ in the world—and this is the apostolate of the layman—then we must expect to suffer. And if we are not willing to do this, then we cannot hope to renew the world in Christ. So, as Christians, we need to take a stand on violence, brutality, the killing of the innocent, the damaging of private and public property. War, as it is fought today, cannot be tolerated, much less glorified. The hatred of labor for management must stop. Yes, abuses must be corrected, but in a spirit of genuine brotherly love. As a Christian, I cannot sit idly by and watch millions of fellow human beings starving because of politics. The list could go on and on. But let me conclude. Before I do, please do not ''cop out'' on your Christian responsibility by asking for someone to show you what to do. The only One to ask, really, is the Spirit of God, and he it is whom we invoke in this Mass. To summarize, let's hear once again Cardinal Cushing's ''if's'' (*Read again the opening paragraph*).

O.J.M.

## Twenty-Fourth Sunday of the Year (C)

Suggested Use: First Eucharistic Prayer

## *IMPORTANCE OF THE INDIVIDUAL*

(*Note to Homilist:* The parable of the "Prodigal Son" is found for the fourth Sunday of Lent. It is repeated for this Sunday, under the long form. This homily is written on the short form for today, which does not include this parable.)

To Christ, the individual was extremely important. To make his point quite clear, Jesus gave up his life for each one of us. But before he did so, he taught the importance of the individual in many acts and teachings: the widow of Naim and her son, Peter's mother-in-law, Mary Magdalene, the story of the prodigal son, and the two stories just read in today's gospel, that of the lost sheep, and of the lost coin. Those whom Christ appointed to take his place also learned the importance of the individual. For example, the early Church reflected on the Old Testament accounts of Moses' acceptability as an individual in the sight of God. Look at the mercy he obtained for his people, as we heard in the first reading. And Paul is not ashamed to use his own life as an example of the care and concern God has for an individual like himself.

Close attention to the parts of the Mass that refer to us will show how important we are in the eyes of God. Time after time in the Eucharistic Prayer (Roman Canon), our importance as individuals, as well as a group of people assembled in God's name, is brought out. We not only pray by name for the Pope and the Bishop, but immediately after for those whom we especially mention. Individuals find their greatest importance in the family. So, we ask God to accept this offering from his whole family. In the words of Christ at the consecration of the blood, I say to each of you: "This blood is to be shed for you and for all so that sins may be forgiven." Even the dead retain their individual importance, as we pray for them in the remembrance of the dead. And then we recognize that the reality of the importance of each individual is not based on "what we truly deserve" but rather on God's "mercy and love."

There is a tendency to think in terms of numbers. So many thousands killed in the Asian conflicts. Unless one of these boys is someone from our family or friends, then he is just a number, not an individual with personal dignity, a smile, the ability to love, destined for eternal life.

Christ is opposed to considerations of people simply as numbers, statistics, figures on a chart, results of a poll. He speaks of *one* sheep, of *one* lost coin. Each is valuable, not because it is just one more of something, but because of itself. That's the main point of the gospel, regardless of whether we consider one sheep out of a hundred, or one silver piece out of ten, worth all the trouble to recover it. Christ did not die for us as groups of people, but as individuals worthy of his love.

In the troubles that beset us at this present time, it is necessary for us to check our attitudes toward other people. There is a tendency to look at people first according to the groups in which we place them. Is he white or black? Is she Catholic or Jewish? Does he have a foreign accent? Does he belong to the union? Is she a Sister or a laywoman? Is she beautiful? Blond? Brunette? Does he have money? A degree? Good position? It is because we ask these and similar questions first and foremost, and not in their proper perspective, that we fail to consider the value of each human being according to the value God gave him, the value that Christ indicates in the gospel reading for today.

The revelation of God in today's liturgy asks us to consider our attitudes toward our fellow man. He is worth the lifeblood of Jesus Christ. As we stand at the altar of sacrifice, does each human being have the worth in our eyes that he has in the eyes of Christ?

O.J.M.

## Twenty-Fifth Sunday of the Year (A)

# *THE GENEROUS EMPLOYER**

* Commentators are by no means in agreement as to the occasion of this parable, either as told by Jesus or as retold in the primitive Church. It may reflect on the problem of the disciples who were first called and those called later, or on that of the first Jewish converts and later Gentile converts, or perhaps even Old Testament election and New Testament election. Considering the reading of this Sunday, it would seem that the liturgy wishes to emphasize that God's generosity cannot be judged by human standards: "My thoughts are not your thoughts." In any case, allegorical interpretations miss the point; for example, there is no sense in trying to determine what the hour of dawn represents in contrast to the later hours of the day. The parable teaches that no one should complain about God's generosity.

Today's gospel presents a perplexing parable, which looks like a case of gross injustice. The laborers all worked for a different amount of time, but all got the same wage. These days, such action by an employer would probably bring on a strike or at least a demonstration.

But if we look closely at the parable, we see that no injustice was done. The workmen hired at dawn reached an agreement with their employer for the usual daily wage, a perfectly just arrangement. All they were entitled to, both according to the economic standards of the day and their personal contract, was a full day's pay for a full day's work. And that is exactly what they got. When they found out that the others had also received a full day's pay, which was really none of their business, they became indignant and demanded more. But they did not have a leg to stand on. Their contract had been fulfilled to the letter. The shamefulness of their complaint is revealed in the answer of the owner: "Are you envious because I am generous?"

Within the parable, the owner is shown to be both just and generous. He was just to the first workers. He was generous to those who came later. The owner knew that the first workers would have enough money for their daily needs; he had concern for the later workers, as he worried about their having to go home to wife and family with less than enough to keep them going for another day. His action was not arbitrary; it was motivated by pity for the poor workers. And yet, we may feel uncomfortable about the parable. Something is wrong. To begin with, employers do not pay wages out of pity. If one ever did, he probably would not stay in business very long, not to mention that his regular employees would revolt. In life, things just don't work out the way they did in the parable. It is precisely in this realization that we come to the lesson Jesus had in mind. There *is* something wrong—something wrong with our human smallness and pettiness. As we heard God say in the first reading, "My thoughts are not your thoughts, nor are your ways my ways." Jesus was in effect saying: "Do you want to know what God is like? He is kind, merciful, and generous—much more so than any human being would ever be!"

Still, we may say that the reaction of the first workers in the parable was natural. It was indeed. In fact, it was so natural that we must constantly be on guard against it, lest we find ourselves complaining about God's incomprehensible generosity. We have agreed with God to live a life of fidelity and love for him, and he will give us a just reward.

Meanwhile, we should not be looking around to see what others are doing or not doing, or what gifts others may have from God. Every now and then, we hear about the "deathbed conversion" of someone who has lived a pretty wild life, and perhaps we are moved to feel that it is simply not fair. We try to live our whole lives as good Catholics, and somebody comes along and in a few minutes makes his peace with God and goes to heaven, as apparently the good thief on the cross did. If God wants to be overly generous with such people, that is his business and we have no right to complain. After all, nothing has been taken away from us.

Sometimes we may be tempted to be distressed about people who seem to be "getting away with murder." We work hard, try to be good and to do the right thing all the time, while those who seem to care little for God or anyone but themselves prosper and have everything their own way. We may think that we are better than them morally, and yet they are better off than us financially, socially, and in every other natural way. Maybe we feel not only envious of such people, but also a little spiteful toward God because of their good fortune. If such be the case, we must open our ears and listen to God saying to us, "I am free to do as I please, am I not? Or are you envious because I am generous?"

There is another reality we must face. Does God deal with *us* in strict justice alone, or is he also very generous toward us? Is there anything, when you come down to it, that we can do to merit the reward of heaven in strict justice? Certainly not! Even a full lifetime of work for God is more than amply repaid with the eternal life of heaven. The greatest saints received a richer reward than they deserved. In other words, we too are the recipients of God's great generosity.

In the preface of the Mass, we proclaim that we do well always and everywhere to give God thanks. We should be grateful that God is just, but we should be ecstatic in our thanksgiving that he is also generous—more generous than any human being ever could be. God's generosity, no matter to whom it may be extended, is something we should never complain about.

C.E.M.

**Twenty-Fifth Sunday of the Year\* (B)**

## *PEOPLE ARE PRECIOUS*

When many of us were young, we were often reminded that children should be seen and not heard. That was a way of telling us that children had a place, and that they had better learn to keep it. The "place" was perhaps not very exalted in the minds of some, but in our Lord's own day children were underprivileged indeed. They enjoyed no clear rights in society. They were almost totally dependent on the good will of their elders, and were treated quite impersonally, like an "it" rather than a "he."\*\*

The scene in today's gospel is a very touching one. Jesus took a little child and put his arms around him. The words that followed, however, came as a shock to the disciples: "Whoever welcomes a child such as this for my sake welcomes me." Were children suddenly to become very important people? Was there to be an almost complete change in the way children were regarded? Yes, that is what Jesus was demonstrating for his disciples both by his words and by his actions. But Jesus wanted to teach a more extensive lesson: if even a child, this "it" of that day's society, must be treated with respect and love, then *every* human being must be treated with respect and love. Jesus was saying in effect that all people are important: big people and little people, rich people and poor people, clean people and dirty people, black people and white people.

Jesus gave a reason why all people are important: he said, "Whoever welcomes a child . . . welcomes me." The book of Genesis teaches us that God made man in his own image and likeness. That image, that idea which God has is a Person, God the Son. Human beings are made in the image and likeness of God the Son. This conformity to God the Son is the first and primary source of their dignity and worth. Moreover, God the Father sent his Son into the world to be human like us in all things except sin, and thereby elevated and sanctified human life. God de-

---

\* Both last Sunday's gospel and today's contain a prediction of the passion. Moreover, today's declaration, "If anyone wishes to rank first, he must remain the last one of all and the servant of all," finds a more complete treatment in the gospel for the Twenty-Ninth Sunday of the Year. The homily presented here, therefore, concentrates on the theme of welcoming even a child.

\*\* Bruce Vawter, C.M., *The Four Gospels*, p. 206.

mands respect for human beings as he demands respect for his own Son.

Respect for human life is quickly being reduced in our society. The reason is that we are experiencing a creeping atheism all around us: not just a theoretical atheism which says there is no God, but more significantly a practical atheism which acts as if there is no God. Without God, there is no sound basis for human dignity. Christianity teaches that man is made a little less than the angels, but atheism puts man in a position which is little better than that of animals.

There are several symptoms of the effect of creeping atheism. The first of these is the abortion movement. No informed person in his right mind can pretend that the child in the womb is not a human being. Science has proven that the product of human conception is a human being right from the beginning, that human life is a continuum from conception until death. But if the child is not made in the image and likeness of God, why should anyone worry about him? If that child is not of great worth in the sight of God, why should anyone inconvenience himself for the sake of that child? No one is going to make any considerable sacrifice to safeguard the life of an alley cat, but without God an unborn child is but little better than an animal.

Take the problem of racial prejudice. Why shouldn't I look down on other people if I do not believe that God has created all men equal? There would be no need for civil rights organizations if we all lived according to the words of the Declaration of Independence, which states "that man has been endowed by the Creator with certain inalienable rights." The problem of parental authority fits into the same context. There is no real reason for a child to respect and obey his parents if he does not believe that God has created him through those parents. Atheism implies that conception and birth are biological accidents, not the work of God. Moreover, when a parent tries to persuade his child that he should not use dope, there is no good argument without God. If a human person has no divinely given dignity, why shouldn't he do with his body whatever he wants, even if it be to destroy that body with drugs? And why shouldn't he use another person sexually solely for his own pleasure? How can there be anything seriously wrong with murder, rape, and all the rest, if there is no belief in God?

It is imperative that we overcome creeping atheism in our society. The primary way to do so is not by arguments and debates, but by living our faith. As believers in God, as followers of Christ, we must respect all human beings, big people and little people, rich people and poor people, clean people and dirty people, black people and white people. To do less is to be an atheist in practice, if not in theory.

C.E.M.

## Twenty-Fifth Sunday of the Year (C)
Suggested Use: Long Form of the Gospel

# *THE DEVIOUS MANAGER*

Of all the gospels of the year, today's is one of the most puzzling. With the old translation we used to refer to it as the parable of the unjust steward, but with the new translation I suppose that we would think of it as the parable of the devious manager. In either case, we are shocked to think that Jesus could praise such a man.

It is true that the manager was irresponsible in his care of his employer's property. The gospel says that he dissipated the rich man's possessions, which implies that he mishandled his affairs, probably for his own profit. When he received notice that he was going to be fired, he struck upon a plan to win favor with his employer's debtors. He called each one and reduced their debt. This action, which is the heart of the parable, did not constitute another act of dishonesty, as we may be led to believe. The debt owed included the manager's commission, and what he apparently was doing was giving up that commission which belonged to him. Even today some promissory notes are written not in the amount of the principal, but with the interest and commissions totaled in. In other words, what the manager did was to give up his commission as a favor to the debtors, so that when he was fired they would befriend him. And so the employer gave the manager credit, not for being dishonest, but for showing initiative.

It was from the enterprise and initiative of the manager that Jesus drew his lesson. The manager not only had the good sense to realize that his future was in jeopardy, but he also decided to get some insurance for that future. He did a great favor for the debtors so that they would have to return the favor. As the manager himself said, "Here is a way to make sure that people will take me into their homes when I am let go."

But Jesus does not want us to be just like the manager because, after all, he did make a big mistake. He was correct in worrying about his future; his mistake was in not looking far enough into the future. In other words, he was preparing only for temporal security when he would lose his job, but he should have been thinking about eternal security when he would lose his life.

It is really a shame that we do not work harder at our own eternal security. Jesus says that we are to use this world's goods to gain a lasting reception in heaven. Money is not an end in itself. Money is supposed to be used to support one's family, to help the poor, to spread religion. Frankly, money is a great danger. We can make our whole lives an effort to build up wealth, and forget about the needs of others who are worse off than we. This was the kind of thoughtless greed condemned by the prophet Amos in the first reading today. Money can even make us forget about God and think that we can do without him. Even for those who are poor, money can be a problem—because we can easily be trapped into thinking about little else than getting more money.

But the gospel story continues; we have just a small part of a complete episode in today's reading. It goes on to say that the Pharisees, who were fond of money, were listening to what Jesus was saying and they began to sneer at him. No doubt, some of us today may be tempted to sneer at this teaching of Christ that money is not the end of life, or at least we may be inclined to feel that it isn't very practical. We live in a society that canonizes the wealthy and forgets about eternal life. As Christians we must remember that our true wealth, our lasting wealth, is spiritual. Our time and our money must be spent in building up treasures in heaven. That is the kind of wealth which no one, not even someone like the devious manager, can steal from us.

In every Mass we have a reminder of true spiritual values. In our memorial of the death of Christ we recall that, though he died penniless, Christ earned for us the greatest wealth possible, the riches of eternal life in heaven. As Christ renews the offering of himself in sacrifice to God the Father, he invites us to join with him as victims. That means that we must offer not only ourselves, but our money and all our possessions as well. We must profess in that offering, that all our worldly goods come from God and are to be used for his glory and our salvation. If we then live in accord with that offering, we can be confident that God will give us a lasting reception in heaven.

C.E.M.

**Twenty-Sixth Sunday of the Year (A)**

## *LOVING OBEDIENCE*

These days, obedience is not very popular for the simple reason that authority is not very popular. Young people especially have become disillusioned with authority figures in all phases of life. As they look at their world, they judge that those running things have not done a very good job. They say that their elders have had their chance, and have pretty well botched up practically everything they have turned their hand to. Rightly or wrongly, many young people have lost trust in authority.

In addition to the unique situation of our day, there is a perennial problem with obedience and authority. Every human being has at one time or another felt that the obedience required by authority tends to crush human freedom. It certainly is true that when you are under an authority you cannot always do what you want, the way you want to do it, or when you want to do it. At work, you have to do the job as the boss requires. On the highway and streets, you have to drive your car as the law prescribes. Even on a football team, you have to play according to the rules and the game plan of the coach. Authority means restrictions and obedience demands self-discipline.

It is no wonder that history is filled with revolutions against authority, but have all revolts been simply a rejection of authority as such? Hardly. In many instances the real problem has been with a lack of trust in a specific authority figure, either because of incompetence or bad faith, not with authority as such. When the American colonies broke with Great Britain, they immediately set about forming another government, one they thought they could trust. In the famous story, *Mutiny on the Bounty*, when Captain Bligh was removed from authority, Mr. Christian immediately took over and was accepted by the crew because they trusted him. The point is that thinking men do not revolt against authority simply because it restricts their freedom. They recognize that some authority is necessary. But they do revolt against an authority that is incompetent or of bad faith.

Today's liturgical readings are concerned with God's authority and our obedience. But since the problems with human authority figures are uppermost in many people's minds these days, it is necessary to remember that none of their human shortcomings can be ascribed to God.

That is something about which we must make no mistake. God is fully competent because of his wisdom. He knows better than we or anyone else what is best for us. God is also of perfect good faith, because in his supreme love he wills only the best for us.

Jesus has given us the perfect example of obedience to God, and he exemplifies its results. Though he is divine himself, Jesus took on our human condition and made himself subject in loving obedience to the authority of his Father. And what was the result of his complete trust in the competence and good faith of his Father? Was he crushed? To the unwise it may appear so, since his obedience led him to death on a cross. But it was precisely because of his total obedience that God highly exalted him in the glory of his resurrection. The Father in his inscrutable wisdom determined what was best for his Son, and in his infinite love gave him the highest possible personal fulfillment.

We cannot always determine easily what it is that God asks of us. We have God's revelation as taught us by the Church, and we must follow it, but even this leaves many gaps for us concerning details. Our lives are a constant search for God's will. The important thing, however, is our attitude. And St. Paul instructs us today that our attitude must be like that of Christ. We are here at this Mass to tell God that we will obey his wishes. That is one thing that our offering should say. But we must not be like the son in the gospel parable who, when told by his father to go and work in the vineyard, replied, "I am on my way," but never went. Words are not obedience; actions are. Words, even the beautiful words, "Thy will be done," which we will pray in the "Our Father" are not enough. "Thy will be done on earth as it is in heaven," we will say. And how is God's will done in heaven? With perfect, unquestioning obedience. It is our attitude, then, that matters, our readiness to accept God's will for us, whatever it may be.

In honesty, we must admit that problems with human authority will continue simply because the authority is human. To God's authority, however, we can and must respond with perfect, unquestioning obedience. Our attitude must be like that of Christ. If it is, then we can be sure that our reward will be like his too, because God's authority is competent and of good faith.

C.E.M.

**Twenty-Sixth Sunday of the Year\* (B)**

## *STARFISH AND CHRISTIANS*

The starfish is a fascinating marine animal. From its central disc radiate five armlike projections. What is so remarkable about the starfish is its ability called autotomy. If some underwater creature has gotten a firm grip on one of its arms, the starfish can break off the captured arm in order to escape to freedom, thereby disappointing its hungry adversary. What is even more remarkable, the starfish can later grow an entirely new arm, a process known as regeneration.

In comparison with starfish, we as human beings have only limited powers of regeneration. Cut areas of the skin or a broken bone can be regenerated, but not an entire structure such as an arm or even a finger. You wouldn't mind cutting off a hand or foot or even tearing out an eye, if you could simply grow back the missing part. And yet Jesus today in the gospel is talking to us as if we were starfish!

Of course Jesus did not wish to be taken literally. His words about cutting off a hand or foot and tearing out an eye represent a typically Semitic way of making a point by means of exaggeration. But Jesus did want to make a point, and he wanted to make it quite emphatically: nothing is more important than eternal salvation; no sacrifice is too great to attain it.

The Jesus we hear in the gospel today seems somewhat out of character with our usual picture of the gentle, loving Savior, the good shepherd, the divine physician. His words sound somber and threating. Jesus pronounced them, however, only because he does love us and has our eternal welfare at heart. His words contain a truth which from time to time we really need to be reminded of. Heaven is the goal of life; it would be a terrible thing to fail to attain that goal. What a tragic mistake it would be to place anything or anyone above our eternal salvation! Jesus does not want our lives to end in tragedy.

Of course we believe that heaven is our goal. If we did not, we

---

\* Since today's gospel pericope is a collection of Jesus' sayings rather loosely connected and combined by the evangelist through means of verbal associations, it is difficult to treat it as a unified whole. And though the reading from Numbers focuses on the first verses of the pericope, it seems that the attention of the people would be caught by the later verses which speak of cutting off hands and feet and tearing out eyes.

wouldn't even bother to be here in church today. And yet, isn't it true that sometimes we are tempted to think that we really don't have to be too strict with ourselves, that we can get by with a bare minimum? Or maybe we become envious of people who seem to get along just fine without any kind of moral code, as they do whatever they please. Sometimes we may even feel that we are missing something. Perhaps we are like the little child who finds a fascination in matches, simply because he has been warned not to play with them.

There is a certain amount of tension in the life of every one of us. I am not talking about the anxieties brought on by modern problems, the kind of nervous tension we see depicted in television commercials for "Compoz" and the like. I am referring to the fact that we are pulled in two directions at the same time—outward toward God and inward toward ourselves. We know that we should lead lives centered on the love of God, that we should be unselfish and loving toward others, but all the while we are tempted to think only of ourselves. If you pick up a rubber band and pull it in opposite directions, you create a tension. Once you let go of one end, there is no longer any tension. God is trying to draw us to himself, but we are pulling in the opposite direction. That makes for tension, and consequently unhappiness for us. In one sense, what life is all about is learning to let go from our end.

I can't tell you what you should let go of. Each person has to discover that for himself. He has to honestly admit what it is, that is holding him back from God. Then he must pray for the courage to make the necessary sacrifice, to give up anything to find God, even if it be something or someone as precious as a hand, or a foot, or an eye.

When we have let go, we will learn that we have done the right thing. The starfish sacrifices an arm, a temporary disadvantage, so that he can survive and later regenerate a new arm. Actually, we are better off than the starfish. We have a much higher form of spiritual regeneration. It is called "resurrection." In this Mass, we profess our faith in the resurrection of Christ and we express hope for our own resurrection. Any temporary disadvantage we may suffer now as a sacrifice will be more than compensated for. We will rise with Christ to a new, a better life, a life of perfect and complete happiness which will never end.

C.E.M.

**Twenty-Sixth Sunday of the Year (C)**

## *THE PARADOX OF POVERTY*

There is a paradox about poverty in the New Testament. On the one hand, Jesus praises poverty. He tells us that a poor man is blessed, fortunate. In many places he insists that money is a danger to us. On the other hand, he is aware that poverty is an evil which must be overcome, and he teaches that we should help to alleviate the poverty of others.

This paradox appears in today's parable about the rich man and the beggar. Jesus obviously does not approve of the condition of the beggar, who is in a pitiable situation. And yet he equally disapproves of the rich man, who by worldly standards was a great success. What then is the ideal? Is it to be found somewhere between wealth and destitution in a kind of compromise? Not necessarily. Wealth is an extremely relative thing. Someone who may pass for a poor man in this country would be counted extremely well off in a country like Nigeria, and the wealthy landowner of Laos might find it difficult to make ends meet in the economic system of the United States. Jesus is not concerned with bank accounts or the lack thereof. His preaching about poverty does not center around quantity of money. Rather, it zeroes in on a quality necessary for Christian living, and that quality is freedom.

Look at the rich man in today's gospel. There is no hint that the man had acquired his wealth dishonestly by stealth or fraud or even at the expense of the downtrodden. And yet our Lord condemned him. Why? Because he had lost his freedom. He had become so enamored of wearing fine clothes and enjoying a splendid banquet every day that he had no time for God or for his fellow men. He was so wrapped up in his pleasures that he was living like an atheist, as if there were no God to whom he would have to answer for his conduct. His fault was not merely that he used his money for selfish ends, but that he refused to use it to help a destitute man like Lazarus, who was so pitiably in need that he longed to eat the scraps that fell from the rich man's table. Apparently, in his attachment to material things the rich man did not even think to offer the scraps to Lazarus. The rich man had indeed lost his freedom. He was a slave to his wealth.

On the other hand, the beggar was in a very dangerous position. His danger was not primarily that he might die of starvation, but rather that he too might lose his freedom. We need God's material gifts in order to have the leisure of time and mind to worship God and to be concerned about others. If a person has to spend all his time and effort in trying to acquire the bare necessities of life and must literally wonder where his next meal is coming from, he can scarcely turn his attention to God and his interest to others. Jesus laments a poverty which is sheer destitution, because it too destroys freedom.

Most of us here today could not be counted as being either extremely poor or extremely rich. Most of us fit somewhere in the middle. But remember that the ideal does not necessarily come between wealth and destitution in a kind of compromise. The question is how free are we. Are we satisfied with moderation, or deep in our hearts are we constantly yearning for more and more? Most Americans seem to live to the extent of their income, even after that income increases. Inflation is not the only reason. In our society, we are pretty well geared to spending our money on ourselves.

One of the best tests of our freedom from attachment to money is our willingness to help others who are in need. It's true that we hear many appeals for money, both in and outside church. It is easy for us to quiet our consciences by telling ourselves that we really don't have anything to spare. But remember that wealth is relative. What may seem like scraps to us, represents a means of survival for others. The least we can do is to share something of our abundance with others—that is the very least, for we must keep in mind that our material goods are a gift from God. The comfortable circumstances that most of us enjoy in this country are given us by God, so that we may be free to practice charity to others and to enjoy the mental leisure we need to be mindful of God, as we are here at this Mass. Our worship of God, the source of all goodness, must overflow in a generosity toward others. That overflow should be motivated by love, but it helps to remember, as the rich man in today's parable failed to do, that there is a God who will judge us in our use of his material gifts.

Whenever Jesus speaks about poverty or wealth, his main concern is with freedom. The rich man in today's gospel was condemned not because he was wealthy, but because he was selfish. His selfishness destroyed his freedom to worship God and to share with others. Rich or poor, how really free are we?

C.E.M.

**Twenty-Seventh Sunday of the Year (A)**

## *WHO'S REJECTING HIM NOW ?*

One of the most incredible things in the life of Jesus is the fact that so many people rejected him. Jesus went about doing good, trying to lead people to everlasting happiness. Not only did he preach the goodness and love of his Father for men, but he himself revealed that goodness and love by his actions. Jesus was disappointed by rejection, but not surprised. Rejection was part of the long, sad history of his people, a history which Jesus of course knew very well.

Jesus reflected on the ministry of Isaiah, the prophet, some seven hundred years previously. He recalled the first reading we heard today, in which Isaiah gently tried to persuade the people to turn from their wicked, fruitless lives. Isaiah started with a point of agreement. He observed that a man who carefully prepared a vineyard and planted the best of vines was right in expecting fine grapes from his vines. A fruitless vine deserved only to be rooted up. Everybody had to agree with that. Then slowly, Isaiah revealed the hard truth: the people were the fruitless vine which had received so much care and attention from God. Jesus took a cue from Isaiah. He too spoke of a vineyard and began with a point of agreement, but he made his lesson more personal. Instead of speaking of an expectation from the vines, he referred to the duty of the tenant farmers. It was their obligation to make a return to the owner on his investment. The slaves sent by the owner represented the prophets of the Old Testament, such as Isaiah. The son sent as a last resort represented Jesus himself. It was bad enough to mistreat the slaves, but it was intolerable to kill the son of the owner. This was a clear warning which was to go unheeded.

It is indeed incredible that the prophets and even Jesus himself were rejected by so many people. There are many complicated reasons, but one reason is that the truth can hurt—not indeed the truth about the goodness and love of God, but the truth that God demands and deserves a response to his goodness and love. That response means a complete change in life, a way of acting that is different. When the truth makes us face our own failures and inadequacies and our own need for change, we put up defenses. The simplest is to ignore or deny the truth. When a teacher, for example, informs irresponsible parents that their child is both a scholastic and a disciplinary problem in school, that evaluation is a judgment of the parents as well as the child. Rather than face their own failure and the need to do something about the child, the parents take the easy way out and reject the teacher's report.

Who's rejecting Jesus now? We might say that the answer is obvious—all the irreligious, unbelieving people in the world. But it is informative to note that today's parable was not addressed to irreligious, unbelieving people. Jesus told the parable to the scribes and Pharisees, who prided themselves on the exactness of their religious observances. The problem was that their piety was merely external, not from the heart.

The teaching of Jesus is really very demanding, even frightening. Have we really listened to it, or have we put up our defenses? Real listening means nothing less than constantly admitting that we have not yet put into practice what we profess or believe. Remember what Jesus has taught in the gospels just during the past five Sundays: take up your cross and follow him; have the courage humbly to correct the faults of others; be so eager to forgive others that you forget what they have done to hurt you; be content with God's generosity to others when the last come first; give God complete obedience like that of Christ, which led him to suffering and death.*

That sampling is not an easy teaching to listen to. Who wants to give up comfort and pleasure to take up a cross of illness, or loneliness, or frustration? The cross seems a crazy approach to life. And that stuff about correcting the faults of others—well, just try it and you'll see that it never works anyway. As for this business of forgiving and forgetting, that's fine for someone to talk about who hasn't really been deeply hurt. And why should bad people always seem to be better off? It isn't right. And if God is so loving, how can he demand an obedience that leads to suffering and death?

Are we listening to the teaching of Jesus Sunday after Sunday, or have we dismissed it as impractical or irrelevant, or as directed to others but not to us? If we let that teaching come through, we open ourselves to the possibility of having to change our lives.

The truth can hurt, even the truth preached by Jesus. That truth demands that we be different from others; it requires that we accept suffering and self-denial, and that we abandon our selfishness to be

---

* The references are, in order, to the gospels of the 22nd through the 26th Sundays of the Year.

generous in our love and of service to God and our fellow men. Don't think about the scribes and the Pharisees. Don't look around at anyone else. Ask yourself the question: "Who's rejecting Jesus now?"

C.E.M.

**Twenty-Seventh Sunday of the Year (B)**

## *GOD'S IDEA OF A LOVE STORY*

In many quarters these days, there is a concern over the rapidly increasing divorce rate. Some psychologists are pointing out that divorce does not solve problems, but only opens up an avenue of temporary escape, an avenue with a dead end. They observe that after divorce a trauma of failure remains, with loneliness and guilt as constant reminders of what might have been. Family counselors have long maintained that children need the love and guidance of *both* parents, and they insist that divorce destroys a part of children's birthright and jeopardizes their future happiness. There is a growing awareness, among some at least, that the relaxation of divorce laws is a favor to no one.

In the gospel we saw Jesus take a strong stand against divorce, despite the practice of his day. His stand was unpopular then and it is unpopular today, but he continues to be opposed to divorce. His position on the permanence of marriage is not based on a legalistic approach—on whether there is a law which either forbids or allows divorce. It is not even based primarily on the harm done to children and society by divorce. Rather, it is based on the fact that sex and its fulfillment in marriage are God's idea, his creation, and that from the beginning God intended marriage to be a lasting relationship between one man and one woman. Jesus has in mind the beauty and meaning of the sexual relationship as expressed in the words from the book of Genesis, "They are no longer two but one flesh."

"They are no longer two but one flesh"—this simple statement, as understood and developed by the long tradition of the Church, means that in God's plan sex is supposed to say something. It is intended to express a relationship so profound that mere words are inadequate for it. Sex says, "I love you completely, exclusively, and forever." "I love you completely—I give myself to you without any holding back, and I accept you just as you are, with all of your wonderful thrilling qualities as well as with your human shortcomings." Let me speak very plainly but quite seriously. We are clothed here today, not only to keep warm or to follow the styles, but because we do not belong to each other. When a husband and a wife express their sexual love, they appear before each other unclothed, naked, because they hold nothing back, they belong entirely to each other. "I love you exclusively—since I have given myself to you completely, I cannot give myself that way to anyone else. This does not mean that I am not interested or concerned with anyone else, but it does mean that my relationship with you is unique. There is no one in the whole world toward whom I feel as I feel toward you." "I love you forever—you are so precious, so valuable to me, that I never want to lose you."

When you love someone this way, you think that person is really special. But you also think that you are pretty good yourself, since you would not want to give something worthless to the person you love uniquely. And since you think you are both very worthwhile people, you instinctively wish to see yourselves repeated and continued in others, your children. Children are not an intrusion on married love, but its finest expression and completion.

"I love you completely, exclusively and forever." This represents a very high ideal of love. The relationship God has in mind cannot be entered into lightly or on a temporary basis. And because it is such a high ideal, we should expect to find that the ideal is not easily reached, that there are many failures along the way. Erich Segal in his popular novel, *Love Story*, which became an equally popular Paramount movie, painted a contemporary picture of a relationship as old as the human race. He made famous the statement, "Love means not ever having to say you're sorry." Some people, while admitting a certain beauty in this statement, have objected to it on the grounds that people do hurt the one they love. Real deep love is not something that happens all of a sudden. It is something which must grow, even amid personal shortcomings. When a wound or hurt has been inflicted, it is vital that the wound be treated with real sorrow; otherwise it leaves a permanent scar. Too many scars destroy the beauty of marriage and lead to the divorce court. Loving someone completely, exclusively, and forever demands bigness, a bigness that can say and mean "I'm sorry." You see, sex is rightly rated "X"—adults only. It is for mature, generous, unselfish people.

In the Mass, we should praise and thank God for the wonderful gift of sex. We should also pray that we and everyone may see what God had in mind, when he created sex to be an expression of a love which is complete, exclusive, and forever.

C.E.M.

**Twenty-Seventh Sunday of the Year (C)**

## *FAITHFULNESS*

There are many fascinating characters in the Bible, people like Abraham, Moses, Isaiah, Jeremiah and so on through a long list. One rather obscure prophet, with the unusual name of Habakkuk, is a man I would like to have met. Perhaps I am interested in him because there have been times when I have wished for a courage like his to stand before God and complain. "How long, O Lord? I cry for help but you do not listen!"

In a sense, Habakkuk represents all of us during those times when everything seems to be going wrong, when perhaps we feel that God is indeed in heaven but far distant from our very real, very troubled world. Frankly, I would not dare speak to God as Habakkuk did, with the courage to complain to God and even the audacity to suggest that God should wake up and look to his business of governing the world and directing the affairs of men. We are fortunate that Habakkuk spoke to God as he did, reflecting a concern that is or can be ours, because through him we have a response from God. Apparently, God was not displeased with his prophet, since he answered him in gentle, understanding tones. In effect God said: "Be patient with me. I have a plan. What I ask of you is faith, and because of your faith you will live."

The faith God asked is not the kind we ordinarily think of, a mere belief that there is a God. Obviously Habakkuk believed in God; otherwise he would not have called upon him. What God meant by faith is a loyalty and trust, a steadfastness especially in the face of difficulties. Such faith is a combination of love and confidence. Perhaps the best single word in English for this quality is "faithfulness."

It is easy to be faithful to God when everything is going well for us, just as it is easy to be loving and kind to pleasant, cooperative people. A young married man thought he knew the meaning of faithfulness and love, until his attractive and affectionate wife was seriously injured in an automobile accident. Instead of coming home after work to a well-prepared dinner and the responsive love of a vibrant woman, he found that he had to be housekeeper and nurse during the long weeks of her convalescence. He slowly went from generous service to impatience, almost exasperation. He resented the heavy burden that had been placed upon him, as he forgot that he had married for better or for worse, in sickness as well as in health. During one of his darkest moments, his father pointed out that his wife, weak and frustrated on a bed of pain, had not uttered a single word of complaint. His father added these simple words: ''Your wife is a very strong woman. If your roles were reversed, don't you believe that she would not hesitate to do anything for you?'' Later that night, the husband stood over his sleeping wife with tears in his eyes and prayed for forgiveness. He resolved that he would be faithful to her, no matter what.

At this moment God is asking that we be faithful to him, especially during our most turbulent and frustrating moments. Like the apostles, we should turn to Jesus during this Mass and pray: ''Lord, increase our faith.'' The apostles, whom Jesus had sent forth to preach, were apparently overwhelmed by the demands of their apostolate and dismayed by the people's lack of response. At that time the apostles did not know that Jesus himself, during the hours of his passion, would be in a situation which would tax the limits of even his endurance. They could not foresee that on the cross, Jesus the man would feel abandoned by his Father and would nonetheless remain faithful as he cried out in a dying gasp: ''Father, into your hands I commend my spirit'' (Lk 23:46). And though he died, Jesus was raised to the fullness of life because of his faithfulness.

In this Mass, we celebrate the death and resurrection of Jesus. We are invited to thank God not only for the salvation which has come to us through the death and resurrection of his Son, but also for the example he has given us. Today as we pray ''Lord, increase our faith,'' we should do so with the realization that our difficulties in life can never match the sacrifice of Jesus. Jesus will never ask more of us than he actually gave himself. His faithfulness should stand as a motive for our own confidence and trust. Like our brother Jesus, we have taken the Father as our God for better or for worse, in sickness as well as in health, but faithfulness means our belief that all will yet be well. With Jesus, we will pass through the passion and death of this world to the fullness of life in the resurrection.

C.E.M.

## Twenty-Eighth Sunday of the Year (A)
Suggested Use: Short Form of the Gospel*

## *WE'VE BEEN INVITED*

We have an old saying that a bird in the hand is worth two in the bush. This saying means, of course, that having something right now is better than holding out a hope for something more in the future. This saying may be true of hunting, but it is certainly not true about life itself.

As Catholics, our approach to life is based on the belief that what lies before us after death, even though unseen, is better than what we have in this world, no matter how good or bad things may seem right now. We believe that God calls us to be happy not merely in a passing way, but forever in heaven. We are basically on a journey to a promised land. We profess to believe that heaven in the future is better than this earth in the present.

In today's gospel, Jesus compares heaven to a great banquet. The imagery was not new. It was used in the Old Testament, as we heard in the first reading from Isaiah, because a splendid banquet is a symbol of joy and happiness, as well as mutual union and love. Even in our own experience, we can recall a special dinner at Thanksgiving or Christmas at which everyone enjoys not only all the fine food and drink, but also the conversation and the feeling of friendship and love. As Jesus told the

---

* The story of the man without a wedding garment poses special problems if read in conjunction with the parable in vv. 1-10. One wonders how a man who has been dragged off to a celebration could possibly be expected to appear in proper attire. Some maintain that it was usual for the host to supply invited guests with a wedding garment (cf. 2 K 10:22), but there is no evidence of such a practice in Jesus' day. The best explanation appears to be that the incident was actually a separate parable, and so we should not expect consistency with the previous episode. It seems better, therefore, to use the short form of the gospel which omits the second parable, rather than attempt a long explanation of how and why these two parables came to be joined together.

parable, he described how the king made elaborate preparations for his dinner and then sent out his invitations. To the amazement of the king, some ignored the invitation and went off to attend to business and personal affairs. To the absolute indignation of the king, others rose up in rebellion against him and murdered his servants. Those invited represented both the Jewish people of the day and their leaders, some of whom in rebellion killed Jesus himself. If we did not know how the people and especially their leaders reacted to Jesus and his invitation to his kingdom, we would think the parable farfetched. Jesus told the parable as a warning to the people of his time, but also as an indication to us that we too have received an invitation, for we are the people who were later called to the banquet.

We have not ignored this invitation; otherwise we would not be here at Mass today. But we are still on our way to the banquet. Since we have not yet arrived, we have to make sure that we do not turn aside on the way. A danger to us is that we may allow the affairs of this life, our pleasure, as well as our obligations, to blot out our vision of heaven as the real goal of life. This life, the bird in the hand, is very real. Its attractions are appealing and its duties compelling. Heaven, the two birds in the bush, seems very unreal and far away. We believe it is there and we know it is our goal, but we are not quite sure what it is all about. None of us has ever seen God, and so we cannot appreciate him. We know that he will give us an unending life of perfect happiness, but we can't get a picture of that in our imagination. Faith, and faith alone, can keep us moving toward heaven.

The Mass is the closest thing to heaven on earth. I don't mean that the Mass is close to what heaven is like, in the sense that the thrill we get from Mass is like the happiness in heaven—often we don't get any thrill at all. I mean that since Jesus has rightly compared heaven to a banquet, the Mass as a spiritual banquet is intended to be a preview of heaven. The Mass is the celebration of God's family, like our own family dinner at Thanksgiving or Christmas.

Frequently, grandparents have the Thanksgiving or Christmas dinner in their home. They invite their own adult children together with all their grandchildren. Often there are so many people that it is a bedlam, but it is really great to get a chance to talk to each other—and of course the grandparents especially want to have a word with everyone who comes. Usually everybody brings something for the meal; one will bring the salad and another the dessert and so on. It's a practical thing, with so many mouths to feed, but it is also a way of showing love and respect for the grandparents, for the food is really a form of gift. Then the climax of the celebration comes when everyone sits down at the table to share the fine dinner.

In the Mass, God our Father calls us together in his home, the Church. Here he wants to speak to us, and he does so in the scriptures and the homily. He also wants us to speak to him, and we do so in the prayers and hymns. We even bring some of the food that will be used in the dinner, as the procession with the bread and wine to the altar symbolizes. But that is more than a practical thing, because we want to give a gift to God to show our love and respect. The gift we give, however, is not bread and wine, but bread and wine changed into the body and blood of Christ as a sign of his great love on the cross, the kind of love we want to have for God. Then in the climax of our celebration, God calls us to his banquet table where we all share in the spiritual food of Holy Communion.

Heaven is God's eternal home, where he wants to have a great big family celebration, an everlasting banquet of joy and happiness. We have been invited. And through all the cares and distractions of this life, and even with a bird in the hand, the way in which we celebrate Mass together with faith and devotion is a sign that we accept the invitation.

C.E.M.

**Twenty-Eighth Sunday of the Year (B)**

## HAPPINESS AND THE EYE OF THE NEEDLE

Almost every little boy at some time has said, "When I grow up I want to be a fireman." How thrilling it seems to stand on the back of a big red truck as it races toward a fire, with its sirens sounding and its lights flashing! How dramatic to climb a precarious ladder into a blazing home to rescue a child, carry him to safety, and place him in the arms of his anxious parents! How satisfying to be acclaimed a hero with your picture in the newspaper! Or so it seems to a little boy. For the veteran fire fighter, the romance has ended long ago. He has made thousands of trips in the middle of the night and climbed as many ladders, breathed immeasurable quantities of poisonous smoke, suffered injuries and burns, and seen his fellow firemen die. He knows better than anyone else why hell is described in terms of fire.

Many firemen have asked themselves whether it is all worth the limited pay or the expectation of a pension still far in the future. Why does such a man continue in his job? One fireman gave his answer: "I know that I could not do anything else with such a great sense of accomplishment." His answer reflects the spirit of wisdom presented in our first reading today. It is much like the attitude of the nun who was a nurse in a Louisiana hospital for lepers. A man watched her changing bandages on the ulcerated legs of a patient and said, "Sister, I would not do what you do for a million dollars." The sister, barely looking up, replied, "Neither would I."

Psychologists have conducted studies on the source of the most elusive of human qualities which we call happiness. Their conclusion has been summarized this way: "Happiness is not in proportion to wealth and leisure, but comes with a sense of accomplishment." It is not without reason that we have developed the saying, "Money can't buy happiness." Many widows, despite comfortable financial means, have discovered that with their husbands dead and their children grown, they feel that their lives are without purpose and value. They are unhappy. Men have retired hoping to enjoy a life of leisure, only to find that there is a hollowness in having nothing worthwhile to do. They are unhappy. Yet people like the fireman and the nun have found happiness, not in wealth or leisure, but in a sense of accomplishment.

You know, the world did not have to wait for psychologists to determine that happiness does not come from wealth and leisure. Jesus taught that very truth a long time ago. In fact, he repeatedly warned that riches are a threat to achieving eternal happiness in heaven—not the only threat but certainly a major one. That is why he invited the rich man to sell what he had and give to the poor so that he would have treasure in heaven. Throughout the history of the Church, some men and women have taken the words of Jesus literally and embraced the vow of poverty. Not every follower of Christ, however, can become a Trappist monk or a cloistered nun, for if everyone did so no one would be left to carry on the ordinary life of society in a Christian manner. And yet everyone can, and must, take as his own the spirit of the words of Jesus. Everyone can acquire a sense of detachment from wealth, a realization that money is not the end and goal of life, but only a means for supporting life.

No one can deny that it is nice to have enough money to do things and go places and not have to worry about making ends meet. Isn't it true, though, that after you have taken a trip or enjoyed some entertainment there is a certain emptiness when it's all over? The pleasure soon fades. But when you do something for someone else, when you have followed the teaching of Jesus to love your neighbor as he has loved you, the satisfaction does last. And the reward will last forever. A camel trying to pass through a needle's eye is no more ludicrous than a greedy person trying to squeeze into the kingdom of heaven. Only by ridding ourselves of the bloated hump of selfishness and the excess baggage of riches, can we hope to make it.

In the Eucharist we have a living memorial of the sacrifice of Jesus Christ: his body given up for us and his blood shed for the forgiveness of our sins. That sacrifice was the greatest accomplishment in the history of the world. Today we are celebrating this Mass because of the command of Jesus, "Do this in memory of me." We will keep his command, not only by celebrating the Mass, but also by trying to lead lives which reflect his sacrificial spirit. That spirit led Jesus to lay down his life for all of mankind. It should lead us to be generous and unselfish with others. It is that spirit alone which gives us what we all seek, that elusive quality which we call happiness.

C.E.M.


## Twenty-Eighth Sunday of the Year (C)
Suggested Use: Fourth Eucharistic Prayer

## *THANKS AND PRAISE*

To experience the ingratitude of someone we have helped is one of the most distressing of human experiences. We have all felt its hurt and pain. When we have done a favor for someone, great or small, we expect at least a "thank you." And we realize that we ourselves should never be remiss in showing our gratitude to others.

The gospel scene today, then, is almost incredible to us. How could the nine men, after being cured by Jesus of a horrible disease, fail to return and thank him? It is very difficult to understand. All of us would like to think that in our relationship with God we are like the Samaritan who returned to give thanks and praise to God. As a matter of fact, thankfulness like that of the Samaritan is the very basis of what our worship of God should be here in the Mass.

In the early days of the Church, people were keenly aware of their need to give thanks to God, and they realized that the best way for them to do so was through the Mass. Their favorite word for the Mass was "eucharist," a word that referred not only to the sacrament of the body and blood of Christ, but also to the whole action of the Mass. It is a Greek word which means "to give thanks." As the early Christians used it, however, the word had a broader meaning than simply a response of gratitude for a favor received. It reflected a usage of the Jews, who did not really have a word which was the exact parallel of our word, "thanksgiving." Among the Jews "to give thanks to God" meant to praise and glorify him. God's showing of his favor toward his chosen people was a sign to them of his goodness and greatness, which made him, in their minds, worthy of worship. Notice that the leper in today's gospel who wanted to show his thanks "came back *praising* God in a loud voice." Jesus himself interpreted that praise of God as a form of thanks. Consequently in our new translations, two words are usually joined together: thanks and praise. For example, at the beginning of the preface your response is, "It is right to give him thanks and praise."

When the early Christians celebrated the Eucharist, their worship was based on this biblical notion of thanksgiving. They realized that God has done good and loving things for people throughout the history of the world. We call these good and loving actions of God in the world "salvation history." The most ancient form of the Eucharistic Prayer, going back to the earliest days of the Church, was based on salvation history.

Our fourth Eucharistic Prayer is a condensed form of that method of prayer, and is modeled on the ancient tradition of the Eucharistic prayers of Antioch, a Christian center founded by St. Peter himself. The theme of our prayer is set by the words: "Father, we acknowledge your greatness; all your actions show your wisdom and love." Actions speak louder than words. We acknowledge God's greatness, that is, we worship him, because all his *actions* show his wisdom and love. This prayer briefly summarizes God's saving actions, from which we too derive benefit today. First is creation itself. Then comes the realization that God did not abandon us in sin, but promised in solemn covenants to send a savior, who in the fullness of time was born of Mary.

Next we briefly recount the public life of Jesus as he went about preaching the news of salvation and communicating aspects of that salvation by doing good. The healing of the ten lepers in today's gospel is one specific example of the good our Savior did. In a climax we recall the great paschal mystery of his death for us and his resurrection from the dead. By his death and resurrection, Jesus destroyed death in the sense that when we die we will rise with him in glory—that is salvation, God's great blessing and kindness toward us. The healing of the lepers was but a partial sharing in the salvation that will completely free us from the effects of sin and death in both body and soul. We also recall Pentecost, the sending of the Holy Spirit to spread the Church, our means of gaining salvation as well as our means of giving thanks and praise to God for our salvation.

This fourth Eucharistic Prayer requires close attention and much thought on our part, since the words are so rich with allusions to what God has done for us. It supplies us with the ancient approach to thanksgiving, the kind of gratitude that our Lord commended in the Samaritan leper. The point to remember, however, is very simple. Actions speak louder than words. We know that God is good because he has done good things, and because he is good he is worthy of the thanks and praise we are privileged to offer him in the celebration of the Eucharist.

                                                                C.E.M.


**Twenty-Ninth Sunday of the Year (A)**

## . . . AND TO GOD

During his public life Jesus was recognized as a moral teacher, and so it was not surprising that he was consulted on the matter of whether Jews should pay taxes to a foreign power. Were the Jews, by acknowledging the dominance of a foreign government, denying God who alone was ruler of Israel?

Those who posed the problem to Jesus, however, were not sincere. They did not hope that he would solve the problem to everyone's satisfaction; rather, they wanted to trick Jesus by means of a dilemma so that they could be rid of him. A simple reply that the tax should be paid would have made him look like a traitor to God. A simple denial would have left him open to the danger of being denounced to the Romans as a seditionist. But Jesus refused to be trapped. When he asked to see the coin used for the tax, one of his adversaries produced, of course, a Roman coin. The possession and use of the Roman coin was itself a sign that the Jews had submitted to Roman authority. Actually, it was at the invitation of the Jews that the Romans first entered Palestine, establishing a protectorate when the land was in a state of bloody anarchy. The people had received and continued to receive benefit from Roman rule, and as a result had assumed obligations as well. Moreover, some in the crowd surely should have remembered that God had previously used foreign rulers to guide the destiny of his people without any abdication of his own kingship over them. For example, today's first reading spoke approvingly of Cyrus, who was king of Persia. Cyrus had conquered Babylon and liberated the Jews. He allowed them to return to their native land, but continued to exercise authority over them.

So the answer of Jesus, as the questioners stared at the Roman coin, was no evasion of the issue. It clearly implied that it was not only lawful to pay the tax but also of obligation in conscience. "Give to Caesar what is Caesar's," Jesus said. Then he added another admonition, one his questioners had not bargained for: "Give to God what is God's." The gospel goes on to say that they were "taken aback by this reply." After all, they thought, who had to tell them to give to God what was God's? Jesus' statement insinuated that they had asked the wrong question and that they were remiss in their religious duties. Considering the insincerity of the questioners as well as their smugness in matters religious, it is not unlikely that such an insinuation was precisely what Jesus intended by his unexpected remark.

As a matter of fact, the Jews were going to pay the tax, no matter what they thought about its propriety. The Romans would see to that, by force if necessary. But God asks only for a service that is freely given. God forces no one to be religious. The questioners, then, needed to be reminded that a legalistic approach to religion and a merely external observance of the law were hardly ways of giving God what is his.

Does this gospel have an application today? Well, you can look at any coin in your pocket or purse and see that the inscription on the back says "United States of America." Since we enjoy benefits from our government, we owe taxes. But whether you think taxes are just or not, whether you approve of the way the government is using the money or not, you will still have to pay taxes. The Internal Revenue Service will see to that, as well as the merchant who simply will not sell you something without collecting the sales tax.

Very frankly, the point we all need to be concerned with is that we must give to God what is God's. And what does that mean? If you tune in at this same time next week, you will hear the answer in the gospel. As they usually do on TV, I will give you a preview. Next week you will hear Jesus say, "You shall love the Lord your God with your whole heart, and with your whole soul, and with all your mind." To put it another way, *everything* belongs to God: our bodies, our souls, our talents, even our possessions. It takes a lifelong, constant effort to give to God what is his, and it is a supreme obligation in conscience of which we must be frequently reminded. God will not force us to give him his due, for he wants a loving service that is freely given from the conviction of faith.

Today in faith, we come before God to offer ourselves completely to him in union with Jesus on the altar. At the conclusion of the Eucharistic Prayer, we will profess that all honor and glory belong to God through, with, and in Christ. Fix firmly in your minds the words of that profession: all honor and glory belong to God. Try to live according to those words during this coming week, as you make a conscious effort to give to God what is God's—in a word, everything.

C.E.M.

## Twenty-Ninth Sunday of the Year (B)
Suggested Use: long form of the gospel

# THE SERVANT AND HIS SERVANTS

The Pope has many titles: Bishop of Rome, Primate of Italy, Patriarch of the West. But the title most in keeping with his role as the vicar of Jesus Christ is "Servant of the Servants of God." Jesus said, "I have come not to be served but to serve." The dictionary defines a servant as one who exerts himself for the benefit of another. Jesus certainly fulfilled that definition.

The first reading today is from a section of the book of Isaiah known as the Songs of the Suffering Servant. We have just heard the word of God from this section proclaiming, "Through his suffering my servant shall justify many and their guilt he will bear." The Suffering Servant is Israel, the faithful people of the Old Testament; but in a larger sense he is Jesus Christ, who served by giving his life in atonement for sin. To say that Jesus exerted himself for the benefit of others is indeed an understatement. Jesus gave all that he had.

The apostles James and John had misunderstood the mission of Jesus as a servant. They thought that he was about to establish a glorious new kingdom in Israel, and they wanted to make sure that they had a place of honor. That is what they had in mind when they asked a favor of Jesus: "See to it that we sit, one at your right and the other at your left when you come into your glory." Little did they realize that Jesus would come into his glory only through his sacrificial death, which Jesus referred to as the cup he had to drink, the bath in which he would be immersed. Good Friday came as a terrible shock to James and John, as well as to the other apostles, and it was only in the light of the resurrection on Easter Sunday that they learned the meaning of Jesus' words in today's gospel. Then they realized that as his followers they too had to become servants, exerting themselves for others even to the point of death. James, as a matter of fact, was beheaded by Herod Agrippa about 44 A.D., the first of the apostles to endure martyrdom. John was not martyred, but he was tortured and exiled to the island of Patmos, where he served his fellow Christians until his death.

It is one thing to appreciate Jesus as a servant and to be grateful for his generosity on our behalf. It is quite another to recognize that we too must be servants, that exerting ourselves for others is the only way to satisfaction and fulfillment in this life, as well as the means for attaining everlasting happiness. Last week we heard Jesus proclaim that happiness does not come from money or leisure but from a sense of accomplishment. Today he wants us to see our accomplishments in terms of service to others. Jesus is very much interested in our having the right attitude in what we do.

We may suspect that to become a servant means doing extraordinary favors for others, special good deeds that are outside the area of our everyday occupations. To some extent that suspicion is correct, but on the other hand we must first get the Christian attitude about our ordinary activities. The Second Vatican Council teaches that "while providing the substance of life for themselves and their families, men and women are performing their activities in a way which appropriately benefits society."* In other words, as fathers and mothers you should not look upon the care of your families as worthless routine or sheer drudgery. Fulfilling your duties is a way of becoming a true servant, and of sharing in the generous spirit that moved Jesus to sacrifice himself for the benefit of the whole world.

Men and women are also engaged in work outside the family. We refer to this work as a job, a word which suggests activity done in order to make money. Money must be earned, but we should look upon our jobs as a way of serving our fellow men. This outlook may appear obvious in the vocation of people like doctors or teachers or social workers, but it is an outlook that should be shared by all in the course of their needful occupations, whether they be bank tellers, sales clerks, truck drivers or garbage collectors. Again the Vatican Council teaches us that the norm of human activity is this: "that in accord with the divine plan and will, it should harmonize with the genuine good of the human race, and allow men as individuals and as members of society to pursue their total vocation and fulfill it."** Whatever our job is, it has come into being because of needs in society. In meeting those needs, we are servants of our fellow men.

As Christians, we must learn to look upon our works as our way of fulfilling our vocation to be servants as was Jesus Christ. We too, like the Pope himself, should cherish as our own the title, "Servant of the Servants of God."

C.E.M.

## Twenty-Ninth Sunday of the Year (C)

## *CATHOLIC PRAYER*

I suspect that most of us have had the experience of getting tired of praying for the same intention again and again without any apparent results. Jesus understood this problem and he was concerned about it. In

---

\* *The Church in the Modern World*, 34.
\*\* *Ibid.*, 35.

today's parable about the widow, he insists on the necessity of praying always and not losing heart.

The emphatic teaching of Jesus is the best reason to pray. And we should see that the example of Jesus clearly indicates that the prayer he has in mind should be not only for ourselves as individuals, but for all people. Dying on the cross, he prayed: "Father, forgive them." His prayer was not just for those present at the crucifixion but for all sinners, which in effect means everyone. And his death itself was in a sense a prayer, an offering to the Father for all mankind. The words of consecration in the Mass proclaim: "This is the cup of my blood . . . shed for you and for all . . ." In the liturgy, the Church has taken its inspiration from the persevering prayer of Jesus for all mankind. The Prayer of the Faithful, following the Creed, is a universal prayer. While there is always room in this prayer for individual petitions, the Church wants us never to omit praying for the needs of the entire Church, for civil rulers and for the salvation of the whole world (see *General Instruction on the Roman Missal*, 45). Notice too, how today in the Eucharistic Prayer we will say: "Lord, may this sacrifice, which has made our peace with you, advance the peace and salvation of all the world" (Third Eucharistic Prayer). Our prayer should be Catholic in accord with our faith, but it should also be catholic in the sense of universal: a generous, unselfish kind of prayer.

Think for a moment back to the scene described in the first reading from the Old Testament. Moses prayed for all the people in a conflict with their enemies. He prayed with his hands held up toward God, after the manner in which the priest holds his hands while praying at Mass. Moses was so persevering in this prayer that his arms grew weary, and in order to continue he needed the support of his brother Aaron, and his companion Hur, who joined him in prayer.

Let me tell you something about my prayer here at Mass as a priest. I hold out my arms to embrace all your prayers, and I raise my hands to heaven to direct them to God. It is my duty as a priest to persevere in this prayer, but the truth is that I sometimes get discouraged as you do. I sometimes get tired of praying, often for the same intentions over and over again, as you do. God, however, calls me as a priest to direct your intentions to him. He wants me to speak in the name of all of you. To fulfill this call, I need your support. I need you to join with me in a spirit of prayer. As you see my arms raised up toward God, you should think of yourselves as supporting my arms by attentively and devoutly identifying yourselves with the prayers I offer in your name to God.

Pope Pius XII said that the faithful should participate in the Mass "not in an inert and negligent fashion, giving way to distractions, but with earnestness and concentration" (*Mediator Dei*, 80). That was the Pope's way of telling us to put into effect the teaching of Jesus in today's gospel on the necessity of praying always and not losing heart. In the Mass the priest is like Moses, but you are like Aaron and Hur. The priest cannot pray effectively alone, any more than Moses could. If my prayer is to be what Jesus wants, you must identify with that prayer through earnestness and concentration.

Jesus wants us to pray with perseverance, and he wants us to pray with an unselfish spirit for others as well as for ourselves. Let our prayer, then, be Catholic, in accord with our faith in Jesus Christ. And let our prayer be catholic, universal, for all mankind.

C.E.M.

## Thirtieth Sunday of the Year (A)
Suggested Use: Third Eucharistic Prayer

# WITH YOUR WHOLE HEART

I think we all recognize that the love we have for a person can find its best expression in time of crisis. A husband may tend to grow thoughtless of his wife and fail to show signs of tenderness and affection, but just let her go into the hospital for a serious operation and he will show how deep his love really is by his worry and concern. Or a mother becomes annoyed with her child who seems always to be complaining, "There's nothing to do around here." After the child is sent out to play he is struck by a car, and in that terrible moment all the love of the mother goes out to her child. It seems a shame that sometimes we wait until a time of crisis to show how great our love is.

Several years ago, a five-year-old girl came down with an extremely rare disease. The doctors understood little about her condition, but they did know that a blood transfusion was imperative, and they wanted her to receive blood exactly like her own, a very rare type. Neither parent had the right type, so the doctors tested the little girl's eight-year-old brother. His type was perfect, but it occurred to the doctor in charge that it would be frightening for a boy of that age to be asked to give blood. The doctor sat the boy down and explained that his sister needed his blood in order to live. The boy's eyes grew bigger and bigger during the explanation, but when the doctor had finished, the boy consented and his parents signed the necessary papers. They wheeled the boy into his sister's room and effected the transfusion. When it was all over, the little boy looked up at the doctor and asked, "Doctor, when do I die?"

That little boy thought that to give blood to his sister meant that he had to die. How heroic he was! But I am sure that he bickered with his sister and teased her as older brothers do. There were times when he did not want her around as he played with his buddies. But despite all that, he did build within his heart a great love for his sister. In one sense, it seems a shame that he waited until a time of crisis to show it.

And it is a shame too, if we wait until a time of crisis to show our love for God. In our daily lives we can tend to drift away from God, to forget about him, to fail to show the love and tenderness that we should. Sometimes, when God's law gets in the way of what we want to do, we may even wish that he were not around. Today Jesus tells us that we must love God all the time, in little things as well as big things. We should not wait until we come face to face with some great problem. Nor can we afford to wait, because we do not know how much love we have built up within ourselves to meet the crisis. Love grows in only one way—by loving.

The Mass is the best means we have both for expressing our love of God and for growing in that love. Mass makes us think about God. We hear his words in the scriptures and the homily. If a person is not on your mind, you are not really going to be concerned about him. The Mass is also our way of telling God we love him through the prayers and hymns. A husband and wife can actually increase their love by saying that they love each other. A good husband doesn't need some special occasion to bring home a little gift to his wife. In the Mass we give God the best gift possible, the body and blood of Jesus Christ in sacrifice. We pray that Jesus may make of us an everlasting gift to his Father. That means that our love for God should be so great that we are willing to die for him, as the little boy was willing to die for his sister.

Of course, the Mass will not automatically help us grow in our love

for God, just as human relationships do not grow automatically. People
in a family can talk to each other without really communicating. They
can physically dwell together under the same roof like boarders, without
any real personal relationship. They can even eat at the same table
without feeling any more sense of intimacy than do people at the same
lunch counter in a coffee shop. Growth in love demands effort, especially the effort on your part. You must get involved. God is talking to
you, and you must listen. When you talk to God, you must mean what
you say. When Jesus renews his sacrifice through the action of the priest,
you are not just a spectator. You must actively join with the priest in
offering yourself as a victim with Christ. At Communion time, you must
be thinking about the fact that Jesus wants to draw you to himself so that
you may share in his own family-like relationship as a child of God the
Father.

The Mass should never be just routine. It is too vital to our
relationship with God. The real test of our love for God will come on a
day of crisis. Meanwhile, let us use the Mass as our means for growing in
our love for God, a love so strong that we will be willing to die for him.

C.E.M.


### Thirtieth Sunday of the Year (B)
Suggested Use: Fourth Eucharistic Prayer

## FAITH AND THANKSGIVING

Today's first reading was addressed to Jews who were living in
exile in Babylon. Perhaps ''existing'' in Babylon is a better way to put it,
for there they were an oppressed people, slaves in a foreign country far
removed from their home in Palestine. During the period of the exile,
their religious spirit was almost entirely absorbed in a constant plea that
God would remember them and set them free. Above all they yearned to
return to their own country, to their beloved city of Jerusalem, and
especially to their temple of worship. God, in today's reading from
Jeremiah, promised that he would indeed free his people and lead them
back safely to their homeland. God kept his promise. After he had done
so, however, a strange thing happened. The people's appreciation of
God's goodness started to erode. They began to drift away from him.

While in exile, when they were in great need, they thought of nothing but God. When that need was met, even though they were once again near their temple, they practically forgot all about God.

In today's gospel we encountered, not a whole people in great need, but a single person. Bartimaeus was blind. From St. Mark's vivid description of the incident, we get the distinct impression that he was a young man, not an elderly person whose sight had gradually failed and for whom only a few years of life were left on earth. A whole lifetime lay before him, and yet he was oppressed by his affliction, a slave of constant darkness. It is no wonder that he did not hesitate to make a scene when he heard that Jesus was passing by. When some people tried to quiet him, he shouted all the louder, "Son of David, have pity on me!" At the moment, he could think of nothing except the possibility that Jesus would cure him. And Jesus did so. In time of great need, Bartimaeus turned to Jesus, but one has to wonder what happened after his cure. Did his appreciation slowly erode after he was freed from blindness, as did that of his ancestors after they had been delivered from exile? We have no indication that he was one of the few who became faithful followers of Jesus. Considering human nature, the odds are pretty heavy that after he got what he wanted, he forgot all about Jesus.

I think we will all admit that when we are in deep trouble, when we really need help, we turn almost instinctively to God for help. Such prayer is a good thing, but why do we find it so hard to remember to express our gratitude to God? Maybe one reason is that we have the idea that prayer is primarily asking God for things we need. Prayer means much more than that. It includes praising God for his goodness and power, and thanking him for extending that goodness and power to us.

Maybe the reason we do not thank God the way we should goes deeper than mere forgetfulness, or even a failure to realize that prayer includes thanksgiving. Deep down, we may just feel that there is actually precious little to be grateful for. Life is hard—trying to make a marriage happy, doing your best to raise kids when modern circumstances seem to be so much against you, working to make financial ends meet when those ends are miles apart, and wondering whether it is all worth it. We can develop a form of myopia, a spiritual nearsightedness, as we see only present problems under our noses and fail to focus on all the wonderful things God has already done for us and promises us in the future.

Today in the Fourth Eucharistic Prayer, we will recall the wonderful things God has done for us. It is a long list, going back to the beginning of time and reaching out into an era without end. Creation—salvation—eternal life—these are indeed great things for which to be grateful, but they seem so distant, so fuzzy, almost unreal. Yes, our problem is spiritual myopia. If we want to ask for something in prayer, we should ask Jesus to clear up our spiritual vision, as he cured Bartimaeus of his physical blindness. Faith is the only cure for spiritual nearsightedness, a deep faith which enables us to see clearly the truth of today's responsorial psalm: "The Lord has done great things for us."

The suggestion that we pray for faith may seem simple, almost commonplace. Yet there is no cure other than faith. Without real faith, we will see religion as if it were a child's balloon, which is brightly colored on the outside, filled only with air on the inside, and which the prick of human problems can easily pop. With faith, we can see through externals and realize that the balloon is filled with the power and goodness of God, and that the balloon will constantly expand without ever bursting. Only with faith can we see clearly that the "Lord has done great things for us," and that we have profound reasons to praise and thank him for his power and love.

C.E.M.

**Thirtieth Sunday of the Year (C)**

## THE PRAYER OF THE LOWLY

The Gospel of St. Luke, which we have been reading every Sunday during this year, is very concerned with prayer. Earlier in the gospel, Jesus taught us how to pray by giving us the "Our Father." Two Sundays ago, through the story of the ten lepers he reminded us of the need for praise and thanks in our prayer. Last Sunday, in the parable about the widow he indicated the necessity of praying always and not losing heart. Today he presents the foundation for all prayer, its starting point, which is humility.

Notice that the words of the Pharisee are not a prayer at all. They are an unabashed proclamation of his supposed virtues. The Pharisee uses God as a sounding board for his own praise as he takes all the glory and credit for himself. Since deep down the Pharisee really feels no need for

God, he does not ask God for anything. And as a result, he receives nothing from God except condemnation. In striking contrast, the tax collector can only recognize that before the all-holy God he is a sinner. His prayer is from the heart, a simple plea for mercy. Jesus attests that this prayer fulfills the words of our first reading today: "The prayer of the lowly pierces the clouds; it does not rest till it reaches its goal. . . ." The Pharisee looked only at himself, but his eyes were blind to his self-righteousness. The tax collector looked toward God, and his eyes beheld God's goodness of which everyone is unworthy, including ourselves.

Before God we must be humble. There is no doubt that we should feel relaxed and comfortable with God when we come to pray. There is no reason to think of God as wrathful and forbidding. After all, God is our Father and we are his children. Since the church is the house of God, it is our home. But we can never forget that God is God. We are not and never will be his equal. We are invited into his home to eat of the Lord's Supper, but it is not the same as going to McDonald's for hamburgers. The church is a sacred place wherein we hear the holy word of God, and share in the sacrifice of his divine Son. No human being can be worthy of this privilege. Moses was one of the greatest figures in the Old Testament. God appeared to him in a burning bush, and when Moses came to look at the bush more closely, God called out to him, "Remove the sandals from your feet, for the place where you stand is holy ground" (Ex 3:5). Moses did so, and as a further sign of his respect he hid his face in his hands. No human person is greater than Mary, but when the angel told her that she was to be the mother of Jesus, she humbly responded: "I am the servant of the Lord" (Lk 1:38).

The liturgy attempts to put us in the right disposition for prayer at the beginning of Mass, by means of the penitential rite. The priest says: "To prepare ourselves to celebrate the sacred mysteries let us acknowledge our sinfulness"* Before God we are all sinners, and are unworthy of him. At the beginning of Mass, we figuratively take off our shoes. We profess that we are God's servants. This act of humility is the necessary prerequisite for pleasing prayer. As such, it is not depressing

---

*The present translation, "let us call to mind our sins," is very misleading. The verb in Latin, "agnoscamus," means "let us acknowledge." The penitential rite is not meant to be an examination of conscience, nor is it a time for the priest to suggest specific sins to the people. The purpose of this rite is simple: to stand before God and humbly admit our unworthiness.

or self-defeating. Rather, since it is honest, it is healthy. Since it is truthful, it is pleasing to God and opens his ears and his heart to our prayers.

Remember that the Pharisee in the parable felt no need for God, and so asked for nothing. The tax collector knew that he needed God. Listen again to his prayer: "O God, be merciful to me, a sinner." Doesn't that sound like the penitential prayer the Church give us: "Lord have mercy"? But the Church wants us to keep this spirit even beyond the time of the penitential rite. In fact a humble plea for mercy is so vital that during the breaking of the bread we sing (or say): "Lamb of God, you take away the sins of the world, have mercy on us," and just before receiving Communion we admit: "Lord, I am not worthy to receive you . . ."

This humbling of ourselves will bring exaltation by God, as Jesus teaches in the gospel. How true are the words of our first reading: "The prayer of the lowly pierces the clouds; it does not rest till it reaches its goal. . . ."

C.E.M.

**Thirty-First Sunday of the Year (A)**

## *ONE IS YOUR TEACHER*

A priest once remarked, "I know that it is a shame that I do not practice what I preach, but it would be far worse if I were to preach what I practice." The statement was made in good humor and by a very fine priest who did practice what he preached. And yet, it reflects rather well what Jesus is talking about in today's gospel. Jesus does not condemn preaching, only bad example. He does not repudiate authority, only authoritarianism.

As a matter of fact, we are not inclined to have a very favorable attitude toward anyone who does not practice what he has to say. You can imagine how you would feel if your doctor were to insist that you give up tobacco for your health's sake, as he blows cigarette smoke in your face. But think about your reaction for a moment. What the doctor is telling you about the danger of smoking is based on pretty solid evidence and research. If you were to reject his advice simply because he is not following it himself, whom would you be harming except yourself?

The scribes and the Pharisees were spiritual doctors, some of whom were not practicing what they preached. In that, they were definitely wrong. On the other hand, since they had succeeded Moses as spiritual leaders in Israel, as Jesus pointed out, their teaching should be followed, but not their example. To allow their bad example to obscure the truth of their teaching was only to do harm to oneself.

Sometimes you hear about people who have left the Church because they maintain that bishops and priests do not practice what they preach. Even if their claims were true, such people should remember that our Lord himself in today's gospel told the people to follow the teaching of their leaders because they had succeeded Moses, even though they did not follow that teaching themselves. But wait a minute. Who really is the teacher of our faith? Who really is the preacher to whom we must listen? "One is your teacher." It is Jesus Christ. The pope, the bishops, the priests only hand on the word of Christ. Notice that Paul the Apostle commended the people of Thessalonica because they received his preaching, not as the word of men, but as it truly is, the word of God (second reading).

The real question, then, centers around the example of Jesus, the Teacher. And he certainly was one who practiced what he preached. Jesus told us to love our enemies, and he redeemed those who by sin were his enemies. He said that we should do good to our persecutors, and he forgave those who put him to death. He proclaimed that no one could have greater love than to lay down his life for a friend, and he died out of love for his Father and us. The very best sermon at any Mass is still the example of Christ, which is made present on our altar: the sacrificial offering of himself to his Father.

There is a lesson in today's gospel for all of us. Those of us who are ordained ministers must recognize our obligation to practice what we preach. You are right in reminding us of our failures to do so. Moreover we must remember what Jesus said about avoiding titles, such as "rabbi," "teacher," or "father." These titles were applied at various times to Jesus himself, who never rejected them; and of course there was nothing wrong in them. What makes them wrong for us is taking them seriously as titles of personal excellence, as if Jesus were not the true teacher of the Church, or as if the purpose of priestly fatherhood were not to draw people only to God the Father in heaven, and not to ourselves. Jesus does not condemn authority, for he gives it to his ministers. But he does condemn authoritarianism, the attitude that authority is a personal characteristic to be used without regard for the teaching of Christ and without reliance on his grace.

There is also a lesson for you who have been baptized into the faith. You must heed the word of God, no matter who the preacher may be. And you too must give good example by practicing that preaching. Frankly, the best stimulus I have to be a better priest is the faith and devotion I see in the people I serve. You also owe mutual support to each other. It is a sad, discouraging experience for a person to find that he stands almost alone in his practice of the faith, among those with whom he lives and works and prays. What will bring others to Christ is your own good example in all the circumstances of your life.

I hope and pray that no one will ever have to say of any priest, "It is a shame that he does not practice what he preaches, but it would be far worse if he were to preach what he practices." I also hope and pray that all of you will always receive the Christian message, not as the word of men, but as it truly is, the word of God, for one is your Teacher, Jesus Christ.

C.E.M.

### Thirty-First Sunday of the Year (B)
Suggested Use: Fourth Eucharistic Prayer

## *HEART SPEAKS TO HEART*\*

A five-year-old girl had been mischievous and disobedient most of the day. As her mother was putting her to bed, she noticed tears in her daughter's eyes and asked, "What is the matter?" The girl replied, "Nobody said they loved me today." The mother smiled and said, "Honey, that's not true. Don't you remember that daddy told you to eat all your vegetables at dinner? That was his way of saying that he loves you." The language of the heart has its own vocabulary, but all too often we miss the message. And that is tragic, because unless we hear and understand the language of the heart, the language of love, we cannot love in return. We love those whom we know love us.

\* John Henry Newman's motto as a Cardinal, *Cor Ad Cor Loquitur*.

Sometimes, something special has to happen to tune us in to the language of the heart. It may be that we take a friend or neighbor for granted, until one day we become seriously ill and confined to bed at home. The first person who comes to offer help, somewhat to our surprise, is the person we have taken for granted. He or she proves to be very generous and completely unselfish in cooking for you and in nursing you back to health. Through this experience, you come to realize something which has been true all along: this person has a great love and affection for you.

After you have recovered, your relationship with this person is different from what it was before your illness. You now appreciate him. You value his friendship. And you find it easy to return love.

The fact is, that we all were indeed seriously ill, sick unto death. God sent his beloved Son to us to care for us, to nurse us back to health, and to nourish us spiritually. We can never leave off reflecting on the truth of our salvation. It is the great sign of God's love for us. The message of today's Mass is that we must love God with our whole being and let this love overflow into our love for others. But we are not moved to this kind of love if we do not know that God loves us. We must not fail to understand the language of God's heart. The language of his heart is made up not primarily of words, but of deeds. That is what we will profess in the Fourth Eucharistic Prayer: ''Father, we acknowledge your greatness: all your *actions* show your wisdom and love.'' God is a loving Father who has created us and called us to be his children. As a Father, he has love for us. We should feel his concern in the air we breathe, in the food we eat, in the whole earth upon which we live. We should sense his kindness in every new dawn, his gentleness in every breeze, and his care in every restful night. We should see his goodness shining through the eyes of those we love. As his children, we await an eternal inheritance.

Above all, we must never forget that something special has happened to tune us in to the language of God's heart. He has lifted up his own Son on the tree of the cross. ''God so loved the world that he gave his only Son.'' We just cannot find a greater sign of love than that. But God is not satisfied with leaving that great sign of love lost in the past of history. So that we won't forget, he renews the sacrifice of his Son for us as a living reality in every Mass we celebrate. God's heart speaks to our heart if we only listen.

C.E.M.

**Thirty-First Sunday of the Year (C)**

## *ACCEPTANCE OF CHRIST*

It is interesting to note the difference between Zacchaeus' acceptance of Christ the grown man, and the rejection of Christ the child by the inn keeper of Bethlehem. One has room for Christ, the other does not. Isn't that pretty much the treatment Christ receives today? Not so much in his person, but in his members. We accept Christ in the people we like, and reject him in those who don't appeal to us. I am sure that most of the crowd was displeased that Christ would talk with Zacchaeus, or that he would allow Zacchaeus to invite him into his house, and accept the invitation.

Zacchaeus was a prominent official. This didn't keep him from climbing a tree in order to catch a glimpse of Jesus. He was a taxgatherer and collected duties over the entire district of Jericho. As we know, this did not make him popular with the people. Whatever the crowd saw in Zacchaeus, Jesus saw in him a son of Abraham, a true Israelite without guile, whose single-mindedness and ingenuous conduct was evidence of something that went deeper than mere curiosity—whatever Zacchaeus himself may have thought of it at the time. Legally, Zacchaeus could not have been held to repay back fourfold where he may have cheated others. This was voluntary on his part. And this voluntary commitment Jesus accepted on its face value.

So, here we have mutual acceptance. Christ offered salvation to Zacchaeus, and the taxgatherer offered his friendship to Christ. The words of the second reading could have been used by Christ as a prayer for Zacchaeus. "We pray for you always that our God may make you worthy of his call, and fulfill by his power every honest intention and work of faith. In this way the name of our Lord Jesus Christ may be glorified in you and you in him. . . ."

The first reading could also stand as a beautiful religious poetic expression of Zacchaeus' acceptance of Christ. "But you have mercy on all, because you can do all things; and you overlook the sins of men that they may repent . . . But you spare all things, because they are yours, O Lord and lover of souls. . . ." This beautiful mutual acceptance of Christ and Zacchaeus can be a prototype of our mutual acceptance of one another.

In the Pastoral Letter of the American bishops, *Human Life in Our Day*, the problem of accepting or rejecting Christ in our own time and according to our own problems is taken up. The first idea is that the human life of an individual is valuable. "We honor God when we reverence human life. When human life is served, man is enriched and God is acknowledged. When human life is threatened, man is diminished and God is less manifest in our midst."

Zacchaeus was not perturbed by negative reactions against his desire to see Christ and be friends with him. And he seems to have acted out of a right conscience. This does not mean a perfect one, but one which was honest. Christ taught him much by word and example, and Zacchaeus seems the kind of man who would readjust his life accordingly. So it is with us. Conscience is our practical judgment, by which we judge here and now what is to be done as being good, and what is to be avoided as evil. Our acceptance of Christ demands that we form a right conscience in regard to his teachings as recorded in the scriptures, and as interpreted by the Church down through the centuries. The problem is to form a right conscience. This must be done through prayer, study, consultation, and an honest facing of the facts. This is especially true of such difficult matters as birth control and the education of children. These are difficult matters to discuss here in a few short minutes. The main purpose of mentioning them is that they do touch upon our relationships with Christ. They are crucial to our acceptance of one another. They do deserve careful consideration. Otherwise, we may be accepting Christ only partially.

The keynote to acceptance of Christ is the Mass. Once we learn to accept Christ as he comes to us in the sacred signs and symbols of love in the Eucharist, then there is a stronger possibility that we will be able to accept him in the human signs of our fellow man. The liturgy presents him to us in word and sacrifice, just as in his lifetime. Sunday by Sunday, we get more glimpses of him, as did Zacchaeus. Sunday by Sunday, he tells us that he will eat with us. Let us learn to accept him here, so we can accept him in daily life.

O.J.M.

**Thirty-Second Sunday of the Year (A)**

## *HEAVEN, NOT HOLLYWOOD*

A master of surprise was Alfred Hitchcock. Moviegoers are glued to their seats waiting for the bizarre element that throws everything into chaos. But movies seldom are real life. Most of us follow the familiar bit of wisdom, "Always be ready for the unexpected." Everyone from automobile safety councils to the Boy Scouts suggests preparedness.

Yet in spite of all the warnings, we occasionally wind up being caught off-guard. So it isn't unusual in all the planning for a big wedding feast, as we have in the gospel, that some discovered late in the evening that they were running low on torch fuel. Jewish wedding celebrations were all-night affairs. And the local customs suggested that the groom had to "collect" his bride at her family's home and then bring her to his home. Meanwhile, the guests went to the groom's home to prepare for the dusk-till-dawn party. Once everyone arrived, the doors and windows were bolted down and barred for the night. The process involved in opening up was so awkward and troublesome that no one in his right mind ever expected the doors to be opened at night.

Taking all this into consideration, the situation of the slow-bridesmaids-being-locked-out isn't a problem. But the attitude of the groom is. The groom represents Christ. And the banquet is heaven. His reaction is hardly filled with "Christian" pity. To bar the careless from a banquet is a small thing. To bar them from a joyful eternity is something serious.

But evidently Christ intends the lesson to be painfully clear. When it is a matter of the Second Coming and entrance into the heavenly kingdom, the criterion won't be pity, but justice. We either have what it takes, or we can't come in. So often we're tempted to say there couldn't be a hell. God wouldn't be that mean. But the simple fact is that God the Father doesn't and won't, choose hell for us. We have to do this for ourselves. Anyone who goes to hell isn't forced. He has to buy his own ticket, get on the train and go. You have to want to go to hell to get there.

But St. Paul suggests we look at the brighter side. God the Father intends that Jesus bring with him those believing in him. And for those who are friends of Christ, the Second Coming will be a joyful banquet. St. Paul was looking beyond cinemascope and stereo sound when he suggested "eyes have not seen, nor ears heard what God has in store for us." Nor do we have to fear if we're the good ones or the "bad guys." It's not too hard to tell those who are earnestly trying to be good Christians from those not bothering to try.

But we do have to be careful. The Lord is still the Director and Producer of our lives. He'll decide when our life-movie is to end. It might be an abrupt ending which no one in the "audience" was expecting. Keep your eyes open, for you know not the day or the hour. Even make a few preparations now, to avoid being caught short. Try a little extra penance and prayer.

The moral is: don't be so confident and lighthearted about heaven that you sit down on the job and stop working. St. Paul warned the early Christians against this. But don't be afraid of hell, either. A person who is reasonably trying to be good, lovingly receiving Christ each Sunday, can be confident about heaven, like the child who deep down knows he is loved and wanted by his parents, in spite of the occasional threats of the "wood shed."

The outcome of the last reel of our lives shouldn't be a mystery. Nor should we fear a Hitchcock surprise ending. If we're good Christians, we can be certain that at the Second Coming the Lord himself will come down to meet us, and we shall be with the Lord unceasingly. Console one another with this message.

C.E.M.

## Thirty-Second Sunday of the Year (B)

Suggested Use: Third Eucharistic Prayer

## *THE WIDOW'S MITE*

Jesus praised the poor widow who put only two small coins into the collection box of the temple, because she gave all she had. We can quite readily identify with the reaction of Jesus since most of us have, in one way or another, had the same reaction. It is the joy in the heart of a mother when her four-year-old daughter presents her with a dandelion and sincerely says, "A pretty flower for you, Mom." A splendid bouquet could not satisfy her more. It is the pride felt by a father when his young son earnestly says, "Gee, Dad, you can really throw that football." Being named the most valuable player in the N.F.L. could not please him more.

Yes, most of us at some time have received a gift or a word of praise, small or insignificant in itself, which has taken on a special value, a preciousness, in our eyes. The value was derived, not from what was given, but from the sincerity and earnestness of the giver. Today, however, we should think about whether we have been like the widow in her relationship with God. I am not talking about putting money into the collection basket, important though that be. Money is necessary for the support of your parish and its many activities, but there is something more vital. God wants not only our generosity in giving money. He wants our generosity in giving ourselves.

I think that as Catholics we have often heard the idea that we should offer ourselves to God in the Mass, that we should make a gift of all that we have done, as well as all our joys and sorrows, together with a promise to try to lead a life in the future worthy of giving to God. The gift of ourselves is an act of love and praise of God. How valuable, however, is our gift? We may feel that its intrinsic worth is not much more than that of a dandelion from the little girl, or a word of praise from a small boy. We know that sincerity and earnestness are important, but are even they sufficient to transform our offering into something truly significant to God? Actually, within the Mass our lives can take on a whole new value.

Catholic doctrine teaches us that within the Mass, Jesus renews the offering of himself on the cross, the gift of himself to his Father. The death of Jesus was the most excellent act of love and praise the world has ever known. It was an act truly worthy of God the Father. Nothing that has happened on this earth has pleased and satisfied God more. But where do we come in? Through the Mass, Jesus makes the offering of himself to the Father a *living* sacrifice, so that his offering becomes the Church's offering, *our* offering. Notice what happens at Mass: during the Preparation of the Gifts at the altar, a drop of water is placed in the chalice. That drop of water mingles with the wine and becomes part of it. The tiny, almost worthless drop of water now shares in the nature of wine, as it takes on its color and flavor. In somewhat the same way, Jesus takes our human lives and transforms them in the Mass so that they become a part of his sacrifice. Jesus renews the offering of himself in the Mass, not for his sake, but for ours—so that he may catch up our ordinary human joys and sorrows, our work and our play, and give them a new, extraordinary meaning.

The entire Eucharistic Prayer is an act of worship of God, but it is particularly at the time of the consecration that Jesus makes himself present as a victim of sacrifice. During those moments, you should not be merely passive spectators. You should be aware of the fact that something is happening—that Jesus is renewing the offering of himself to the Father and he is inviting you to offer yourselves with him. The expression of that offering reaches its culmination in the great doxology: "Through him, with him, in him, in the unity of the Holy Spirit, all glory and honor is yours, almighty Father, for ever and ever." Your strong and fervent "Amen" is your way of proclaiming in one word that you share with Christ the offering of himself in praise and love for the Father.*

The point is that we can do something very worthwhile here at Mass. The two coins which the widow put into the collection box of the temple pleased God because of her sincerity and generosity, but all the sincerity and generosity in the world could not make those two coins actually worth more than their face value. Our offering in the Mass needs our sincerity and generosity to make it pleasing to God, but Jesus himself gives our offering a real value which it could never have by itself.

C.E.M.

## Thirty-Second Sunday of the Year (C)
Suggested Use: Long Form of the Gospel

## IS THERE A RESURRECTION ?

We are drawing very close to the end of this liturgical year. After today, there are only two Sundays left for the current year. As we think about the scripture readings we have heard since the first Sunday of Advent, it is obvious that there has been great emphasis on the problem of death and its solution in the resurrection of Jesus. The resurrection of

---

* "Let the faithful consider to what a high dignity they are raised by the sacrament of baptism. They should not think it enough to participate in the Eucharistic Sacrifice with that general intention which befits members of Christ and children of the Church, but let them further, in keeping with the spirit of the sacred liturgy, be most closely united with the High Priest and his earthly minister, at the time the consecration of the divine Victim is effected, and at that time especially when those solemn words are pronounced, 'Through him, with him, in him,' etc. To these words in fact the people answer 'Amen.' Nor should Christians forget to offer themselves, their cares, their sorrows, their distress and their necessities in union with the Divine Savior upon the Cross" (*Mediator Dei*, 104).

Jesus from the dead is a sign and a guarantee of our own resurrection from the dead.

It is very appropriate, as we draw near to the end of the liturgical year, that this whole topic of death and resurrection come before us again. The Sadducees, who questioned Jesus in today's gospel, did not believe in a resurrection from the dead. When they asked Jesus whose wife the woman who had had seven husbands would be after the resurrection, they were not looking for an answer at all. They were trying to reduce the idea of the resurrection to the absurd, to show that it was ridiculous. As far as the Sadducees were concerned, the whole idea of a resurrection from the dead was childish. As a matter of fact, they never thought of the resurrection except in childish terms, as though it meant bringing to life corpses which would take up once again all the present processes of eating and drinking, loving and hating, giving in marriage and taking wives.

Some people today are like the Sadducees. They ask how God can put together a body that has disintegrated in the grave, or worse still, a body that has been blown to pieces in an atomic explosion at Hiroshima or Nagasaki. The question is often asked with a sophisticated sneer, which implies that the idea of resurrection is ludicrous. Such people do not realize that our resurrected bodies, though real and physical, will exist in a newer and better manner far beyond our powers to imagine. As Jesus stated in today's gospel, "They become like angels and are no longer liable to death. Sons of the resurrection, they are sons of God."

Our resurrected bodies will be as different from our present body as a full-blown plant is different from the seed. Our risen body will be in a state of perfection by the power of God, a power not limited to what our human minds can imagine or comprehend. Faith in our own resurrection from the dead is both a belief that God has almighty power, and a confidence that in his goodness he will use that power to raise us from the dead to a new life.

Our faith in the resurrection should influence our lives. The first reading today, taken from the Old Testament, gives us an example. The seven brothers and their mother were asked to abandon their religion and God, but their faith in the resurrection from the dead was so strong that, rather than do so, they eagerly went to their deaths. One brother said to the king, "You are depriving us of this life, but the King of the world will raise us up to live again forever." Another brother said, "It is my choice to die at the hands of men with the God-given hope of being restored to life by him.''

Such is the influence faith in the resurrection should have on us—a willingness to suffer death rather than abandon God. But the influence should be more extensive. A person who is planning to get married goes about the ordinary duties of his life with a lightness in his step and a glow in his eyes, because of the joyful expectation of a new way of life in marriage. As we go about the duties of our lives, we should do so with a certain lightness and happiness that comes from the expectation of our resurrection from the dead, a new life with God forever. Our faith in the resurrection should color our otherwise drab lives in joyful hues.

That faith, remember, is both a belief that God has almighty power, and a confidence that in his goodness he will use that power to raise us from the dead to a new life.

C.E.M.

## Thirty-Third Sunday of the Year (A)

## *PURPOSE AND VALUE*

Jesus found it necessary to tell the parable you have just heard, because as human beings we often fail to use our God-given talents. There are no doubt many reasons why we so fail, but I am convinced that one of the greatest obstacles to progress in our lives is not a lack of opportunity, or inability, or even laziness. It is boredom. Boredom is cold water on the fire of enthusiasm and enterprise. But why are we bored? We get up in the morning and go to bed at night, and in between it is just the same thing over and over again. Is repetition the reason for our boredom? I really don't think it is quite that simple. Actually, we can do routine things without finding them monotonous, provided we see purpose and value in them. Boredom comes with repetition only when repetition seems pointless.

Think for a moment about God in his act of creation, as he brought something out of nothing; as he made the universe from a void, as he produced life from stillness. Now there is work with a purpose. If we may speak humanly of God, what a thrill creation must have been for him, what a feeling of accomplishment! But in one sense his work of creation is still going on, and God wills to give each of us a share in continued creation through our human work. God could have made this world to operate like some kind of massive computer without any human involvement, but he didn't want to do it that way. God has put the world and all its marvelous resources into our human hands. He entrusts to us the responsibility of actualizing its potential. Exalted though that may sound, and is, it includes not only the stunning accomplishments of modern science, but all the ordinary chores of everyday life as well. It means earning a living and doing housework, going to PTA meetings and Pop Warner football games, repairing your car and washing the dishes.

Listen to this official teaching of the Church, in the words of the Second Vatican Council: "While providing the substance of life for themselves and their families, men and women are performing their activities in a way which appropriately benefits society. *They can justly consider that by their labor they are unfolding the Creator's work"* (*The Church in the Modern World*, 34). This teaching should give a sense of purpose to all that we do, however simple—for human work is truly a sharing in the thrilling act of God's creation itself.

But there is more. Human work not only has a supreme purpose. It is also holy with a great spiritual value. Jesus gave it that value when he became a human being like us. Listen again to these important words of the Second Vatican Council: "By his incarnation the Son of God has united himself in some fashion with every man. He worked with human hands, he thought with a human mind, acted by human choice, and loved with a human heart. He blazed a trail, and if we follow it, life and death are made holy and take on a new meaning" (*The Church in the Modern World*, 22). Yes, if we only follow the trail blazed by Jesus, everything will take on a new meaning. If we could only keep firmly in mind that human activity has purpose and value, then even the most ordinary, routine matters should not be boring. We should approach them with the enthusiasm of God in his act of creation, and with the zeal of Jesus in his human life.

Our celebration of Mass is a constant reminder of the meaning and value of our lives. In the Mass, God takes the most ordinary things possible, bread and wine, made food and drink by the work of human hands, and gives them a whole new meaning and value as they are changed into the body and blood of Christ. Their new meaning is that as a gift to God they become an act of worship. Their new value is that they are the most precious gift possible. What could be more precious than the body and blood of Jesus Christ! But the Mass is more than a reminder, for God invites us to offer our lives too as a gift to him. In the Mass,our gift becomes one with that of Christ, and thereby takes on a special meaning and a precious value, far above that of simple human activity. Our offering should include everything: our joy and our sorrow, our successes and our failures, our pains and our pleasures—and, oh yes, our feelings of boredom too. Our celebration of Mass should make Sunday the brightest day of the week.

Of course, tomorrow will be Monday again as we return to our weekly routine, but it need not be a blue Monday. Monday and all the other days of the week can each be a Sun-day if we illumine them with the brightness of their true meaning and value in God's plan. Let's try to take from this Mass a sense of the worth of human activity. Then we have a chance of overcoming the obstacle of boredom, and we will have the hope of hearing from Jesus when he comes in judgment: "Well done! You were dependable in small matters. Come, share your master's joy!"

C.E.M.

## Thirty-Third Sunday of the Year (B)

## *A PILGRIM PEOPLE GOING HOME*

Although we are only in the middle of November, the Church in this Mass is looking toward the end of the liturgical year, which occurs next Sunday, and consequently to the end of time when Jesus will come again. Whether that great day is close at hand or still far in the future, we simply do not know. Nonetheless, that day is important to us and we are constantly moving toward it.

The first reading today and the gospel tell us, in very complex images, of the final coming of the Lord. This final coming is a concern in every Mass we celebrate. We pray following the "Our Father" that we may be protected from all anxiety as we wait in joyful hope for the coming of our Savior, Jesus Christ. "Anxiety" is a well-chosen word. It indicates a painful uneasiness, a nervousness, a fear about what is going to happen. Such feelings should not be ours as faithful people. Rather, we should look forward to the coming of Christ as people who have been on a very long, arduous journey looking forward to arriving home. Home means rest and comfort, and an end to all the burdens and inconvenience of travel. Home is the end of the journey, but it is the beginning of contentment.

As we travel through this life, we need to have a balanced attitude. We cannot think only of heaven as if this life were devoid of value and purpose, but on the other hand we would be foolish indeed to live with only this present existence in view.

Since we are so caught up with the necessities and worries, as well as the pleasures, of this life perhaps most of us need to remember that there is much more to existence than what we experience in the present. There are two times, which occur with alternating frequency for most of us, when we should most remember that there is more to come. The first time is when life is bleakest, when we are suffering the most, when we are totally frustrated and near despair. It is quite proper for a person of faith to seek to find some solace in the hope that God does plan something better for us, that we must suffer and even die as Jesus himself did so that we may enter into the unending happiness God has prepared for those who love him.

The second time is when life is most pleasant, when things are going so well for us that we perhaps fail to think of God since we feel no need for him, quite content with the satisfaction which is ours. It is not uncommon for some people to turn to God in prayer only when there is great need, as during a war or after a terrible catastrophe such as an earthquake or cyclone. We should view good times as a foretaste of what is to come, and so praise and thank God during the experience because of his goodness to us.

Put as simply as possible, in good times and in bad it is quite proper for a person of faith to live with one eye fixed on heaven. We are people on a journey, and we should never lose sight of our destination.

On the other hand, we should not live with both eyes fixed on heaven. This life and this world have meaning and purpose. We are God's children and to us he has entrusted his creation. His plan is that all of creation will slowly move toward a time of perfection, and we are part of that plan. What we do through God's grace helps to contribute to the upbuilding of creation, until Jesus Christ completes the work through the redemptive power of his death and resurrection.

Listen to this beautiful teaching of the Second Vatican Council: "While providing the substance of life for themselves and their families, men and women are performing their activities in a way which appropriately benefits society. They can justly consider that by their labor they are unfolding the Creator's work" (*Church in the Modern World*, 34). This life is meaningful as part of God's plan.

In every Mass we celebrate, we have a reminder that we are a pilgrim people. Walking in procession to receive Communion is a liturgical sign of our spiritual journey. And as a pilgrim people we have a food to sustain us, the Eucharist. We stand to receive Communion these days, because standing is the ancient sign in the Church of the resurrection of Christ. And this food is the pledge, the promise of sharing in the resurrection of Christ who promised, "He who eats my flesh and drinks my blood has everlasting life and I will raise him up on the last day" (Jn 6:54). We are indeed on a journey, not to a place, but to a destiny—the gift of everlasting life through our sharing in the resurrection of Christ.

Live this life we should, but let us do so with no anxiety, as we believe that all the while we are headed for home.

C.E.M.

## Thirty-Third Sunday of the Year (C)

# *WORKING FOR THE END*

The liturgy of the word today puts before our minds once again the coming of Christ at the end of the world. This doctrine is an integral part of Christian belief and hope. We believe that Christ will come again, and we have the hope that we will then share with the Risen Christ the glory he already enjoys.

The early Christians were keenly aware of this doctrine. Apparently, some of the Thessalonians were so convinced that the second coming was just around the corner, that they concluded it was useless to work. The second reading of today's Mass, in which St. Paul stated that anyone who did not work should not eat, was originally addressed to them.

As a matter of fact, we simply do not know when Christ will come again. Jesus simply never gave an indication of the time of his second coming. *When* Jesus will come again does not matter; *that* he will come is the object of our belief and the source of our hope. Meanwhile, until Jesus does come to perfect the world, we must not sit around in idleness like some of the Thessalonians.

The Catholic doctrine on the second coming, as drawn from sacred scripture, is summed up in this statement of the Second Vatican Council:

> We do not know the time for the consummation of the earth and of humanity. Nor do we know how all things will be transformed. As deformed by sin, the shape of this world will pass away. But we are taught that God is preparing a new dwelling place and a new earth where justice will abide and whose blessedness will answer and surpass all the longings for peace which spring up in the human heart. . . . The expectation of a new earth must not weaken but rather stimulate our concern for cultivating this one. For here grows the body of a new human family, a body which even now is able to give some kind of foreshadowing of the new age. (*The Church in the Modern World*, 39)

What all this means to us can be symbolized in the aborted flight of Apollo XIII. You may remember that as the astronauts sped through space toward the moon, their space ship was rocked by a tremendous explosion. The original plan of landing on the moon had to be abandoned. With help and directions from Mission Control, the astronauts were able to develop a plan for returning to the earth safely. Though they could not repair their space ship perfectly, through imagination and diligence they worked at making the ship as functional as possible. They did not merely aim the ship toward earth, where all would be well, and sit back and hope they would have a safe landing. Though the earth was their goal, they had a lot of work to do out there in space. Above all, they had to guard against any further damage to their space ship.

Our world is like Apollo XIII, and our history like its journey through space. The terrible explosion of sin nearly wrecked our world for good. With help and direction from Jesus Christ, our Savior, we are working at making this world as functional as possible. We are not moving through space toward a planet, but we are moving through time toward a moment when all will be well. That moment is the second coming of Christ. Though that moment is our goal, we must not spend our time in idleness. There is much work to be done on our space ship, this world.

Though Christ will come again to perfect our world, it is our Christian duty to work now to repair our world as much as possible, and to guard against any further damage. For example, it is Christian to work to clear up the pollution of our atmosphere, to safeguard natural resources, to improve human living conditions. More important, we should work to clear up another kind of pollution, the pollution of the human mind and spirit. That pollution is manifested in the preoccupation with mind-destroying drugs, but it is a pollution brought on by the despair of not knowing the Christian message of salvation or, worse still, by the frustration of seeing professing Christians not living up to the teachings of Christ. That pollution is manifested in racial prejudice, a filth worse than any amount of smog. It is generated by our failure to fulfill Christ's command that we love all without exception.

So there is much to do before the second coming. Christ has died; Christ is risen; Christ will come again. That is the object of our faith and the motive of our hope. But we cannot afford to sit in idleness until Christ comes again.

C.E.M.

### Thirty-Fourth and Last Sunday of the Year (A)
(Christ the King)

## *STEWARDS OF CHRIST THE KING*

On November 22, 1963, the people of the United States and indeed of almost the whole world were shocked at the news that President John Kennedy had been shot to death. For four days, from the day of the assassination until the day of burial, most Americans sat stunned before their television sets as the aftermath of the terrible tragedy was revealed before their eyes. At the time, some people asked the question, "How could God, who rules the world, allow such an evil thing to happen?"

God the Father has absolute power and control over his creation. It is also true, as we will hear in the preface today, that the Father has anointed Jesus Christ, his Son, as universal king. Today's feast, however, brings out the fact that Jesus has chosen to exercise the fullness of his kingship only at the end of the world, when he will come again in all his glory. That is one reason why we celebrate this feast of Christ the King on the last Sunday of the liturgical year.

Meanwhile, Jesus has put the world into our hands in trust. We are stewards of the king. A steward does not have dominion over his master's goods; he cannot do whatever he wants with them. He must use them carefully and prudently, as his master wishes. In other words, what we have does not belong to us in any absolute way. This is not the doctrine of communism, which denies the right to private property. Such a denial is not in accord with Christian teaching. On the other hand, the man who says, "I earned it; it's mine and I can do with it whatever I want," does not know whereof he speaks. This world with all of its resources belongs to God. Without those resources, we could never survive. Moreover, it is God who has given us the intelligence we use in developing the goods of this world. It is God who gave us the strength we use in earning a living. So whatever we have, even though it was acquired at the expense of our arms and in the sweat of our brows, belongs really to God. He has entrusted these things to us until Christ comes in glory at the end of time to claim his kingdom.

When Christ does come at the end of time, he will demand an accounting of our stewardship. He will want to know whether we have used his goods carefully and prudently. He will want to know whether we have been selfish and greedy, or loving and generous. Actually, however, Christ will not wait until then to check up on us. Frankly, you might even say that he is just a little sneaky about checking up on us all the time. You see, he is not confined to heaven. He is still walking this earth in our fellow human beings. In a special way he is present in the poor and the needy, and in and through them he will know how we are using the things he has entrusted to us.

Recall the gospel you heard proclaimed a few minutes ago. Jesus declared that when he comes in glory, he will judge us on how we have treated him as he is found in his brothers. How mysterious are his words: "I assure you, as often as you did it for one of my least brothers, you did it for me." Mysterious words, yes, but true. There is no reason to water down this truth: Jesus somehow is really present in our fellow human beings, even in those in whom we might least expect to find him.

When you think about it, those in need have even some kind of a right to be helped by us. I don't mean a right in strict justice, as a man has a right to a day's pay for a day's work. It is a right without a special name. It is a right based on the fact that Jesus lives within others, especially the needy. And remember, whatever we have, we hold in trust as stewards; it all belongs to Jesus. When he asks us for help in his poor, he is only asking for what belongs to him. We have to stop thinking exclusively of our own rights. We must soberly listen to the words of Jesus: "I was hungry and you gave me no food. I was thirsty and you gave me no drink. I was away from home and you gave me no welcome, naked and you gave me no clothing. I was ill and in prison and you did not come to comfort me." We must not dare to protest: "Lord, when did we see *you* in such need and neglect you?" because if we do, he will answer, "I assure you, as often as you neglected to do it to one of these least ones, you neglected to do it to me."

When President Kennedy was shot, some people looked up to heaven and asked, "How could God allow such an evil thing?" Maybe we all at times, disturbed and uncomfortable about the poverty and need in our own country, have asked: "How can God allow such an evil?" Both questions are wrong. We should not look up to heaven to God. We should look at ourselves and ask, "How can we allow evil? Why have we not overcome hatred with love? Why have we not overcome poverty with generosity?"

On this feast of Christ the King, we must recognize that we share in Christ's kingly power, that he has entrusted us with his earthly kingdom until he comes in judgment. We must pray that we will live in accord with the truth we proclaim to Christ: "The kingdom, the power, and the glory are yours, now and forever." Then we will indeed be protected from "all anxiety as we wait in joyful hope for the coming of our Savior, Jesus Christ."

C.E.M.

**Thirty-Fourth and Last Sunday of the Year (B)**
(Christ the King)

## *THE KING AND HIS NOBLES*

To say that Jesus is a King does not mean a whole lot to us these days. Our ideas of a king, surrounded by his court of nobles, are rather jumbled and confused, a conglomerate from historical data, fairy tales, and old Disney movies. Even the people of our Lord's own day did not have very clear ideas, because they compared Jesus and his kingdom with their own human experience. It was somewhat like comparing a Boeing 747 with the simple airplane flown by the Wright brothers at Kitty Hawk back in 1903. The people had to make a tremendous jump in their thinking before they could begin to understand what Jesus really intended.

In today's gospel episode, Jesus recognized that Pilate had failed to make that jump. "Are you the king of the Jews?" Pilate asked, and he was thinking only of a type of person who was a military and political leader, a man who could possibly be a threat to Roman authority in Palestine. "My kingdom does not belong to this world," Jesus replied, and he meant that he was not the kind of king Pilate imagined, not a ruler whose followers would fight for him as soldiers in a war or whose domain was limited to one nation.

Of course, Jesus does have a domain. It is a universal kingdom, for Jesus has authority over all creation. This domain is well described in today's preface: "a kingdom of truth and life, a kingdom of holiness and grace, a kingdom of justice, love and peace." That certainly sounds like a fitting kingdom for Jesus Christ, but it also sounds very ideal and quite futuristic with a reality only in heaven. To some extent, this evaluation is correct. The perfect kingdom is yet to come, and we are the people who "wait in joyful hope for the coming of our Savior, Jesus Christ." Jesus will come again when the world is at an end. The end of the world, however, does not mean catastrophe but fulfillment. To say that a house or building is finished and the work ended, does not imply destruction but perfection. That is the kind of end to which our world, and indeed the whole universe, will be brought.

Right now, the condition of the kingdom is similar to that of a child who has a lot of developing to do before he becomes a mature man, grown to full stature in the prime of life. Christ will come to claim his kingdom and present it to the Father when its perfection in the divine plan has been reached. Meanwhile, we are not to sit around and hope that our King will get this work done all by himself. Not one of us is a mere pawn or peasant; we are all nobles, "a people set apart, a chosen race, a royal priesthood." We are called to be close cooperators with the King in making the kingdom reach its ideal. We should not expect Christ to replace our present world with some kind of prefabricated paradise. We ourselves have to work for a better world, prepared and fit to come fully under God's dominion as a kingdom of justice, love and peace.

Though we have to be realistic about the many imperfections of our world and our society, it is unchristian to be pessimistic and tragic to be apathetic. The Catholic who does nothing to better world conditions is a scandalous cop-out. The present time should be one of tremendous dynamism, hope and enthusiasm. But where do we start? For one thing, we should see that, since Christ has dominion over all of creation, the ecological movement, though fraught with complications, is fundamentally Christian. We should be active in ecological programs, with a Christian perspective that God has put the resources of this world into our hands to be used properly, not abused for greedy and selfish purposes. Part of this perspective is the truth that the earth and all its resources are intended by the Creator to help people fulfill their destiny, and that, to put it bluntly, the welfare of human beings is more important than preserving some endangered species of alligator in Florida or condors in California.

Ecology, moreover, is not our greatest problem. Because Christ's kingdom is to be one of justice, love and peace, the biggest obstacles to its growth toward perfection are injustice, hatred and war. These seem to be such momentous evils that one wonders what a single person can do. We must remember that if everyone thought he was powerless, then indeed nothing would ever be accomplished. You may feel that there is nothing you can do to overcome the grave injustices in this world or the inequities of wealth, but in your own life you can try to respect all human beings without exception, and you can be more generous and unselfish with the material goods God has given you. You may not be able to put a stop to war, but war is in reality the worst expansion of hatred between individuals. What you can do is to work for love and peace within your own home and with the people you see every day. Our sign of peace in the Mass is a simple reminder that Christ calls us to spread his kingdom and love to the whole world.

Jesus is a King who wishes to conquer the world, but not through war or by means of trampling on the rights of others. Rather, he wants to bring peace and happiness through justice and love. He has entrusted the spreading of his kingdom to us, the nobles of his court. He could do it all himself, but he wants us to work with him in bringing the world to fulfillment. We wait in joyful hope for the coming of our Savior Jesus Christ. But right now, our labors for a better world give meaning to our words addressed to Christ the King: "The kingdom, the power, and the glory are yours now and forever."

C.E.M.

## Thirty-Fourth and Last Sunday of the Year (C)

# *CHRIST THE KING*

Today is the feast of Christ the King. Originally, the kingship of Christ was associated with Holy Week and Easter. On Palm Sunday the kingship of Christ was heralded by the people during the triumphal procession into Jerusalem, and on Easter Sunday it was manifested and confirmed by God the Father in raising his Son from the dead. Jesus won the victory over sin and came into possession of his kingdom by means of his death and resurrection.

In order to proclaim Christ as king of all men and even of the whole universe, Pope Pius XI in 1925 instituted a special feast in honor of Christ the King. As a matter of fact, however, Jesus has chosen not to exercise full reign over this world, his kingdom, until he comes again in glory at the end of time. To symbolize this fact that Jesus will exercise his full reign only at the end of time, the Church has now moved the feast from October to this Sunday which marks the end of the liturgical year (*Calendarium Romanum*, p. 63).

The idea of Christ the King is one that is very familiar to us, and yet Christ is very different from earthly kings. The kings we have heard and read about have often had to win their kingdoms in the blood of battle. Frequently one king met another in individual, mortal combat. The survivor was the victor. Though some kings have been benevolent rulers, many became tyrants, exacting heavy taxes and tribute and giving few benefits in return to their subjects. One thing all kings, no matter how powerful or extensive their kingdom, have had in common is this: death has been the end of their kingship.

How different is Christ the King! To begin with, Jesus did not win his kingdom in the blood of a battlefield, but "through the blood of his cross," as the second reading today tells us. His enemy was not another king, but sin itself. Though Christ died in the struggle, it was Christ and not sin who was the victor. After his victory Christ, far from becoming a tyrant, has shown that he is most benevolent toward his subjects. As we will hear in the beautiful preface of this Mass, his kingdom is one of "truth and life, a kingdom of holiness and grace, a kingdom of justice, love and peace." Most striking of all is the fact that death was not the end of Christ's kingship, but in one sense only its beginning.

If Christ has already won the battle for his kingdom, and if his kingdom has so much good to offer people for their happiness, why is it that many people still fail to recognize and accept Christ as their King? Why is it that the justice, love and peace of his kingdom are not in great evidence in our world? The reason is that sin, despite the victory of Christ, still has power in the world.

The situation is somewhat like the one following the war with Japan. In that war, the decisive battles had been fought and won by the United States in the summer of 1945. On August 14, 1945, Japan officially surrendered. Though there was no doubt then that the United States had won the war, some fighting continued in a few islands of the Pacific in what the military referred to as "mopping-up" operations. We are like men in the final stages of a war. Christ has fought and won the decisive battle against sin and evil, and we are now in the mopping-up period. We long for the day when this struggle will be over and done with, so that all people may enjoy the justice, love and peace of Christ's kingdom. The second coming of Christ will mark the end of this transition period, and then will begin in all its perfection the eternal and universal reign of Christ the King.

Today in this Mass, we should profess our faith and trust in Christ as our King, and proclaim before the whole world our loyalty and our devotion to him. We should also renew our resolutions to persevere in the mopping-up operations against sin and evil until that day when Christ will come again in all his glory to take full possession of his eternal and universal kingdom.

C.E.M.

# PROPER OF THE SAINTS

**Solemnity of the Assumption (A)**

## *KEEP A-GOIN'*

The long, hot days of the summer can often be a drag as the heat and humidity drain your energy and enthusiasm. Here we are in the middle of August, with your vacation probably behind you and little to look forward to. Once in a while, life itself seems to be as draining as an unpleasant August day, and you need someone to give you a friendly slap on the back and say, "Keep a-goin'! It's all worth it."

Today we have come together to celebrate a great event, Mary's assumption into heaven. After her earthly life, Mary was taken up body and soul into heavenly glory. Because Mary enjoyed the power of Christ's redemption to the full, preserved as she was from all guilt of original sin, she did not have to wait until the end of time to share in Christ's resurrection. We should praise God for this marvelous thing that he has done for Mary. But there is more. We should also take great encouragement from our celebration of Mary's assumption.

Mary is the "great sign that has appeared in the sky, a woman clothed with the sun."\* Mary's assumption into heaven is a sign of what our own destiny is in God's plan. By our faith, we believe that Christ overcame death in his resurrection from the dead. Mary's assumption, body as well as soul, assures us that we will share in Christ's resurrection. The reason is that Mary is the model of the people of God. She is not only a model of what our lives should be in virtue, but also of what our lives, in body and soul, will one day be in heaven.\*\*

Just before the turn of the century, a man by the name of Frank Stanton in a playful mood wrote a poem of encouragement. Some of his

---

\* Though these words of the book of Revelation refer to God's people in the Old and New Testaments, the liturgy rightly accommodates them to Mary since she is the model and exemplar of the Church, the people of God.
\*\* Cf. Vatican II's *Constitution on the Church*, 53, 63, and 65.

verses were these: "If you strike a thorn or rose, / Keep a-goin'! / If it hails or if it snows, / Keep a-goin'! / When it looks like all is up, / Keep a-goin'! / Drain the sweetness from the cup, / Keep a-goin'!" That poem isn't much as literature, but it says something we sometimes need to hear. In a very real sense, today's celebration of Mary's assumption tells us much the same thing. In all the distressing, discouraging days of life, we should look to Mary in her assumption for encouragement. Her assumption tells us, "Keep a-goin'! It's all worth it."

C.E.M.

## Solemnity of the Assumption (B)

### *ABUNDANT LIFE*

Today's celebration of the Assumption, together with its ennobling and uplifting scriptural readings, stands in striking contrast with a mood of our times. All around us we see apathy, depression, pessimism. Frustrations and disappointments seem to be endless and yet leading nowhere. Even many young people, caught in a world of conflict and confusing change, are giving up on life.

What a pity these young people, and those who once were young, cannot experience the meaning of the abundant life which Christ promised and gave to his mother. Our celebration of Mary's assumption body and soul into eternal life should help all of us feel the worth of every effort to live life to the full here and now. Only in this way can we hope to live life to the full eternally. The cynic will probably respond to today's feast, with its promise of life, by saying that it is all nice poetry and fancy but a far cry from reality with all its harshness and drabness. Well, a lot depends on one's view of reality. Mary's view can be summarized in the opening words of her song of praise as found in today's gospel: "My being proclaims the greatness of the Lord, my spirit finds joy in God my savior."

One big mistake some people make is that they try to get through life on their own. They think that religion is a sign of weakness, a crutch, and they prefer to stand on their own two feet. They are proud. But Mary was humble. She exclaimed: "God has looked upon his servant in her lowliness; God who is mighty has done great things for me." She knew that all her privileges came from God, and that his power alone was making her life worthwhile. She went through her life, with all its problems and difficulties, in a spirit of complete trust in God. She had to see her son leave their home in Nazareth to begin his public ministry. With a mother's sympathy, she shared in the ridicule, the disdain, and the rejection which her son had to endure. She stood on Calvary and witnessed her son die a criminal's death. And through it all she never gave up on life, for her trust was not in herself but in God.

Was Mary's trust misplaced? Were her hopes only fantasy? Certainly not! Because Mary trusted that the Lord's words to her would be fulfilled, she was raised body and soul to the abundance of life. Her son had drawn human life from her womb, but she drew eternal life from his death on the cross. Like Mary, our happiness in life comes from our acceptance of God's promise of life. Like Mary, we can draw life from the death of Christ. Our Eucharistic acclamation of faith is: "Dying you destroyed our death; rising you restored our life; Lord Jesus, come in glory."

Lew Sarett in his poem, "The World Has a Way with Eyes," after describing the various things a young girl sees, strikes this encouraging note:

Keep a long, long look on pine and peak that rise
Serene today, tomorrow—when the world's eyes go
To socketed dust; keep a long look on the hills.
They know something, child, they know.

At this moment, let us take a long look at the hill of Calvary where Mary stood at the foot of the cross. When Christ opened his arms on the cross, he also opened the door to eternal life for himself, for Mary, and for us. That hill in our own time is the altar. To the altar we come for life here and hereafter.

O.J.M.
C.E.M.

**Solemnity of the Assumption (C)**

## *SOUL AND BODY, ONE PERSON*

The feast of the Assumption is one of the oldest liturgical celebrations in honor of Mary, but it has a vital importance to us in our own day.

This feast praises God who through his Son took Mary, soul and body, into heaven when her life on this earth had ended.

The feast proclaims God's attitude toward the material or physical aspect of human beings, which we usually call the "body." God's attitude toward the body stands in the middle between two extremes.

The first extreme says that the physical aspect of people is all that really counts. It is derived from a lack of faith and manifests itself in a cult or worship of the human body, which eventually leads to varied abuses. One abuse is a preoccupation with physical health: "If you have your health, you have just about everything," states a commercial on TV. That is the outlook of some people who are concerned only with their body, who are unwilling to endure any kind of pain or hardship and who strive to preserve their lives on this earth as long as possible. That is the first abuse of this extreme.

A second abuse sees pleasure as the only worthwhile goal in life. This pleasure takes many forms, such as overindulgence in food and drink, excessive gambling, a search for constant distraction in movies, TV and other forms of entertainment. A symptom of this abuse is a fear of silence and solitude. A person must always be with others or be distracted by a radio or hi-fi. There is a fear to face our inner selves and some possibly deeper meaning to life.

A third abuse is to view man in effect, if not in so many words, as little more than an animal. Without some spiritual view of human beings, a corrupt image emerges which manifests itself in such distortions of human dignity as pornography and prostitution.

That is one extreme view of human nature. The opposite extreme says that the spiritual side of people is all that really counts. This extreme is derived from faith—but a false or distorted kind of faith, which says that the only goal of life is to "save our souls," as if the body does not matter at all. This distortion results in a suspicion about anything physical or material. It manifests itself in a fear of our emotions and a suppression of them, and in an attitude that sex, even in marriage, is something just a little dirty and unworthy of human beings.

The proper outlook, God's outlook, is a balanced one. Our faith in God should help us to see that we have come forth from his creating hand in our entire being, body as well as soul. All that God has made is good. Moreover, God sent his eternal Son to be human like us in all things except sin, thereby giving a new and elevated holiness to our human condition. Today's feast shows us that we have been redeemed, body as well as soul, in the blood of Christ; made holy by the coming of the Holy Spirit; and destined for eternal happiness in heaven. Yes, we are destined for heaven as complete beings, including our physical or bodily aspects.

Mary did not have to wait until the end of the world to be taken body and soul into heaven. Her whole being was especially precious to God because she had come fully under the redeeming power of Christ, even to the extent of being preserved free from all sin. That is why God did not allow her body to corrupt in the grave.

We have to wait for the resurrection of our bodies. But today's feast is a sign and a pledge that we too are precious in the eyes of God, soul and body, and that the privilege which Mary enjoys now will, someday, be ours as well.

C.E.M.

## Solemnity of All Saints (A)

## *INSPIRATION AND STRENGTH*

The eighteenth century English poet, Alexander Pope, wrote: "Be not the first by whom the new is tried." That is advice which most of us probably follow. It is difficult to be the first at almost anything, particularly at something which is demanding and challenging.

The call to be a follower of Christ is indeed demanding and challenging. If we really listen to the gospel message of Jesus, we know that he asks much of us. The beatitudes proclaimed by Jesus today are a complete antithesis of worldly wisdom. To a person without real faith, it just does not make sense to think that one can find happiness in being poor in spirit, sorrowful or persecuted.

We need faith, but we also need inspiration and strength from someone who has embraced the gospel message. It is true that Jesus does not ask of us more than he himself has given, that he does not require that we do anything which he has not done himself. From him, we draw our inspiration and strength. Even though we believe that Jesus was human like us in all things but sin and entered fully in our human situation, we may be a little distracted by supposing that being divine made his human life easy. Such a distraction is off the mark theologically, and yet I believe that most of us can benefit by reflecting on the example of the saints, ordinary mortals in every respect.

One thing the saints mean to us is that we do not have to be the first to follow Christ. Other men, women and children, in vast numbers, have gone before us in deep faith and heroic love. What they have accomplished, we can accomplish as well by the grace of God.

Let me tell you about one saint in particular. I suspect most Catholics realize that St. Vincent de Paul was a great saint, the patron of charitable works for the universal Church. But he was not born a saint. It was a lifelong struggle for him, and he had to come to grips with the same weaknesses which most of us also possess in different degrees.

Vincent had to struggle against the attraction of money. He admitted that when he was ordained a priest, his motives were not unmixed. He had been born into an extremely poor family. He thought that by becoming a priest, he would be in a position to come into enough money to help support his family. He was not entirely ignoble in this intention, but as a young priest he went so far in his desire for financial gain as to enter into lawsuits with certain persons who owed him money. Although what he did was within the law of the land of France, he regretted his action for the rest of his life since he felt he had failed to follow the law of love taught by Jesus.

At one period in his life, Vincent was subjected to terrible temptations against faith. The more he prayed and mortified himself, the denser seemed to be the darkness within his soul. The trial lasted for several years. Exhausted and near despair, he wrote out the Creed and placed the sheet of paper next to his heart. He asked God to understand that as often as he placed his hand on his heart, this gesture was to be taken as his act of faith. He also promised God that he would abandon his greed and work for the poor. It was then that the temptation left him.

Perhaps we think that the saints are people who have never had any of the difficulties we experience. St. Vincent de Paul is but a single example of the opposite. Today's feast should help us to realize that thousands of men and women like ourselves have been drawn to holiness by God's grace only through a lifetime of struggle. Nor should we think that their progress was unimpeded by occasional lapses. They too had their ups and downs, their good days and their bad days.

God has been very good to the saints. He is also very good to us. The Father has loved us so much that he has called us to be his children, brothers and sisters of Jesus Christ. Ours is a family so large that it cannot be counted. We have many older brothers and sisters who have gone before us in faith and love. They serve as inspiration and strength to us, as we travel the same journey through life as they.

C.E.M.

## Solemnity of All Saints (B)

# *THE SAINTS GO MARCHING OUT ?*

On a Sunday afternoon, eighty thousand people are seated in an arena which resembles the ancient Roman Colosseum. They rise to their feet, and with great gusto sing out, " . . . the saints come marching in. . . ." Onto the field trot a number of men who resemble the Roman gladiators more than they do the saints who met a martyr's death centuries ago. They are members of the New Orleans Saints, a professional football team.

With the recent reduction of saints' days in the Church's calendar, it may seem to some that soon the only thing the word "saints" will suggest is a struggle between two teams in the N.F.L. Recent liturgical reform has indeed de-emphasized saints' days, but it has done so only in order to restore the mystery of Christ as the center of liturgical celebration. This is as it should be. But though saints' days have been "played down," they will continue to form part of the liturgical year and we will continue to celebrate today's feast of All Saints. The real question is not why saints' days have been de-emphasized, but rather why they should be celebrated at all.

Actually, the reason for the continuance of saints' days is precisely the fact that Christ is the center of all liturgical celebration. We must remember that Christ is present and active in the world in many ways. He continues not only in the Eucharist, not only in the words of Sacred Scripture, but also in people. All Christians are called to continue the life of Christ. In the second reading today, we were told that we are God's children. As children of God, we are like God's child by excellence, God's unique son, Jesus Christ. Through baptism, we were given a participation in the life of Christ.

It is not that we are called merely to imitate Christ, as a modern president of the United States may try to imitate, say, Abraham Lincoln. Lincoln is dead. He cannot communicate anything of himself to the living. But Jesus is very much alive, and he does communicate his life to people. Every person in union with Christ by faith and baptism continues his presence in the world. Jesus lived the perfect human life, and his followers continue that life in varying degrees. Some people have lived the Christ-life in an eminent degree. They are the people we call saints.

In the early Church, the first saints to be honored were the martyrs. The Church saw that martyrs were conformed to Christ most specially and heroically in dying as he did. When persecutions ended, the Church broadened its vision of how people live the Christ-life. Every Christian death, even though not heroic, is a conformity to Christ in his death. Moreover, all the aspects of the Christ-life are lived out by Christians: his preaching, his healing ministry to the sick, his love and concern for all classes of people, his devotion to children, his intense life of prayer. Saints tend to "specialize" in reliving certain aspects of the life of Christ. In St. Vincent de Paul, we feel Christ's concern for the poor. In St. John Chrysostom, we hear Christ the great preacher. In St. Teresa of Avila, we see Christ once again spending whole nights in prayer. And today we honor those many unnamed saints, those little people like you and me, who through all the ordinary chores and pleasures of life tried to let Christ and his love radiate from their lives.

Today we honor Christ in his saints. We should praise God whose power is so great that he has made the wonderful life of his Son continue among us in human persons, and we should thank him for this tremendous favor. We should also pray that we may cooperate with his grace, which can make saints of us too. And finally, we should ask pardon for our failures in not letting the life of Christ take over our own being.

The saints are not marching out. On the contrary, we can with appreciation, joy and even gusto, see them come marching into the liturgy as another way of celebrating the great central mystery of Jesus Christ.

C.E.M.

**Solemnity of All Saints (C)**

## *LITTLE PEOPLE ARE SAINTS TOO*

A certain man died at the age of sixty-two. He had been a loving husband, and a devoted father to four sons and a daughter. For most of his adult life, he worked as a clothing salesman. He tried to lead a good life and to do what he believed was right. When he died, he left behind him the memory of a warm, friendly human being. Today is his feast day.

A woman died at the age of seventy-four. She had been a good wife and mother. Most of her time was spent in the home, taking care of her husband and her six children. Her life was simple and basically happy. Her greatest sorrow was to see her youngest daughter leave the Church, marry a much older man, and then end her marriage in divorce. She was a widow for about seven years, the hardest time of her life. She was lonely, left with no one to care for and almost nothing to do. But she was a good woman. She tried to pray a lot for others, especially her youngest daughter. Today is her feast day.

A three-year-old boy was killed near his home when, in the twilight, a car struck him down. He had been baptized, but had never had the happiness of receiving Jesus in Holy Communion. Today is his feast day too.

Throughout the year, we celebrate feast days in honor of the saints. They are the "name" saints, the "big" saints like St. Joseph, the Apostles, the martyrs. Today we celebrate the unnamed saints, the "little" saints. They are the people who quietly tried to lead good, Christian lives, and who in God's plan never had the occasion to do anything really spectacular or extraordinary. They were the people our Lord referred to in today's gospel: the poor in spirit, the sorrowing, the lowly. They were the people like us.

Today in this Mass, we should praise and thank God for the little saints. And we should pray that one day, we may be among them in heaven. Then this feast, the solemnity of All Saints, will be our feast day too.

C.E.M.

**Solemnity of the Immaculate Conception (A)**

## GOD CAN DO IT

They say that history tends to repeat itself. I suppose that is true mainly because human nature does not change. The first reading today tells us that our first parents were sinful. And when they sinned, they looked around for excuses—the old human foible of "passing the buck." Adam said, "Don't blame me; blame that woman you gave me." And Eve said, "Don't blame me; blame that snake in the grass."

We are not really much different from our first parents. It is just very hard to admit that we are weak, that we are imperfect, that we have faults. Even in little things, we make excuses. If we knock over a glass and break it, we protest that it is the fault of someone who left it where they shouldn't have. If we run out of gas, we try to blame someone else for having forgotten to fill the tank. And when it comes to sin, the degree of our guilt is exceeded only by the imagination we use in finding excuses.

All of us can use a great big dose of honesty in admitting that as human beings we are far from perfect. The problem is that we are engaged in a bitter struggle against evil. God warned that from the time of the first sin, enmity would exist between the devil and the human race. Enmity means all out war to the end. We simply cannot afford to underestimate the devil. And making excuses, pretending that we are stronger and better than we are, is playing right into the devil's plans—as did Adam and Eve. He is more subtle and clever than we can ever be.

If we had to fight this battle alone, we would simply have to give up in despair. But we need not fight alone, provided we stand before God in honest humility and say, "We can't do it alone; we need your help." God will help us, and with him on our side we cannot lose. That is one meaning of today's feast, the Immaculate Conception.

With Mary, God showed how powerful he really is. Mary was just as human as we are. But she was humble. When the angel appeared to her, she didn't say, "Oh, I know I'm great. I will get God's work done for him." No, she humbly professed, "I am the maidservant of the Lord." A maidservant, she said—one who completely depends on her master. And God brought his almighty power to bear on the person of Mary. Through his power, she was conceived without sin and remained without sin throughout her whole life.

What God did for Mary should give us hope. God has the power. Will he use it for us? Will he be on our side? Yes, he will—for, as we heard in the second reading, God has chosen us to be his children. And God will not abandon his children. He will help us through the struggle with sin if we first admit we need his help by not making excuses, and if we turn to him with confidence and trust. We must stand before God naked like Adam and Eve—naked without any clothing of excuses to try to cover over our human weakness. And we must say to him, "We need your help to overcome sin. We know you can do it because we have seen what you have done for Mary Immaculate."

C.E.M.

## Solemnity of the Immaculate Conception (B)

# *FOLLOW THE LEADER*

In 1941 on this day, in a small town on an island in the Pacific, the skies were aglow and there was ferocious activity. But it wasn't a celebration. The imperial war machine the morning before had gutted Pearl Harbor. Twenty-four hours later, fires were still burning and men were being hauled out of partially submerged ships. The shock of war had touched American soil. These were to be days of sadness, waste and destruction, but also times for unusual bravery. And the bravest heroes seem to have been the ones who thought they couldn't do much; but they started and others followed. Bravery seems almost contagious. Yet someone has to volunteer first.

Two thousand years ago, the world faced a great crisis. A cosmic power was needed to straighten our life and make some sense of human suffering. A brave person was needed to begin the process; an instrument chosen by God and made fit by him through an immaculate conception; someone who could be both humble and effective. Courageously a young woman, so chosen and made fit by God, volunteered—a young woman who took credit for nothing, "the maidservant of the Lord," but who with God's grace could say, "Let it be done to me as you say."

Someone has to be bold and go first to show the rest of us what is possible. Mary had to take the great leap of faith, and trust totally in God's will. The one to go first seems to have the hardest road. Mary had to care for a child and see the Son of God. Mary had to hear her son ridiculed as a madman and see the Messiah. She had to experience his death as a criminal and know her son to be a king. But she did it. So it's not so hard for us to follow the lead. Mary's faith strengthened the apostles, and it should strengthen us.

We blame mother Eve for foolishly blazing the trail of listening to Satan, of having faith in pride and self-power. But as the early Church Fathers shouted, we praise mother Mary for making a path for the humble pilgrim to have faith in Jesus Christ as our total answer, the real way of becoming "like God." We have been "predestined through Christ to be adopted sons," and we have been predestined through Mary to be believing pilgrims.

During this Mass, simply ask Mary to gently hold your hand, as only a mother can, and guide you through any shadows you may be experiencing. Think about the events in Christ's life, and consider how Mary responded. Ask her Son to share his Spirit with you, as he did with his mother. And ask the Holy Spirit dwelling in Mary to fill each of us with the courage to believe Jesus is Lord, to be strong enough to live openly as dedicated Christians.

There may not be visible wars in your neighborhood demanding bravery, but the war of Satan, enflamed by man's pride, continues to saturate us. Go ahead: take up Christ and wave the banner of faith.

M.M.R.

**Solemnity of the Immaculate Conception (C)**

## *PATRONESS OF OUR COUNTRY*

Today we are celebrating a feast which is significant for us not only as Catholics, but also as Americans. Mary, immaculately conceived, is the patroness of our country. As such, she has an important lesson to teach us.

Mary was free from sin—not only original sin, but all sin throughout her entire life. This was a great gift from God, as Mary herself heard the angel proclaim: "You have won God's favor." Mary recognized that all her gifts came from God and that in gratitude she belonged entirely to God, and so she responded, "I am the Lord's handmaid."

Mary's recognition of God as the source of her gifts is in accord with the tradition of our country. One of the greatest spokesmen for the ideas of our country was Thomas Jefferson. In the Declaration of Independence, he wrote these famous words: "We hold these truths to be self-evident, that all men are created equal, that they are endowed by their creator with certain unalienable rights, that among these are life, liberty, and the pursuit of happiness." Yes, we are endowed by our creator, by God. God is the source of our most treasured gifts, as Jefferson so well wrote.

In our nation's capitol stands the Jefferson Memorial. On the interior marble walls are inscriptions from Jefferson's writings. On the northeast wall can be read these magnificent words: "God who gave us life gave us liberty. Can the liberties of a nation be secure when we have removed a conviction that these liberties are the gift of God?" Thomas Jefferson indeed recognized God as the source of our gifts, and he feared that our gifts would not remain secure if men failed to make the same recognition. Experience with godless rulers of our own times has shown us how atheism leads to a denial of the basic human rights to life, liberty, and the pursuit of happiness. At the birth of our country, Jefferson warned, "Can the liberties of a nation be secure when we have removed a conviction that these liberties are the gift of God?"

Magnificent though the words of Jefferson be, they are merely an echo of the inspired words of St. Paul in today's epistle, "Praised be the God and Father of our Lord Jesus Christ, who has bestowed on us in Christ every spiritual blessing in the heavens." St. Paul then goes on to say that we are to praise God for his gifts to us.

In this Mass, together with Mary, let us recognize God as the source of all our gifts. On this patronal feast of our country, let us also pray that all our fellow Americans will join us in seeing God as the source of all our blessings, as did the patroness of our country, Mary Immaculate.

C.E.M.

# OTHER ALBA HOUSE PUBLICATIONS

*OPENING THE TREASURES:* A Book of Daily Homily Meditations
by: Rev. Charles E. Miller, C.M.                    $12.95, paper

'What I found most appealing in Father Miller's work is the excellent way in which he connects the readings to other areas of human knowledge and life. This will, no doubt, help the parish priest to make such connections on his own. Father Miller clearly indicates that these meditations are not meant to be a substitute for the priests' own reflections. They are a starter which each preacher must develop and incarnate. Such wise caution in preaching is as welcome as is this book. A good parish resource and one that will help in priestly ministry and spirituality.''

PASTORAL LIFE MAGAZINE — Rev. W. Maestri

---

*LIVING IN CHRIST:* Sacramental and Occasional Homilies
by: Rev. Charles E. Miller, C.M.                    $2.95, paper

Priests will welcome this work. From Baptism to Labor Day to Renewal of Vows to Parish Finance Sunday, his words offer genuine help and inspiration to other preachers of the Word.

TODAY'S CATHOLIC TEACHER

---

*LOVE IN THE LANGUAGE OF PENANCE:* A Simple Guide To The
New Rite Of Penance.
by: Rev. Charles E. Miller, C.M.                    .50¢

The purpose of this booklet is to present one means to grow in appreciation and love for the Sacrament of Penance so that one may be reconciled as fully and fruitfully as possible.

The approach is not scholarly but pastoral.

Available in Spanish: AMOR EN ELLENGUAJE DE PENITENCIA — .50¢

## WORDS OF POWER

by: Rev. James F. McNulty, O.S.A.                        $8.95, paper

This book comprises a wide selection of Father McNulty's homilies, eulogies, prayers, invocations and talks on various themes. The material is suitable for personal reflection and may also be used as a basis for specialized homilies such as the funerals of priests, religious, outstanding lay men, women and youth.

The topics covered are timely and diverse as seen from this partial listing: "Being Human," "Marriage," "Women and the Church," "Reconciliation," "Call to Parenting" and many more. The topics would be suitable for graduations, anniversaries of priests, religious and married couples.

---

## PRAY TODAY'S GOSPEL: Reflections on the Day's Good News

by: Rev. Bernard C. Mischke, O.S.C., and
    Rev. Fritz Mischke, O.S.C.                          $9.95, paper

"This is a collection of reflections on the scripture readings found in the Lectionary for each weekday of the year. The authors present some fine reflections on the daily Gospels. This is a volume of solid spiritual insights."

                                                        THE PRIEST

---

## BIBLICAL CATECHETICAL HOMILIES FOR SUNDAYS AND HOLY DAYS

Based on the Lectionary and Reflecting the Syllabus of the Pastoral Homiletic Plan—Cycles A, B & C

by: Rev. David Q. Liptak                                **$10.95, paper**

"Father Liptak's work helps the homilist treat practically all the key Catholic teachings against the background of the Scriptural readings assigned for the different Sundays and holy days. Each homily outline announces the aim of this homily, a service for the preacher and a blessing for the people."

                                                        THE PRIEST